'At a time when the Europea[illegible] from some corners of the continent, this book p[illegible]ides a timely reminder of the value of a European perspective. This edited collection contains contributions from Austria, Belgium, Ireland, Norway, Portugal, Slovakia, Sweden and the UK with chapters addressing topics that are fundamentally trans-European such as human rights law and trafficking.

The book maintains a strong focus on children and young people's involvement in domestic violence and abuse. It provides up-to-date explorations of a wide range of diverse experiences encompassed within the term "domestic violence", including LGBT young people's experiences of abuse and those of older women, child to parent violence, digital IPVA, FGM and forced marriage.

A particular strength is the breadth of the collection which includes incisive accounts of research processes, training, policy and service development. The book will provide an invaluable resource for all those who work or study in the field of domestic violence.'

– Nicky Stanley, Professor of Social Work,
University of Central Lancashire, UK

of related interest

Helping Babies and Children Aged 0–6 to Heal After Family Violence
A Practical Guide to Infant- and Child-Led Work
Dr Wendy Bunston
Foreword by Dr Julie Stone
ISBN 978 1 84905 644 1
eISBN 978 1 78450 138 9

Child to Parent Violence and Abuse
Family Interventions with Non Violent Resistance
Dr Declan Coogan
ISBN 978 1 84905 711 0
eISBN 978 1 78450 231 7

Working with Violence and Confrontation Using Solution Focused Approaches
Creative Practise with Children, Young People and Adults
Judith Milner and Steve Myers
ISBN 978 1 78592 055 4
eISBN 978 1 78450 312 3

Domestic Violence and Protecting Children
New Thinking and Approaches
Edited by Nicky Stanley and Cathy Humphreys
ISBN 978 1 84905 485 0
eISBN 978 0 85700 875 6

Values in Health and Social Care
An Introductory Workbook
Ray Samuriwo, Stephen Pattison, Andrew Todd and Ben Hannigan
ISBN 978 1 78592 063 9
eISBN 978 1 78450 320 8

RESPONDING TO DOMESTIC VIOLENCE

EMERGING CHALLENGES FOR POLICY, PRACTICE AND RESEARCH IN EUROPE

Edited by **Stephanie Holt**, **Carolina Øverlien** and **John Devaney**

Jessica Kingsley *Publishers*
London and Philadelphia

First published in 2018
by Jessica Kingsley Publishers
73 Collier Street
London N1 9BE, UK
and
400 Market Street, Suite 400
Philadelphia, PA 19106, USA

www.jkp.com

Library of Congress Cataloging in Publication Data
A CIP catalog record for this book is available from the Library of Congress

British Library Cataloguing in Publication Data
A CIP catalogue record for this book is available from the British Library

ISBN 978 1 78592 261 9
eISBN 978 1 78450 549 3

Printed and bound in Great Britain

FSC www.fsc.org MIX Paper from responsible sources FSC® C013056

CONTENTS

ACKNOWLEDGEMENTS

The impetus for this book arose from the inaugural European Conference on Domestic Violence held at Queen's University Belfast in September 2015. The key people behind the conference were John Devaney, Stephanie Holt, Davina James-Hanman, Anne Lazenbatt, Carolina Øverlien and Nicky Stanley. We would like to thank everyone who participated in the conference, and subsequent events in Porto, Portugal, in 2017 and Oslo, Norway, in 2019.

INTRODUCTION

Stephanie Holt, *Associate Professor of Social Work, Trinity College Dublin, Ireland*

Carolina Øverlien, *Associate Professor, Stockholm University, Sweden, and Researcher, Norwegian Centre for Violence and Traumatic Stress Studies, Oslo, Norway*

John Devaney, *Centenary Chair of Social Work, University of Edinburgh, Scotland*

Responding to the challenges domestic violence presents for practise, policy and research, this book provides a critical and much needed debate on the concerns that resonate across Europe, while simultaneously providing a platform for divergence and innovation. As editors, our vision with this book is bold, perhaps even audacious. We believe that by viewing domestic violence through a European lens, we can raise awareness of domestic violence, promote the evidence base, encourage the development of effective policy and good practise, and develop methods and tools that can be beneficial both on a European and wider international level. As such, our aim is for the book to be an inspired source of new knowledge for researchers, policy-makers, practitioners, service providers, activists and survivors, across Europe as well as around the globe.

Policy, practise and research are not easily distinguishable, as they, rightfully, intertwine, connect and influence one another. Indeed, while the relationship between the three is considered complex, as authors, however, we aim for this publication to act as a 'knowledge platform' that has the potential to play a 'brokering role' between the three activities (de Haas and van der Kwaak 2017, p.11). We also acknowledge that we are not starting with a blank slate. Tracing the history of how the issue of domestic violence became one of the priorities of the Council of Europe, the role of research for the development of policy, and vice versa, becomes eminently clear. At the Fourth World Conference of Women in Beijing in 1995, the issue of domestic violence against women was defined as one of the 12 areas of concern, and as such provided an opportunity for European advocates to influence policy-makers to place the issue on the agenda of the European Union (EU). To raise awareness of the issue of domestic violence in Europe, two early studies stand out as particularly important. In 1999, the European Commission published *Eurobarometer 51.0: Europeans and Their Views on Domestic Violence*, where over 16,000 Europeans in 17 member states were surveyed about their views on domestic violence against women. The results revealed that 96 per cent of respondents had heard of the phenomenon, 50 per cent thought it was fairly common, and 96 per cent agreed that it was not acceptable, highlighting both high levels of awareness and low levels of acceptability of domestic violence in Europe (Gracia and Herrero 2006). The same year, the European Women's Lobby launched the study *Unveiling the Hidden Data on Domestic Violence in the European Union*, as part of an awareness-raising campaign. Gathering and analysing data from 15 member states, this study highlighted, among other things, flaws in the judicial systems, lack of services and poor crime statistics across Europe, which revealed almost nothing on domestic violence, despite estimates that one in five women in Europe had been victims of domestic violence. The issue of domestic violence as a significant problem in Europe emerged with clarity from both of these studies, as did the necessity for policy and practise to be developed and implemented in order to meet the needs of the people of Europe. The campaign headed by the European Women's Lobby ended with a conference in Lisbon in May 2000, where one of the key messages conveyed was that the EU must take a more active role in eliminating violence against women (Montoya 2013).

Between the years 2006–08, the Council of Europe ran a Europe-wide awareness-raising campaign, targeted against domestic violence and violence against women. By the end of this campaign, the Committee of Ministers set up an expert group to work out a draft text of a new convention, the Council of Europe *Convention on Preventing and Combating Violence against Women and Domestic Violence* (Istanbul Convention). The Convention, which was opened for signature in May 2011 and has, to date, been signed by 44 countries (and ratified by 23), states that it is the obligation of each state to address violence against women and domestic violence, to prevent it, protect its victims and prosecute the perpetrators. It also includes an obligation for countries to support research and the collection of data in the field of violence against women and domestic violence (Article 11).

In 2014, three years after the opening of the Istanbul Convention, the first study that could document the extent and nature of physical, sexual and psychological violence against women in all 28 member states was launched. Unlike many EU-wide surveys where questions are changed to meet the specific policy needs of individual countries, the EU Agency for Fundamental Rights (FRA) employed the same questionnaire in all member states, collecting data on 42,000 women aged between 18 and 74 across the EU, representing an average of 1500 women in each member state. The FRA study found that a substantial number of women in Europe become victims of violence at some point in their lifetime. Similar to the findings from the European Women's Lobby's study from the end of the previous century, the FRA study found that much of the violence remains hidden as victimised women tend not to report the violence to the authorities; hence perpetrators are never confronted and held accountable for their actions. Although the EU, with its complex body of institutions, has, since the end of the century, taken an active role in combating violence against women, the FRA study highlights that in many European countries it is still difficult to talk openly about violence. There is a dearth of services and support for victims, and violence is not perceived as a mainstream policy issue. To a large extent, domestic violence is still understood as a private matter, and as such, an issue that should be dealt with within the walls of the family home, even if what constitutes a family has changed significantly in the last two decades (Toulcmon 2016). Not least among these changes is the move away from the dominance of the nuclear family model, largely based on marriage, to family arrangements that are based on co-habitation, those headed by lone parents, reconstituted families and same-sex family partnerships.

When we talk of Europe we are discussing both the political project that is the European Union, and the geographical continent that includes countries outside the Union. As such, the Council of Europe, an international organisation comprising 47 member states and covering approximately 820 million people that focuses on human rights, democracy and the rule of law, is probably a more inclusive and accurate representation of the many countries and citizens who see themselves as European. In this context Europe is a continent of many countries and a multitude of cultures and languages, each with its own laws, policies and traditions, and at differing stages of economic development. Individual nation-states determine how their national laws respond to domestic violence. Similarly, how well individual countries respond to the needs and rights of victims, while simultaneously providing treatment interventions for perpetrators, varies greatly. It is worth noting, however, that domestic violence is reported to a large extent by women in all countries, regardless of issues such as differential levels of equality and awareness, and differences in the operation of judicial systems (FRA 2014).

In line with the Council of Europe (2011), we define domestic violence as 'all acts of physical, sexual, psychological or economic violence that occur within the family or domestic unit or between former or current spouses or partners, whether or not the perpetrator shares or has shared the same residence with the victim'. In this book, we understand domestic violence as a gendered phenomenon, given the research evidence that men are more likely to be perpetrators of such abuse, and that women tend to suffer more severe abuse over longer periods of time (FRA 2014). At the same time, we acknowledge that domestic violence can be perpetrated by women against men, as well as in same-sex relationships, and that the victims can be children and adults of any gender. As discussed in several of the chapters in this book, domestic violence is not a phenomenon affecting men and women of a certain age. Children of all ages have been shown to be negatively affected by the violence that takes place in their homes and indeed, in the post-separation period, when the perpetrator continues the abuse through the facility of child contact, adolescents can be victimised by their peers, and violence may be exerted against older people by an individual with whom they are in a close relationship or dependent on. Furthermore, violence can be perpetrated by and against any person regardless of ethnic and social background or religion.

Today, there exists a substantial body of literature on the issue of domestic violence against women, literature that, to a large extent, has contributed to put the issue of domestic violence on the European policy agenda. Inspired by the breadth and depth of new knowledge captured by the FRA 2014 survey, this book sets out the European context and showcases the evidence base, the development of effective policies and of innovative practise responses in Europe. In doing so, it confirms that violence against women continues to be a significant and complex social problem, and one that has become increasingly diverse over time and across Europe and elsewhere. While research on other closely linked issues such as men and children as victims of domestic violence, teenagers' victimisation by peers, and violence in lesbian, gay, bisexual, transgender and queer (LGBTQ) relationships continues to develop, they are still, to a large extent, under-researched and, as such, less acknowledged in policy and practise. This book goes some way to addressing those knowledge gaps while maintaining the focus on practise, policy and research. As editors, we have been in a unique position to appreciate the measure of progress in the field across Europe. Moving from chapter to chapter, we assert that while many of the age-old challenges inherent in violence against women persist, employing an intersectional approach supports our evolving understanding of the increasingly diverse nature of more recent aspects of domestic violence and abuse that have emerged.

This publication, which emerged out of the inaugural European Conference on Domestic Violence in 2015, is the first of its kind to present a coordinated focus on domestic violence through a three-way European lens of practise, policy and research. To that end it contains a collection of 17 high-quality chapters authored by both leading and emerging experts across Europe, who were carefully selected for inclusion in this text. As editors, our aim was that this publication would reflect the diversity of the experience of domestic violence, would represent, in so far as that was possible, a breadth of European research, policy and practise, and finally, that our authors were experts in their field. The outline of the structure of the book that follows illustrates that we have achieved this aim.

The book is divided into four parts. We begin in Part One with Joanna Goodey's chapter focusing on policy development at a pan-European level. Specifically, her chapter argues that the European response to domestic violence is explicitly rights-based, in contrast to other jurisdictions around the world. It recognises that 'duty bearers', that is, the State and State actors, such as the police and other public bodies, have a duty towards 'rights holders', who are the ordinary citizens whose rights have been violated. This has resulted in the European response to violence against women and girls being framed around the United Nations' (UN) structure-process-outcome model, which has been developed to assess the application of the law, policies and practise on the ground. However, such a process requires good-quality data to inform both policy and practise, and in the absence of comprehensive 'outcome' data in many European countries on the extent and nature of women's experiences of violence, which includes rates of reporting to the police and other services, it has been encouraging to see the FRA's Violence Against Women survey provide a unique dataset that has furnished data at the EU and member state level. The challenge going forward is to build on this approach, with more consistent data collection and replicable research approaches across and between individual countries.

The second chapter, by Philip McCormack, moves from the pan-European focus to one that reflects on the journey of strategy and policy development in one country, Ireland. In this chapter, McCormack outlines the role of Cosc, Ireland's National Office for the Prevention of Domestic, Sexual and Gender-based Violence, in devising, implementing and reviewing a national strategy on domestic, sexual and gender-based violence, and in working towards a second national strategy. While a number of achievements arising from the first national strategy are highlighted, he suggests, however, that the strategy may have been overly ambitious and did not anticipate the changing economic environment. Both points strongly support the need to prioritise, so that the new strategy contains realistic and achievable actions. In developing the second national strategy, emphasis is being placed on improved coordination between State and non-State services as well as improvement in the collection, collation and analysis of data in the sector(s).

Part Two includes six diverse contributions on the perspectives of children and young people who have experienced domestic abuse. The first chapter reports on a research project undertaken in Slovakia, concerning the mother–child relationship in the context of domestic violence. Using a bilateral model of mother–child relationships when analysing interviews with mothers and children who are victims of intimate partner violence, Zuzana Ocenasova and Hana Smitkova argue that both mothers and children can be understood as active agents who are capable of meaning construction and intentional actions during and after a violent relationship. Close, mutual mother–child relationships contribute highly to the resiliency of both mothers and children, and may serve as an important basis for future interventions from helping professionals.

Chapter 4 also focuses on the agency of children and young people, with Claire Houghton's participatory action research project with a national advisory group of young experts in Scotland, identifying both challenges and opportunities for the inclusion of young survivors in the policy-making process. She concludes that in order for that participation to be meaningful, adult experts needed to recognise the expert voice of young survivors, and young survivors needed to be supported to have their voice heard. The importance of the voice of the child being heard in the research process is the focus of the next chapter by Carolina Øverlien and Stephanie Holt. This discussion reflects on the challenges inherent in both the ethical demand for children to be permitted and facilitated to participate in research, which is about them, and the challenges researchers can encounter in conducting ethically sensitive research with what can be considered a vulnerable population. They conclude by asserting that research with children demands an environment that is respectful, considerate and attentive to the child's needs, a context where the child is in control of what to answer, when to take breaks, and when to end the interview, with the expressed freedom to withdraw from the research process at any time without penalty.

The next two chapters by Sibel Korkmaz and Maria Pentaraki focus on the issue of teenage intimate partner violence. Korkmaz provides a comprehensive literature review on the issue within a European context, concluding that the inclusion of an intersectional perspective would allow us to understand how teenagers are shaped by the interaction of different social positions (ethnicity, gender, class, age, sexuality, etc.), and how these create interdependent forms of privilege and oppression (Hankivsky 2014). Pentaraki also calls for an intersectional perspective, with her chapter drawing selectively on a qualitative research project in Northern Ireland with LGBT youth experiencing relationship abuse. Pentaraki concludes by asserting that the barriers to help-seeking faced by LGBT young people involve multiple intersecting forms of oppression, marginality and discrimination. Consequently, LGBT youth are less likely to get the help needed in a Northern Ireland context, not only because of their sexual orientation, but also because of how it intersects with their age, their geographical setting and their religion, among other factors.

The final chapter in Part Two returns to a focus on practise, and is reflective of a growing appreciation that perpetrators of domestic violence have many roles – including that of parent in many situations. As such, Nicola McConnell, Julie Taylor and Matt Barnard argue that there is a need to engage with men who have been violent and abusive towards to their current or former partner, about their parenting role as fathers, and the impact of their behaviour on their child(ren). The trial of the Caring Dads programme, imported to the UK from Canada, is a welcome development. As the authors note, such approaches seek to engage fathers through their motivation to be better parents. While not successful with everyone, the intervention shows promise, and this chapter highlights the importance of working with the complexities of many children's realities, whereby even though their parents may be separated, they continue to have both parents involved in their life.

Part Three, which we have titled 'New Understandings on Domestic Abuse and Violence', contains five contributions that introduce both emerging and diverse areas of concern in the field of domestic violence. Reflective of the nascent nature of the issues discussed, the empirical knowledge base and policy development are largely considered to be in their infancy, with practitioners struggling to provide best practise responses and services considered underdeveloped. Chapter 9 explores the relatively recently acknowledged problem of child-to-parent violence and abuse (CPVA), both at a European level and also focusing on research conducted in the west of Ireland. Declan Coogan describes CPVA as a pattern of behaviours and as an abuse of power through which a son or daughter under the age of 18 coerces, controls or dominates parents or carers. As a response to CPVA, a non-violent resistance (NVR) model of intervention challenges us to shift our focus from the individual child and his/her behaviour to the responses of parents and an extended network. In his chapter, Coogan asserts that training in non-blaming and solution-focused models such as NVR can significantly enhance practitioners' awareness of CPVA, and further develop practitioner skills in working with parents living with CPVA. By accepting the possibility that some parents may be victimised by their children under the age of 18, by asking parents about their experiences and about those who can stand in solidarity with them against abuse/violence, practitioners and researchers take the first steps in supporting families to resolve the problem of CPVA.

Per Moum Hellevik's chapter on digital intimate partner violence and abuse among young people presents a systematic review of the literature on factors that increase or decrease the likelihood of a person being exposed to such violence and abuse. Focusing specifically on policy-makers, Hellevik concludes that a key component in the implementation of prevention and intervention strategies should be a holistic perspective on young people's intimate relationships, sexuality and online proficiency, as these factors are interrelated. In Chapter 11, Nusha Yonkova and Gloria Kirwan highlight how despite a range of legal and policy initiatives at national and international levels designed to prevent and combat trafficking in human beings, each year thousands of people are traded as commodities within and across European borders. While considerable effort has been devoted in recent years to coordinating security and legal strategies across Europe, the authors posit that there is still a long way to go before national and European systems are properly equipped and resourced to effectively deal with this problem. While much of the focus has been on saving victims, they argue for greater attention to awareness raising and education among the wider population. Going forward, they assert that while national strategies should be informed by the specific needs in the distinct national contexts, demand reduction has to be recognised as a transnational issue, where measures to address demand should involve cross-border cooperation and coordination at European and global levels.

Dalila Cerejo's chapter on the complex issue of female genital mutilation/cutting (FGM/C) provides an overview of the phenomenon's extent throughout the globe, and articulates the subject within the European context. Using Portugal as a case study, data from the estimated prevalence of FGM/C and the methods used to estimate that prevalence are presented. A fundamental argument articulated in this chapter is the centrality of prevalence studies in order to assess and comprehend the phenomenon of FGM/C, and to continue to design and implement effective national and international integrated public policies. Related to this, Cerejo asserts, is the critical need to develop a common transnational methodology for the estimation of the prevalence of FGM/C that can be adopted by all member states with the aim of producing comparable statistics. Cerejo concludes that this goal is not possible by simply reeling in administrative data that is neither systematically collected nor centrally stored.

There is a growing recognition of the nature and prevalence of forced marriage in Europe, supported by the provisions within the Istanbul Convention. While Els Leye states in Chapter 13 that legislation outlawing this practise is helpful, it also requires the education of professionals from across a range of disciplines, and an engagement with communities in a way that does not undermine their culture, and develops long-term and sustainable solutions. As Leye notes in her thoughtful chapter, there is a notable difference in the openness of second- and third-generation immigrants to discuss the issue of forced marriage, and to conform to both the legal and social norms within Europe.

The final part of the book is concerned with responding to domestic violence and abuse. Ingunn Rangul Askeland and Marius Råkil outline the differing theoretical positions informing our conceptualisation of why individuals perpetrate violence and abuse against current or former intimate partners, and how this shapes the nature of interventions, using the case example of Alternative to Violence from Scandinavia. They argue for an integrated theoretical explanatory framework, and interventions that address the perpetration of domestic violence at both individual and structural levels.

Developing this theme on intervention, Lucy Potter and Gene Feder reflect on both the cultural and organisational changes required within healthcare systems to both better identify and respond to the needs of victims of domestic violence. This is within a context whereby many healthcare systems are already feeling overworked and sometimes overwhelmed. While some high-quality research has now been conducted in relation to identifying and responding to domestic violence within the health context, most of this has been undertaken in economically developed countries in Europe, and it cannot be assumed that the learning from such studies is readily transferable to other contexts.

Elizabeth Martin, John Devaney and Gemma Carney's chapter on older women's experience of domestic abuse asserts that older women are doubly disadvantaged as a consequence of society's antipathy towards both being old and being a victim of domestic violence and abuse. Drawing on results from European studies, this chapter highlights the lifelong impact of domestic violence across the life course, and the continuing experience of it in later life. Linking research with practise, the authors suggest that professionals working in health, social care and criminal justice as a whole therefore have a central role in both identifying domestic violence and understanding the particular experiences and needs of older women affected by this issue. The chapter concludes by calling for increased awareness and recognition of the abuse of older women, but also an explicit acknowledgement of society's obligations to both protect and support victims of domestic violence, and the particular needs brought on by being older, for both the experience of services and response to domestic violence.

The final chapter in this part is focused on frontline practise and reflects on Davina James-Hanman's three decades of experience of working on the issue of domestic violence throughout the UK. To this end it provides a fascinating whistle-stop historical narrative on the development of practise and service provision, policy and legislative reform, highlighting both the achievements and the challenges encountered over that time period. James-Hanman calls for a recognition of survivors as whole people with complex lives, of which domestic violence may only be a part.

We conclude this introductory chapter with a reflection on the above invitation by James-Hanman to consider the complexity inherent in domestic violence. The chapters that follow unpick and unpack that complexity as it manifests itself in a myriad of ways, across and within European contexts. As with any similar publication, it is not within our gift to include all relevant aspects of domestic violence, nor is it possible to have representation from all European countries. We are aware that significant issues such as children's experiences of post-separation contact alongside the concerning issue of femicide, for example, are noticeable by their absence. Subsequent editions of this text will have ample opportunities to address that deficit.

It is worth noting that while the growth of evidence and practise is uneven across Europe, there is an increasing desire to share good practise and to engage in undertaking high-quality and robust research to inform our understanding of the many aspects of domestic violence, its varying impact and the effectiveness of different interventions for adult and child victims, and perpetrators. We have travelled a long way in the recognition of domestic violence over the past 20 years. Our ambition should now be to make significant reductions in both the incidence and prevalence of this social ill over the next two decades.

REFERENCES

Council of Europe (2011) *Convention on Preventing and Combating Violence Against Women and Domestic Violence.* Strasbourg. Available at www.coe.int/en/web/conventions/full-list/-/conventions/treaty/210

de Haas, B. and van der Kwaak, A. (2017) 'Exploring linkages between research, policy and practise in the Netherlands: Perspectives on sexual and reproductive health and rights knowledge flow.' *Journal of Health Research Policy and Systems 15*, 40, 1–13.

European Commission (1999) *Eurobarometer 51.0: Europeans and Their Views on Domestic Violence Against Women.* Brussels. Available at http://ec.europa.eu/commfrontoffice/publicopinion/archives/ebs/ebs_127_en.pdf

EWL (European Women's Lobby) (1999) *Unveiling the Hidden Data on Domestic Violence in the European Union.* Brussels. Available at www.familyviolence.gov.cy/upload/20091217/1261037273-32239.pdf

FRA (European Agency for Fundamental Rights) (2014) *Violence Against Women: An EU-wide Survey.* Luxembourg: Publications Office of the European Union.

Gracia, E. and Herrero, J. (2006) 'Acceptability of domestic violence against women in the European Union: A multilevel analysis.' *Journal of Epidemiology and Community Health 60*, 2, 123–129.

Hankivsky, O. (ed.) (2014) *An Intersectionality-based Policy Analysis Framework.* Vancouver, BC: Institute for Intersectionality Research and Policy, Simon Fraser University.

Montoya, C. (2013) *The Othering of Domestic Violence: The EU and Cultural Framings of Violence Against Women.* New York: Oxford University Press.

Toulemon, L. (2016) 'Fifty Years of Family Change in Europe: Diversifying Partnerships.' In D. Mortelmans, K. Matthijs, E. Alofs and B. Segaert (eds) *Changing Family Dynamics and Demographic Evolution: The Family Kaleidoscope* (pp.25–50). Cheltenham: Edward Elgar Publishing.

Part One

THE POLICY FRAMEWORK FOR RESPONDING TO DOMESTIC VIOLENCE IN EUROPE

Chapter 1

DOMESTIC VIOLENCE – A RIGHTS-BASED RESPONSE

DRAWING ON RESULTS FROM THE FRA'S VIOLENCE AGAINST WOMEN SURVEY

Joanna Goodey, *Head of the Freedoms and Justice Department, European Union Agency for Fundamental Rights, Vienna, Austria*

INTRODUCTION: WHY A RIGHTS-BASED RESPONSE TO DOMESTIC VIOLENCE?

This chapter outlines why it is important to place our understanding of and responses to domestic violence in a rights-based framework, which, in the context of this chapter and the data presented in it, is specifically with reference to domestic violence against women in the European Union (EU). This rights-based approach serves to underpin the role of the State, and hence State services, in its duty to acknowledge and effectively respond to domestic violence as it impinges on certain rights.

The chapter is divided into two parts, with the first introducing a rights-based framework, which was developed by the Office of the United Nations High Commissioner for Human Rights (OHCHR), as a useful tool for understanding how the State responds to violence against women. Having outlined this rights-based framework, the chapter proceeds to place responses to domestic violence within the wider legal context of recent responses to victims of crime in the EU. The second part presents selected findings from *Violence Against Women: An EU-wide Survey*, published by the EU Agency for Fundamental Rights (FRA) in 2014, which interviewed 42,000 women across all EU member states, focusing on psychological violence by a woman's partner, and presenting an overview of the services women contact in the aftermath of partner and non-partner violence. The survey's results highlight the role that data can play in providing 'evidence' for responding to domestic violence as a human rights abuse.

DEVELOPING A RIGHTS-BASED RESPONSE

Duty bearers and rights holders

A rights-based response to domestic violence acknowledges both 'duty bearers' – that is, the State and State actors, such as the police and other authorities – as well as 'rights holders', ordinary women whose rights have been violated. The international human rights legal framework, which came to fruition at the end of the Second World War, has sought to ensure that States uphold their duties to individuals, to respect, protect and fulfil their human rights. Traditionally, these rights were focused on ensuring people's civil and political rights, such as the right to vote or freedom of assembly, but increasingly the scope of rights has extended to encompass areas such as economic and social rights. In the context of domestic violence against women (by men), it is only relatively recently that this has been addressed within a human rights framework as the extreme manifestation of inequality between women and men, and as violating core human rights such as the right to life and human dignity, as well as the right to a fair trial and to an effective remedy – where the State has a responsibility to ensure that women's abuse is recognised and effectively responded to in line with existing law. In turn, the State's human rights duties have increasingly included recognition of both negative and positive obligations of the State, that is, not only must the State not violate individuals' rights, it must also proactively protect individuals' rights. To this end, human rights case law has evolved in the last decade in recognition of States' failures in their duty to protect women from abuse, because of, for example, failures by the police or courts to intervene in domestic violence cases.

Arguably, the recognition of violence against women as a form of human rights abuse is relatively recent in comparison with other areas of human rights law, such as political and civil rights, because of the traditional divide between the public and private spheres of life and, hence, where the State has been seen as having a duty to act (European commission 2010; McQuigg 2014). Since the 1970s, the grass-roots women's rights movement, including practitioners working with victims of domestic violence, together with academic feminists and legal scholars, have progressively sought to highlight this dichotomy between the public and private sphere, and have been instrumental in bringing violence against women high on the agenda to ensure that it receives legal recognition as a human rights abuse. Herein, it is notable that the United Nations *Convention on the Elimination of All Forms of Discrimination against Women* (CEDAW), which was adopted in 1979 and came into force in 1981, does not make explicit reference to violence against women. It is only with General Recommendation 19 of the CEDAW Committee, in 1992, that violence against women – in both the public and private domains – was squarely put within the remit of human rights law. At the regional level, the Council of Europe *Convention on Preventing and Combating Violence against Women and Domestic Violence* (the Istanbul Convention), which was opened for signature in 2011 and entered into force in 2014, is the most comprehensive international legal instrument to date to specifically address violence against women and domestic violence, and demonstrates how far the law has developed over the span of several decades.

The importance of ensuring recognition in law of violence against women as a form of human rights abuse is essential for a number of reasons, paramount among which is that violations of international human rights law demand a response by the State, and international human rights law – unlike public policy, which can be changed from one government administration to the next – cannot be considered as something temporary. To this end, the importance of a rights-based framework for victims of domestic violence is that they have the law, rather than simply policy, on their side. However, as all good socio-legal books acknowledge, the law in the books is only as good as the law in practise, which necessitates that legislation is upheld by policy and the implementation of law in practise. The Group of Experts on Action against Violence against Women and Domestic Violence (GREVIO) is the independent body that is responsible for monitoring the implementation of the Council of Europe's Istanbul Convention, and is one example of how countries that have signed up to international human rights law can be held accountable. However, to ensure that rights are enforced in practise means looking at the complex intersection between law, policy and practise. A framework for doing this has been developed by the Office of the United

Nations High Commissioner for Human Rights (OHCHR), which has constructed a 'structure-process-outcome' model (FRA 2011; OHCHR 2012) for looking at the application of international human rights law in practise. Figure 1.1 illustrates this model with specific reference to European legislation that addresses violence against women and domestic violence.

Source: FRA, based on the OHCHR

Figure 1.1: Structure-process-outcome model

Another way of describing the UN's three-pronged 'structure-process-outcome' model is to think of each element, in turn, as 'law', 'policy' and 'practise' on the ground. Here, the structural indicators refer to each State's acceptance of and commitment to legal instruments, such as the Istanbul Convention, which addresses violence against women and domestic violence, and captures the legal framework to which an individual State has signed up to. In turn, process indicators capture concrete efforts to enact law through policies that address violence against women. This means establishing and adequately funding support systems for victims of violence, and ensuring that victims can report abuse by training the police and other services to respond effectively to victims. Finally, outcome indicators measure the results of these efforts by providing data that shows the number of victims and how they, as rights holders, experience reality. This data can be collected as administrative data by the State, and can also be collected by both the State and other actors in the form of criminal victimisation surveys. The FRA's Violence Against Women survey is based on criminal victimisation survey models, and captures the extent of women's experience of violence, including whether they report abuse to the police and other services. In this way, surveys, such as the FRA's, provide a useful comparator between what official criminal justice statistics indicate about the extent of violence against women and a more realistic picture of the 'true' extent and nature of violence as women report it in a survey – which, as a reflection of women's under-reporting to the authorities, shows significantly higher levels of victimisation than official data.

Ideally, this UN model should be populated by data at the level of individual countries that shows how they are addressing violence against women through the provision of structural, process and outcome indicators. The reality is that while data is relatively straightforward to collect on a country's accession to international law and corresponding national legislation to address violence against women, it becomes harder to document policies and funding that target violence against women, and harder still to provide 'outcome' indicators that can paint an accurate picture of the phenomenon beyond official criminal justice data (EIGE 2014). Herein, the FRA's survey presents a unique dataset that serves to fill a gap at the EU and individual member state level, particularly for those member states that do not have regular and comprehensive surveys on violence against women (Martinez and Schröttle 2006; UN 2015), by capturing the diverse range of women's experiences of physical, sexual and psychological violence, as reported in the survey.

It is through such 'outcome' indicators, which include data on whether women report to the police and other services – and importantly, if 'not', then 'why not' – that we are able to see whether the State is meeting its duty, with respect to law and policies, to address violence against women. However, in the absence of regular and comprehensive surveys collecting this data, which can be read alongside official statistics and reports from non-governmental organisations (NGOs), it remains difficult to establish whether services and support for women are improving in practise.

Looking at responses to domestic violence in a wider context

In parallel with the growth in recent decades of the women's rights movement and calls for increased recognition of violence against women – focusing initially on domestic violence – has been the growth of practitioner and academic-based work on victims of crime in general. This generic victim rights 'movement' emerged from the framework of international human rights law, and was built on the back of responses to the Holocaust and the mass victimisation of the Jewish population (as well as other groups, including Roma and homosexuals) by the State. In addition, grass-roots movements by individuals in different countries began to address the apparent imbalance between the status of victims and offenders in the criminal justice process, notably in Common Law jurisdictions, where the victim's status was simply that of the 'witness' in criminal proceedings (Goodey 2000, 2005) rather than being given the status of an active and equal party. In comparison, in other jurisdictions the victim had a more active role to play in the criminal justice process, at least in law, if not always in practise, for example in the form of the *partie civile* in France and as a *Nebenklager* in Germany (Dearing 2017).

The UN was at the forefront of trying to increase recognition of the status of victims of crime, with the 1985 Declaration of Basic Principles of Justice for Victims of Crime and Abuse of Power being a ground-breaking move in this direction. At the same time, at the level of the Council of Europe, Recommendation (85) 11 on the Position of the Victim in the Framework of Criminal Law and Procedure saw increased recognition of the place and role of victims. While more recently, at the EU level, the 2001 Framework Decision on the standing of victims in criminal proceedings, which was surpassed in 2012 with the Victims' Rights Directive, has seen a significant shift towards greater recognition of victims in law.

The EU Victims Directive is a major development for victims of crime, in general, in the EU. It moves the victim centre-stage from the 2001 Framework Decision that referred to the 'standing' of victims to a Directive that refers to 'victims' rights'. With this, the language of rights is now centre-stage in binding legislation for victims that addresses victims' needs – as rights – which range from the right to information through to the victim's treatment by the police and other services. Importantly, the Directive makes specific reference to the following groups, namely victims of terrorism, organised crime, human trafficking, gender-based violence, violence in a close relationship, sexual violence, exploitation or hate crime, victims with disabilities, and children. While the Directive's various references to 'gender-based violence', 'violence in a close relationship' and 'sexual violence' are all significant for their recognition of gender-based violence or for violence that disproportionately impacts on women, some commentators critique the fact that violence against women still does not have its own specific legislation at EU level (Montoya 2013). However, alongside the Victims' Rights Directive, the EU does have legislation that targets certain types of crime that disproportionately impact on women and that has a strong 'cross-border' element that clearly denotes where the EU has the legal 'competence' (mandate) to act, such as trafficking in women for sexual exploitation (the anti-trafficking Directive from 2011), and the Regulation on mutual recognition of protection measures in civil matters and the accompanying Directive on the European Protection Order under criminal law, which can assist women who are victims of relational abuse in cross-border situations. However, while the EU is not proposing specific legislation addressing violence against women, the European Commission has now signed up to the Council of Europe's Istanbul Convention, which is the most advanced legal instrument at the regional level to specifically address violence against women and domestic violence (Goodey 2017).

The deadline for transposing the Victims Directive into law at the level of individual EU member states was November 2015, and by November 2017, member states have to communicate to the Commission on the basis of available data 'how victims have accessed the rights set out in this Directive' (Article 28), which will form the basis of a report by the European Commission on the implementation of the Directive across the EU. This report should critically assess the extent to which member states have met their obligations in law to respond to the needs of all victims and specific groups of victims, including victims of gender-based violence, violence in a close relationship, and sexual violence (among others). Every three years after first reporting to the Commission, member states are required to submit data showing how victims have accessed their rights as set out in the Directive, which underlines the need for good administrative data, alongside criminal victimisation surveys, that can furnish the Commission with the overview it needs to assess progress towards meeting victims' rights in practise. The Commission can be supported in this regard by the European Institute for Gender Equality (EIGE), which has indicated its intention to closely follow the collection of administrative and criminal justice data on violence against women at the level of member states. In addition to the data generated by the Violence Against Women survey, the FRA is conducting qualitative research interviewing victims of violent crime in selected member states, which includes women who are victims of domestic violence, the results of which will look at the extent to which victims' needs have been met in line with the rights provided in the Victims' Rights Directive. These findings can directly support the Commission and individual member states to assess progress to date in meeting the standards set out in the Directive.

Whether looking at the Victims' Rights Directive, the anti-trafficking Directive and other legislation at EU level that variously addresses different groups of victims, ranging from children through to victims of terrorism, it is notable that there is increasing reference to 'rights' in the legislative text. The Charter of Fundamental Rights of the EU contains many articles that are of direct relevance for victims of crime, ranging from Article 1 on 'human dignity' through to Article 47 on the 'right to an effective remedy and a fair trial', and is increasingly referenced in EU law since the Charter entered into force in 2009. Even where not directly referenced (as in the case of the Victims' Rights Directive), it is nevertheless applicable when member states adopt or apply national law implementing an EU Directive. In sum, the interplay between generic recognition of victims' rights and increased recognition of the specificities of women's rights as victims of gender-based violence is increasingly interlinked as we look across EU law. It is also reflected by developments at the level of the Council of Europe with respect to take-up by individual EU member states of the Istanbul Convention, alongside the Commission becoming a signatory to the Convention.

Turning once again to how we can measure the impact of rights – in law – with respect to practise on the ground, the next section looks at the work of the FRA and the specific role that survey data plays as 'outcome' indicators.

ROLE OF DATA: EXAMPLES FROM THE FRA'S VIOLENCE AGAINST WOMEN SURVEY

Data to inform policy

Not only has legislation at EU level increasingly come to refer to 'rights', but there is also increasing recognition of the role that data has to play in monitoring the application of the law in practise. To this end, the fact that Article 28 in the Victims' Rights Directive refers to the 'provision of data and statistics' is a significant step towards recognition of the importance of 'evidence', which was missing from the Framework Decision on victims that preceded the Directive. The Council of Europe's Istanbul Convention goes one step further by referring to 'data collection and research' in Article 11 and, specifically in paragraph 2 of this article, to the need for 'population-based surveys' to be able to assess prevalence and trends in all forms of violence against women covered in the Convention.

The survey by the FRA was undertaken in order to fill an existing gap in EU-wide population-based survey data on the extent and nature of violence against women, which had been remarked on over several years by international organisations through to NGOs. The results of the survey present 'outcome' data – in the framework of the UN structure-process-outcome model – that informs us about women's experiences of physical, sexual and psychological violence since the age of 15 (lifetime prevalence) and in the last 12 months. In addition, the survey collected data about women's experiences of violence in childhood at the hands of adult perpetrators (Till-Tentschert 2017). The survey also included questions about newly recognised forms of violence against women that have not been captured to date at an EU-wide level or at the level of many individual countries, namely 'cyber-harassment' and 'cyber-stalking', which involve new tools such as text messages, email and social media to victimise women, including in the context of domestic violence, and in the aftermath of relationships ending when women are at high risk of abuse.

Importantly, unlike some surveys that ask very general questions about experiences of violence, the FRA survey used a version of the 'conflict tactics scale' to ask women a series of questions that built up a picture of their experiences of violence, namely by asking about each individual act of violence in turn. For example, with respect to physical violence, women were asked in turn for each of the following:

'Since you were 15 years old until now/in the past 12 months, how often has someone: Pushed or shoved you? Slapped you? Thrown a hard object at you? Grabbed you or pulled your hair? Beaten you with a fist or a hard object, or kicked you? Burned you? Tried to suffocate or strangle you? Cut or stabbed you, or shot at you? Beaten your head against something?' The same approach was adopted for other types of violence asked about in the survey. Using a variation of the conflict tactics scale produces a more accurate picture of the extent and nature of violence as it is experienced, which is also shown by other surveys that have adopted this approach (Garcia Moreno *et al.* 2005). In addition, women were asked in the FRA survey whether specific incidents had occurred in the past 12 months, and how often, and were asked who the perpetrator was and the nature of their relationship with them; they were also asked about reporting and non-reporting of incidents to the police and different organisations. In this way, when asking about specific acts of physical and sexual violence, and who the perpetrator was, the dataset is able to show the extent of 'domestic violence' experienced by women by either current or former partners.

In sum, the FRA survey interviewed a random sample of 42,000 women aged between 18 and 74 across the 28 member states of the EU, which represented an average of 1500 women in each member state. The selection of women for interviewing was based on the best available sampling frame in each member state, and all interviews were conducted in person by female interviewers. Whereas some countries benefit from established, regular and large-scale surveys that ask about violence against women – such as the Italian crime survey and the crime survey for England and Wales – this is not the case in many EU member states, where surveys are sporadically conducted, and where sample sizes can be small (in a number of cases, smaller than that of the FRA survey). This means that, for a number of member states, the FRA survey is the most up-to-date and comprehensive population-based survey on the prevalence of different forms of violence against women.

Unlike many EU-wide surveys where questions are changed to meet the specific policy needs of individual countries, the FRA survey used the same questionnaire in all member states. While comparison between historically and culturally diverse countries presents challenges when looking at the results of any number of international surveys, the fact that the FRA survey asked the same questions does allow for comparison of results between countries that are closer in terms of their political, social and economic standing, including in relation to gender equality and with respect to responses to violence against women. Herein, as suggested in the FRA's *Main Results Report* from the survey, comparisons of the survey results can be more meaningfully made between countries that are more closely 'matched' – for example, Sweden can compare its findings with Finland and Denmark; Spain with Portugal; and Bulgaria with Romania. In addition, the *Main Results Report* indicates some possible explanations for variations in reported rates of violence between member states (FRA 2014, pp.22-26); however, as noted by Nevala (2017) in his in-depth analysis of the survey's results with respect to coercive control, high rates of violence do not always hold across countries when different types of violence are explored in detail.

What the data shows and how it can be used

Turning to the survey's results with respect to data at the level of the EU, the following 'headline' figures can be noted that encompass different aspects of women's experiences of 'domestic' or 'intimate partner' violence, namely among those women in the survey who indicated they have a (current or previous) partner:

- 22 per cent of women have experienced some form of physical and/or sexual violence by a partner since the age of 15
- 7 per cent of women have experienced physical violence by a current partner, and 24 per cent by a previous partner
- 34 per cent of victims of physical violence by a previous partner experienced four or more different forms of physical violence, with the most common forms involving pushing or shoving, slapping or grabbing, or pulling a woman's hair
- 43 per cent of women have experienced psychological violence by a partner, 23 per cent by a current partner and 48 per cent by a previous partner
- 18 per cent of women have experienced some form of stalking, most often by a previous partner.

While the data indicates higher levels of violence with respect to former partners, this can be a result of women having had more than one previous partner, and could also reflect women's willingness to report violence perpetrated by previous (rather than current) partners. Different chapters in the survey's *Main Results Report* look at the above and additional findings in detail, while in the remainder of this chapter the following results are presented with reference to a rights-based response: first, findings on women's experiences of psychological violence by a partner, as this represents one of the most widespread forms of abuse that women experience, and an area that until recently was relatively under-researched in comparison with physical violence in intimate partner relationships; and second, women's contact with the police and different services in the aftermath of violence by a partner or someone else.

Psychological violence by a partner

In the survey a series of 17 questions was asked about a broad range of 'psychological partner violence' that is variously encapsulated under the following general categories, namely (1) 'controlling behaviour', such as trying to keep a woman from seeing friends, family or relatives, or jealousy beyond normal concern; (2) 'economic violence', such as preventing a woman from making decisions on family finances or shopping independently, or forbidding her to work outside the home; (3) 'abusive behaviour', such as forbidding a woman to leave the house or locking her up, or scaring or intimidating her on purpose, or threatening her with violence; and (4) 'blackmail with/abuse of children', such as threatening to take the children away, or threatening to hurt the children, or actually hurting the children.

Overall, noting that 43 per cent of women indicated that they had experienced some form of psychological violence by a current and/or previous partner, the prevalence rates were as follows across the four general categories referred to above: controlling behaviour, 35 per cent; economic violence, 12 per cent; abusive behaviour, 32 per cent; and blackmail with/abuse of children, 8 per cent. Looking across the 17 questions on psychological violence asked about in the survey, the results indicate that the most common forms involve a partner belittling or humiliating a woman in private, insisting on knowing where she is in a way that goes beyond general concern, and getting angry when she speaks to other men. Among women in the survey who indicated they were currently in a relationship, 7 per cent said they had experienced four or more different forms of psychological violence by their current partner. In turn, most women who experience four or more forms of psychological violence by a current partner also indicated in the survey that their current partner had been physically and/or sexually violent towards them, which indicates the connectedness of different forms of abuse.

The extent and nature of psychological violence by a partner, as outlined in the FRA's survey results, can have a significant impact on a woman's life. In recognition of core fundamental rights that are undermined by such abuse, such as 'respect for private and family life' under Article 7 of the Charter of Fundamental Rights of the EU, the FRA's report on the survey's findings states: 'Multiple and repetitive forms of psychological violence by intimate partners need to be recognised as undermining a woman's autonomy, which equates to the loss of an autonomous and family life' (FRA 2014, p.79). The FRA report outlines the following 'opinions' as examples of where 'duty bearers' could act in response to psychological violence – namely:

- Those who have a duty to care, such as employers in relation to their staff, should consider adopting awareness-raising and related training activities to be able to identify and respond to the needs of staff who are suffering from psychologically controlling behaviour.
- EU member states should review legislation to assess if it encompasses the various forms and impact of repetitive psychological abuse on victims.
- The police and other services should be trained to recognise and understand the impact of psychological abuse on victims.
- Controlling and abusive behaviour by offenders may require that the police intervene directly to protect victims and to refer them to victim support services, rather than waiting for a victim to seek assistance herself. (FRA 2014, pp.79–80)

The Council of Europe Istanbul Convention requires that State parties to the Convention pay due attention to various forms of psychological violence, namely Article 33 requires States to take measures to ensure that intentionally impairing a person's psychological integrity is criminalised, and Article 46 requires that repeated offences and causing severe psychological harm are considered as aggravating circumstances when sentencing. Therefore, States that have signed up to the Convention will need to ensure that these elements are reflected in national law. Some countries, such as the UK, have introduced legislation recognising psychological violence in the form of 'coercive control', which is referred to in the UK's Serious Crime Act 2015 as 'controlling or coercive behaviour in an intimate or family relationship'. These developments illustrate that the law is now acknowledging the very real problem of abuse in the form of psychological violence. However, while these 'structural indicators' are falling into place, very few countries collect administrative or other data – 'outcome indicators' – on women's actual experiences of this form of abuse. Therefore, the FRA's data can play a vital role in making this information available for countries, which can encourage responses at the level of legislative reform and policy provisions.

Contacting the authorities

A key finding from the FRA survey was the low rate at which women reported different forms of abuse to the police, as well as to other organisations, a finding that is supported by other research (ONS 2015). For example, women who indicated in the survey that they were a victim of violence were asked whether they had contacted the police or other services following the most serious incident of violence (if there was more than one). Table 1.1 presents a breakdown of the survey's results on contacting the police and other services on the basis of whether the perpetrator was a partner or someone else, and according to whether the incident was related to physical or sexual violence.

As the data shows, overall rates for contacting any service in the aftermath of an incident of violence are low, with 39 per cent of incidents of sexual violence and 31 per cent of incidents of physical violence by a partner resulting in contact with a service, in comparison with 30 per cent of incidents of sexual violence and 24 per cent of incidents of physical violence perpetrated by someone else resulting in contact. One of the reasons for higher rates of contact with respect to partner violence could be the repetitive nature of 'domestic' violence, which means that a number of women could be reporting abuse after having experienced several incidents. What is particularly notable from these results is that 'healthcare providers' – combining hospitals, doctors, health centres or other healthcare institutions – represent, collectively, those services that are most often turned to for help. In comparison, rates of reporting to the police never exceed 15 per cent. The involvement of a lawyer or legal service reaches 15 per cent in the case of sexual violence by a partner and 10 per cent in cases of physical violence by a partner, which could reflect the initiation of proceedings such as divorce. Of particular note is the fact that only 3 per cent of women contacted a women's shelter as a result of physical violence by a partner, which rises to 6 per cent with respect to sexual violence by a partner, whereas it might be expected that these services, which are aimed at women who are victims of domestic violence, would be contacted more frequently, a finding that is explored further below.

Table 1.1: Contact with the police and other services after the most serious incident of violence (%)

	Any partner		Non-partner	
	Physical violence	Sexual violence	Physical violence	Sexual violence
Police	14	15	13	14
Hospital	11	12	9	12
Doctor, health centre	15	22	10	16
Social services	5	7	2	2
Women's shelter	3	6	0	1
Victim support organisation	4	4	1	4
Church/faith-based organisation	3	4	2	2
Legal service/lawyer	10	15	4	6
Another service/ organisation	3	5	3	3
Any of the above	31	39	24	30

Source: FRA (2014, p.59)

These results can be read in different ways, but are informative for those services that have a public duty to respond to the needs – and hence the rights – of victims of crime in accordance with the law. For example, the EU Victims' Rights Directive contains specific articles relating to the 'right to receive information from the first contact with a competent authority' (Article 4), the 'right to access victim support services' (Article 8), to receive 'support from victim support services' (Article 9) and on 'training of practitioners' (Article 25), while the Council of Europe's Istanbul Convention – under Chapter IV covering 'protection and support' – contains several articles that are directly relevant to contact with the authorities and different services.

Low rates of contact with the police and other authorities indicate that more needs to be done by these services – through personnel training and public outreach – to ensure that women feel they can approach them for support, and to make certain that women who contact services and report abuse are responded to in an appropriate way. This is particularly the case with respect to the police, as women indicated lower rates of satisfaction with the assistance they received from the police in comparison with other services (FRA 2014, p.65). At the same time, high rates of reporting to health services, in comparison with low rates of reporting to women's shelters or victim support services, may reflect the reality in many countries that specialist services are geographically few and far between, and are also relatively under-funded when compared with health services. There may also be less 'stigma' attached for women to contact their local doctor or health service as a result of abuse, as opposed to the decision to contact specialist services.

In the survey, women were asked why they did not contact a range of services in the aftermath of violence. The main reason given was because women dealt with the incident themselves or involved a friend or other family member, with this response being highest for cases of physical violence by a woman's partner. What this indicates is the extent to which violence against women is still regarded by many women as something that should not or cannot be addressed by a range of services, and as something that remains in the 'private' sphere and does not warrant intervention by the State. Given that reporting to the police is low, at 15 per cent or under, depending on the type of incident, and also very low for a range of other services, it is clear that the role of 'duty bearers' to effectively respond to violence against women – including cases of domestic violence – will remain under-developed if women do not feel willing or able to contact the police and other services. As reporting rates to combined health services are higher than for other services, it is apparent that attention can be paid to increasing the role of doctors and other medical staff in recognising and responding to cases, or suspected cases, of violence against women – including domestic incidents. Here, it is worth noting that among all the women interviewed for the survey, 87 per cent indicated that they would find it acceptable if doctors routinely asked about violence when patients exhibited certain injuries or symptoms.

To summarise, the FRA's report from the survey includes 'opinions' of where 'duty bearers' could act in response to women's experiences of violence. For example, with respect to healthcare and to specialist victim support services, the report states:

- Healthcare professionals can play an enhanced role in identifying and channelling cases of violence against women; confidentiality rules should be clarified so that healthcare professionals can report abuse (under appropriate conditions).
- In line with the EU Victims' Rights Directive and the Istanbul Convention, there is a pressing need across the EU to enhance resources for specialist victim support services that are able to respond to the needs of women who are victims of violence. (FRA 2014, p.69)

CONCLUSION

A rights-based response to domestic violence that is framed around the UN's structure-process-outcome model – which has been developed to assess the application of the law, policies and practise on the ground – requires data to populate the model. In the absence of comprehensive 'outcome' data in many countries on the extent and nature of women's experiences of violence, which includes rates of reporting to the police and other services, the FRA's Violence Against Women survey provides a unique dataset that can furnish data at the EU and member state level.

The FRA's survey presents a starting point for encouraging more comprehensive data collection by individual countries that do not already have regular population-based surveys on violence against women. In 2017, the EU's statistical office – Eurostat – is piloting a survey in selected EU member states, building on the FRA's survey, that will collect data on women and men's experiences of violence.

Also in 2017, the Office for Security and Cooperation in Europe (OSCE) is replicating the FRA's survey in ten non-EU countries to measure women's experiences of violence, including their experiences of violence in post-conflict settings. The results of the FRA's survey, alongside that of the OSCE's, can be read in combination with administrative data on violence against women – from the police and other sources – to better understand the 'true' extent and nature of violence as women experience it. In turn, these 'outcome' indicators on violence against women need to be looked at in the context of existing law and policy to see the extent to which the 'law in the books' and policy commitments are being met in practise. Ideally, if surveys are repeated over time, trends in rates of violence will be available to assess whether progress is being made to address violence against women, which includes indicators as to whether victims are more frequently reporting violence to the police and different services and, in turn, whether these services are recording incidents. Only with the regular provision of data that can populate the structure-process-outcome model will we be able to see if a rights-based response to domestic violence is in place, from which the State and other actors, such as NGOs, can assess the performance of those who have a duty to respond to victims.

Disclaimer: The views expressed in this chapter are solely those of the author and do not necessarily reflect the views or position of the European Union Agency for Fundamental Rights.

REFERENCES

Dearing, A. (2017) *Justice for Victims of Crime: Human Dignity as the Foundation of Criminal Justice in Europe.* Basel, Switzerland: Springer International Publishing.

EIGE (European Institute for Gender Equality) (2014) *Administrative Data Sources on Gender-based Violence Against Women in the EU: Current Status and Potential for the Collection of Comparable Data.* Luxembourg: Publications Office of the European Union. Accessed on 16/6/2017 at http://eige.europa.eu/rdc/eige-publications/administrative-data-sources-gender-based-violence-against-women-eu-report

European Commission (2010) *Feasibility Study to Assess the Possibilities, Opportunities and Needs to Standardise National Legislation on Violence Against Women, Violence Against Children and Sexual Orientation Violence.* Brussels: Directorate General for Justice, Directorate B – Criminal Justice. Accessed on 16/6/2017 at http://bookshop.europa.eu/en/feasibility-study-to-assess-the-possibilities-opportunities-and-needs-to-standardise-national-legislation-on-violence-against-women-violence-against-children-and-sexual-orientation-violence-pbNE3209188

FRA (European Union Agency for Fundamental Rights) (2011) *FRA Symposium Report: Using Indicators to Measure Fundamental Rights in the EU: Challenges and Solutions.* 2nd Annual FRA Symposium, Vienna, 12–13 May. Accessed on 16/6/2017 at http://fra.europa.eu/en/publication/2012/fra-symposium-report-using-indicators-measure-fundamental-rights-eu-challenges-and

FRA (2014) *Violence Against Women: An EU-wide Survey – Main Results Report.* Luxembourg: Publications Office of the European Union. Accessed on 16/6/2017 at http://fra.europa.eu/sites/default/files/fra-2014-vaw-survey-main-results-apr14_en.pdf

Garcia Moreno, C., Jansen, H., Ellsberg, M., Heise, L. and Watts, C. (2005) *World Health Organization Multi-country Study on Women's Health and Domestic Violence Against Women.* Geneva: World Health Organization. Accessed on 16/6/2017 at http://cdrwww.who.int/gender/violence/who_multicountry_study/Introduction-Chapter1-Chapter2.pdf

Goodey, J. (2000) 'Overview of Key Themes.' In A. Crawford and J. Goodey (eds) *Integrating a Victim Perspective within Criminal Justice: International Debates* (Chapter One). Aldershot: Ashgate Publishing.

Goodey, J. (2005) *Victims and Victimology: Research, Policy and Practise.* Harlow: Pearson Education Limited.

Goodey, J. (2017) 'Violence against women: Placing evidence from a European Union-wide survey in a policy context.' *Journal of Interpersonal Violence 32,* 12, 1760–1791.

Martinez, M. and Schröttle, M. (2006) *State of European Research on the Prevalence of Interpersonal Violence and Its Impact on Health and Human Rights.* CAHRV-Report 2006. Co-ordination Action on Human Rights Violations funded through the European Commission, 6th Framework Programme, Project No. 506348. Accessed on 16/6/2017 at www.cahrv.uni-osnabrueck.de/reddot/CAHRVreportPrevalence(1).pdf

McQuigg, R.J.A. (2014) 'The European Court of Human Rights and Domestic Violence: Valliuliene v Lithuania.' *The International Journal of Human Rights 18,* 7–8, 756–773.

Montoya, C. (2013) *From Global to Grassroots: The EU, Transnational Advocacy, and Combating Violence Against Women.* New York: Oxford University Press.

Nevala, S. (2017) 'Coercive control and its impact on intimate partner violence through the lens of an EU-wide survey on violence against women.' *Journal of Interpersonal Violence 32,* 12, 1792–1820.

OHCHR (Office of the United Nations High Commissioner for Human Rights) (2012) *Human Rights Indicators: A Guide to Measurement and Implementation.* New York and Geneva, Switzerland: United Nations. Accessed on 16/6/2017 at www.ohchr.org/EN/Issues/Indicators/Pages/documents.aspx

ONS (Office for National Statistics) (2015) 'Chapter 4: Violent Crime and Sexual Offences – Intimate Personal Violence and Serious Sexual Assault.' Accessed on 16/6/2017 at http://webarchive.nationalarchives.gov.uk/20160105160709/http://www.ons.gov.uk/ons/dcp171776_394500.pdf

Till-Tentschert, U. (2017) 'The relation between violence experienced in childhood and women's exposure to violence in later life: Evidence from Europe.' *Journal of Interpersonal Violence 32,* 12, 1874–1894.

UN (United Nations) (2015) *The World's Women 2015: Trends and Statistics.* New York: UN. Accessed on 16/6/2017 at http://unstats.un.org/unsd/gender/downloads/WorldsWomen2015_report.pdf

Chapter 2

DEVELOPMENT, COORDINATION AND IMPLEMENTATION OF NATIONAL STRATEGIES FOR THE PREVENTION OF DOMESTIC, SEXUAL AND GENDER-BASED VIOLENCE IN IRELAND

LESSONS LEARNED AND UNLEARNED

Philip McCormack,[1] *Cosc – The National Office for the Prevention of Domestic, Sexual and Gender-based Violence, Dublin, Ireland*

INTRODUCTION

This chapter aims to share some of the learning Cosc (Ireland's National Office for the Prevention of Domestic, Sexual and Gender-based Violence) has had in devising, implementing and reviewing a national strategy on domestic, sexual and gender-based violence, and in working towards a second National Strategy. As most of the detailed material is available online at cosc.ie, this chapter doesn't spend a lot of time describing the history or the content of the strategy, but does both very briefly to start, before moving on to describe some of the successes. Finally, the chapter draws out a number of themes that were learning experiences for the work of Cosc, and may be of interest and use to policy-makers in other jurisdictions.

1 Any views expressed in this chapter are not necessarily those of Cosc or the Department of Justice and Equality.

Cosc was established in June 2007. After extensive consultations with the voluntary sector and state stakeholders, the National Strategy on Domestic, Sexual and Gender-based Violence, 2010–2014, was agreed by the Government and published. The mid-term review of the strategy was published in the autumn of 2012. An end-of-term review and issues arising in the context of the second National Strategy was completed in September 2014. Work is currently underway to implement the second National Strategy on Domestic, Sexual and Gender-based Violence, 2016–2021.

FIRST AND SECOND NATIONAL STRATEGIES ON DOMESTIC, SEXUAL AND GENDER-BASED VIOLENCE

There has been significant learning arising from both the development and implementation of the first National Strategy. Key milestones in its development were the call for submissions, an all of Ireland conference with international representatives, national and regional consultations and circulation of the outline Strategy. Work focused on consideration of the direction or approach of the Strategy to ensure that the high-level goals, objectives, actions and activities were reasonable, and capable of achieving the overall goal of the development of a strong framework for sustainable intervention to prevent and effectively respond to domestic, sexual and gender-based violence. In the light of the mainstream approach taken in the outline Strategy, particular attention was given at that stage to consideration of the suitability of the actions to meet the needs of particularly vulnerable groups. Final phases of Strategy development involved the drafting of the narrative to contextualise the actions. Further consultation was required to consider any adjustments necessary, the insertion of timescales, further identification, where necessary, of the details of implementation and the formal agreement of the various responsible public service bodies to carry out the actions in the draft leading to the completion of the Strategy.

Following a process of research, submissions and consultations, Cosc gathered a wealth of material by the end of 2008. Some of the submissions had been submitted using the thematic headings suggested viz. strengthening of preventative mechanisms; the development of support services for victims; dealing with offenders; protection of victims; and ensuring the effectiveness of action. Submissions ranged from short personal views to referenced and detailed documents.

The material was combined with material gathered at the consultations, and was summarised into a table that ran to over 85 pages.

Some suggestions were relevant to more than one theme, and it quickly became clear that maintaining the thematic approach was adding to the complexity of the analysis. The material was then divided into sectoral and multisector issues. The various sectoral tables developed were then used as a basis for discussion with the relevant responsible public sector bodies. The general approach taken in these discussions was an explanation of the context, the suggested action and feasibility of the implementation of the action in the short, medium and long term, or if it posed a major policy difficulty.

During this period, consideration was also given to the conceptual model suitable for the Strategy. This included examination of various World Health Organization (WHO) models and the general approach taken in domestic and sexual violence strategies in other jurisdictions. Given the medium-term constraints on the Irish economy at the time, as well as the state of development of interventions in Ireland, it became increasingly clear that the most sensible approach would be to aim for the development of a solid framework, which would deliver a strong foundation for more expansive work in the future. The model chosen was one that was seen as being capable of making a significant impact on prevention and the cohesion of activity as well as basic improvements in services. The strength of the model was in its simplicity and its emphasis on impact.

Following the choice of model, the Strategy development took shape by placing the various actions under a series of goals and objectives. It cascaded from the overall strategic objective to the various activities to be carried out under the Strategy. These included the *primary intervention* step covering *prevention and awareness* (including sensitisation of relevant staff, public and victim awareness, etc.); the *secondary intervention* step covering all the actions that directly concern *service delivery* (including common information across organisations and sectors, disclosure/routine enquiry, etc.); and the *policy and planning* step level that draws on primary and secondary intervention, thereby bringing it all together (covering improvements to data, monitoring and evidence-based planning).

The first Strategy had four high-level goals:

- Promoting a culture of prevention and recognition of such violence

- Effective and consistent service to victims
- More effective policy and service planning
- Efficient and effective implementation.

Under these goals were 59 activities. There were also monitoring structures and a twice-yearly monitoring exercise in relation to progress on the activities. These activities continued to be the activities at the end of the Strategy five years later. At least one of these activities, for example some related to training and education, proved to be unachievable, but remained as part of the Strategy. This was because the Strategy and its separate Executive Summary were bound volumes that were printed.

There have been many positive developments arising from the implementation of the first National Strategy, and other activities under it have been carried over into the second National Strategy, although much remains to be done. There was, however, some disappointing slippage in the first National Strategy, for a number of reasons, in relation to target dates and in relation to revised target dates.

The overview of the analysis of submissions received as part of the end-of-term review discussed the impact of reduced resources on implementation of the Strategy. It was suggested that the original Strategy may have been overly ambitious and did not consider the changing economic environment. A changed financial climate, changes to the ways in which support services were funded and issues around ownership of the Strategy all contributed to significant challenges in the implementation of the first National Strategy, and would then have to be taken into account in the shaping of the second. These points strongly support the need to prioritise, so that the new Strategy contains realistic and achievable actions.

On 13 January 2016 the Government approved the second National Strategy on Domestic, Sexual and Gender-based Violence, 2016–2021. The Minister for Justice and Equality formally launched the Strategy on 20 January 2016. The multi-annual Strategy contains a range of actions to be implemented by State, voluntary and community sector organisations aimed at preventing and responding to domestic, sexual and gender-based violence over its lifetime.

The overall aims of this Strategy are relatively simple to state:

- Change societal attitudes to support a reduction in domestic and sexual violence

- Improve supports available to victims and survivors
- Hold perpetrators to account in order to create a safer Ireland.

In support of these objectives data will be gathered, research encouraged and monitoring engaged in.

The actions have a four-fold genesis:

- There are worthwhile actions from the first National Strategy that warrant continuation.
- There are actions agreed by the Government that must be implemented to enable Ireland to ratify the Council of Europe *Convention on Preventing and Combating Violence against Women and Domestic Violence* (the Istanbul Convention).
- Relevant actions to implement the EU Victims Directive are also included.
- Finally, new actions that resulted from the consultation process to develop the Strategy have been included.

Three elements contributed to the activities of the second National Strategy. First, it was essential that worthwhile activities not completed in the timescale of the original Strategy were carried forward into the new Strategy. Second, an action plan with timelines was set out in the second Strategy for all policy and legislative changes and actions needed to enable Ireland to ratify the Council of Europe Istanbul Convention. Third, activities required to transpose the EU Victims Directive of relevance to victims of domestic and sexual violence made up part of the activities in the new Strategy. Cosc is driving its implementation. In order to ensure its successful delivery, appropriate monitoring structures have been put in place. Those consist of a monitoring committee comprised of key stakeholders (non-governmental organisations (NGOs) and the State), and an interdepartmental Strategy oversight committee of high-level officials to ensure actions are delivered on time and address any problems that may arise in implementation.

New actions contained in the second National Strategy include:

- A national awareness-raising campaign

- A range of legislative measures including the new Domestic Violence Bill, the Criminal Justice (Victims of Crime) Bill and the Criminal Law (Sexual Offences) Bill
- Provision of education and training of public sector staff involved in this area, by An Garda Síochána (Irish Police Force), Courts Service, Probation Service, Tusla (the Child and Family Agency) and the Health Service Executive
- Addressing gaps in academic and professional education for service providers in the community and voluntary sectors
- Initial training and ongoing developmental training for legal professionals by the Law Society, Bar Council and King's Inns
- A range of measures to be undertaken by An Garda Síochána to improve the service provided to victims including implementing a risk assessment for all victims of domestic violence and sexual crime
- Focusing on the recidivist perpetrator
- A planned and managed approach by An Garda Síochána to each report of a domestic violence incident
- Building a new family court complex in Dublin
- Establishing a family court system throughout the country.

The overall goals of the new Strategy were, at the time, unlikely to change radically over a number of years, but circumstances may change and new opportunities emerge, which the activities of the Strategy should reflect. In other words, the strategic focus may remain broadly the same over time, but the tactics to achieve these strategic aims may change. In particular, it may be that in a number of years' time resources may not be as constrained as they were. Cosc, therefore, envisage the Strategy as a so-called 'living document'. The launch document of the second National Strategy was edition 1. Cosc anticipates that any member of the monitoring structure is able to propose a modification or termination of an activity for stated reasons or is able to propose the inclusion of a new activity. This will give rise to successive editions of the Strategy. It is primarily a web-based document that can be printed if required.

WHOSE STRATEGY?

The first National Strategy was described in its own terms as a 'whole of government' approach to domestic, sexual and gender-based violence. However, it was often also described as the Cosc Strategy. Loosely speaking, it was the Cosc Strategy in that Cosc endeavoured to promote a wide range of the activities under it, and undertook the monitoring and organised the relevant committee meetings. However, the use of this terminology suggested a lack of requisite ownership by state organisations.

Another perception was that the Strategy was a State Strategy, with the voluntary sector holding the State side to account in relation to its delivery of activities. Of course, the voluntary sector has a valid national advocacy role in relation to victims of violence. Tusla, the statutory national child and family agency, provide approximately €20 million to voluntary organisations working in the sector. In addition, resources are provided to An Garda Síochána and the Legal Aid Board to enable them to respond to domestic and sexual violence. Funding is also available for various support services such as the Sexual Assault Treatment Units. Relevant court services are also funded. The organisations in the voluntary sector have a key role as service deliverers. The implementation of the second National Strategy needed to acknowledge this role.

ACHIEVEMENTS

Cosc identified a long list of achievements arising from the first National Strategy. Before going on to look at learning, it is important to highlight and comment on a handful of those achievements. Some relate to how the Strategy had facilitated dialogue both between sectors (e.g. Government and the voluntary sector) and also within sectors (e.g. different parts of different Government departments). This has resulted in services being more joined-up (e.g. services available through the courts). Other emerging themes relating to the achievements of the first National Strategy include an enhanced dialogue on gender and another on using evidence and information for meaningful analysis and reflection on both policy and practise in the sector as a whole.

The first achievement, however, is that the first National Strategy was agreed and implemented. A previous attempt some years earlier failed to get as far as a strategy. The *Report of the Task Force on Violence Against Women*, published in April 1997 by the Oifig an Tánaiste (Office of the Tánaiste, Deputy Prime Minister), recommended a national strategy for Ireland. However, attempts to implement this recommendation failed. At the time there were many complex factors at play as to why this was the case, but these remain beyond the scope of this chapter.

A second noteworthy achievement is that the Dublin Family Law Courts at Dolphin House are now housing voluntary sector resident support services for victims of domestic violence. These complement the legal protections available through the Courts Service, the Legal Aid Board and the Family Mediation Service in the same building. Support services are also available in Dundalk Court and will become available in other venues in due course. This is a significant achievement, which is claimed for the first National Strategy, even though it happened as the result of a conversation in the margins of the National Steering Committee meeting between the Courts Service and Women's Aid, Dublin.

A further plus of the Strategy, which is highlighted by this serendipity, is the opening up and consolidation of relationships between actors in different sectors and different organisations. It also marked a deepening of the appreciation on some sides of the distinct and complementary roles that different players had in the system. It gave access to policy-making and service planning to the voluntary sector. Policy-makers, too, learned a greater appreciation of the complexity of service delivery and practise.

Major strides were also made during the currency of the first National Strategy in the development of sexual violence perpetrator programmes, the establishment of a Sex Offender Risk Assessment and Management (SORAM) office, and the use of Stable and Acute 2007 and Risk Matrix 2000 as standard tools in Ireland for use by the police and probation services in relation to convicted sex offenders. While these actions were listed under the first National Strategy, the impetus for their development and delivery came not from Cosc, but from a joint commitment between the Irish police force and the Probation Service, and a champion in the Department of Justice and Equality. The actions occurred because they made sense to the main actors concerned and addressed a real issue, and not necessarily because they were part of a national strategy.

With a relatively modest budget there was much innovation in the area of awareness-raising and the harnessing of the creativity of the voluntary sector service providers at all levels in this regard.

A major learning in all that was achieved by the sector was full recognition of the fact that there is a difference between the approaches of State and voluntary sector organisations generally, which applies not just in this sector. Voluntary sector organisations produce a range of documents, but value face-to-face contact, oral communication and dialogue, both structured and unstructured. The State sector is able to articulate its positions orally and to engage with and resolve issues in this way. However, when dealing with complex processes, it sees the necessity to capture what is happening in some written form, whether that is a report or a spreadsheet.

The lack of engagement with the six-monthly progress report in the form of a table on all strategy activities was noticeable under the first Strategy. Perhaps the voluntary sector found the 20-page spreadsheets unduly bureaucratic, and found debates with invited experts on a particular topic more congenial. And perhaps the State side was happy to keep their heads down and wait for criticism under separate agenda items. In any event, at this level there was little strategic discussion in the monitoring structures on how the Strategy was going.

THE ISSUE OF GENDER

When Cosc was established, the issue of violence against women moved from the gender equality side of the Department of Justice and Equality to the crime side. Crimes of violence including assault, assault causing harm, harassment and coercion are gender-neutral on the statute books. Either gender can be a victim or a perpetrator. This simple paradigm shift appears to have been profound in the eyes of the voluntary sector.

In the structures, resources and activities of the first National Strategy, implementation and response was focused more on women as victims and men as perpetrators, while acknowledging the possibilities of men as victims and women as perpetrators. It is noteworthy as an aside that Amen, the sole, dedicated voluntary sector organisation dealing with male victims of domestic violence, spent €190,000, according to their 2015 published accounts. This is 0.6 per cent of the expenditure of all domestic violence voluntary sector services in the same year. Some of those who sit around the table regard violence against women exclusively as another and pernicious manifestation and enforcer of women's longstanding inequality with men in Irish society, and are reluctant to accept alternative analyses.

The tension between the two views came to the fore in discussions from time to time. It sometimes also had other impacts. The National Steering Committee on Violence against Women reluctantly agreed to the addition of a single member representing the domestic violence perpetrator programmes for men. All of these programmes work closely with the women's domestic violence services at a local level through partner contact mechanisms. On the ground, these contacts have benefited the perpetrators, their victims and the organisations, helping both. The National Steering Committee on Violence against Women predates the first National Strategy. Its establishment was recommended by the *Report of the National Task Force on Violence Against Women* in 1997. This structure was co-opted as an advisory committee for the National Strategy. The inclusion of Amen on the National Steering Committee was explored. However, a less happy outcome has been the establishment perforce of the National Steering Committee on Violence against Men, which is effectively a bilateral meeting between Cosc and Amen.

STRUCTURES AND POLITICAL OVERSIGHT

The breadth of the issue of domestic and sexual violence along with the complexity of the relationships between stakeholders involved required the establishment and maintenance of committees, sub-committees, ongoing meetings and relationship-building. Hence a considerable network of formal and informal structures between agencies had been developed. Some changes in these structures over the lifetime of the first National Strategy did present challenges for both State and non-State stakeholders involved.

Cosc, as an executive office of the Department of Justice and Equality, is undertaking the monitoring process of the second National Strategy. Cosc, as stated, has established a monitoring committee involving all relevant State bodies and non-State actors. Under the second National Strategy Cosc will commission mid-term and end-of-term reviews. There are 15 State bodies involved in implementing the Strategy. At the time of writing, the main bodies include An Garda Síochána, Tusla and the Department of Justice and Equality. Tusla is now the primary funder of the approximately 60 domestic and sexual violence service providers in the voluntary sector.

The work of Cosc and the second National Strategy is complemented by the Irish Observatory on Violence Against Women that operates under the auspices of the National Women's Council of Ireland (NWCI) since its formation as part of an EU Daphne initiative in 2002. The Irish Observatory links into the European Women's Lobby (EWL) European Observatory on Violence against Women. The EWL Observatory's main objectives are to identify critical and emerging issues in order to feed the policy work of the EWL to advocate for improved policies and service provision for the prevention and support of women victims of male violence.

Members of the National Observatory are AkiDwA (Swahili for sisterhood), Sexual Violence Centre Cork, Rape Crisis Centre, Dublin, EWL through the Irish Representative on the European Observatory, Immigrant Council of Ireland, National Women's Council of Ireland Ltd, Pavee Point Travellers and Roma Centre, Ruhama and Women's Aid.

Regarding political oversight, the second National Strategy has been approved by the Government and subsequently published. Various ministers have their efforts to progress legislation under the new Strategy monitored and reviewed. It is a matter for the Government to decide on the appropriate structures to support and advise on the new Strategy.

LOCATION OF THE COORDINATING BODY

The mid-term review of the first National Strategy summarised the position in relation to the location of Cosc and the home of the National Strategy in the following two paragraphs:

> The role of Cosc as a lead agency with a focus on coordination of strategy implementation is widely accepted. Cosc should continue to focus its energy on coordination of the strategy, ensuring clarity with regard to progress and working to enhance the quality of services and information. There was a view raised by some respondents as to whether the Department of Justice and Equality is the most appropriate 'home' for Cosc, as much of the funding support is channelled through the health services. In this context, the establishment of the Child and

Family Support Agency early in 2013 provided an opportunity for an examination of more general arrangements for family and domestic support services with a view to considering if the location of Cosc should remain as it is.

There are some strong arguments for Cosc remaining within Justice and Equality, given the centrality of crime and crime prevention to the strategy. Though conversely a case can be made for the area providing the greatest level of funding hosting the coordinating body, in this case the Department of Health. However, ultimately, location of the hosting department is unlikely to be the most crucial aspect determining Cosc's effectiveness. Rather, it is the willingness of participating bodies to engage and provide the necessary resources to support the implementation of the national strategy, with Cosc ensuring coordination and monitoring of progress.[2]

INFLUENCE OF EUROPEAN DEVELOPMENTS

Outside the National Strategy there were three significant developments that will have a large impact in the future:

- The Council of Europe *Convention on Preventing and Combating Violence against Women and Domestic Violence* was adopted in April 2011 (the Istanbul Convention), and came into force on 1 August 2014 for the initial 11 countries that had ratified it.
- The EU Agency for Fundamental Rights (FRA) published the results of an EU-wide survey on the incidence of violence against women across all 28 EU member states in March 2014.
- The EU Victims Directive was adopted in October 2012, and Ireland opted in to its negotiation and its terms. This was transposed into Irish legislation by November 2015.

Istanbul Convention

The Convention provides for a range of legislative and administrative protections for women affected by gender-based violence. It is an important instrument in tackling violence against women. At the time

2 Available at www.cosc.ie

of writing (June 2017) only three members of the Council of Europe have yet to sign the Convention – Armenia, Azerbaijan and the Russian Federation. Twenty-four members of the Council, including Ireland, have yet to ratify it. In many cases there are local legislative changes that need to be made before some members can ratify it.

On 13 October 2015 the government gave approval to Ireland signing the Istanbul Convention. Ambassador Gunning signed it on 5 November 2015 on behalf of the State.

The signing by Ireland of the Istanbul Convention reaffirms the commitment of the Government to foster a culture and to implement meaningful changes that can help reduce the incidence of violence against women, better support victims and bring their perpetrators to justice.

While current Irish legislation already implements many articles contained in the Convention, the Government also gave approval to a multi-annual action plan brought to cabinet by the Minister, which, when implemented, will enable Ireland to ratify the Convention. The second National Strategy also includes those actions required to ratify the Istanbul Convention.

EU Victims Directive

This Directive, which took direct effect from 16 November 2015, sets out to provide minimum standards across the EU on the rights, support and protection of victims of crime, including victims of sexual offences.

The EU Victims Directive represents a change in the way that victims will be dealt with as they make their way through the criminal justice system. It provides for information to be given to victims from first contact with the criminal justice agencies. It provides for much additional information to be given in the course of the investigation and court process if the person opts in to receive that information.

The criminal justice agencies have been working to provide a service to victims in line with the standard set out in the Victims Directive. An Garda Síochána have trained members of all ranks to implement the new policies and procedures that they have put in place to ensure that victims of crime across all 28 police districts receive a comprehensive and consistent response. The Courts Service and Office of the Director of Public Prosecutions have also put in place new procedures and practises to enable victims to receive the rights provided by the Directive.

As well as the administrative policies and procedures already put in place by various criminal justice agencies to give effect to the Directive, legislation has also been updated to transpose the Victims Directive into Irish law. The committee stage of the Criminal Justice (Victims of Crime) Bill was taken in the Seanad (the upper house of the Irish legislature) on 17 May 2017. This legislation will strengthen the rights of victims of crime and their families and ensure that victims and their needs are at the heart of the justice process. It also transposes into Irish law an EU Directive, which came into effect from 16 November 2015, establishing minimum standards on the rights, support and protection of victims of crime.

The legislation will entitle victims to comprehensive information on the criminal justice system and their role within it and the range of services and entitlements they may access from their first contact with An Garda Síochána. They will also receive a written acknowledgement of the making of a complaint, as well as contact details as to where further information can be obtained. On request, victims will be provided with information concerning the progress of the investigation and any court proceedings. They will also be provided, if they so request, with information from the Prison Service of the release or escape from prison of an offender serving a sentence for an offence against the victim.

An individual assessment to establish what measures, if any, are necessary for the protection of the victims from further victimisation is provided for under the legislation. Victims of crime will be able to access support services and interpretation, translation or other linguistic assistance where it is necessary to help participate in the criminal justice process.

The sector had also received funding of €300,000 per annum from Cosc for awareness-raising projects. The focus has now switched to a national awareness-raising campaign under the National Strategy. In that regard, the Minister for Justice and Equality secured funding of €950,000 for 2016 for this campaign. A fundamental aim of this campaign is to change societal attitudes to domestic and sexual violence. After seven years of awareness-raising programmes where in the region of 300 projects were supported, Cosc are trying a new approach with a single multi-annual national campaign. The process will involve the voluntary sector. The aims of the campaign are to bring about a change in long-established societal behaviours and attitudes in relation to domestic and sexual violence, and to activate bystanders where it is safe to intervene. The campaign shows the unacceptability and the effects of domestic and sexual violence.

The anticipated outcomes are:

- More recognition and understanding of the incidence of domestic and sexual violence among the general public
- Bystander intervention if safe to do so
- A decrease in domestic and sexual violence
- Increased reporting by victims and others
- Perpetrators/potential perpetrators being made aware of sanctions for offending.

In addition, in 2016 the Victims of Crime Office allocated €536,200 funding for the domestic violence sector for 2016 and €174,000 for the sexual violence sector.

CONCLUSION

This chapter has provided a brief overview of the development of the first National Strategy on Domestic, Sexual and Gender-based Violence in Ireland, some achievements under the Strategy and plans for the development and implementation of the second National Strategy. Work is ongoing, with much emphasis being placed on improved coordination between State and non-State services as well as the improvement of collection, collation and analysis of data in the sector(s).

Over the course of developing both National Strategies and in their planning and implementation, there have been many learnings and (at times) some unlearnings on the part of Cosc. The material above refers to a great many of these, including the importance of:

- Maintaining an eye on shifts in context: economic, political, changing relationships
- Facilitating flexibility in certain actions so as to accommodate the different views of a myriad of stakeholders and policy decision-makers

- Building in a measure of elasticity in the overall framework of any strategy so as allow for a marrying of simplicity with more complex issues
- The learning involved in the appreciation of the complexity of domestic violence service delivery and practise
- Sharing information across all interested parties along with the development of requisite protocols for managing this sharing of information, for example data protection
- The availability of standardised data on the extent and nature of the issues at hand and measures of the efficacy of response
- The allocation of ownership of actions by stakeholders, thereby enabling the holding of agencies to account
- Managing expectations in partnerships – not just an exercise in cynicism, but as a way of bringing people along
- Recognising (and working within) contested spaces where a variety of stakeholders claim expertise framed by their alternative worldviews, position or 'take' on the issues, that is, every agent has their take on this highly emotive issue and so it is important to work with that rather than attempt just to win them over
- Understanding that when it comes to aspirational strategising, losses are inevitable...wins are not
- Locating and working with identifiable champions across the sector
- Sustaining ongoing discussion around monitoring how the Strategy is going
- The inappropriateness of simply superimposing so-called 'best practise' models applied elsewhere
- Recognising and utilising unexpected outcomes and unplanned offshoots and by-products of work undertaken, such as research networks and new overlapping national and international relationships.

In its ongoing implementation of Ireland's National Strategy on Domestic, Sexual and Gender-based Violence, 2016–2021, Cosc will, no doubt, continue to learn (and unlearn) while working with partners in the sector. Coordinating work efforts with purpose will benefit all including policy-makers, civil society network organisations, support service providers, and victims and their families.

REFERENCES

Council of Europe (2011) *Convention on Preventing and Combating Violence against Women and Domestic Violence*, November. Accessed on 29/6/2017 at www.coe.int/en/web/conventions/full-list/-/conventions/treaty/210

Council of the European Union (2012) 'Directive 2012/29/EU of the European Parliament and of the Council of October 2012 establishing minimum standards on the rights, support and protection of victims of crime, and replacing Council Framework Decision 2001/220/JHA.' *Official Journal of the European Union* L 315/57, 14 November. Accessed on 29/6/2017 at www.refworld.org/docid/52eb66354.html

Oifig an Tánaiste (Office of the Tánaiste) (1997) *Report of the Task Force on Violence Against Women.* Dublin: The Stationery Office. Accessed on 1/8/2017 at www.justice.ie/en/JELR/dvreport.pdf/Files/dvreport.pdf

Part Two

CHILDREN'S EXPERIENCES OF DOMESTIC VIOLENCE

Chapter 3

MOTHER–CHILD RELATIONSHIP IN THE CONTEXT OF INTIMATE PARTNER VIOLENCE

Zuzana Ocenasova, *Coordination and Methodological Centre for Prevention of Violence against Women, Bratislava, Slovakia*

Hana Smitkova, *Department of Psychology, Comenius University, Bratislava, Slovakia*

INTRODUCTION

Intimate partner violence (IPV) is a problem that disproportionately affects women. In the European Union (EU), 28 per cent of women have experienced some form of physical and/or sexual violence by their intimate partner during their lifetime, and 43 per cent have suffered from various forms of psychological violence (FRA 2014). Although women are seen as the primary victims of IPV, children are increasingly recognised as suffering from it, either directly or indirectly, by living in a violent household. According to a review by Apple and Holden (1998), 30–60 per cent of children exposed to IPV have also suffered from physical abuse. Nevertheless, being exposed to IPV against their mothers can be similarly traumatic for children (Fanetti *et al.* 2015). Whether direct or indirect victims, children experience various adverse outcomes such as higher levels of aggression, depression, anger, anxiety and increased risk of post-traumatic stress disorder (PTSD) symptoms (Øverlien 2010). Therefore some authors advocate that children should not only be understood as witnessing or being exposed to IPV, but rather as experiencing it and being survivors similar to their mothers (Callaghan *et al.* 2015; Katz 2015c; Mullender *et al.* 2003). This fact has been acknowledged by several European policies (e.g. Opinion of the European Economic and Social Committee 2006/C 325/15 or Istanbul Convention (Council of Europe) 2011).

Although the research on children surviving IPV against their mothers focuses primarily on its impact, the agency of children and their perceptions and reactions to IPV is becoming increasingly recognised (Callaghan *et al.* 2015; Izaguirre and Calvete 2015; Mullender *et al.* 2003; Øverlien and Hydén 2009). Children actively respond to violence against their mother, and create various emotional and behavioural strategies for coping with it, such as protecting their mother or younger siblings, attempting to avoid conflict and seeking help (Mullender *et al.* 2003; Øverlien and Hydén 2009). Despite increasing awareness of children's agency, the concept has rarely been applied to an analysis of the mother–child relationship.

A positive mother–child relationship is considered to be one of the most important factors influencing the recovery of children from the adverse effects of IPV (Katz 2015b; Létourneau, Fedick and Willms 2007; Levendosky, Bogat and Martinez-Torteya 2013; Øverlien 2010). Nevertheless, the emphasis of research and practise interest has been on studying the impact of mothers' parenting that either protects or further harms children. This approach has been repeatedly criticised as it often holds mothers solely responsible for the wellbeing of their children and subsequently failing to do so (see, for example, Johnson and Sullivan 2008; Katz 2015a; Semaan, Jasinski and Bubriski-McKenzie 2013). Conversely, fathers' parenting is scrutinised to a much lesser extent (exceptions are Bancroft, Silverman and Ritchie 2012 or Cater and Sjögren 2016), despite the fact that fathers often continue to behave violently, and post-separation violence has been identified as having a detrimental impact on children (Bancroft *et al.* 2012; Thiara and Humphreys 2015). Additionally, as Katz (2015a) has highlighted, this perspective also construes children as objects, dependent on their mother's behaviour, and as such denied of agency and the potential to reflect on their situation. As a result, Katz argues for the need to include children's agency when studying mother–child relationships, and to use a bilateral model to achieve this, as proposed by Kuczynski, Harach and Bernardini (1999). In the bilateral model, both the mother and child are considered as active agents 'capable of meaning construction and intentional actions', although they may not exercise an equal amount of power (Kuczynski *et al.* 1999, p.25). Thus, the relationship is seen as two-directional, with both parties mutually influencing it.

THE PRESENT STUDY

This study contributes to the research on children's agency in IPV, and extends this understanding of the mother–child relationship in IPV cases. Following Katz (2015a), we used the bilateral model of the relationship as it reflects the findings of developmental psychology on parent–children relations as well as the knowledge about the agency of children living with IPV. The findings are based on a qualitative study of six women and their eight children who have experienced IPV in Slovakia. The interviews were carried out separately with mothers and with children in order to grasp the children's experience and to provide them with a space for expression. The study primarily focused on the children's behaviour and perceptions of IPV against their mothers, and on how the experience of IPV influences the mother–child relationship. The purpose of this analysis is to explore the strategies that mothers and children employed during IPV, and the positive and negative influence of IPV on the mother–child relationship in the aftermath of violence.

To date, research on children surviving IPV has predominantly been carried out in Anglo-Saxon and Nordic countries, while, in the context of Central and Eastern Europe, IPV is studied mainly from the woman's perspective (the exception is Barvikova and Paloncyova 2016), with children understood merely as witnesses to violence or where the focus is on adverse outcomes of IPV for children. In Slovakia, IPV has primarily been studied employing quantitative methods, although a qualitative methodology was used within the VICTIM project that focused on mothers and children. Nevertheless, only mothers were directly interviewed and children were tested for any negative impact of IPV (Karkoskova 2012). To the authors' knowledge, the present study is the first in Slovakia concentrating on children's experience of IPV and the mother–child relationship within this context. The findings have implications for designing interventions for mothers and children experiencing IPV. As Humphreys, Thiara and Skamballis (2010) pointed out, in practise, interventions are often offered separately for mothers and children, and fail to recognise the interlinkage of issues they face; this also seems to be the case in Slovakia. Service providers focus mostly on women (although parenting can be one of the interventions' issues). However, on the grounds of the Council of Europe's *Minimum Standards for Support Services* (Kelly and Dubois 2008), assistance to children has become increasingly available.

METHODS

Recruitment and participants

The recruitment of participants was carried out through counselling centres and refuges for women experiencing IPV in Slovakia. The form of recruitment was selected on the basis of the accessibility of the target group as well as in consideration of research ethics, since service providers can better assess the appropriateness of clients' participation in the research on safety and welfare grounds. Additionally, if needed, women and children could have been referred to services for further intervention following participation in the research. The criteria for the selection of participants included the following: (1) women with children living separated from the perpetrators for a maximum of three years; (2) children aged 5–18; (3) no further potentially stressful processes going on within the family (e.g. court procedures); and (4) forthcoming consent and voluntary participation by both the woman and child.

Six women participated in the research with their children. In all cases the mother and child's interviews were paired; in two cases, we interviewed two siblings. The women were aged 38–43, while their children covered the whole age spectrum – two were aged 5, three were 11, one 14, one 16 and one 17. Three girls and five boys were interviewed. In five cases the perpetrator of IPV was the child's father; in three cases, it was the mother's subsequent male partner.

Procedure

Due to the participation of children in the research and the sensitivity of the topic, the authors followed Fontes' (2004) recommendations on ethics in Violence Against Women research. Further key resources for ethical research with children included the Ethical Research Involving Children (ERIC) compendium, which emphasises that ethical consideration should be ongoing throughout the entire research project (Graham *et al.* 2013). Service providers were also consulted in the early stage of the research in order to tailor its design and procedures. The research was carried out using semi-structured interviews conducted by psychologists; in the case of children, these were experienced child psychologists. Four interview guides were developed – one for women and three for children, depending on their age group. They comprised of open-ended questions about their experience of IPV, perceptions of the mother–child relationship, common activities, and life after separation from the violent perpetrator.

Counselling centres and refuges were informed about the selection criteria, based on which they contacted suitable clients or former clients and informed them about the purpose and nature of the research. The mothers were also provided with an information sheet explaining the aims, duration and limits to confidentiality of the study. Informed consent was obtained prior to the interview from both mothers and children; consent forms were adjusted according to the age division of the children. Process consent (Fontes 2004) was applied, and all participants were informed about the possibility of withdrawal at any time without penalty. The mothers and children were interviewed separately. Data collection was conducted between December 2015 and May 2016. Interviews were digitally voice-recorded, with participants' permission, and transcribed verbatim for subsequent analysis.

Data analysis

The transcripts were coded on the basis of axial coding according to the methods of grounded theory by Strauss and Corbin (1998). The method was selected in order to avoid prior structuring of data and to let the findings 'emerge' from the interviews. Two researchers coded the transcripts, codes were compared and discrepancies discussed. Later, codes were grouped into thematic categories separately for the interviews with the mothers and with the children. In the final stage, categories for both groups were examined and overlaps identified. Final categorisation comprised of common categories for the mothers and children, and special categories for each group. Both inductive and deductive analytical methods were used during the process of categorisation (Miles and Huberman 1984).

FINDINGS

The analysis of women and children's interviews revealed several common themes. Below we present and illustrate those that occurred in both groups and are relevant for the mother–child relationship.

Strategies of mothers and children in IPV

Living with IPV, the mothers as well as the children reported on how they created various strategies on how to protect themselves and avoid any conflict escalating. Corresponding with the other studies mentioned above, children proved to be agentic in IPV situations. Both children and mothers described situations of children's agency, of their attempts to intervene in the situation of direct violence either by trying to communicate with their father/mother's partner or to defend the mother physically, as the following boy explains:

> 'Dad pulled her [mother] on the bed and beat her up. I came and I cried for half an hour, they were fighting and then I started hitting papa, too. There, in the groin and it started to hurt him. I then stood on the table kicking him all the time.' (Tomas, aged 11)

As apparent, Tomas tried to intervene in two ways: first, by merely being present and crying and, later, desperate from not succeeding, he attacked his father physically. Although not all children reported that they directly defended their mothers, almost all described attempts to stop violence by being present, talking to their father/mother's partner or trying to distract their father's attention prior to violence. Children, particularly the older ones, also contributed to leaving the violent household either by letting relatives know what was going on or by talking about the situation at school, which led to securing a place in a refuge.

Older children also described how they protected their younger siblings from experiencing violent behaviour towards their mother, as Lily explains:

> 'Sometimes I really did not know what I should do. I tried somehow to lull him [younger brother] to sleep for him not to hear anything and stay quiet. So I tried to comfort him somehow. I held him in my hands and talked to him about something nice.' (Lily, aged 14)

Lily further explained that her oldest sister went to conciliate the violent situation while she took care of the youngest brother. The examples often illustrated the responsibility children felt to monitor safety for themselves, siblings or mothers, or to avoid conflict escalations by direct interventions, or simply by being present at home. Children often adopted the adult role that was reflected by mothers acknowledging that their children were more mature for their age.

All of the participating mothers asserted that protecting their children was their upmost priority, and that they had developed various tactics for protecting them from direct violence or from witnessing the abuse of their mother, as well as tactics for preventing them from seeing their emotional suffering and exhaustion. This mother explains:

> 'We were in the children's room and...they combed my hair... And I was grateful that he then didn't yell at them. Girls were quiet, no noise, no banging, they did not throw a ball, because he couldn't stand such things... They were playing with me. I was a doll with whom they played.' (Maria, aged 39)

As this quote demonstrates, mothers and children described how they sometimes invented mutual strategies for avoiding violence, either initiated by mothers, as in the former case, or as commonly created, such as preparing for school together, and preventing the father participating. The common strategies reported, whether among siblings or between the mother and children, were found to contribute to the development of the sense of family and maintaining a level of closeness in mother–child or sibling relationships.

Strengthening of mother–child relationship in the aftermath of violence

Both mothers and children considered that what they had to go through deepened their mutual relationship and often also the relations among siblings, particularly if they felt mutual support during IPV. In the interviews, some children acknowledged the support and protection that their mothers provided them with during IPV. The following interview extract illustrates this:

> Interviewer: 'Do you think that it has influenced your relationship – the way your mother reacted, did it influence the relationship?'
>
> Monika (aged 15): 'Yeah... I think it strengthened it even more, the way she supported us.'
>
> Interviewer: 'You consider it as supportive and you think it made your relationship stronger?'
>
> Monika: 'Yes, that mum is willing to do everything for us. She proved it then and she proves it every day.'

Furthermore, it is possible that the psychological counselling that some children underwent contributed to the framing of the IPV experience and acknowledgement of their mother's support, both during and in the aftermath of the violence. In other cases, the difficult family situation, post-separation, strengthens mutual ties, as the following quote illustrates:

> 'It is difficult for each of us, because we lost everything practically overnight… And then Christmas came but we did not celebrate it because we could not afford it. But together with my daughter we tried to make Christmas for the youngest, so at least he could have it… So the youngest did not feel…to make Christmas for him so that at least he would feel it was Christmas.' (Lena, aged 41)

Despite the difficult economic situation described above, the mother describes the attempts the family made to protect at least the youngest member from its impact. Mothers also reported being concerned about the psychological wellbeing of their children. They explained how they strived to compensate them for what they had experienced during IPV by spending more time together, doing things the coercive perpetrator did not allow them to do, and creating a safe home. Barbara explains:

> 'I do what I can [to]…since the beginning I tried to change my kids' thoughts, to mentally change the mood. We tried a lot… We went to the pool, we did lots of activities, ice creams and such. We had our rituals, so we could function somehow, in some daily routine.' (Barbara, aged 40)

Children also reported being aware of their mothers' efforts, and expressed appreciation of those efforts. They similarly reported spending more time together, playing and having fun.

In the interviews, children often spoke very passionately about their mothers; they considered them as friends, trusted them, and felt that they could rely on them to protect them. Some of the children perceived their mothers as 'being a great mum' or 'probably the best in the world'. In their statements, they reflected on how they worried about their mother, for example the mother has wrinkles on her face due to stress, she works a lot, or she is tired due to the court procedure with the father. On the other hand, they perceived their mother as happier since they had left the perpetrator and said that she deserved it. All these examples illustrate how children are quite sensitive about how their mother feels.

Correspondingly, the participating mothers characterised their children as agentic in their mutual relationship; they described situations in which children, even at a very young age, attempted to soothe their mother, cheer her up and support her emotionally, as the following examples demonstrate:

> 'Later, it was him [son] who calmed me down: "Look, he has a restraining order so he cannot come here for sure."' (Anna, aged 39)

> 'When she finds out that I was crying or so, she [daughter] tries... She is very sad about it and tries to find a way to change it... I consider her as a strong and wonderful person; she copes better than us. She is extremely positive, she believes that I will manage, that we'll be OK; she does not consider any other option.' (Lena, aged 41)

Besides the emotional support that children were reported to exercise, they were also highlighted as motivating mothers to continue the struggle of the post-violence situation, as the last quote illustrates. In addition, they also were reported to aid pragmatically by taking care of younger siblings or helping with housework.

Some of the children, particularly the older ones, presented as having a remarkable understanding of IPV and an understanding of how their mother experienced it. From the children's narrative, the mothers who experienced IPV were perceived as strong women, able to resist the perpetrator and to start a new life. In other terms, the children recognised their mothers as survivors, as Lily explains:

> 'Respect, I do respect her for what she had suffered and really, I couldn't survive what she had went through... She is a fighter, she speaks her mind, her word stands and she's right. But then, she was, she wouldn't fight back, she would rather bear it so that we didn't have to listen to it and watch it.' (Lily, aged 14)

None of the participating children blamed their mother for the violence and, from their interviews, all were very clear about the responsibility of the perpetrator – the father or their mother's partner – for the abuse.

Deterioration of the mother–child relationship in the aftermath of violence

Despite the majority of examples reflecting positive mutual mother–child relationships, some mothers described deteriorating relationships with their children as a consequence of violence. In three cases, the relationship with one of their children deteriorated due to the violence experienced. Mostly it was described as being accompanied by a deterioration in the relationship between the siblings or where the relationship had been already negatively impacted during IPV, when the father treated the siblings differently. Some children were reported to respond to violence by diverting their anger towards their mother, accusing her of having caused the partner's rage or of staying in a violent relationship. One child opted to live with their father (the perpetrator of violence was the mother's subsequent partner), and another child (now adult) was reported to be not in contact with the family at all. These cases concerned children who did not participate in the research due to the age limit, or because they were not living within the family at the time the research was conducted, so their experience is not included.

Some mothers stated they were aware of behavioural issues they faced with their children that could be attributed to the violence experienced, such as the child's increased aggression towards the mother or other children, or the loss of the mother's respect by a child. Anna explains:

> 'She [daughter] does not take me seriously at all, sometimes, when I tried to give her advice or so. Also, my ex-husband told me that we have to work it out, because it is not good. She does not respect me, makes fun of me, but on the other hand, she communicates, we are in contact, we talk on the phone or Skype, but I know it is in her.' (Anna, aged 39)

The question of parental authority was raised several times during the interviews. Some mothers stated that they strived to balance parental authority, compensation for the IPV experience and being responsive to children's needs.

Communication about IPV

Most mothers participating in the research stated that they tried to openly communicate with their children about the violence, appropriate to their age. In one case the mother used the method developed by a counselling centre for facilitating this. Open communication certainly contributed to improved relationships, as she explains:

> 'I talked about everything with my older daughter. I have never hidden from them the fact that I went to court or to meet their father. I have never spoken badly about him, that "your father is so and so". No. I just told them that I have to solve the problem with him and I have to meet him, but they had to know about it. I never kept it a secret... We have always openly communicated with the girls; they knew what I was going through and so on... We have always openly spoken about everything.' (Maria, aged 39)

On the other hand, not all the children confirmed that they talked about IPV in the aftermath of violence. Some stated that they either do not communicate with their mother about it or do not feel positive about the conversation regarding IPV or their father, as Jan and Monika explain:

> 'We do not talk about it; we want to forget it all.' (Jan, aged 11)

> 'It helps me that we do not talk about him [father] at all. Even when my mum and sister came from the court and spoke about it, I went to my room, put earphones on and played some music. I ignored what they were discussing and what had happened... I just did not want to deal with it at all.' (Monika, aged 15)

The mothers and children seemed to apply both strategies identified in the literature – open communication about IPV and its aftermath, or doing the opposite, not talking about the violence in order to forget about it.

DISCUSSION

In this research focusing on the mother–child relationship in the context of IPV, we studied both actors – the mother and the child – and considered them as agents capable of intentional actions and meaning construction of situations and relations (Kuczynski *et al.* 1999). This was confirmed by the findings of this study. Children as well as their mothers were able to interpret situations and to react to them during and after IPV. Similarly, both actively contributed to the development of a mutual mother–child relationship, and promoted each other's recovery.

The findings of the current study contribute to the research on children's agency during IPV (Callaghan *et al.* 2015, Mullender *et al.* 2003; Øverlien and Hydén 2009). Children used various communication and behavioural strategies in order to defend their mother, to avoid conflict escalation or to protect themselves or their younger siblings. Children were able to comprehend IPV, interpret it, and intentionally reacted to it. Children, mainly the older ones, had a clear understanding of IPV, and attributed responsibility for it to the perpetrator. Nevertheless, it has to be acknowledged that the majority of the children underwent counselling in the centres or spent some time in a refuge, and this may have affected their framing of the responsibility for violence. Accordingly, mothers were found to prioritise the wellbeing of their children, and developed strategies on how to protect them from experiencing IPV, which is consistent with previous studies (Izaguirre and Calvete 2015; Lapierre 2010). In some cases, mothers and children created mutual strategies on how to avoid conflicts, or siblings divided tasks during violent incidents – one intervening in the situation while the other protected the younger sibling. As apparent, both mothers and children are active agents in IPV situations and use various tactics for mutually protecting themselves, by which they contribute to the development of their relationship and provide mutual emotional support. Similarly to Katz (2015c), the findings indicate that mothers and children surviving IPV can seek opportunities to maintain levels of closeness in their relationship and promote each other's wellbeing.

Furthermore, in the aftermath of the violence, the children remained agentic in the development of the mother–child relationship and in promoting each other's recovery. Both mothers and children confirmed in the interviews that they have a close relationship and support each other. Mothers reported that they intentionally worked on the safety and wellbeing of their children, were aware of the possible adverse effects of violence, and tended to compensate for them (similar to Goldblatt, Buchbinder and Cohen 2014). Children highlighted positive relationships with their mother and recognised and appreciated her efforts. Correspondingly, children were reflective of their mother's emotional state and situation, and responded to it according to their age and capacities in order to improve it. Mothers considered their children to be highly supportive, and described situations where children were sympathetic and encouraging. Support and protection often involved not only their mother but also younger siblings. Comparable to the situation of IPV, after the violence mothers and children used various tactics of mutual support, which they asserted contributed to their recovery. Strategies that were applied were similar to those described by Katz (2015b) – attunement to one another's emotional state, support and the development of feelings of safety, lifting the mood, spending time together and 'just being there'. Similar to Izaguirre and Calvete (2015), mothers' attempts to openly communicate about IPV were found to contribute to positive relationships and recovery. Nevertheless, it is important to note that not all children welcomed such communication, with some choosing a 'conspiracy of silence' (Humphreys *et al.* 2006).

Despite many examples of positive mutual relationships and of assisting in each other's recovery among mothers and children, in some interviews the narrative suggested evidence of deteriorating relationships. However, mother-blaming or diverting the rage against the mother (identified also by Mullender *et al.* 2003) was reported to subside during the recovery process, although in two cases the alienating effect of IPV was found to remain. As we were not able to interview the children concerned in those two cases as they were not living with the family at the time of the research, it was impossible to analyse the causes.

Consistent with Katz's (2015b) findings, the current study shows that both mothers and children are active in developing mutual relationships and are capable of promoting each other's recovery if supported by professional help. All of the women participating in the interviews received professional assistance and acknowledged its importance for the process of recovery for them and for their children. Considering the limitations of the study, it is not possible to assess how the recovery process is influenced when professional services are not provided or how it can be hindered despite the help received. Nevertheless, together with Humphreys *et al.* (2006) or Katz (2015b), we advocate for inclusion of the interventions on the mother–child relationship into social services provided to women and children surviving IPV. These interventions need to concentrate on supporting the relationship in the bilateral model framework that helps mitigate the consequences of IPV and to sustain the resilient strategies of children and their mothers.

LIMITATIONS OF THE STUDY

The main limitation of this study is that a relatively small number of interviews were conducted, which, in combination with the heterogeneity of particular life situations of participating women and children, does not allow for generalisation of the sample. Second, it is important to consider the fact that most of the participants underwent counselling processes in refuges or centres for women experiencing IPV. Finally, it is presumable that women and children with resilient strategies tended to participate in the interviews while families experiencing more adverse effects and problems caused by IPV refused to do so. Future studies examining the mother–child relationship and its effects on recovery from IPV should therefore include a more diverse population of women and children experiencing IPV.

CONCLUSION

Research on mother–child relations in IPV is scarce, particularly in Central and Eastern Europe. The study reported on in this chapter is, in many regards, consistent with studies from other European regions. It contributes to the awareness of children's agency, both in situations of IPV and also after violence. Similarly, it shows that the mother–child relationship constitutes an important factor for recovery promotion for IPV survivors – for children as well as for mothers. Mutual support, promotion of each other's wellbeing and in some cases mutual strategies during and after IPV contribute to resiliency and reduction of the negative impacts of IPV. Therefore it is necessary to continue exploring this relationship in IPV research and to further analyse the dynamics and factors leading to resiliency and recovery promotion of IPV survivors as well as the factors hindering it. A bilateral model of the mother–child relationship seems to be particularly suitable for providing a complex understanding of the process.

Note: The research reported was financed by the EEA and Norway Grants and national budget of the Slovak Republic in the scope of the project 'Coordination and Methodological Centre for Gender-based and Domestic Violence' within the Programme SK09: 'Domestic and Gender-based Violence'.

REFERENCES

Apple, A.E. and Holden, G.W. (1998) 'The co-occurrence of spouse and physical child abuse: A review and appraisal.' *Journal of Family Psychology 12*, 4, 578–599.

Bancroft, L., Silverman, J.G. and Ritchie, D. (2012) *The Batterer as Parent: Addressing the Impact of Domestic Violence on Family Dynamics.* London: Sage.

Barvikova, J. and Paloncyova, J. (2016) *Děti, rodiče a domácí násilí.* Praha: Výzkum klientely Acorusu, z.ú. Výskumní ústav práce a sociálních věcí.

Callaghan, J.E.M., Alexander, J.H., Sixsmith, J. and Fellin, C.H.H. (2015) 'Beyond "witnessing": Children's experiences of coercive control in domestic violence and abuse.' *Journal of Interpersonal Violence* 1–31. doi: 10.1177/0886260515618946

Cater, A.K. and Sjögren, J. (2016) 'Children exposed to intimate partner violence describe their experiences: A typology-based qualitative analysis.' *Child and Adolescent Social Work Journal 33*, 6, 473–486.

Council of Europe (2011) *Convention on Preventing and Combating Violence Against Women and Domestic Violence (Istanbul Convention).* Accessed on 23/3/2017 at www.coe.int/en/web/conventions/full-list/-/conventions/treaty/210

Fanetti, M., O'Donohue, W., Happel, R.F. and Daly, K. (2015) *Forensic Child Psychology: Working in the Courts and Clinic.* Hoboken, NJ: John Wiley & Sons, Inc.

Fontes, L.A. (2004) 'Ethics in violence against women research: The sensitive, the dangerous, and the overlooked.' *Ethics and Behavior 14*, 131–174.

FRA (European Union Agency for Fundamental Rights) (2014) *Violence Against Women: EU-wide Survey – Main Results Report.* Luxembourg: Publications Office of the European Union.

Goldblatt, H., Buchbinder, E. and Cohen, R. (2014) 'Re-experiencing motherhood: Transformation of relationships between formally abused women and their children.' *Violence Against Women 20*, 5, 561–580.

Graham, A., Powell, M., Taylor, N., Anderson, D. and Fitzgerald, R. (2013) *Ethical Research Involving Children.* Florence: UNICEF Office of Research-Innocenti.

Humphreys, C., Mullender, A., Thiara, R.K. and Skamballis, A. (2006) '"Talking to my mum": Developing communication between mothers and children in the aftermath of domestic violence.' *Journal of Social Work 6*, 1, 53–63.

Humphreys, C., Thiara, R.K. and Skamballis, A. (2010) 'Readiness to change: Mother–child relationship and domestic violence intervention.' *British Journal of Social Work 41*, 1, 166–184. https://doi.org/10.1093/bjsw/bcq046

Izaguirre, A. and Calvete, E. (2015) 'Children who are exposed to intimate partner violence: Interviewing mothers to understand its impact on children.' *Child Abuse and Neglect 48*, 58–67. http://dx.doi.org/10.1016/j.chiabu.2015.05.002

Johnson, S.P. and Sullivan, C.M. (2008) 'How child protection workers support or further victimize battered mothers.' *Affilia 23*, 3, 242–258.

Karkoskova, S. (2012) 'Týrané matky a ich vnímanie najlepšieho záujmu dieťaťa.' In K. Kardis and M. Kardis (eds) *Zborník religionistických a sociologických štúdií* (pp.261–272). Prešovská univerzita v Prešove.

Katz, E. (2015a) 'Domestic violence, children's agency and mother–child relationships: Towards a more advanced model.' *Children and Society 29*, 69–79. doi: 10.1111/chso.12023

Katz, E. (2015b) 'Recovery promoters: Ways in which children and mothers support one another's recoveries from domestic violence.' *British Journal of Social Work 45*, 1, i153–i169.

Katz, E. (2015c) 'Beyond the physical incident model: How children living with domestic violence are harmed by and resist regimes of coercive control.' *Child Abuse Review 25*, 46–59. doi: 10.1002/car.2422

Kelly, L. and Dubois, L. (2008) *Combating Violence against Women: Minimum Standards for Support Services.* Strasbourg: Council of Europe.

Kuczynski, L., Harach, L. and Bernardini, S.C. (1999) 'Psychology's Child Meets Sociology's Child: Agency, Influence and Power in Parent–Child Relationships.' In S. Shehan (ed.) *Through the Eyes of the Child: Revisioning Children as Active Agents of Family Life* (pp.21–51). Stamford, CT: JAI Press.

Lapierre, S. (2010) 'Striving to be "good" mothers: Abused women's experiences of mothering.' *Child Abuse Review 19*, 342–357.

Létourneau, N.L., Fedick, C.B. and Willms, J.D. (2007) 'Mothering and domestic violence: A longitudinal analysis.' *Journal of Family Violence 22*, 649–659.

Levendosky, A.A., Bogat, G.A. and Martinez-Torteya, C. (2013) 'PTSD symptoms in young children exposed to intimate partner violence.' *Violence Against Women 19*, 2, 187–201. doi: 10.1177/1077801213476458

Miles, M. and Huberman, A. (1984) *Qualitative Data Analysis: A Sourcebook of New Methods.* Beverly Hills, CA: Sage.

Mullender, A., Hague, G., Imam, U., Kelly, L., Malos, E. and Regan, L. (2003) *Children's Perspectives on Domestic Violence.* London: Sage.

Opinion of the European Economic and Social Committee on Children as indirect victims of domestic violence (2006/C 325/15). Accessed on 23/3/2017 at http://eur-lex.europa.eu/legal-content/EN/TXT/?uri=CELEX%3A2006IE1577

Øverlien, C. (2010) 'Children exposed to domestic violence.' *Journal of Social Work 10*, 1, 80–97. doi: 10.1177/1468017309350663

Øverlien, C. and Hydén, M. (2009) 'Children's actions when experiencing domestic violence.' *Childhood – A Global Journal of Child Research 16*, 4, 479–496.

Semaan, I., Jasinski, J.L. and Bubriski-McKenzie, A. (2013) 'Subjection, subjectivity and agency: The power, meaning and practise of mothering among women experiencing intimate partner abuse.' *Violence Against Women 19*, 1, 69–88.

Strauss, A.L. and Corbin, J.M. (1998) *Basics of Qualitative Research: Techniques and Procedures for Developing Grounded Theory.* Newbury Park, CA: Sage.

Thiara, R.K. and Humphreys, C. (2015) 'Absent presence: The ongoing impact of men's violence on the mother–child relationship.' *Child & Family Social Work 22*, 137–145. doi: 10.1111/cfs.12210

Chapter 4

VOICE, AGENCY, POWER

A FRAMEWORK FOR YOUNG SURVIVORS' PARTICIPATION IN NATIONAL DOMESTIC ABUSE POLICY-MAKING

Claire Houghton, *Researcher and Expert Adviser, School of Social and Political Science, University of Edinburgh, UK*

INTRODUCTION

> There's a lot of work for children to do...if you've got the drive and the will to change something, you can do it. We've proved it. We hope the spirit of Voice Against Violence lives on. (VAV, Our Messages to Young People)

Voice Against Violence (VAV), a group of young survivors of domestic abuse, significantly changed the service, research and policy landscape in Scotland. Their role as young expert advisers to Government with direct, regular access to senior politicians has no precedent. Ministers invested in VAV, a national advisory group pilot, as a response to young survivor-led critiques of tokenistic participation, inviting the young people themselves to set the terms for political engagement. This chapter explores the unique perspectives of young survivors on their sustained involvement in the policy-making process. It contributes the lens of a child, and a young survivor, to debates about participation, including a child's right to be involved in collective decision-making. From the onset of engagement, young survivors feared their status as a child, and as a victim, could prevent and hinder such engagement, mainly due to adults' (mis-)conceptions about children as well as domestic abuse. Further, often related, challenges emerge over time that contribute key lessons and challenge key established tenets for children and young people's participation in national policy-making.

In this chapter I recommend a framework for national participation of young survivors in policy-making: the key tenets are voice, agency and power, and young survivor-set conditions are support and impact.

BACKGROUND

A small group of young survivors were consulted on the development of Government policy (see Houghton 2008) and, along with peers, critiqued its one-off, limited and tokenistic (if impactful) nature. Ministers responded at the Scottish Parliament by inviting them to recruit a group of young advisers and issue directives to Government on how a 'national advisory group' should work. This group assisted me in advertising and targeted recruitment of young experts through specialist support agencies. Agreed criteria set by this group, in dialogue with the Scottish Government, were that the young person was aged 15–18, had a support worker and was at a good, safe stage in 'moving on' from domestic abuse (while recognising continued contact meant that young people were still subject to coercive control). Furthermore, it was felt beneficial to have previous research/participation/activism experience in the subject area, as both a stepping-stone to participation in policy-making, and also to bring knowledge of the priorities of a wider range of children and young people. Specific agencies were targeted to put forward one young person each – to ensure experience of a diverse range of services and that young people were not rejected.

Eight 'young experts' were recruited to the national advisory group that they named 'Voice Against Violence'. Each of the young members had experienced domestic abuse and homelessness alongside their mothers. They had received specialist support and had previously been active participants in research, research advisory groups, political activism, influencing policy, service evaluation or training (Fitzpatrick *et al.* 2003; Houghton 2008; Stafford, Stead and Grimes 2007). I was appointed as VAV's manager and the young experts defined the role, making clear the manager did not speak for them and was their equal, with specific responsibilities.

VAV demanded, and was given, direct, regular access to senior politicians and national representatives of Scottish local authorities. VAV was given equal status to the adult board in relation to governance and implementation of domestic abuse policy. A specific directive ensured that sensitive and safe ethics/rules of engagement were co-developed with young survivors, initially prioritising safety and confidentiality (see Houghton 2015). Through two-and-a-half years of engagement, the young experts reflected and acted on their experience of national policy-making, alongside myself as their manager-researcher. This chapter explores their unique perspectives on key challenges for young survivors' sustained involvement in national policy-making.

A framework of voice, agency and power emerges from their critique, and provides the structure for this chapter. The literature review briefly explores each of these concepts through domestic abuse research with young survivors, participation challenges from childhood studies and the emerging facilitative political context in Scotland. A participatory action research methodology then brings us young experts' reflections and action in relation to the challenges they perceived. The chapter concludes through recommending a framework for young survivors' participation in national policy-making, and a call for time for children and young people to claim their political space for action.

LITERATURE REVIEW

Voice

How children and childhood are seen is interlinked with their participation in collective decision-making (Tisdall *et al.* 2014). In domestic abuse theory, policy and, to some extent, practise, the issue has been whether children are seen at all. Domestic abuse literature exploring young survivors' perspectives has given children voice; it has developed our recognition of children's active participation in their own and their family's survival, protection and recovery (Buckley, Holt and Whelan 2007; Katz 2015; Mullender *et al.* 2002; Øverlien and Hyden 2009). Children's lack of voice in practise responses emerges as a critical issue in women and children's safety (Eriksson 2011; Holt 2016; Mackay 2013). In relation to collective voice, researchers have begun to involve young survivors as research advisers and, more rarely, as active participants in developing and piloting interventions (see, for example, Barter *et al.* 2015; Humphreys *et al.* 2006). Yet, in theorising about the quest for social justice, children's political voice remains silent. Calls are to reclaim abused women's voices as a political asset (Stark 2007), that feminist methodologies remain politically engaged (Harding 2012) but not, yet, that we, as practitioners, researchers and policy-makers, engage with young survivors' political voice.

Lundy (2007) asserts that space and voice are two of four critical elements in realising a child's right to participation in collective decision-making under Article 12 of the United Nations Convention on the Rights of the Child (UNCRC). The inauguration of a Scottish Parliament, following devolution in the UK, substantially increased feminist political representation and henceforth feminist activists' access to the invited spaces of national decision-making. Scottish Women's Aid's (SWA) alliances with feminist-elected politicians resulted in opportunities for children and young people to be invited into that space (SWA's Listen Louder Campaign; see Houghton 2006):

> We have moved as a nation from ignoring children to recognising that they are affected by domestic abuse and need support in their own right. Young people have shown they can eloquently state their needs. (Scottish Parliament 2006, col. 29209)

Although the campaign was effective, influencing models of refuge and the establishment of a central government fund for specialist support workers for children and young people, the children were outsiders, activists, achieving only temporary access to power. Shifting their position to that of political actors, with consistent access to power, would entail tackling several generic participation challenges that are now briefly discussed.

Before children can express their views, Lundy (2007) argues, those views must be actively sought, and this requires political will and investment (Byrne and Lundy 2015). Participation can be dismissed as unrepresentative (Cockburn 2010; Tisdall 2015), lacking in diversity (Lundy 2007), and often excludes vulnerable children through adults elevating protection over agency (Hanson 2016). If asked at all, children are asked about adult-defined 'children's issues', rather than defining for themselves what impacts on them (Lundy 2007). It is usually powerful adults whose terms define invited spaces for young people (Cockburn 2010), forcing young participants into adult-centric ways of working (Prout 2003), rather than defining what is safe, inclusive and effective for themselves. For those spaces to become transformative, both individually and collectively, time is required to learn about oneself and the world (Freire 1970; Tearney and Hinton 2014). For young survivors, this necessitates safe, empowering and non-traumatising ways of (co-)developing a critical consciousness of individual and collective experiences of abuse, structures that perpetuate domestic abuse and action that may change it. Furthermore, as Lundy (2007, p.927) asserts powerfully, '"voice" is not enough': children's views require 'audience' and 'influence' to ensure they are given due weight in decision-making.

Agency

Lundy (2007, p.937) argues for children's 'right of audience' – the opportunity to communicate their views to someone with the power to make decisions. A national young advisory group demands exploration of opportunities for sustained communication and actual involvement in decision-making and policy-making. Such participation of young survivors requires consideration of their agency, its relational and embodied nature, not only as a child but also as a victim of coercive control. Active participation in decisions about their everyday lives emerges from domestic abuse literature as 'crucial to their ability to cope' (Mullender *et al.* 2002, p.100), central to validation, support and recovery (Eriksson 2011). Re-focusing on agency (Stark 2007) and women's 'space for action' (Kelly, Sharp and Klein 2014, p.4) is deemed essential for adult survivors, but needs to be extended and explored with young survivors, not only in their everyday lives, but also in their participation in collective decision-making.

In Scotland, Ministers have publicly committed to children's 'voice' in domestic abuse policy development: 'the work has and will continue to be informed by young people' (Scottish Parliament 2007, col. 3742). It is notable that the real 'work' remains an adult domain, and children, although key, are passive informants, which reflects critiques in generic participation literature (see Lansdown 2010, p.13). Children and young people are deemed not to have the competence to take an active part in public debate (Malone and Hartung 2010), and opportunities to join the political decision-making structure are usually unavailable (Shier 2001). Tisdall (2017, p.67) argues that 'co-production' could provide the shift required for children to find a place in decision-making through recognition of children 'as potential experts and creators of knowledge'. This chapter explores co-production's potential for deeper engagement than decision-making (see Stephens, Ryan-Collins and Boyle 2008), uniquely whether young survivors can use their skills and experience to help the Government deliver. This challenges policy-makers to have the competence and capacity to work with children collaboratively, to achieve real dialogue with 'mutual respect and recognition' (Thomas 2009, p.195).

Power

It is rare for children to have direct access to power as 'children have no formal place at the decision-making table' (Theis 2010, p.350). The Scottish Parliament and its participative structure increased opportunities for access, and recent legislation outlines a (somewhat caveated) duty on Ministers to take account of any relevant views of children (Children and Young People (Scotland) Act 2014, Part 1, Section 1 (2) and (5)). Transforming structures to enable meaningful, effective and, most elusive, sustained participation of children and young people remains the challenge (Tisdall *et al.* 2014). Should children's views be actively sought, they need to be given due weight (Lundy 2007), impact on decision-making (Tisdall 2017) and actively translate into change (Johnson 2011). Transformation of adult-controlled spaces and mechanisms (Theis 2010) could lead to real power for children in decision-making, in co-creation of solutions, and in governance (Tisdall 2017). Considerable time, effort, political will and investment is required for this, and perhaps might only be secured through accountability mechanisms (see Byrne and Lundy 2015; Lansdown and O'Kane 2014; Theis 2010).

There remains a need to shift perceptions about children involved from 'technical actors who can provide useful information...[to] citizens or political actors with rights to uphold and interests to defend' (Theis 2010, p.350). This chapter contributes young survivors' perspectives on becoming political actors, on 'vulnerability' and power when claiming their political space for collective action.

METHODOLOGY

Eight young experts were recruited (aged 15–19 at the onset; four self-identified as male, four female, two minority ethnic, one learning disabled, two LGBT) and agreed to a participatory action research process over a two-and-a-half-year period. This allowed for reflection on challenges as they arose, young and adult expert action to address issues, as well as respect for young people as expert and equal in the development of participation principles.

Young experts created templates and activities to reflect on issues within the process that included direct contact with politicians; collaborating with civil servants; fact-finding with young and adult experts; and peer empowerment projects. They co-designed a final review. Thematic analysis was undertaken together for the young people's chosen outputs – a film of key messages[1] and a 'snakes and ladders of participation' presentation to the Scottish Government. Young experts gave me permission to further analyse using my own expertise and insights in relation to the wider research study (Houghton 2013), literature and theoretical debates (Alderson 2009), and did not want a part in that 'boring' endeavour.

Ethical codes and situated ethics

Initial (and regular) interviews with young people, their support workers and their mothers included risk assessment, safety planning and identifying access to a local specialist support worker for the duration. Their perspectives on safe and happy involvement informed the research ethics established using Mullender *et al.*'s (2002) 'three Cs' of 'Consent, Confidentiality and Child protection' and 'three Ds' of 'Danger, Distress and Disclosure'. This study co-developed ethical standards throughout the process,[2] culminating in a model that re-focused the Cs and Ds on children's agency and added the 'three Es' of 'Enjoyment, Empowerment and Emancipation' (see Houghton 2015).

INTRODUCTION TO THE FINDINGS

Voice Against Violence identified two key challenges to participation from the onset that they defined as two adult-held prejudices. The first related to being a child. Adults would undoubtedly question their competence and ability to participate within the political system, expressed here through a wonderful skit on politicians, played by Raya and Jack:

1 See https://vimeo.com/46353009

2 See https://voiceagainstviolence.org.uk/wp-content/uploads/2012/07/standards-booklet.pdf

Minister 1: 'Thanks very much, very interesting, very moving, aye you keep it real.'

Minister 2: 'Key to budget setting you are, key information, excellent ideas.'

[VAV leave Parliament]

[Ministers laugh]

Minister 1: 'Who the f*ck are *they* to tell us what to do?'

Minister 2: 'Aye, a bunch of kids? Nae chance!'

The second related to being a child 'victim' of domestic abuse. VAV felt keenly that they might be perceived as 'doomed' – stigmatised as problem youth or labelled perpetrators/victims of the future. They also feared being ignored, reflecting their experiences of agency responses, because they weren't the 'real' victims of domestic abuse. As Chloe relates:

> 'After all these years, people still think abuse is between adults, but we see and hear more than you think. We get hurt ourselves. Our lives are controlled. We are all frightened.'

VAV actively challenged these perceptions throughout their two-and-a-half years as young experts, and since, through involvement in a recent Economic and Social Research Council (ESRC) IMPACT project with myself. The status of being a child, being a young survivor, now permeates their perspectives on collective voice, action and power. Their chosen pseudonyms are used or '(VAV)' where quotes were collectively agreed in the co-analysis and resources produced.[3]

Collective voice

Young experts resisted pressure from adult policy-makers that a national advisory group should be larger and more 'representative'. They felt strongly that small groups of young people, of a similar age and with shared experiences (the experience of domestic abuse with their mother), were important, to ensure they could build the trust, relationships and confidence necessary to speak out about

3 See www.voiceagainstviolence.org.uk/category/resources

abuse to powerful strangers. It was important that young experts had received support and were safe with their mother, both to be able to speak about tackling domestic abuse and to commit to two years in the group. This was caveated with recognition that abuse and its effects could be ongoing, particularly if there was contact with the perpetrator; that VAV participation workers were skilled in specialist support was a young survivor-led prerequisite.

That group members had experience of a range of services was also considered important, with recruitment targeting previously unheard groups of young people, for example those experiencing the justice system and 'new' services such as CEDAR[4] groupwork or Women's Aid outreach. Actively seeking young people with previous involvement of domestic abuse studies/participation projects (Fitzpatrick *et al.* 2003; Houghton 2006; Stafford *et al.* 2007) meant group members were informed by the priorities of a wider range of children and young people. It was important to the young people (and the Government) that VAV itself was independent from those services, hence they chose VAV's neutral base at the university. They defined the role of the research-manager as like a band manager, not the boss. It was incredibly important that they sang their own song, spoke for themselves and were not controlled or silenced by adults, as these young people explain:

> 'Young people led our independent projects, there was no one sort of pushing us to do them.' (John)
>
> 'Yes, no one telling us what to do, our own priorities, our own words.' (Chloe)

Within the group, an equal number of male and females was considered vital to reflect children's experiences of domestic abuse and the importance of promoting gender equality to end abuse. Striving for diversity was important and, to that end, VAV was proud that they included young people who identified as black and minority ethnic (BME), lesbian, gay, bisexual and transgender (LGBT) and learning disabled, but recommended specific action research with these and other excluded groups.

4 'Children Experiencing Domestic Abuse Recovery', Concurrent Programme for children and mothers (www.cedarnetwork.org.uk).

VAV chose the singular word 'voice' for their name to represent that they were a voice, not the voice or all voices. They recognised that many children were silenced through abuse and too scared to speak out, but also that many other children just needed the opportunity. They felt valued as 'experts through experience' but that ongoing participation required an increased mandate through listening to others, learning about children's situation across Scotland and empowering others to speak out.

> 'VAV wants to...be a voice and give a voice to children and young people experiencing domestic abuse...amplify children and young people's voices to campaign for their rights...empower all children and young people.' (VAV)

VAV developed an action research model of working to engage other young experts currently experiencing services in fact-finding projects (e.g. on housing, justice), to reflect on their issues and solutions, to seek and share information (e.g. interviewing adult experts, talking to researchers), to co-create recommendations and then empower (other) young people to challenge Ministers. This could be done anonymously (e.g. VAV presenting illustrations and thought bubbles comparing old and new refuges) or through mentoring children's direct engagement with people in power.[5] These quotes from Marc and Karen illuminate this further:

> 'Real participation for me is when VAV leads our participation projects for young people to directly be involved and have their voices heard...' (Marc)

> '...yeah, when children and young people of Scotland came to the Big Bang event and had the opportunity to ask the people in power what they wanted to.' (Karen)

VAV felt shorter-term engagement with real outcomes and access to power could suit children with recent and traumatising experiences of abuse, particularly in chaotic housing circumstances. It was obvious to them that each priority area of domestic abuse policy impacted on children and should therefore include participation of (other) young survivors and even introducing measures to monitor this. VAV also

5 See www.voiceagainstviolence.org.uk/question-time-peer-education-project

recommended other national advisory groups (e.g. younger children, teenagers experiencing abuse in their own relationships); a future model linking national with local authority/themed projects; and national action research with unheard groups, all of which would identify and empower young experts of the future. They were frustrated by Government lack of action on these recommendations that they perceived as policy-makers' 'tick-box' approach to participation:

> 'It feels like "we've got VAV, we've done it".' (Declan).
>
> 'Their whole point was to make sure that children were participating in every single stage and they severely failed in that task.' (VAV)

Agency

> 'We are not here just to "make it real".' (John)

While young participants felt policy-makers did need to develop their understanding of what experiencing domestic abuse is really like for children, VAV were frustrated at perceptions that theirs would be a passive role, as the next quotes from Declan and Chloe articulate:

> 'Adults see us as people with problems, not problem-solvers; we've got ideas, solutions.' (Declan)
>
> 'They also need us as quality assurance, to check that something actually happens.' (Chloe)

They did not 'just' want to present young people's issues but to help set priorities for Government action, be part of that action and to monitor it. They were confident that they brought a unique contribution to policy-making, as young survivors and also as young people with fresh ideas and perspectives:

> 'We convinced people we were as important as adults...told adults what needed changed...listened to others...got some allies (choose adults that can help/experts)...listened to other children...read stuff...went on fact-finding trips...developed our arguments...got equal status as advisers to people at the top.' (VAV)

VAV recommended and were given equal status to the adult board in the policy structure. This meant that young survivors, as well as the board, had direct regular access to Ministers. Monitoring progress on policy priorities was a shared responsibility, as was re-setting those priorities over time. Young experts felt this relationship was strained; communication could be poor:

> 'They were nae interactive...they lacked giving us information and giving us criticism...never really a two-way relationship.' (Chloe).

VAV came late to the process into adult-centric structures that they felt were very un-child friendly. They were critical that some members did not share their passion for change, were 'just' there as part of their job, and felt that some civil servants lacked knowledge on the subject. Young experts also stated that they felt patronised by some adults, as Raya and Karen explain:

> 'I don't want them to just nod and be nice, yes, yes, aka poor wee victim.' (Raya)
>
> 'Yes, I haven't got time to be fucking nice.' (Karen)

VAV did feel that they played an active role in monitoring progress and felt young experts' perspectives were crucial. They were more critical about progress than the adults, and responded when children's top priorities were considered to be under threat, as Karen asserts:

> 'Real participation was campaigning for support workers and influencing the budget to ensure there was funding for them – justifying their importance and significance to a young person.'

Through fact-finding with young and adult experts, giving evidence to the board and dialogue with the chair, VAV fought off numerous threats to the multi-million Scottish Government fund for specialist workers across Scotland: de-centralisation of funds from national to local government; recommendations to mainstream such support, that is, make it the responsibility of generic statutory services; and the effects of broader financial cuts through austerity agendas. While they were keen to retain their own voice and 'not sound like the adults we're trying to influence' (Declan), they designed a workshop with board members using the 'spend to save' argument (which was perfectly clear to them, unlike much government jargon). As John explains:

> 'Individual support workers was all of ours' top priority – some of us didn't get any support at all, leading to loads of problems and costs to the health and justice service and to our education.'

They also influenced funding reach and conditions of grants, such as specialist support and advocacy within the justice system and expanding outreach to young people aged 16+ (male and female). VAV felt other examples of 'real participation' included:

> '[When] young people are involved right from the start of a project to the end...their views are respected and taken on board.' (Jack)

> 'Yes, our ideas, our work, our product.' (Declan)

These included being co-clients for a national advert with the Government;[6] co-authoring a survey with a Government researcher;[7] and creating their legacy film,[8] which was funded by the Government without any conditions:

> 'They trusted us by then, it's our film, our messages.' (Chloe)

Key to this were adults, especially civil servants, with a deep understanding of domestic abuse, skills in participation and expertise in the subject area. These civil servants shared power and were clear about the power they and the young people had, such as VAV's right of veto over the advertising campaign. There was a definite shift in adult/child relations over time, and VAV felt that they played an active part in government action, as illuminated by these next quotes:

> 'We've proved that we can have active roles in helping decide things.' (Raya)

> 'That we know what we're talking about and that we're wanting things to be changed.' (Chloe)

> 'Yes, we were actually *doing* policy.' (Marc)

> 'That's what we're about, actually changing things.' (John)

---

6 See www.youtube.com/watch?v=Sf5yjJq7ubU

7 See https://voiceagainstviolence.org.uk/wp-content/uploads/2012/03/Shaping-the-Future-Voice-Against-Violence-Survey-Report.pdf

8 See https://vimeo.com/29908502

Power

VAV agreed that the pinnacle of success in participation was young survivors' direct access to power. This was not only their sustained, successful relationship with senior politicians as young experts, but also using that position and status to enable other young survivors to access power, as Declan describes:

> 'We inspired them, mentored them, trained them a wee bit and they spoke up to those in the highest power; it was awesome.'

VAV chaired and set the agenda for regular meetings with the same three politicians, through which they built an ongoing relationship as 'critical friends', developing a genuine camaraderie, a shared quest for straight talking, and a sense of urgency in changing policy. Politicians said VAV became critical to decisions on priorities and budget setting, and VAV noted a shift in openness, a willingness to act on what they said and to include VAV in the discussion on action. They felt all their achievements directly related to this access to power. This direct relationship was rated by far the most successful by young survivors, the most effective use of their time and energy and requiring a great deal of preparation and research. Raya and Jack reflect:

> 'I wanted to influence the people at the top because direct access I feel is the only way we can achieve real change.' (Raya)

> 'It's a great feeling to know that you're influencing where the money goes, what decisions are made, what those pieces of paper called policies say. Because for us, before, those policies just did not work.' (Jack)

Furthermore, VAV felt this direct access, and the 'expert' status senior politicians conferred to them, legitimised their presence in the policy-making system to other adult political actors. Without it they felt policy-makers, including senior professionals, would not have spared the time to meet them, attempt equal dialogue or work alongside them on priorities. They felt strongly that people in power needed to help challenge the stereotypes that young people were too young to participate, or that they should be treated in a certain way because they were victims. VAV felt that they constantly had to prove the competence of children, that their voice was worth listening to and that they could contribute to debates, as these next two quotes elaborate:

> 'Showing that just because we're young or maybe we don't have certain things that adults do, we can still do a fine job. And you don't need, I don't know, material sort of things to make a difference.' (John)

> 'Many adults said we'd be too young to handle such responsibility but we've proved we're not.' (VAV)

They also felt they needed to show that they were good people, advocates against violence, and implored politicians and the media to urgently challenge the myth that child victims would automatically go on to hurt others or be abused.

VAV's reason for being was to change children's lives. In fact, their ethical stance was that participation should not be undertaken with young survivors if change was not possible (see Houghton 2015 for a discussion on this). Their key priorities for change at first related to improved responses: an awareness of children as victims; access to specialist support and housing; mandatory teacher training and gender equality/abuse education in schools; improved journeys through the justice system including safe contact; appropriate, safe, respectful information sharing; and improved multi-agency responses. This expanded over time to include changing attitudes (of society, of politicians) and enhancing children's democratic participation, as Raya's quote illuminates:

> 'We want to challenge the political system and raise the platform for children and young people on the political level, but in doing so inspire other children and young people as well to feel empowered that their opinions count too...create more opportunities for participation...just so it's not so elitist.'

They felt it was particularly difficult for young survivors to access political power structures, including those set up as elected bodies. For example, school pupil councils were not experienced positively by the young people, as for each of them their education was severely disrupted by abuse and they were not the 'chosen kids' for such activity. Similarly, national youth parliaments were experienced as inaccessible and irrelevant to their chaotic and disrupted lives (although VAV became a stepping-stone for such engagement). VAV recommended young survivors' direct access to power, without intermediaries, as the most empowering, successful and effective relationship they could have. They felt strongly that such participation needed to be sustained and had a firm belief in the capabilities of the many young survivors they had worked with to be the next VAV. This is asserted here by Karen and Chloe:

> 'We've built it in stone – the structure, the standards, the goals – not to be knocked down...this is wasted if participating in this way is not done over and over, rolled out just like all the projects we've been fighting for.' (Karen)

> 'We've proved ourselves already, Nicola Sturgeon [now Scotland's First Minister] said that we need to get on with it, children are suffering out there.' (Chloe)

When this did not happen immediately they came back as young adults to share their template with policy-makers and young people, then co-developed ways of sustaining participation in gender-based violence policy for the future:

> 'We had to come back, advise on "Equally Safe",[9] otherwise it was all for nothing.' (Karen).

A FRAMEWORK FOR YOUNG SURVIVORS' INVOLVEMENT IN POLICY-MAKING: VOICE, AGENCY, POWER, SUPPORT, IMPACT

This unique opportunity for sustained involvement in policy-making allowed us to identify and tackle inherent challenges of participation while developing an ethical framework to support young survivors. This not only pertains to their 'vulnerabilities', but also injects agency into protective measures of Consent, Confidentiality and Child protection: Danger, Distress and Disclosure (Mullender *et al.*'s 3 Cs and Ds, 2002). It necessitates a fuller exploration of how participation can be Enjoyable, Empowering and Emancipatory (Houghton's 3 Es, 2015). This chapter recommends a framework for young survivors'

---

9 Equally Safe: Scotland's strategy for preventing and eradicating violence against women and girls https://blogs.gov.scot/equally-safe/wp-content/uploads/sites/18/2016/03/ES-update-18-April1.pdf

sustained participation in national policy-making: voice, agency and power are its key tenets, while support and impact are conditions young survivors set.

In relation to voice, a national advisory group can be an effective voice over time can increase its mandate through conducting action research thereby giving voice to those not (yet) in the position to be involved over time. A consistent national voice proved vital in increasing, monitoring and critiquing opportunities for participation across policy priorities. Ultimately it enabled many more young survivors to have a voice in service and policy development. Furthermore, a national voice helps sustain participation. In Scotland, once that voice disappeared, children's rights and participation became invisible in policy-making. Political investment in a continuous process, where experienced young experts mentor and hand over to new members after time, would counter this.

In relation to agency, young survivors and policy-makers can work together to monitor and co-produce policy: this is acutely dependent on the space developed and the capacity of adults to collaborate. Time for adults and children to develop their 'critical consciousness' (Freire 1970) about domestic abuse, the national situation for children, the structures that perpetuate abuse, gender equality and the denial of children's rights is important. They need time together to co-develop transformative spaces for collaboration on action. Then, a national youth advisory group brings a unique contribution to governance: distinct perspectives on progress, real measuring of participation and clear priorities for budgetary decisions. This path is not easy and requires improved youth-led communication and creative dialogue with small numbers of skilled, powerful policy-makers.

In relation to power, young survivors' direct access to power is key. The establishment of friendly, critical relationships with powerful politicians over time is the most effective route to impact and empowerment, and the best use of survivors and politicians' limited time. Young people need status as young experts and a defined, independent space and role within collective decision-making and delivery. If time and investment is limited, the pre-eminent route for participation is meaningful, and sustained dialogue with politicians holding the most power to change children's lives.

There are two critical conditions for young survivors to be involved at all: support and impact. A national advisory group requires investment in local and national skilled support workers throughout the process. Participation needs to play a part in the therapeutic process and is not distinct. The standards young survivors set ensure involvement contributes to redressing harm, restoring agency and a newfound confidence in the collective power of young people to make the world a better place. If participation does not impact on (other) children's lives, it risks disrupting recovery from abuse, compounding young survivors' distrust in adults and disaffection with politics.

IT IS TIME...

It is time to co-develop space for young people's collective and sustained participation in national policy-making. A shift is needed to co-create transformative space for children and young people to become political actors over time: to ensure an audience and influence then active, continual involvement in decision-making and delivery. It is time for young survivors to claim their space for political action, should they choose to. It can help redress and prevent the collective harm domestic abuse does to children. It can challenge deficit constructions of children and child victims. It can enhance policy. It proves without doubt the amazing competence, capabilities, strengths, skills and expertise of young people, of young survivors. It is time to break the silence of young survivors: in their personal and political lives. It is their right. It is our duty.

This exciting pilot demonstrates what is possible with political will and investment. It provides a framework for countries to adapt and evidence from young survivors and politicians that working together works. Scotland's First Minister elaborates:

> Voice Against Violence is unique, the first group of Young Experts to participate as equal partners in the development and implementation of policy on domestic abuse anywhere in the world. Individually they are all very impressive young people, and together they are a force to be reckoned with. They have proved that genuine participation of Young People is not only possible; it is a vitally important part of developing good policy.
>
> The Scottish Government is very proud to have supported this ground-breaking and important initiative, and to have proved that working together really works. (Nicola Sturgeon MSP, VAV 2011)

The challenge across countries is to assert, then sustain, young survivors' collective right to participation in national, and then international, policy-making.

Dedication: Thank you to the eight wonderful young experts of Voice Against Violence; you are an inspiration to us all.

REFERENCES

Alderson, P. (2009) 'Rights-respecting research: A commentary on the "Right to be properly researched: Research with children in a messy, real world".' *Children's Geographies 7*, 233–239.

Barter, C., Wood, M., Aghtaie, N., Larkins, C. *et al.* (2015) *Safeguarding Teenage Intimate Relationships (STIR): Connecting Online and Offline Contexts and Risks.* EU: DAPHNE III and NSPCC (PI). [See http://stiritup.eu/young-people]

Buckley, H., Holt, S. and Whelan, S. (2007) 'Listen to me! Children's experiences of domestic violence.' *Child Abuse Review 16*, 296–310.

Byrne, B. and Lundy, L. (2015) 'Reconciling children's policy and children's rights: Barriers to effective government delivery.' *Children and Society 29*, 266–276.

Children and Young People (Scotland) Act (2014). Edinburgh: Scottish Government.

Cockburn, T. (2010) 'Children and Deliberative Democracy in England.' In B. Percy-Smith and N. Thomas (eds) *A Handbook of Children and Young People's Participation* (pp.307–317). Abingdon: Routledge.

Eriksson, M. (2011) 'Contact, shared parenting, and violence: Children as witnesses of domestic violence in Sweden.' *International Journal of Law, Policy and the Family 25*, 2, 165–183.

Fitzpatrick, S., Lynch, E., Goodlad, R. and Houghton, C. (2003) *Refuges for Women, Children and Young People in Scotland.* Edinburgh: Scottish Executive.

Freire, P. (1970) *Pedagogy of the Oppressed.* New York: Continuum.

Hanson, K. (2016) 'Children's participation and agency when they don't "do the right thing".' *Childhood 32*, 4, 471–475.

Harding, S. (2012) 'Feminist Standpoints.' In S. Nagy Hesse-Biber (ed.) *The Handbook of Feminist Research: Theory and Praxis* (Chapter 3). Thousand Oaks, CA: Sage.

Holt, S. (2016) 'The voice of the child in family law: A discussion paper.' *Children and Youth Services Review 68*, 139–145.

Houghton, C. (2006) 'Listen Louder: Working with Children and Young People.' In C. Humphreys and N. Stanley (eds) *Domestic Violence and Child Protection: Directions for Good Practise* (pp.82–94). London: Jessica Kingsley Publishers.

Houghton, C. (2008) *Making a Difference: Young People Speak to Scottish Ministers about Their Priorities for the National Domestic Abuse Delivery Plan for Children and Young People.* Edinburgh: Scottish Government.

Houghton, C. (2013) 'Voice Against Violence: Young People's Experiences of Domestic Abuse Policy-Making in Scotland.' PhD, University of Warwick. Accessed on 2/8/2017 at http://wrap.warwick.ac.uk/59089/1/WRAP_THESIS_Houghton_2013.pdf

Houghton, C. (2015) 'Young people's perspectives on participatory ethics: Agency, power and impact in domestic abuse research and policy-making.' *Child Abuse Review 24*, 235–248.

Humphreys, C., Mullender, A., Thiara, R.K. and Skamballis, A. (2006) '"Talking to my mum": Developing communication between mothers and children in the aftermath of domestic violence.' *Journal of Social Work 6*, 1, 53–63.

Johnson, V. (2011) 'Conditions for change for children and young people's participation in evaluation: "Change-scape".' *Child Indicators Research 4*, 4, 577–596.

Katz, E. (2015) 'Domestic violence, children's agency and mother–child relationships: Towards a more advanced model.' *Children and Society 29*, 1, 69–79.

Kelly, L., Sharp, N. and Klein, R. (2014) *Finding the Costs of Freedom: How Women and Children Rebuild Their Lives after Domestic Violence.* London: Solace Women's Aid, CWASU, Lottery.

Lansdown, G. (2010) 'The Realisation of Children's Participation Rights: Critical Reflections.' In B. Percy-Smith and N. Thomas (eds) *A Handbook of Children and Young People's Participation* (pp.11–23). Abingdon: Routledge.

Lansdown, G. and O'Kane, C. (2014) *A Toolkit for Monitoring and Evaluating Children's Participation.* London: Save the Children.
Lundy, L. (2007) '"Voice" is not enough: Conceptualising Article 12 of the United Nations Convention on the Rights of the Child.' *British Educational Research Journal 33*, 6, 927–942.
Mackay, K. (2013) *The Treatment of the Views of Children in Private Law Child Contact Disputes Where There Is a History of Domestic Abuse.* Commissioned Briefing Paper. Edinburgh: Scottish Commissioner for Children and Young People. Accessed on 2/8/2017 at www.sccyp.org.uk/ufiles/views-of-children-and-domestic-abuse.pdf
Malone, K. and Hartung, C. (2010) 'Challenges of Participatory Practise with Children.' In B. Percy-Smith and N. Thomas (eds) *A Handbook of Children and Young People's Participation* (pp.24–38). Abingdon: Routledge.
Mullender, A., Hague, G., Imam, U., Kelly, L., Malos, E. and Regan, L. (2002) *Children's Perspectives on Domestic Violence.* London: Sage.
Øverlien, C. and Hyden, M. (2009) 'Children's actions when experiencing domestic violence.' *Childhood 16*, 479–496.
Prout, A. (2003) 'Participation, Policy and the Changing Conditions of Childhood.' In C. Hallett and A. Prout (eds) *Hearing the Voices of Children: Social Policy for a New Century* (pp.11–25). London: RoutledgeFalmer.
Scottish Government (2016) *Equally Safe: Scotland's strategy for preventing and eradicating violence against women and girls.* Edinburgh: Scottish Government. https://blogs.gov.scot/equally-safe/wp-content/uploads/sites/18/2016/03/ES-update-18-April1.pdf
Scottish Parliament Official Report (2006) *Meeting of the Parliament, Session 2, Thursday 9 November 2006.* Edinburgh: Scottish Parliament.
Scottish Parliament Official Report (2007) *Meeting of the Parliament, Session 3, Thursday 22nd November 2007.* Edinburgh: Scottish Parliament.
Shier, H. (2001) 'Pathways to participation: Openings, opportunities and obligations.' *Children and Society 15*, 107–117.
Stafford, A., Stead, J. and Grimes, M. (2007) *The Support Needs of Children and Young People Who Have to Move Home because of Domestic Abuse.* Edinburgh: Scottish Women's Aid.
Stark, E. (2007) *Coercive Control: How Men Entrap Women in Personal Life.* Oxford: Oxford University Press.
Stephens, L., Ryan-Collins, L. and Boyle, D. (2008) *Co-production.* London: New Economics Foundation.
Tearney, K. and Hinton, R. (2014) 'Reflections on Participation and its Link with Transformative Processes.' In E.K.M. Tisdall, R. Hinton, A.M. Gadda and U.M. Butler (eds) *Children and Young People's Participation and its Transformative Potential: Learning from across Countries* (pp. 22–43). Basingstoke: Palgrave Macmillan.
Theis, J. (2010) 'Children as Active Citizens: An Agenda for Children's Civil Rights and Civic Engagement.' In B. Percy-Smith and N. Thomas (eds) *A Handbook of Children and Young People's Participation* (pp.343–355). Abingdon: Routledge.
Thomas, N. (2009) *Children, Politics and Communication: Participation at the Margins.* Bristol: Policy Press.
Tisdall, E.K.M. (2015) 'Children and Young People's Participation: A Critical Consideration of Article 12.' In W. Vandenhole, E. Desmet, D. Reynaert and D. Lembrechts (eds) *The Routledge International Handbook of Children's Rights Studies* (pp.185–200). Abingdon: Routledge.
Tisdall, E.K.M. (2017) 'Conceptualising children and young people's participation: Examining vulnerability, social accountability and co-production.' *The International Journal of Human Rights 21*, 1, 59–75.
Tisdall, E.K.M., Hinton, R., Gadda, A.M. and Butler, U.M. (2014) 'Introduction: Children and Young People's Participation in Collective Decision-making.' In E.K.M. Tisdall, A.M. Gadda and U.M. Butler (eds) *Children and Young People's Participation and its Transformative Potential: Learning from across Countries* (pp.1–31). Basingstoke: Palgrave Macmillan.
Voice Against Violence (VAV) (2011) *One Voice at a Time: Tackling Domestic Abuse Through the Voice of the Young.* Scotland: A Media Coop Production. Accessed on 11/9/2017 at https://vimeo.com/29908502

Chapter 5

INCLUDING CHILDREN AND ADOLESCENTS IN DOMESTIC VIOLENCE RESEARCH

WHEN MYTHS AND MISCONCEPTIONS COMPROMISE PARTICIPATION

Carolina Øverlien, *Associate Professor, Stockholm University, Sweden, and Researcher, Norwegian Centre for Violence and Traumatic Stress Studies, Oslo, Norway*

Stephanie Holt, *Associate Professor of Social Work, Trinity College Dublin, Ireland*

INTRODUCTION

Research and practise interest in domestic violence has, in recent years, expanded to include a consideration of the scope and consequences of children's exposure to violence, resulting in a depth of empirical knowledge about its prevalence, and the impact this experience has on its youngest victims (Hazen *et al.* 2006). This increased awareness of children's needs, and their heightened visibility and prominence in the context of domestic abuse, has been slow to develop, as has their status within the research community.[1] However, the emergence of a more sharply focused research and practise interest in childhood and children's experiences is reflective of the core ethos of the United Nations Convention on the Rights of the Child (UNCRC 1989). A substantive theme within the UNCRC concerns children's participatory

1 We use the terms 'domestic abuse' and 'domestic violence (and abuse)' interchangeably in this chapter, to include all forms of violence, including non-physical.

rights, including the freedom to express an opinion and to have a say in matters affecting their lives.

However, while the traditional focus of this interest and understanding has largely been achieved by eliciting the views of mothers, refuge workers and other professionals as to the impact on the child, more recent inquiry has sought to directly explore children and young people's experience of exposure to domestic abuse from their own point of view (Buckley, Holt and Whelan 2007; Callaghan *et al.* 2015; Holt 2011, 2016; Jensen, Holt and Ormhaug 2017; Katz 2015; McGee 2000; Mossige and Stefansen 2016; Mullender *et al.* 2002; Øverlien 2016; Radford *et al.* 2011). These studies have greatly increased our knowledge about the extent of children's experiences of domestic abuse, the short and long-term consequences, and what it means to be a child and live with violence in their everyday experiences. This knowledge is critical for all practitioners who work with children and adolescents in their everyday life, for researchers who develop and evaluate interventions and treatment methods, and for policy-makers who make decisions that affect children and adolescents' lives. Across the three domains of research, policy and practise, we *need* children's knowledge about their own lives, but children also have a *right* to make their voices heard in matters that concern them. This reflects a commitment to honouring the principle of 'listening to the voice of the child' as demanded by nation-states across Europe, and by recognising and accepting children as active sentient social actors in the unfolding story of their ongoing development in family life. Specifically, Article 12 of the UNCRC states that 'States Parties shall assure to the child who is capable of forming his or her own views the right to express those views freely in all matters affecting the child, the views of the child being given due weight in accordance with the age and maturity of the child' (UNCRC 1989). This means that a child has the right to express his or her views, for example through participating in research, in accordance with his or her age and maturity. While *participation* is one of the categories of the UNCRC, *protection* is another. Article 36, for example, describes how 'States Parties shall protect the child against all other forms of exploitation prejudicial to any aspects of the child's welfare'. This includes every form of potential harm, including harm from participating in research. As such, children's right as research participants to be protected from harm is more extensive than the rights of the adult participants. This balance between an obligation to include *and* to protect, described by Lansdown (1994, p.36) below as an 'inherent tension', is the core of the ethically sensitive child researcher's dilemma:

> [The debate] exposes the inherent tension between a view of children on the one hand, as dependent on adult protection and incapable of taking responsibility for their decision-making, and on the other, as people with basic civil rights including the right to participate fully in decisions that affect their lives.

The philosophical rhetoric underpinning the UNCRC also reflects theoretical developments in the study of childhood, namely the new sociology of childhood where the lens of sociological interest has shifted from viewing children as 'mere objects of enquiry', to dynamic and key participants (Powell and Smith 2009). This acknowledges not only their capacity to operate within 'adult-centred socially constructed meanings of citizenship', but also their capacity to influence them as well (Bacon 2014, p.22).

Despite these debates and developments, children today are far from being included in research to the same extent as adults. According to the European Union Agency for Fundamental Rights (FRA),[2] the extent to which children and adolescents are allowed to participate in research varies greatly in Europe. This is particularly true with regard to the process of ethical approval and the gaining of informed consent. In the absence of internationally agreed-on standards on how to conduct ethically sound research with children, research practise in Europe is governed by the laws, institutional procedures and codes of conduct in each respective country. The FRA (2014) highlights that in Belgium, for example, ethical research codes exist but have almost no implications for research involving children. However, informed consent is always required from parents, unless the research takes place in a school setting. If so, a teacher or a headteacher can give consent in the place of the parent. In Portugal, written consent from parents for all children under the age of 18 is stipulated by the law on data protection, while in Romania, no specific legal framework exists. Although approval from an ethics committee is needed, the procedure depends on the research institute that conducts the research, hence the codes of conduct and practises vary. In France, there are no specific

2 See http://fra.europa.eu/en/theme/rights-child/child-participation-in-research

regulations or guidelines concerning involving children in research, except in the medical field. Furthermore, even within individual countries, there are varying standards and processes.

In this chapter we would like to discuss some of the challenges that we, as researchers, struggle with, when conducting research on/with children and adolescents experiencing domestic violence. We take our starting point in our own studies, where the methods have varied, but where the majority have included children and adolescents as informants with the aim of trying to understand issues of violence and abuse from their perspective. In all of these studies, research ethics, defined here as the moral principles guiding research from designing the research questions to dissemination of the results, have been a primary concern. Drawing on this empirical research, this chapter considers those ethical challenges while maintaining a strong reflective awareness of a growing ethos of respect for the child's position in a process that involves all family members (Buckley *et al.* 2007; Mullender *et al.* 2002).

AN ADULT-DRIVEN CONSENT PROCESS

In a survey responded to by 257 researchers in 46 countries, informed consent was defined as one of four key areas of ethical concern with regard to research involving children (Powell *et al.* 2012). Acquiring consent before the start of data collection is perhaps the most central principle in all research, regardless of methods and research design, and the consent must be clearly informed and voluntary. That is, the potential participant must be given enough information to be able to make an informed decision, and there must be no circumstances that force or persuade him or her into agreeing to participate. In the countries where we conduct our research, children's explicit consent (rather than assent) must also be sought, and along the same lines as with adults, their dissent or withdrawal before or during the data collection process must be respected, without penalty. However, in many countries, along with the children's consent, a (most often) parent or caretaker must also consent. This means that regardless of the issue, the voice of the adult is superior to the voice of the child who is 15, 16 or 18 years old (depending on the regulations in the specific country) and younger. When the first author conducted a study on teenage intimate partner violence, a 15-year-old girl consented to being interviewed about her boyfriend's abuse, but her father did not approve, and dissented. In effect, this negated the voice of that child to be heard and undermined her right to participate. In line with the Norwegian laws regulating research, the ethical board that reviewed and approved the study would not allow any participants under the age of 16 to independently consent regardless of the fact that in Norway a 15-year-old girl can receive counselling or be prescribed birth control pills without her parents' knowledge. She is not, however, deemed to be able to independently decide if she would like to participate in research regarding the abuse she has endured in her own romantic relationship. The issue of children and consent can be understood as a rights-based issue: the right for parents to protect their child and the rights of the child for autonomy and to freely express his/her opinion. In practise, however, in many jurisdictions across Europe, the rights of the parent to protect their child, can hold greater weight and can overrule the right of the child to participate.[3]

There are additional issues that complicate and compromise the consent of the child, such as if one or both parents' consent is required, including the consent of a violent parent, and what the possible implications might be for the safety of the child. Peled (2001) argues that a child who has experienced domestic violence should not participate in research if a parent he/she has contact with objects or may object (if asked) to the child's participation. Since many children today do have contact with their violent fathers, with or against their will, this argument may exclude many children's rights to have their voices heard. At the same time, can a request to a violent father to let his child participate in research about violence and abuse result in more violence? What if he is not asked, and finds out that his child has talked to a researcher about the abuse he subjected the family to?

In research that includes children there are often additional adults, besides the parents, who may interfere with children's participation. These adults, commonly called 'gate-keepers', do not usually have the power to directly consent or dissent on behalf of the child, but may prevent the child (and the parents) from receiving the invitation to participate, on the basis that they do not consider it to be in the child's best interest to participate. As stated in the UNCRC, children

3 See http://fra.europa.eu/en/theme/rights-child/child-participation-in-research

have the right to protection. Therefore, having adults, other than the parents, who protect and care for them, is vital. However, it is problematic that children's participation is conditioned in ways that adult participation is not. In practise, this means that many children, and particularly children who are understood as vulnerable, are never presented with the option of participating or not. Moreover, if doors are opened and the child receives that invitation, we, as researchers, must be sensitive to the power dynamics involved, and ensure that the participation of the child is voluntary. Furthermore, for a child who knows that, for example, the school principal has agreed to let the researcher contact the class teacher, who has asked the parent for permission to let the researcher contact him or her, and the parent has consented and thereby allowed the researcher to contact the child, that child must also be reassured that their participation is fully voluntary, and that declining will have no negative ramifications for the child or his or her parents.

Furthermore, what and how much information do children need to provide an authentically informed consent? The issue of how much is enough is more complex when including children in research, as compared to adults. Children need information adjusted for their age and development. Along the same line as adults, they need to know who will listen to the recording or read the interview notes, and how the results will be disseminated. In research conducted by the second author (Holt 2011), the issue of consent was described for 8- to 11-year-old children as a 'deal' they were making together with the researcher. Their part of the deal was to only answer questions or talk about things that they were happy with, and the researcher's part of the deal concerned issues of confidentiality. Similarly, the first author told the younger children in one of her studies (Øverlien 2012) that she would write a book based on the interviews, thinking that this was easier to grasp than the concept of scientific articles. The questions, however, were many. 'Where will the book be sold? In the supermarket?' 'Who will read it, and if my teacher reads it, will she recognise that it is me?' All these questions must be taken seriously, and explained to the researcher's best ability, in a way that makes it possible for the child to make a decision based on facts. However, the issue of how much and what information is enough to make an informed decision is not just complicated with regard to children, but also adults, as they, too, may have difficulties fully understanding what it means to consent to participating in a research study.

Finally, it is important to point out that consent cannot be given once and for all. Even though a child has given his or her consent, it must always be possible to decline during or after the interview, or filling out the survey, etc. Important terms in this regard include 'ongoing consent' or what Flewitt (2005, p.556) calls 'provisional consent'. To ensure that the child consents throughout the interview, for example that the consent is 'ongoing', is to be sensitive to the child's signals and behaviour before, during and after the interview. A child who is restless, who can't sit still on their chair, may need a break or a drink of water, but may also want to terminate the interview. Because of the power imbalance and inequality between the adult and the child, the child may find it difficult to tell an adult researcher that they do not want to participate or that they want to withdraw from the study. It is therefore the responsibility of the researcher, not the child, to ensure ongoing consent, throughout the interview as well as when the recorder is turned off. Hence, a child's consent, along the same lines as adults, should be open for review throughout the research process.

RE-TRAUMATISATION AS AN ETHICAL CONCERN

An often-debated concern in research is the potential risk of re-traumatisation (Alderson and Morrow 2011; Morris, Hegarty and Humphreys 2012; Mudaly and Goddard 2009). That is, the contested understanding that a child, traumatised from being subjected to violence and abuse, can, through sharing the memories of their experiences, be traumatised again by participating in research. This concern is part of the larger discussion about children's right to protection, and the researcher's obligation to ensure that the research benefits outweigh its risks. According to the World Medical Association Declaration of Helsinki (1964), the subject's welfare must always take precedence over the interests of science and society (Article 5). The primary ethical issue is to weigh the value of the possible knowledge gains of a study against its possible harm to the participants. As little research can be so valuable that it is worth the risk of re-traumatisation, the meaning of the word and the scientific evidence for such occurrence must be further scrutinised.

According to Alderson and Morrow (2011) there are four types of potential risks of harm for children participating in research: children can be physically harmed by the research; they can be physically harmed by their parents for agreeing to participate; they can be physically punished by others for participating; or they can become anxious, experience emotional discomfort or lose self-esteem. Becoming anxious, however, and experiencing emotional discomfort during the completion of a survey or participating in a research interview, is not necessarily the same as being re-traumatised. As is the case with researching children's experience of domestic violence, where the focus is on children who have already been potentially damaged by their experiences (Edleson 1999; Holt, Buckley and Whelan 2008), inevitable ethical questions arise that demand a response that outlines how these children will be protected by, and within, the research process. Therein lies a challenge for social research: to balance the protection of children from harm in a way that does not stifle their involvement, yet discover ways to safely and ethically elicit their opinions and experiences in a way that empowers children while contributing to knowledge.

A related issue concerns the 'appropriateness' of some topics for research with children (Campbell 2008), with the degree of sensitivity in a research topic related to the level of potential emotional upset for the child. Preventing children's participation in research on emotive topics that directly affect them, because of adults' concerns about possible damage to them, not only negates their autonomy and their ability to decide for themselves, but also conceptualises them as incompetent (Campbell 2008).

Although at times claimed in the literature (see, for example, Devries *et al.* 2016) there is little support in research for the theory of re-traumatisation, in recent years, several research studies on children exposed to violence and abuse have included questions about how the children experienced answering questions about abuse, and have found that the potential risks of being harmed by participating in research are minimal. In a telephone interview with 4503 youth (aged 10–17) about their possible experiences of violence and abuse, they were asked whether answering the questions had upset them (Finkelhor *et al.* 2014). The results showed that 4.5 per cent of the children did report being upset, and 0.8 per cent reported being pretty or very upset. More children who reported being victimised by violence and abuse reported being upset compared to children who reported no such experiences. However, only 3 per cent said that they would not participate again if asked, and the majority of these regrets had to do with the length of the study, not the content. Similar findings were reported by Zajac *et al.* (2011), who interviewed children aged 12–17 about a range of potentially traumatic experiences, including being exposed to violence and abuse. A total of 5.7 per cent of the children reported feeling any level of upset, victimised children more than non-victimised. In a Norwegian study, 97 victimised children between the ages of 10 and 18 participated in a clinical study on trauma-focused cognitive behavioural therapy (Jensen 2012). As part of the study, the children were asked on three occasions if they found it stressful or upsetting to be asked questions about their experiences of trauma or trauma-related difficulties. In total, 52 per cent reported that they found it interesting or very interesting to answer the questions; 80 per cent said they were willing or very willing to answer them again; and 2 per cent said that they found the questions very stressful or upsetting. However, they still agreed to complete the study, and stated they would answer the questions again (Jensen 2012). The most common response in several studies where children in the general population are asked about their feelings with regards to answering questions about violence and abuse is that they are slightly positive, indifferent or neutral in participating (Ellonen and Pösö 2011; Fagerlund and Ellonen 2016). These findings support including victimised and non-victimised children as research-informants, considering the small risk of feelings of stress and upset and the absence of research findings supporting the theory of re-traumatisation when participating in research.

In their review of ethical issues in research with traumatised people, Newman and Kaloupek (2005) even argue that the phenomenon of re-traumatisation is not an issue with regards to research, as there is a considerable difference between asking a person to describe their experiences in a controlled and safe environment, where the person is informed of what will take place, consent to it and terminate when he or she wishes, compared to the traumatic event itself, where the victim loses all such rights.

Øverlien argues that 'research not only needs children, but children need research, and research can have an empowering effect on children in need' (2010, p.90). Moreover, the evidence also indicates that both children and adults alike can experience the sharing of their domestic violence history through the research process as therapeutic (Downes, Kelly and Westmarland 2014; Ungar 2004). As authors, we argue for the inclusion of children in research, with this assertion grounded in the evidence that research benefits children and young people who are experiencing domestic violence by garnering valuable insights into how professionals might not only better understand their individual experiences, but also support them to feel and stay safe.

There are, of course, challenges that researchers are presented with in engaging younger children on a sensitive topic such as domestic abuse. Reflecting on their own experiences as children's researchers on domestic violence, Hogan and O'Reilly (2007, p.19) argue that 'even very young children are aware of domestic violence and can offer insights on the services they received'. The experience of the two authors of this chapter also concludes that children are the best authors of their own experiences, and can surprise adults with articulate insightful accounts of what is, after all, their own first-hand account of their lived experience. We believe, however, that this is heavily dependent on the manner and means by which children's views are ascertained. In this regard, our starting point is to concur with Mantle *et al.* (2007, p.792) who argue against a 'naïve positivism underlying any assumption' that the views of the child are simply 'out there waiting to be collected'. It is also pertinent to note that, while on the one hand, the oppressive context of domestic abuse may not have facilitated free expression, resulting in the child's need for considerable support and preparation in order to be able to participate, our experience as researchers nonetheless attests to children's participatory competence (Neale 2002; Smith, Taylor and Tapp 2003). In this regard we wholeheartedly endorse Smith *et al.*'s (2003) criticism of the 'escape clause' against children's participation that is provided for by the imposition of standards of age and maturity, rather supporting the view that the argument should not be one of proving the child's ability to participate but more one of responsibility on adults to be competent enough to elicit those views in the context of a trusting relationship with the child. Similarly, Thomas and O'Kane (2000) argue that when children are judged incompetent to participate in research, we should perhaps, first, question if the methods used to elicit their views were appropriate and, second, if those methods were 'competently' administered. As argued in the early writings in the paradigm of sociology of childhood, if the research methods are adjusted and carried out in a 'child-friendly manner', children and adolescents can participate in research along the same lines as adults (James and Prout 1990).

UNDERSTANDING CHILDREN, CHILDHOOD, ADULTS AND PARENTS

Children's limited rights to give consent to participate in research, combined with a perception that participation in research causes harm to children, or places them at risk, both stem from a positioning of children as more vulnerable and in need of protection when compared with adults, and an understanding of childhood as a period in people's lives that should, as far as possible, be sheltered from all potential pain, suffering or even unpleasantness. As authors, we want to make clear that we agree that children should have extensive rights to protection, rights that are more advanced than the rights of adults. However, with these rights comes taken-for-granted notions of children, childhood, adults and parents, which may not be in the best interest of the child and/or may hinder children's participation in issues that concern them and their lives. For example, by limiting children's rights to consent to take part in a research interview, the child's parents are empowered to consent on their child's behalf. The reasoning here is grounded in the belief that adults are more competent than children, and that parents always know or want what is best for their child, when, in fact, research on violence and abuse shows that this is not always necessarily true. Parents and other carers may have justifiable reasons to limit or even decline children's participation in research. However, the understanding that children are in need of and have the right to protection may be misused as grounds for adults to limit children's participation in research. This, in turn, may deny children their right to participation, or at least the possibility to choose whether or not to make their voices heard. Beneath these notions of children and childhood, we argue, lies an understanding of children as less reliable than adults, and therefore less suitable to participate in research. It is also perhaps as a result of a representation of childhood as unimportant (relative to adulthood) and, as such, merely a 'quarantine' period for adulthood (Christensen and Prout 2005), reflective of a sense of 'becoming' rather than 'being' (Hogan 2005; James and Prout 1990; Mayall 2000).

Children as well as adults may provide answers they believe the researcher wants in order to please him or her. Children as well as adults may also choose not to disclose or change the details of their story. This is all part of the research process, regardless of age of informants, and cannot be reasons to exclude participation. Hence, trustworthiness is a non-justifiable reason to exclude children from research. Furthermore, in contrast to a court of law, the aim of the research interview is seldom to find out 'what really happened', but to shed light on or to capture the participant's understanding of a specific phenomenon or happening. Most often, we as researchers are first and foremost interested in learning about the experiences of our informants from their own perspectives, to the best of our abilities. The aim, consequently, is not to expose 'the truth', but to explore the subjective understandings of our informants, understandings that are situated in a specific time and context. The story of what it is like, for example, to be a young child having to witness one's father abusing one's mother cannot be told more 'truthfully' than by the child him or herself.

WHEN MYTHS AND MISCONCEPTIONS COMPROMISE PARTICIPATION

Children and adolescents have an undisputable right to be protected against any form of harm, including potential harm caused by participating in research. This right, which extends the rights of adults, comes from an understanding that children are vulnerable and less capable, compared to adults, to make independent choices and know what is in their best interest. However, combining the category of 'children' with 'victimisation' and with the issue of violence and abuse that can be understood as 'sensitive topics' may evoke tensions and challenges that could lead to what Downes *et al.* (2014) call 'a dangerous lack of evidence'. If research with children who have experienced domestic violence becomes so difficult, because of age, perceived vulnerability and the understanding of the topic as sensitive, the research might become impossible to conduct. This, in turn, argues Downes *et al.* (2014), may have 'a harmful impact upon women and children and leave specialised violence and abuse services facing a precarious future'.

As noted in the literature, although research with children experiencing domestic violence has increasingly included the voice of the child, there are still a limited number of studies that use children as research participants on equal terms as adults (Holt 2011; Øverlien 2010). However, we must also reflect on whose voices we listen to when gate-keepers keep the doors locked or select our informants, when parents decline consent on behalf of their teenager, when our funders do not allow for a translator or when the most victimised children miss school the day we are there to distribute our survey. What does the absence of their voices mean with regard to the data we collect, to the results we share, to the conclusion we reach or to the methods or programmes we design and implement?

Ethical laws and guidelines are built on notions of risk with the purpose of eliminating any form of potential harm for the participant. As such, they are inevitable. However, we question whether some of the understandings underpinning the laws and guidelines governing ethical research, such as risks of re-traumatisation, are built on common assumptions rather than research data. Furthermore, ethical principles on risk, harm and protection have developed out of the scientific field of medicine, which is problematic, since much research today comes from the social science sector where the risk of harm can be understood as something different than within medicine.

When researchers meet children and adolescents who have experienced domestic violence, the worst thing has already happened. Many of these children may also be at risk again in the future. As researchers, we cannot eliminate this risk, and neither can we guarantee that the study we conduct will not in any way cause discomfort, upset or even harm. What we need to do is to take every precaution possible to make sure that the probable gains outweigh the potential risks in the research we conduct. When we conduct our interviews with victimised children, for example, we need to create a situation that is the direct opposite to the abusive situation or environment the child experienced in the past. That is, a situation which is predictable, agreed on beforehand and clearly structured. We need to create an environment that is respectful, considerate and attentive to the child's needs, that is, a situation that the child is in control of, what to answer, when to take breaks, and when to finish.

Integral to success when conducting research with children is the necessity for the children to feel that their involvement is essential, that they are the experts and what they have to say is important (Aubrey and Dahl 2005; May 2001; Mayall 1996). Hence, without compromising on responsibility, the power must shift in so far as the adult becoming the listener in need of knowledge, while the child is the teller with expertise that needs to be shared. Most importantly, research needs to start from a position that accepts the uniqueness of *each* child and their lived experiences and to commit to practise that values and prioritises the right of children to use their voices to participate in research, which is, after all, about them.

REFERENCES

Alderson, P. and Morrow, V. (2011) *The Ethics of Research with Children and Young People: A Practical Handbook.* London: Sage.

Aubrey, C. and Dahl, S. (2005) 'That child needs a good listening to! Reviewing effective interview strategies.' *Journal of Education 35*, 99–119.

Bacon, K. (2014) 'Rethinking children's citizenship: Negotiating structure, shaping meanings.' *International Journal of Children's Rights, 22*, 1, 21–42.

Buckley, H., Holt, S. and Whelan, S. (2007) 'Listen to me! Children's experiences of domestic violence.' *Child Abuse Review 16*, 5, 296–310.

Callaghan, J., Alexander, J.H., Sixsmith, J. and Fellin, L.C. (2015) 'Beyond "witnessing": Children's experiences of coercive control in domestic violence and abuse.' *Journal of Interpersonal Violence.* doi: http://dx.doi.org/10.1177/0886260515618946

Campbell, A. (2008) 'For their own good: Recruiting children for research.' *Childhood 15*, 1, 30–49.

Christensen, P. and Prout, A. (2005) 'Anthropological and Sociological Perspectives on the Study of Children.' In S. Greene and D. Hogan (eds) *Researching Children's Experiences: Approaches and Methods* (pp.42–60). London: Sage.

Devries, K., Naker, D., Monteath-van Dok, A., Milligan, C. and Shriley, A. (2016) 'Collecting data on violence against children and young people: Need for a universal standard.' *International Health 8*, 3, 159–161. doi: https://doi.org/10.1093/inthealth/ihw009

Downes, J., Kelly, L. and Westmarland, N. (2014) 'Ethics in violence and abuse research – A positive empowerment approach.' *Sociological Research Online.* Accessed on 27/6/2017 at www.socresonline.org.uk/19/1/2.html

Edleson, J.L. (1999) 'Children's witnessing of adult domestic violence.' *Journal of Interpersonal Violence 14*, 8, 839–870.

Ellonen, N. and Pösö, T. (2011) 'Children's experiences of completing a computer-based violence survey: Ethical implications.' *Children and Society 25*, 470–481.

Fagerlund, M. and Ellonen, N. (2016) 'Children's experiences of completing a computer based violence survey: Finnish Child Victim Survey revisited.' *Journal of Child Sexual Abuse 25*, 5, 556–576.

Finkelhor, D., Vanderminden, J., Turner, H., Hamby, S. and Shattuck, A. (2014) 'Upset among youth in response to questions about exposure to violence, sexual assault and family maltreatment.' *Child Abuse and Neglect 38*, 2, 217–223.

Flewitt, R. (2005) 'Conducting research with young children: Some ethical considerations.' *Early Child Development and Care 175*, 6, 553–565.

FRA (European Union Agency for Fundamental Rights) (2014) *Violence Against Women: EU-wide Survey – Main Results Report.* Luxembourg: Publications Office of the European Union.

Hazen, A.L., Connolly, C.D., Kelleher, K.J., Barth, R.P. and Landsverk, J.A. (2006) 'Female caregivers' experience with intimate partner violence and behaviour problems in children investigated as victims of maltreatment.' *American Academy of Pediatrics 117*, 1, 99–109.

Hogan, D. (2005) 'Researching the Child in Developmental Psychology.' In S. Greene and D. Hogan (eds) *Researching Children's Experiences: Approaches and Methods* (pp.22–41). London: Sage.

Hogan, F. and O'Reilly, M. (2007) *Listening to Children: Children's Stories of Domestic Violence.* Dublin: Office of the Minister for Children.

Holt, S. (2011) 'Domestic abuse and child contact: Positioning children in the decision-making process.' *Child Care in Practise 17*, 4, 327–346.

Holt, S. (2016) 'The voice of the child in family law: A discussion paper.' *Children and Youth Services Review 68*, 139–145.

Holt, S., Buckley, H. and Whelan, S. (2008) 'The impact of exposure to domestic violence on children and young people: A review of the literature.' *Child Abuse & Neglect 32*, 8, 797–810.

James, A. and Prout, A. (1990) *Constructing and Reconstructing Childhood: Contemporary Issues in the Sociological Study of Childhood.* London: Falmer Press.

Jensen, T.K. (2012) 'Intervjuer med barn og unge i spesielt vanskelige livssituasjoner. Kan vi snakke med barn om alt?' ['Interviews with children and young people in difficult life situations. Can we talk to children about everything?'] In E. Backe-Hansen and I. Frønes (eds) *Metoder og perspektiver i barne- og ungdomsforskning* [*Methods and Perspectives in Children and Adolescent Research*] (s. 95–120). Oslo, Norway: Gyldendal Akademisk.

Jensen, T.K., Holt, T. and Ormhaug, S.M. (2017) 'A follow-up study from a multisite, randomized controlled trial for traumatized children receiving TF-CBT.' *Journal of Abnormal Child Psychology.* doi: 10.1007/s10802-017-0270-0

Katz, E. (2015) 'Beyond the physical incident model: How children living with domestic violence are harmed by and resist regimes of coercive control.' *Child Abuse Review.* doi: http://dx.doi.org/10.1002/car.2422

Lansdown, G. (1994) 'Children's Rights.' In B. Mayall (ed.) *Children's Childhoods Observed and Experienced* (pp.33–45). London: Falmer Press.

Mantle, G., Moules, T., Johnson, K., Leslie, J., Parsons, S. and Shaffer, R. (2007) 'Whose wishes and feelings? Children's autonomy and parental influence in family court enquiries.' *British Journal of Social Work 37*, 5, 785–805.

May, T. (2001) *Social Research: Issues, Methods and Process.* 3rd Edition. Buckingham: Open University Press.

Mayall, B. (1996) *Children, Health and the Social Order.* Buckingham: Open University Press.

Mayall, B. (2000) 'Conversations with Children: Working with Generational Issues.' In P. Christensen and A. James (eds) *Research with Children: Perspectives and Practises* (pp.120–135). London: Falmer Press.

McGee, C. (2000) *Childhood Experiences of Domestic Violence.* London: Jessica Kingsley Publishers.

Morris, A., Hegarty, K. and Humphreys, C. (2012) 'Ethical and safe: Research with children about domestic violence.' *Research Ethics 8*, 125–139.

Mossige, S. and Stefansen, K. (eds) (2016) *Vold og overgrep mot barn og unge. Omfang og utviklingstrekk 2007–2015* [*Violence and Abuse of Children and Young People. Prevalence and Trends 2007–2015.* NOVA Rapport nr. 5. Oslo, Norway: Norsk institutt for forskning på oppvekst, aldring og velferd [Norwegian Social Research].

Mudaly, N. and Goddard, C. (2009) 'The ethics of involving children who have been abused in child abuse research.' *International Journal of Children's Rights 17*, 261–281.

Mullender, A., Hague, G., Imam, U., Kelly, L., Malos, E. and Regan, L. (2002) *Children's Perspectives on Domestic Violence.* London: Sage.

Neale, B. (2002) 'Dialogues with children: Children, divorce and citizenship.' *Childhood 9*, 4, 455–475.

Newman, E. and Kaloupek, D.G. (2005) 'The risks and benefits of participating in trauma-focused research studies.' *Journal of Traumatic Stress 17*, 383–394.

Øverlien, C. (2010) 'Children exposed to domestic violence: What have we concluded and challenges ahead.' *Journal of Social Work 10*, 80–97.

Øverlien, C. (2012) *Våld i hemmet, barns strategier* [*Domestic Violence, Children's Strategies*]. Oslo, Norway: Universitetsforlaget.

Øverlien, C. (2016) '"Do you want to do some arm wrestling?" Children's strategies when experiencing domestic violence and the meaning of age.' *Child & Family Social Work.* doi: 10.1111/cfs.12283

Peled, E. (2001) 'Ethically Sound Research on Children's Exposure to Domestic Violence: A Proposal.' In S.A. Graham-Bermann and J.L. Edleson (eds) *Domestic Violence in the Lives of Children – The Future of Research, Intervention and Social Policy* (pp.111–132). Washington, DC: American Psychological Association.

Powell, M. and Smith, A.B. (2009) 'Children's participation rights in research.' *Childhood 16*, 1, 124–142.

Powell, M., Fitzgerald, R., Taylor, N. and Graham, A. (2012) *International Literature Review: Ethical Issues in Undertaking Research with Children and Young People.* Oslo, Norway: Childwatch International Research Network.

Radford, L., Corral, S., Bradley, C., Fisher, H., *et al.* (2011) *Child Abuse and Neglect in the UK Today.* London: NSPCC.

Smith, A.B., Taylor, N.J. and Tapp, P. (2003) 'Rethinking children's involvement in decision-making after parental separation.' *Childhood 10*, 2, 201–216.

Thomas, N. and O'Kane, C. (2000) 'Discovering what children think: Connections between research and practise.' *British Journal of Social Work 30*, 6, 819–835.

UNCRC (United Nations Convention on the Rights of the Child) (1989) Accessed on 4/7/2017 at www.ohchr.org/EN/ProfessionalInterest/Pages/CRC.aspx

Ungar, M. (2004) 'The importance of parents and other caregivers to the resilience of high-risk adolescents.' *Family Process 43*, 1, 23–41.

World Medical Association Declaration of Helsinki (1964) *Ethical Principles for Medical Research Involving Human Subjects*, adopted by the 18th WMA General Assembly. Helsinki, Finland, June.

Zajac, K., Ruggiero, K.J., Smith, D.W., Saunders, B.E. and Kilpatrick, D.G. (2011) 'Adolescent distress in traumatic stress research: Data from the national survey of adolescents–replication.' *Journal of Traumatic Stress 24*, 226–229.

Chapter 6

RESEARCH ON TEENAGE INTIMATE PARTNER VIOLENCE WITHIN A EUROPEAN CONTEXT

FINDINGS FROM THE LITERATURE

Sibel Korkmaz, *PhD Candidate, Department of Social Work, Stockholm University, Sweden*

INTRODUCTION

In recent decades, a growing body of research has confirmed dating violence/teenage intimate[1] partner violence as a public health issue and a societal problem that it is important to combat (Barter *et al.* 2009; Brown *et al.* 2007; Foshee *et al.* 2007; Jackson 1999; Viejo *et al.* 2016). Most research on teenage intimate partner violence has been conducted in North America, but in the last few years the phenomenon has received increased attention in Europe (Barter 2009; Hellevik and Øverlien 2016; Leen *et al.* 2013; Viejo 2014). These studies confirm that some teenagers across Europe engage in and are subjected to intimate partner violence (Barter *et al.* 2015; De Puy, Hamby and Lindemuth 2014; Muñoz-Rivas *et al.* 2007). However, a number of researchers (Barter and Stanley 2016; Leen *et al.* 2013) have highlighted the need for further research, as applying results from other parts of the world may be problematic due to cultural factors (Hamby *et al.* 2012).

1 The concepts 'teenage intimate partner violence' and 'dating violence' will be used interchangeably, as will 'teenagers', 'adolescents', 'youth' and 'young people', following the terms used in the studies cited. When not citing a study, 'teenage intimate partner violence' will be used.

A study from the European Union Agency for Fundamental Rights (FRA 2014) confirms that young women (18–29 years) are particularly vulnerable to intimate partner violence. The study shows that during the previous 12 months, 6 per cent of women in this age group had been subjected to violence by a partner. Studies also indicate that girls younger than 18 also experience partner violence. For example, in the UK, Barter *et al.* (2009) found that a quarter of the girls (13–17 years) in their study reported being subjected to some form of physical partner violence. Moreover, a recent extensive five-country European study, 'Safeguarding Teenagers' Intimate Relationships' (STIR) (Barter *et al.* 2015), showed that legislation, public policy and action plans disregard teenage intimate partner violence (online and offline) or acknowledge it to only a limited degree. However, there are recent examples of increased governmental awareness across Europe. In 2013, for example, the UK government revised its definition of domestic violence and abuse to include young people in the age group of 16–17, arguing that the change would raise awareness that this age group can also be victims or perpetrators of intimate partner violence, and hoping to encourage young people to come forward and seek support (Home Office 2013). Intimate partner violence among youth has also been acknowledged to some degree in Sweden as well. In 2014, the Swedish National Board of Health and Welfare presented binding regulations (SOSFS 2014: 4) for social services and the healthcare sector on domestic violence. The regulations concern intimate partner violence among young people under the age of 18. They make it mandatory for social services to assess the need for help and support of people in this age group subjected to violence or other forms of abuse by their partners (SOSFS 2014: 4). The National Board concluded that 'even though teenagers by definition still are children, they can be subjected to partner violence in the same ways as adults' (Socialstyrelsen 2015, p.97; author's translation). During the autumn of 2016, the Swedish government also presented a ten-year national strategy to prevent and combat men's violence against women (Regeringens skrivelse 2016), with young women specifically identified as a vulnerable group. These examples of governmental awareness indicate that intimate partner violence among teenagers is an emerging issue that some European countries have defined as a societal problem that needs to be addressed and combated.

This chapter offers an overview of European research on teenage intimate partner violence, looking at studies that draw on a sample with a mean age of 19 or lower. The aim of this literature review is to present the main themes and findings of this research, to discuss its implications and to describe future challenges and contemporary knowledge gaps. The chapter begins by shedding light on the lack of common terminology on violence perpetrated within teenagers' romantic relationships, moving on to describe the method used when conducting this literature review. Thereafter, prevalence rates on victimisation and perpetration of violence are presented, followed by a discussion on gender differences, risk factors, perpetrator characteristics, adverse consequences and tolerance issues. Finally, some implications for future research and the challenges ahead are discussed, alongside reflections on implications for policy and practise.

LACK OF COMMON TERMINOLOGY

The field of research on violence perpetrated in intimate relationships between young people and the first studies of the phenomenon were conducted in North America, (e.g. Kanin 1957). On that side of the Atlantic, such violence is frequently called 'dating violence' or 'teen dating abuse', by both academics and practitioners. In Europe, terminology has been a topic of debate among researchers (e.g. Barter 2009; Viejo 2014), and European research has employed different terms from those used in North America. These include the terms 'partner abuse' and 'violence in teenage relationships' (Barter 2009) and 'teenage intimate partner violence' (Hellevik and Øverlien 2016). Some European studies, however, have also used the terms 'dating aggression' (e.g. Fernández-González, O'Leary and Muñoz-Rivas 2014) and 'dating violence' (or variations of it) (e.g. Bowen *et al.* 2013; De Puy *et al.* 2014; Diaz-Aguado and Martinez 2015; Rodríguez Franco *et al.* 2012; Viejo 2014). All of these terms seemingly aim to identify the same phenomenon: violence in young people's intimate relationships. However, their definitions and the age of the sample and populations studied can vary, making it difficult to compare research results and policy initiatives. Stonard *et al.* (2014) provide a definition of what they term 'adolescent dating violence and abuse' that attempts to draw together definitions found in their review of the literature on the nature, prevalence and impact of adolescent dating violence and technology-assisted adolescent dating violence and abuse. They argue for 'a more comprehensive and inclusive definition of ADVA [adolescent dating violence and abuse]...which incorporates all possible violence typologies that may be performed or experienced in person or via ECT [electronic communication technology], that may be relevant to abusive adolescent romantic relationships' (2014, p.393). They define ADVA as:

> ...any behaviours that are threatening, controlling, violent, abusive, harassment or stalking that are directed towards a current or former romantic partner by the other within the context of an adolescent (10–18 years old) dating relationship. This can include either or a combination of physical, psychological/emotional and sexual behaviours and can take place in person or electronically via technology (such as a mobile phone or online) and occurs regardless of gender or sexuality. (Stonard *et al.* 2014, p.393)

The definition acknowledges that violence can be perpetrated both in person and online, something European research has focused on (e.g. Hellevik and Øverlien 2016; Stonard *et al.* 2015). The definition also uses the term 'dating' to describe adolescent intimate relationships, a term that has been questioned especially regarding its applicability outside North America. Barter (2009) argues that the term does not transfer well to the UK, as young people there do not use or indeed recognise it. She also notes that 'dating' seems to imply a degree of formality not necessarily reflective of the diverse range of young people's intimate encounters and relationships. Similarly, Hamby *et al.* (2012) point out that 'dating' has no exact equivalent in Swiss French. The youth in their study preferred to describe these relationships in more casual terms, most involving variations of 'to go out' (Hamby *et al.* 2012). Researchers in the US have also questioned the term 'dating' as potentially outdated, pointing out that sex and intimacy may happen in a variety of relationship contexts (Brown *et al.* 2007).

Outside of Europe, a number of studies argue that research on partner violence among young people requires a concept that encompasses many ways of being in an intimate relationship as a teenager (Chung 2005; Hickman, Jaycox and Aronoff 2004; Jackson 1999). Differences between adult relationship violence and teen violence are also addressed (Cutter-Wilson and Richmond 2011). In the US, Hickman *et al.* (2004) point out that the existing literature often defines partner violence as violence between married or cohabiting partners – a type of relationship uncommon among adolescents (Cutter-Wilson and Richmond 2011). Hickman *et al.* (2004) also stress the need for researchers who study adolescents to operationalise partner violence in the context of non-cohabitating relationships, which can vary widely in their level of intimacy, role expectations and duration. Adding to the challenge, they highlight how young people tend to use specific terms to describe categories of dating relationships, terms that can vary depending on social contexts (Hickman *et al.* 2004). Hence, the concept used needs to be context-bound, acknowledging young people's lifestyles and reflecting their views on intimate relationships. The digital revolution also throws new factors into the mix: new ways of meeting people (e.g. through dating applications and social media), which gives rise to new types of relationships, as well as new arenas for violence to be perpetrated in (Stonard *et al.* 2015). Recognising these challenges is one important step in the effort to combat teenage intimate partner violence, as overall it acknowledges that teenagers, as well as adults, are potential victims and perpetrators of intimate partner violence (Rodríguez-Franco *et al.* 2012a). This may be accomplished by using a youth-specific concept (e.g. dating violence), or by widening the discourse and concept of intimate partner violence to include youth as well.

METHOD

To find European studies on teenage intimate partner violence, a search of databases (Web of Science, ASP, Criminal Justice Abstracts, CINAHL, Sociological Abstracts, Social Services Abstracts, Scopus, PsycINFO, JSTOR, IBSS) was conducted for peer-reviewed scientific journals. The search was two-fold. One part used key search terms such as 'dating violence' and 'teenage intimate partner violence' (concepts that are specific to violence in youth relationships) in combination with each country or nationality in Europe[2] (e.g. 'Norway' OR 'Norwegian'). This was found to be the only way to retrieve research conducted in Europe, while excluding research from other parts of the world. The other part used more general violence-related key search terms, such as 'partner violence', in conjunction with youth-specific

2 Referring to the member states of the Council of Europe.

terms such as 'adolescents', 'teenagers' and 'boys/girls'. The compound search (a general violence-related term plus a youth-specific term) was then combined with every country or nationality in Europe (e.g. 'partner violence' AND 'teenagers' AND 'Norway' OR 'Norwegian'). The search was set to scan titles and abstracts, aiming to find research conducted in Europe during the last decade (2006–January 2017). Reference lists were scanned from the retrieved literature in order to maximise the collection of available studies. European researchers who publish frequently were contacted through email, or lists of their published work were gathered from their websites, to make sure that all of their peer-reviewed articles on teenage intimate partner violence were included in the search results. The articles obtained were read to see if they met the criteria established for this overview, which were: (1) the full text of the study must be published in English; (2) the study must draw on a sample of young people in Europe; and (3) the sample must have a mean age of 19 or lower. Forty-four articles were found to meet the criterion and were included in the review. Finally, a thematic synthesis was used to categorise literature meeting these criteria, in order to identify topics of focus for European researchers. The identified themes were: victimisation and perpetration of violence; risk factors; gender differences; perpetrator characteristics; adverse consequences; and tolerance.

In some cases, studies that did not meet the inclusion criteria (e.g. were conducted in another part of the world, or with a higher mean age, etc.) have been included when it seemed relevant to draw a brief comparison or highlight another point of view. In these instances, the text notes that the study was not conducted in Europe, or that the sample consisted of university students, etc. In the discussion, relevant reports, articles published after the set time period and studies that fell outside the identified main topics, possibly implying a need for a future research, have also been included.

VICTIMISATION AND PERPETRATION OF VIOLENCE

A number of European studies have addressed the prevalence of violence among young people. Some studies have aimed to capture violence victimisation from a broad perspective, including violence within an intimate relationship alongside other forms of victimisation (Danielsson *et al.* 2009; Jackson, Browne and Joseph 2016). Some have focused specifically on partner violence (Barter *et al.* 2015). One study has also focused on whether victims of intimate partner violence label themselves as victims or not (Rodríguez-Franco *et al.* 2012a).

Reported rates of intimate partner violence victimisation and perpetration among European teenagers vary. Partner violence is often classified with regards to a typology of violence that most commonly distinguishes between physical, psychological and sexual violence (Danielsson *et al.* 2009). In addition, some studies also acknowledge digital violence (Hellevik and Øverlien 2016). For general experience of intimate partner violence, van Ouytsel, Ponnet and Walrave (2017) show that 23.1 per cent of their sample of 466 adolescents in Belgium had become a victim of at least one form of dating violence. Rates as high as 42.9 per cent in Norway (Hellevik and Øverlien 2016) and 45 per cent in England (Fox *et al.* 2014a) have also been highlighted. For physical dating violence victimisation, reported results vary widely: 13.4 per cent in a Portuguese study (Machado, Caridade and Martins 2010); 21.7 per cent in a Spanish study (Fernández-Fuertes and Fuertes 2010); about 23 per cent in a study with a sample consisting of young people in Spain and England (Viejo *et al.* 2016); and 48.8 per cent in a study conducted in French-speaking Switzerland (De Puy *et al.* 2014). For perpetration, results vary from 7 per cent (Fox *et al.* 2014a) to 9 per cent (Wai Wan and Bateman 2007) in two English studies, to 18.1 per cent in a Portuguese study (Machado *et al.* 2010), which is similar to the results in Muñoz-Rivas *et al.*'s (2007) study conducted in Spain. Around 18 per cent of the adolescents stated they had grabbed, hit or kicked and/or shoved their partner in their current or past relationships, compared to 41.9 per cent in French-speaking Switzerland (De Puy *et al.* 2014). In Spain, a psychological dating violence victimisation rate of 95.4 per cent was reported by Fernández-Fuertes and Fuertes (2010), indicating that a large portion of the study sample said that they had been victims of one or more verbal-emotional aggressive behaviours. Meanwhile, 96.3 per cent of participants admitted to perpetrating verbal-emotional aggression in their romantic relationships (Fernández-Fuertes and Fuertes 2010). Concerning sexual violence victimisation, de Bruijn, Burrie and van Wel (2006) distinguish between unwanted sexual behaviour of a verbal nature, non-verbal/intimidating sexual behaviour and physically violent sexual behaviour. Over 75 per cent of their sample of 1700 Dutch adolescents said they had been subjected to the first type, 60 per cent to the second type and 23 per cent to the third type in the preceding 12 months. In the same group, 1.6 per cent reported being forced into sexual intercourse. Regarding perpetration, 63 per cent of the adolescents had been a perpetrator of unwanted verbal sexual behaviour during the last 12 months, 36 per cent said they had engaged in non-verbal/intimidating behaviour, and 28 per cent had engaged in physically violent sexual behaviour. Nearly 1 per cent reported forcing another person into sexual intercourse (de Bruijn *et al.* 2006). It is important to note, however, that for respondents who reported being victimised, it is not clear who their perpetrators were or whether they were in relationships with the respondents, or whether respondents who perpetrated violence did so within intimate relationships. One study in Spain found a large difference in the percentage of youth who reported having sustained sexual violence (42%) and those who reported having perpetrated it (8.8%), a finding the authors note differs from other studies (Sebastían, Verdugo and Ortiz 2014).

European studies have also investigated where individuals were simultaneously the perpetrator and victim of at least one act of violence, presenting data on reciprocal involvement. For example, an Italian-Spanish study (Menesini *et al.* 2011) reported that about 50 per cent of adolescents studied were involved in reciprocal forms of aggressive acts toward their partners. Similarly, in Spain, Viejo (2014) has suggested that both boys and girls involved in aggressive behaviour are generally aggressors as well as victims. This tendency is cited by Viejo to support a theoretical perspective suggested by Ortega *et al.* (2008) and Ortega and Sánchez (2011), which describes the establishment of an erotic-aggressive pattern early in dating relationships that brings forms of reciprocal aggressive behaviours, so-called 'dirty dating', into the partners' communication processes. Viejo notes the lack of gender difference here, and suggests that reciprocal involvement in mild violence especially, is characteristic of both boys and girls. For more severe forms of violence, there are observable gender differences. Viejo concludes that adolescent dating is a phenomenon whose characteristics justify independent study within the context of, using the author's own wording, 'marital violence research' (Viejo 2014, p.797): milder forms of violence within these relationships seem to result from inexperience at dating on the part of both boys and girls, but can nevertheless be a risk factor for gender-based violence, and can precipitate the phenomenon of more severe marital violence.

Digital media

In relation to teenage intimate partner violence, the digital revolution has highlighted new factors that need to be considered (Hellevik 2017). A limited number of studies separate out the prevalence rates of violence perpetrated online and offline (e.g. Hellevik and Øverlien 2016), offering information on the contextual factors for violence. Studies have also focused specifically on cyber-dating abuse victimisation (van Ouytsel, Ponnet and Walrave 2016a, b), and highlighted the phenomenon of 'sexting' (sending and receiving sexual images and text messages) in relation to teenage intimate partner violence (van Ouytsel *et al.* 2016a; Wood *et al.* 2015). This illuminates teenagers' use of technology and, by extension, makes visible the cultural and social conditions they live in (Furlong, Woodman and Wyn 2011).

Studies cited

As presented, rates on victimisation and perpetration vary across countries as well as studies. Later in the chapter, cultural factors are highlighted as something that may need to be taken into consideration when comparing results. Nevertheless, the sample and selection procedure may also influence the results, making it relevant to highlight them. Many of the cited studies focus on teenagers who have or have had a romantic relationship, presenting subsamples drawn from a larger sample. Often the survey includes a gateway question, asking whether the teenagers had any experience of intimate relationships, excluding teenagers in the analysis who had not.

Table 6.1 provides an overview of cited key studies that bring forward rates on victimisation and perpetration of violence, focusing specifically on teenage intimate partner violence. I have kept the original wording and descriptions used by the authors in the cited articles.

Table 6.1: Key studies cited

Study cited	Sample	Selection procedure	Study design
De Puy *et al.* (2014)	132 school pupils and vocational educational students in French-speaking Switzerland, mean age 17.75 42% girls 58% boys	The study was conducted in several youth centres and one vocational education programme. Not a randomly selected sample	Questionnaire
Fernández-Fuertes and Fuertes (2010)	High school students in Spain, aged 16.6 236 males 331 females	Convenience sample	Questionnaire
Fox *et al.* (2014a)	82.6% of 1065 in England, aged 13–14	13 schools across Staffordshire, seven of which received a school-based domestic abuse prevention educational programme (intervention group) and six of which did not (control group). Separate analyses were conducted for both groups. The findings were identical and are presented for the sample as a whole in the article	Questionnaire
Hellevik and Øverlien (2016)	Draw on data from the STIR project. Students in Norway, mean age 15.2 272 girls 270 boys 7 lacking gender information	Convenience sample	Questionnaire
Machado *et al.* (2010)	4667 participants in Portugal, mean age 18.9 42.2% males 57.7% females	Participants were recruited nationally, through contacts with teachers. Data were collected in eight universities, 12 secondary schools and 16 professional schools. The proportional distribution in terms of geographical area was not achieved	Two questionnaires, one behavioural and one attitudinal

Menesini *et al.* (2011)	304 adolescents in total, 141 from Italy and 163 from Spain, mean age 17.14 Italy: 36.9% male, mean age 17.29 Spain: 35.6% male	The sample was representative of the school distribution in Italy and Spain	Questionnaire
Muñoz-Rivas *et al.* (2007)	2416 adolescents, mean age 17 58.6% women 41.4% men	This representative sample was obtained from a pool of 36 high schools from different areas of the Community of Madrid. Of those, 20 accepted to participate in the present study	Questionnaire
Sebastían *et al.* (2014)	579 students in Spain, aged 12–22, mean age 16.11 319 females 260 males	Five public high schools in a region of Madrid	Questionnaire
van Ouytsel *et al.* (2017)	466 adolescents in Flanders, Belgium, mean age 17.82 71% females	Subsample from the larger Teen Digital Dating Survey in Belgium, which was conducted in seven Flemish secondary schools	Questionnaire
Viejo (2014)	2687 students enrolled in secondary education schools in Andalusia, mean age 16.85 45.8% boys 54.2% girls	Stratified sampling, schools were the sampling unit	Questionnaire
Viejo *et al.* (2016)	Students aged 15–18 in England and Spain Spain: 164 students England: 142 students	The English sample was from two urban secondary schools in South East England; the Spanish sample was representative of schools in South Spain. All selected schools in Spain were mixed, and the sample included equal numbers of boys and girls	Questionnaire

GENDER DIFFERENCES

As a number of studies address the prevalence of violence among young people, many studies also acknowledge gender differences.

Studies indicate that young men are more often subjected to physical violence than young women (Danielsson *et al.* 2009; Jackson *et al.* 2016). Perpetrators of violence against young men, however, are more frequently strangers, while young women more often report a parent or current or ex-partner as a perpetrator (Danielsson *et al.* 2009; Landstedt and Gillander Gådin 2011). As for intimate partner violence, studies suggest the following: that more females than males report abusing their dating partners, and gender (female) is consequently presented as a significant predictor of violence perpetration (Machado *et al.* 2010); that women engage in more mild physical and psychological violence (Sebastián *et al.* 2014); and that a higher percentage of women than men engage in verbal aggression (Muñoz-Rivas *et al.* 2007). On the other hand, studies also show that men are involved in more severe physical aggression (Muñoz-Rivas *et al.* 2007) and perpetrate more sexual violence and aggression (Fernàndez González, O'Leary and Muñoz Rivas 2013; Sebastían *et al.* 2014; Stanley *et al.* 2016). It has been noted that although significant gender differences exist for dating violence perpetration, no significant gender differences are found for victimisation, suggesting that boys and girls are victims of dating violence in equal proportion. Nevertheless, it is argued that such results must be interpreted cautiously, and that gender differences merit further exploration (Sebastían *et al.* 2014).

Studies have also examined whether the consequences of victimisation vary by gender (Hellevik and Øverlien 2016). A study conducted in northern Italy by Romito, Beltramini and Escribà-Agüir (2013), drawing on a sample of 259 males and 327 females who had ever been in a couple relationship, found that 43.7 per cent of the female adolescents and 34.8 per cent of the males reported being victimised through intimate partner violence. The results point out that the adolescent girls exposed to intimate partner violence showed significantly higher adjusted odds ratios for depression, panic attacks, eating problems and suicidal ideation. Concerning alleged motives and the contexts in which aggression occurs, Muñoz-Rivas *et al.*'s (2007) extensive study on prevalence, justification and the health consequences of aggression in adolescent dating relationships in Spain, drawing on self-reported data, indicates that in men, aggressive behaviours are triggered by received aggression (self-defence). In women, violence is usually triggered by emotional moments of intense anger or fury. However, despite the fact that the representation of aggressive men is small and their alleged motives seem to be related to self-defence, health consequences were found to be much more severe and negative for women when compared to men (Muñoz-Rivas *et al.* 2007).

Studies have also been conducted throughout Europe aiming to capture teenagers' attitudes towards intimate partner violence (e.g. Bowen *et al.* 2013; McCarry 2009, 2010), showing gender differences in some aspects. For example, it has been shown that justifications for violence are higher among men (De Puy, Hamby and Lindemuth 2014; Ferreira *et al.* 2014; Muñoz-Rivas *et al.* 2011), and that young men are more likely to ascribe to traditional views of men as more dominant than young women (McCarry 2010). Another gender aspect considers that perpetration of violence by women also seems more often to be perceived as acceptable (Bowen *et al.* 2013; De Puy *et al.* 2014; Muñoz-Rivas *et al.* 2011).

RISK FACTORS, PERPETRATOR CHARACTERISTICS, ADVERSE CONSEQUENCES AND TOLERANCE

Besides prevalence rates and gender differences, a number of European studies have focused on possible risk factors for intimate partner violence among teenagers. Pregnant teenagers and teenage mothers have been identified as a vulnerable group that may need additional support (Brown, Brady and Letherby 2011; Edirne *et al.* 2010; Wood and Barter 2015). In Belgium, van Ouytsel *et al.* (2017) found that adolescents who consume alcohol at a relatively young age, have ever used marijuana, or have committed acts of vandalism, are also more likely to become victims of dating violence than adolescents who have not engaged in these behaviours. For both genders, physical aggression in dating relations is shown to peak during mid-to-late adolescence, thereby displaying a pattern similar to other antisocial and criminal behaviours (Fernández-González *et al.* 2014). In a study drawing on a sample of young people aged 13–29 in Portugal, Machado *et al.* (2010) also noted that older students reported more perpetration and victimisation. Concerning the characteristics of dating violence perpetrators, violent boys have lower self-esteem, more often seek to justify male dominance and intimate partner violence against women, and receive more dominant and violent messages from adults in their family, compared to non-violent boys. This is shown in Diaz-Aguado and Martinez's (2015) comprehensive study, drawing on a probabilistic sample of 4147 boys aged 14–18. Boys' perpetration of sexual coercion and abuse has also been found to be significantly associated with regular viewing of online pornography (Stanley *et al.* 2016).

Teenage intimate partner violence has also been found to result in adverse consequences. A qualitative study examining the experiences of two Swedish adolescent girls who lived in violent relationships as teenagers showed that daily oppression and humiliation were internalised in the girls' self-perceptions, manifesting as lowered self-esteem, feelings of worthlessness and loss of sexual pride. By analysing the girls' narratives in depth, the authors are able to demonstrate that intimate partner violence can have long-term consequences and negatively affect the transition from adolescence to adulthood (Wiklund *et al.* 2010). In Turkey, Unlu and Cakaloz's (2016) study of the effects of perpetrator identity on suicidality and non-suicidal self-injury in sexually victimised female adolescents convincingly shows that sexual dating violence is the strongest predictor of subsequent suicidal ideation.

Focusing on the tolerance of dating violence, Rodríguez-Franco *et al.* (2012b) present results showing how abusive behaviour by a partner provokes little or no discomfort among a notably large portion of their sample of Spanish young women, aged 15–25 (average age 18.7). The authors argue that these findings provide sufficient evidence of the need for new preventive policies throughout the socialisation process.

IMPLICATIONS FOR FUTURE RESEARCH AND THE CHALLENGES AHEAD

In Europe, a number of cross-country studies have found that their results vary greatly across borders (e.g. Barter *et al.* 2017; Leen *et al.* 2013; Viejo *et al.* 2016), further fuelling the discussion as to whether research on teenage intimate partner violence is internationally applicable or whether it can only be studied within a specific societal and cultural context (Hamby *et al.* 2012; Stanley *et al.* 2015). These and other challenges, knowledge gaps and implications for future research are discussed below.

Adding an intersectional analysis

Much of the research on teenage intimate partner violence to date does not incorporate an intersectional analysis to any great extent. Adding an intersectional perspective would allow us to understand how teenagers are shaped by the interaction of different social positions (ethnicity, gender, class, age, sexuality, etc.), and how these create interdependent forms of privilege and oppression (Hankivsky 2014). The present overview, for example, could not identify any European study within peer review journals, focusing specifically on intimate partner violence among LGBTQ adolescents. Nevertheless, the report *Partner Exploitation and Violence in Teenage Intimate Relationships* (Barter *et al.* 2009) highlights young people with a same-sex partner. The 50 young people with a same-sex partner participating in the survey were significantly more likely to experience all three forms of partner victimisation compared to those with an opposite sex-partner (Barter *et al.* 2009). A recent Swedish study shows that young women who belonged to a sexual minority were more often victims of violent acts than heterosexual young women (Palm *et al.* 2016). These results underline the need of future research, focusing on LGBTQ adolescents and teenage intimate partner violence. In general, societal positions and power structures ought to be addressed in an effort to expose the fact that 'teenagers' are not a homogeneous group (Barter and Stanley 2016; Pentaraki 2017; Wood, Barter and Berridge 2011).

Presenting narratives

Another indicated direction for future research is to present more narratives from young people who have experienced violence in an intimate relationship. The field generally lacks qualitative studies of teenagers who have experienced such violence (but see, for example, Wiklund *et al.* 2010; Wood and Barter 2015), and especially studies of young people who perpetrate violence (but see Gadd *et al.* 2015). This approach might fill another knowledge gap by providing insight into teenagers' own perceptions of intimate partner violence. The approach could also be used to gather more well-needed evidence on the immediate and longer-term impact of teenage intimate partner violence. The knowledge gained could be an important step toward combating this societal problem.

Prevalence rates: acknowledging cultural factors

Comparing prevalence rates across countries and between studies presents several challenges. First, aims, methodologies (including terminology used, definition of violence) and samples can vary. Methodological issues need to be taken into account when looking at prevalence rates, as a number of European researchers have pointed out (e.g. Barter 2009; Danielsson *et al.* 2009; Leen *et al.* 2013; Stonard *et al.* 2014), as well as correction factors (Fernández González, O'Leary and Muñoz Rivas 2013). Cultural factors may also be taken into consideration when comparing results (Nocentini *et al.* 2011), as Lysova and Douglas (2008) note in their article on dating violence among Russian university students. They discuss that the significant differences in perpetration rates between men and women and the moderate level of intimate partner violence in their sample, as compared with those reported for other countries, may be explained by the deterrent effect of the Russian army on Russian male students. In Russia, a male student found to have abused a woman may be expelled from university and immediately enlisted into military service (Lysova and Douglas 2008). This exemplifies how external factors may influence informants' willingness to report (Fernández-González, O'Leary and Muñoz-Rivas 2013). Viejo *et al.* (2016) also highlight a cultural consideration, and suggest that in Spain, mild expressions of violence are more culturally accepted than in the UK, and adolescents thus feel freer to engage in them (Viejo *et al.* 2016). In the STIR study, it has been shown that interpersonal violence and abuse prevalence rates were significantly associated with gender in only two out of the five country samples: England and Norway (girls in England and Norway reported higher rates of victimisation compared to boys) (Barter *et al.* 2017). Hence, cultural factors may be important to explore and address when presenting results on both victimisation and perpetration among European youth (Barter *et al.* 2015, 2017; Hamby *et al.* 2012).

The cultural context is also important to acknowledge when designing prevention programmes (Hamby *et al.* 2012; Stanley *et al.* 2016b; Sundaram 2016), at every societal level (Stanley *et al.* 2015). There are some examples of prevention programmes in a European context (e.g. Bowen *et al.* 2014; de Graaf *et al.* 2015) whose aims are to raise awareness (e.g. Bell and Stanley 2006) or change teen attitudes on violence (e.g. Bowen *et al.* 2014). The need to warn teenagers about the dangers associated with certain types of play, underpinned by results showing that aggressive and stimulated play increases the danger of dating victimization, is also brought forward, adding to a discussion on prevention (Gonzalez-Mendez and Hernandez-Cabrera 2009). But is research on attitudes toward violence internationally valid, and should primary interventions, for example, in Europe, focus on similar attitudinal foci as those in North America (Bowen *et al.* 2013)? Cross-country cultural differences within Europe may make the design of prevention programmes even more challenging. Additional factors such as gender and socioeconomic status may also influence the reception of such programmes (Fox, Hale and Gadd 2014b; Gadd, Fox and Hale 2014), and should therefore be explored further.

REFLECTIONS ON POLICY AND PRACTISE

Overall, it is indisputable that research on teenage intimate partner violence is important in order to combat this societal problem. Nevertheless, research is just one out of three important pillars in this endeavour: policy and practise also need to be highlighted. It is clear from research that teenagers across Europe are being subjected to intimate partner violence, underpinning the argument for a robust policy response. Teenage intimate partner violence needs to be addressed in policy work as a public health and societal problem, focusing on preventing teenage intimate partner violence from happening in the first place, as well as providing sufficient means in order for practitioners to help and support those who are victimised and who victimise others. Researchers, policy-makers and practitioners may play different roles in the drive to combat teenage intimate partner violence; however, they need to work together, sharing information and inflict each other's work.

CONCLUSION

In Europe, teenage intimate partner violence has been portrayed both as a phenomenon with characteristics that are significant for adolescents' intimate relationships (Viejo 2014) and as a phenomenon that challenges the previous understanding of intimate violence as a primarily adult problem (Barter 2011). It has sometimes been framed as a gender-neutral phenomenon, and at other times considered in relation to gender and power. In the US, Baker and Stein (2016) point out a shift within the field on teen dating violence. They find that the lack of a gender-based analysis reflects a shift from a feminist framing of violence that focuses on the safety and wellbeing of women and girls based on an analysis of gender, power, and structural inequalities, toward a conservative focus on individualistic solutions to the gendered social problem that violence represents. In Europe, some studies point out that adolescents participate in reciprocal forms of aggressive acts toward their partner, and the violence is not necessarily framed as gender-based (e.g. Menesini *et al.* 2011; Viejo 2014). Others include a more explicit gender dimension, for example, by labelling teenage intimate partner violence as gender-related partner violence (e.g. Wiklund *et al.* 2010), or by pointing out differences between genders, both in terms of the severity of violence, where men are found to perpetrate more severe forms of violence (Muñoz-Rivas *et al.* 2007) and sexual violence (Sebastían *et al.* 2014), and the consequences of victimisation, where women are found to suffer more from being subjected to violence (Barter *et al.* 2009; Hellevik and Øverlien 2016). Overall, it is clear that gender is a key variable to explore in research on teenage intimate partner violence with the potential to expose societal power structures across Europe.

LIMITATIONS

The search for this review was conducted by scanning titles and abstracts, which is acknowledged as a limitation: it requires that researchers address the country or nationality of their sample on the first page of the article. However, this was found to be the only method of including Europe while excluding research from other parts of the world. The overview included only peer-reviewed studies whose full text was published in English in scientific journals. It therefore excluded reports and other publications. Studies drawing on samples outside of Europe or with a mean age over 19 were also excluded. The decision to use mean age instead of actual age was based on the premise that the review should include as many studies as possible. Nevertheless, this should be taken into consideration when looking at the prevalence rates included in this overview.

REFERENCES

Baker, C. and Stein, N. (2016) 'Obscuring gender-based violence: Marriage promotion and teen dating violence research.' *Journal of Women, Politics and Policy 37*, 1, 87–109.

Barter, C. (2009) 'In the name of love: Partner abuse and violence in teenage relationships.' *The British Journal of Social Work 30*, 2, 211–233.

Barter, C. (2011) 'Domestic violence: Not just an adult problem.' *Criminal Justice Matters 85*, 1, 22–23.

Barter, C. and Stanley, N. (2016) 'Inter-personal violence and abuse in adolescent intimate relationships: Mental health impact and implications for practise.' *International Review of Psychiatry 28*, 5, 485–503.

Barter, C., McCarry, M., Berridge, D. and Evans, K. (2009) *Partner Exploitation and Violence in Teenage Intimate Relationships.* London: NSPCC.

Barter, C., Stanley, N., Wood, M., Lanau, A., Aghtaie, N., Larkins, C. and Øverlien, C. (2017) 'Young people's online and face-to-face experiences of interpersonal violence and abuse and its subjective impact across five European countries.' *Psychology of Violence Advance* online publication. http://dx.doi.org/10.1037/vio0000096

Barter, C., Stanley, N., Wood, M., Aghtaie, N., Larkins, C., Øverlien, C., Lesta, S., *et al.* (2015) *Safeguarding Teenage Intimate Relationships (STIR): Connecting Online and Offline Contexts and Risks.* Research Report. Available at http://stiritup.eu

Bell, J. and Stanley, N. (2006) 'Learning about domestic violence: Young people's responses to a Healthy Relationships programme.' *Sex Education 6*, 3, 237–250.

Bowen, E., Holdsworth, E., Leen, E., Sorbring, E., Helsing, B., Jaans, S. and Awouters, V. (2013) 'Northern European adolescent attitudes toward dating violence.' *Violence and Victims 28*, 4.

Bowen, E., Walker, K., Mawer, M., Holdsworth, E., Sorbring, E., Helsing, B., *et al.* (2014) '"It's like you're actually playing as yourself": Development and preliminary evaluation of "Green Acres High", a serious game-based primary intervention to combat adolescent dating violence.' *Psychosocial Intervention 23*, 43–55.

Brown, G., Brady, G. and Letherby, G. (2011) 'Young mothers' experiences of power, control and violence within intimate and familial relationships.' *Child Care in Practise 17*, 4, 359–374.

Brown, L.K., Puster, K.L, Vazquez, E.A., Hunter, H.L. and Lescano, C.M. (2007) 'Screening practises for adolescent dating violence.' *Journal of Interpersonal Violence 22*, 456.

Chung, D. (2005) 'Violence, control, romance and gender equality: Young women and heterosexual relationships.' *Women's Studies International Forum*, 28.

Cutter-Wilson, E. and Richmond, T. (2011) 'Understanding teen dating violence: Practical screening and intervention strategies for pediatric and adolescent healthcare providers.' *Current Opinion in Pediatrics 23*, 373–383.

Danielsson, I., Blom. H., Nilses, C., Heimer, G. and Högberg, U. (2009) 'Gendered patterns of high violence exposure among Swedish youth.' *Acta Obstetricia et Gynecologica 88*, 528–535.

de Bruijn, P., Burrie, I. and van Wel, F. (2006) 'A risky boundary: Unwanted sexual behaviour among youth.' *Journal of Sexual Aggression 12*, 2, 81–96.

de Graaf, I., de Haas, S., Zaagsma, M. and Wijsen, C. (2015) 'Effect of rock and water: An intervention to prevent sexual aggression.' *Journal of Sexual Aggression 22*, 1, 4–19.

De Puy, J., Hamby, S. and Lindemuth, C. (2014) 'Teen dating violence in French-speaking Switzerland: Attitudes and experiences.' *International Journal of Conflict and Violence 8*, 2.

Diaz-Aguado, J.M. and Martinez, R. (2015) 'Types of adolescent male dating violence against women, self-esteem, and justification of dominance and aggression.' *Journal of Interpersonal Violence 30*, 15, 2636–2658.

Edirne, T., Can, M., Kolusari, A., Yildizhan, R., Adali, E. and Akdag, B. (2010) 'Trends, characteristics, and outcomes of adolescent pregnancy in eastern Turkey.' *International Journal of Gynecology and Obstetrics 110*, 105–108.

Fernández-Fuertes, A.A. and Fuertes, A. (2010) 'Physical and psychological aggression in dating relationships of Spanish adolescents: Motives and consequences.' *Child Abuse and Neglect 32*, 183–191.

Fernández-González, L., O'Leary, D.K. and Muñoz-Rivas, M.J. (2013) 'We are not joking: Need for controls in reports of dating violence.' *Journal of Interpersonal Violence 28*, 3, 602–620.

Fernández-González, L., O'Leary, D.K. and Muñoz-Rivas, M.J (2014) 'Age-related changes in dating aggression in Spanish high school students.' *Journal of Interpersonal Violence 29*, 6, 1132–1152.

Ferreira, M., Lopes, A., Aparício, G., Cabral, L. and Duarte, J. (2014) 'Teens and dating: study of factors that influence attitudes of violence.' *Atención Primaria 46,* 187–190.

Foshee, V.A., Bauman, K.E., Linder, G.F., Rice, J. and Wilcher, R. (2007) 'Typologies of adolescent dating violence: Identifying typologies of adolescent dating violence perpetration.' *Journal of Interpersonal Violence 22,* 5, 498–519.

Fox, C.L., Hale, R. and Gadd, D. (2014b) 'Domestic abuse prevention education: Listening to the views of young people.' *Sex Education 14,* 1, 28–41.

Fox, C.L., Corr, M.-L., Gadd, D. and Butler, I. (2014a) 'Young teenagers' experiences of domestic abuse.' *Journal of Youth Studies 17,* 4, 510–526.

FRA (European Agency for Fundamental Rights) (2014) *Violence Against Women: An EU-wide Survey.* Luxembourg: Publications Office of the European Union.

Furlong, A., Woodman, D. and Wyn, J. (2011) 'Changing times, changing perspectives: Reconciling "transition" and "cultural" perspectives on youth and young adulthood.' *Journal of Sociology 47,* 355.

Gadd, D., Fox, C.L. and Hale, R. (2014) 'Preliminary steps towards a more preventative approach to eliminating violence against women in Europe.' *European Journal of Criminology 11,* 4, 464–480.

Gadd, D., Fox, C. L., Corr, M-L., Alger, S. and Butler, I. (2015) *Young Men and Domestic Abuse.* New York: Routledge

Gonzalez-Mendez, R. and Hernandez-Cabrera, J.A. (2009) 'Play context, commitment and dating violence.' *Journal of Interpersonal Violence 24,* 9, 1518–1535.

Hamby, S., Nix, K., De Puy, J. and Monnier, S. (2012) 'Adapting dating violence prevention to Francophone Switzerland: A story of intra-Western cultural differences.' *Violence and Victims 27,* 1

Hankivsky, O. (ed.) (2014) *An Intersectionality-based Policy Analysis Framework.* Vancouver, BC: Institute for Intersectionality Research and Policy, Simon Fraser University.

Hellevik, P. (2017) 'Digital Intimate Partner Violence and Abuse Among Youth: A Systematic Review of Associated Factors.' In S. Holt, C. Øverlien and J. Devaney (eds) *Responding to Domestic Violence: Emerging Challenges for Policy, Practise and Research in Europe.* London, Jessica Kingsley Publishers.

Hellevik, P. and Øverlien, C. (2016) 'Teenage intimate partner violence: Factors associated with victimization among Norwegian youths.' *Scandinavian Journal of Public Health,* 1–7.

Hickman, L.J., Jaycox, L.H. and Aronoff, J. (2004) 'Dating violence among adolescents: Prevalence, gender distribution, and prevention program effectiveness trauma.' *Violence and Abuse 5,* 123.

Home Office (2013) *Domestic Violence and Abuse.* Accessed on 2/8/2017 at www.gov.uk/guidance/domestic-violence-and-abuse

Jackson, S.M. (1999) 'Issues in the dating violence research. A review of the literature.' *Aggression and Violent Behavior 4,* 2, 233–247.

Jackson, V., Browne, K. and Joseph, S. (2016) 'The prevalence of childhood victimization experienced outside the family: Findings from an English prevalence study.' *Child Abuse and Neglect 51,* 343–357.

Kanin, E. (1957) 'Male aggression in dating-courtship relations.' *American Journal of Sociology 63,* 2, 197–204.

Landstedt, E. and Gillander Gådin, K. (2011) 'Experiences of violence among adolescents: gender patterns in types, perpetrators and associated psychological distress' *International Journal of Public Health, 56,* 4, 419–427.

Leen, E., Sorbring, E., Mawer, M., Holdsworth, E., Helsing, B. and Bowen, E. (2013) 'Prevalence, dynamic risk factors and the efficacy of primary interventions for adolescent dating violence: An international review.' *Aggression and Violent Behavior 18,* 159–174.

Lysova, V.A. and Douglas, E.M. (2008) 'Intimate partner violence among male and female Russian university students.' *Journal of Interpersonal Violence 23,* 11, 1579–1599.

Machado, C., Caridade, S. and Martins, C. (2010) 'Violence in juvenile dating relationships: Self-reported prevalence and attitudes in a Portuguese sample.' *Journal of Family Violence* 25, 43–52.

McCarry, M. (2009) 'Justifications and contradictions. Understanding young people's view of domestic abuse.' *Men and Masculinities 11,* 3, 325–345.

McCarry, M. (2010) 'Becoming a "proper man": Young people's attitudes about interpersonal violence and perceptions of gender.' *Gender and Education 22,* 1, 17–30.

Menesini, E., Nocentini, A., Ortega-Rivera, F.J., Sanchez, V. and Ortega, R. (2011) 'Reciprocal involvement in adolescent dating aggression: An Italian-Spanish study.' *European Journal of Developmental Psychology 8,* 4, 437–451.

Muñoz-Rivas, M.J., Graña, J.L., O'Leary, D.K and González, M.P. (2007) 'Aggression in adolescent dating relationships: Prevalence, justification, and health consequences.' *Journal of Adolescent Health 40*, 298–304.

Muñoz-Rivas, M.J., Gámez-Guadiz, M., Fernández-González, L. and González Lozano, M.P. (2011) 'Validation of the Attitudes About Aggression in Dating Situations (AADS) and the Justification of Verbal/Coercive Tactics Scale (JVCT) in Spanish adolescents.' *Journal of Family Violence 26*, 575–584.

Nocentini, A., Menesini, E., Pastorelli, C., Connolly, J., Pepler, D. and Craig, W. (2011) 'Physical dating aggression in adolescence. Cultural and gender invariance.' *European Psychologist 16*, 4, 278–287.

Ortega, R., Ortega-Rivera, J. and Sánchez, V. (2008). 'Violencia sexual entre compañeros y violencia en parejas adolescentes.' *International Journal of Psychology and Psychological Therapy*, 8, 63–72.

Ortega, R. and Sánchez, V. (2011). 'Juvenil Dating and Violence.' In C. Monks, and I. Coyne (Eds.), *Bullying in different contexts* (pp. 113–136). London: Cambridge University Press.

Palm, A., Danielsson, I., Skalkidou, A., Olofsson, N. and Högberg, U. (2016) 'Violence victimization – A watershed for young women's mental and physical health.' *European Journal of Public Health 26*, 5, 861–867.

Pentaraki, M. (2017) 'Fear of Double Disclosure and Other Barriers to Help Seeking: An Intersectional Approach to Address the Needs of LGBT Teenagers Experiencing Teenage Relationship Abuse.' In S. Holt, C. Øverlien and J. Devaney (eds) *Responding to Domestic Violence: Emerging Challenges for Policy, Practise and Research in Europe.* London, Jessica Kingsley Publishers.

Regeringens skrivelse (2016) 'Makt, mål och myndighet – feministisk politik för en jämställd framtid.' 2016/17:10. Available at www.regeringen.se/rattsdokument/skrivelse/2016/11/skr.-20161710/ [in Swedish].

Rodríguez-Franco, L., de los Ángeles, M., Antuña Bellerín, M., López-Cepero Borrego, J., Rodríguez Díaz, F.J and Bringas Molleda, C. (2012a) 'Tolerance towards dating violence in Spanish adolescents.' *Psicothema 24*, 236–242.

Rodríguez-Franco, L., López-Cepero Borrego, J., Rodriguez-Diaz, F.J., Bringas Molleda, C., Estrada Pineda, C., Antuña Bellerin, M.A. and Quevedo-Blasco, R. (2012b) 'Labeling dating abuse: Undetected abuse among Spanish adolescents and young adults.' *International Journal of Clinical and Health Psychology 12*, 1, 55–67.

Romito, P., Beltramini, L and Escribà-Agüir, V. (2013) 'Intimate partner violence and mental health among Italian adolescents: Gender similarities and differences.' *Violence Against Women 19*, 1, 89–106.

Sebastían, J., Verdugo, A. and Ortiz, B. (2014) 'Jealousy and violence in dating relationships: Gender-related differences among a Spanish sample.' *Spanish Journal of Psychology 17*, 1–12.

Socialstyrelsen (National Board of Health and Welfare) (2014) *Våld i nära relationer.* 2014:4. Socialstyrelsens författningssamling. Available at www.socialstyrelsen.se/Lists/Artikelkatalog/Attachments/19441/2014-5-7.pdf [in Swedish].

Socialstyrelsen (2015) *Våld. Handbok om socialtjänstens och hälso- och sjukvårdens arbete med våld i nära relationer.* Stockholm: Socialstyrelsen.

Stanley, N., Ellis, J., Farrelly, N., Hollinghurst, S. and Downe, S. (2015) 'Preventing domestic abuse for children and young people: A review of school based interventions.' *Children and Youth Services Review 59*, 120–131.

Stanley, N., Ellis, J., Farrelly, N., Hollinghurst, S., Bailey, S. and Downe, S. (2016b) '"What matters to someone who matters to me": Using media campaigns with young people to prevent interpersonal violence and abuse.' *Health Expectations*, 1–7.

Stanley, N., Barter, C., Wood, M., Aghtaie, N., Larkins, C., Lanau, A. and Øverlien, C. (2016a) 'Pornography, sexual coercion and abuse and sexting in young people's intimate relationships: A European study.' *Journal of Interpersonal Violence*, 1–26.

Stonard, K.E., Bowen, E., Lawrence, T.R. and Price, S.A. (2014) 'The relevance of technology to the nature, prevalence and impact of adolescent dating violence and abuse: A research synthesis.' *Aggression and Violent Behavior 19*, 390–417.

Stonard, K.E., Bowen, E., Walker, K. and Price, S.A. (2015) '"They'll always find a way to get to you": Technology use in adolescent romantic relationships and its role in dating violence and abuse.' *Journal of Interpersonal Violence*, 1–35.

Sundaram, V. (2016) '"You can try, but you won't stop it. It'll always be there": Youth perspectives on violence and prevention in schools.' *Journal of Interpersonal Violence 31*, 4, 652–676.

Unlu, G. and Cakaloz, B. (2016) 'Effects of perpetrator identity on suicidality and nonsuicidal self-injury in sexually victimized female adolescents.' *Neuropsychiatric Disease and Treatment 12*, 1489–1497.

van Ouytsel, J., Ponnet, K. and Walrave, M. (2016a) 'Cyber dating abuse victimization among secondary school students from a lifestyle-routine activities theory perspective.' *Journal of Interpersonal Violence*, 1–10.

van Ouytsel, J., Ponnet, K. and Walrave, M. (2016b) 'Adolescent cyber dating abuse victimization and its associations with substance use, and sexual behaviors.' *Public Health 135*, 147–151.

van Ouytsel, J., Ponnet, K. and Walrave, M. (2017) 'The association of adolescents' dating violence victimization, well-being and engagement in risk behaviors.' *Journal of Adolescence 55*, 66–71.

Viejo, C. (2014) 'Physical dating violence: Towards a comprehensible view of the phenomenon.' *Journal for the Study of Education and Development 37*, 4, 785–815.

Viejo, C., Monks, C.P., Sánchez, V. and Ortega-Ruiz, R. (2016) 'Physical dating violence in Spain and the United Kingdom and the importance of relationship quality.' *Journal of Interpersonal Violence 31*, 8, 1453–1475.

Wai Wan, M. and Bateman, W. (2007) 'Adolescents and intimate partner violence: Evaluation of a brief school-based education programme.' *International Journal of Health Promotion and Education 45*, 1, 17–23.

Wiklund, M., Malmgren-Olsson, E.B., Bengs, C. and Ohman, A. (2010) '"He messed me up": Swedish adolescent girls' experiences of gender-related partner violence and its consequences over time.' *Violence Against Women 16*, 2.

Wood, M. and Barter, C. (2015) 'Hopes and fears: Teenage mothers' experiences of intimate partner violence.' *Children and Society 29*, 558–568.

Wood, M., Barter, C. and Berridge, D. (2011) *'Standing On My Own Two Feet': Disadvantaged Teenagers, Intimate Partner Violence and Coercive Control.* London: NSPCC.

Wood, M., Barter, C., Stanley, N., Aghtaie, N. and Larkins, C. (2015) 'Images across Europe: The sending and receiving of sexual images and associations with interpersonal violence in young people's relationships.' *Children and Youth Services Review 59*, 149–160.

Chapter 7

FEAR OF DOUBLE DISCLOSURE AND OTHER BARRIERS TO HELP SEEKING

AN INTERSECTIONAL APPROACH TO ADDRESS THE NEEDS OF LGBT TEENAGERS EXPERIENCING TEENAGE RELATIONSHIP ABUSE

Maria Pentaraki, *Lecturer in Social Work, Queen's University Belfast, UK*

INTRODUCTION

It has been widely documented that violence in intimate partner relationships cuts across age, class, race, sexual orientation, disability and national boundaries (WHO 2013). Unlike the widely circulated stories of teenage romantic relationships being characterised by pure love, kisses, kindness and carefree times, young age is not a protective factor from intimate partner abuse (Pentaraki 2002, 2003). Teenage relationship abuse and dating violence, the intimate partner violence abuse that takes place in teenage and young adult couples, has been long identified in Western countries such as Canada, the US and Australia as a pressing social problem (Ashley and Foshee 2005; Black and Weisz 2003; Elias-Lambert, Black and Chigbu 2014). Nevertheless, it is only during the last two decades that it has become an object of scholarly investigation in European countries (Barter 2009; Barter *et al.* 2017; Burman and Cartmel 2005; Fox *et al.* 2014; Hellevik and Øverlien 2016; Pentaraki 2002, 2003; Schütt 2006).

Teenage relationship abuse (TRA) refers to teenagers' experiences of intimate partner violence (IPV), such as physical, sexual, psychological and emotional violence (Pentaraki 2003), which takes place in person, or electronically, via the internet (such as social networking sites) or mobile phones (Stonard *et al.* 2015). Although much of the existing academic literature has focused on heterosexual young people, relationship violence occurs in all forms of romantic relationships, whether in opposite-sex or same-sex relationships, or in relationships where one or both partners identify as genderqueer or transgender (Calton, Cattaneo and Gebhard 2015). TRA has gendered dimensions with the worst consequences being experienced by girls (Barter 2009). However, research with sexual minority adults has documented that the worst consequences are encountered by trans people (Donovan and Hester 2015; Donovan, Barnes and Nixon 2014).

Dating violence/TRA in young couples is a common occurrence with comparable rates for victimisation across Europe and North America (Viejo *et al.* 2015). It is therefore acknowledged as a pressing international issue. TRA is associated with adverse consequences for survivors such as depression, anxiety, suicide ideation, decreased physical health, substance abuse, increased sexual risk behaviours and poor educational outcomes (Banyard and Cross 2008; Gehring and Vaske 2015; Pentaraki 2003, 2004a, b; Silverman *et al.* 2001; Voth Schrag and Edmond 2017). To date, few studies have explored the effects of social support and helpers' reactions in response to disclosure of TRA by young people. However, there is some evidence to suggest that social support can help to protect against the negative effects of TRA (Banyard and Cross 2008; Fortin *et al.* 2012). Further, Weisz *et al.* (2007) have argued that helpers' reactions may influence the victim's decision to continue in an abusive relationship, and Campbell (2008) has reported that recipients receiving inappropriate responses from formal sources may be experienced as a second victimisation. Moreover, research by Gillum and DiFulvio (2012) included examination of the barriers to help seeking faced by LGBT youth survivors of TRA (although this was not the key focus of their study), and highlighted the significance of both societal and internalised homophobia. Societal homophobia, in particular, constitutes an important barrier to help seeking. Specifically, fear and stigma among sexual minority youth related to homophobia within wider society was found to hinder the disclosure of dating violence to informal sources, such as friends and family, and formal sources, including the police.

Research with adult survivors has indicated that they may have concealed their sexual identity from friends and family, due to fear of rejection or homophobic responses, which, in turn, reduces the pool of individuals to whom young people can turn to for support (Gehring and Vaske 2015). Societal homophobia was likewise identified as an impediment to the disclosure of physical abuse to authorities such as the police, due to concerns about not being taken seriously or being subjected to further victimisation by law enforcement agencies (Gillum and DiFulvio 2012). Understanding the context of the process of seeking and receiving help is therefore important, not only to enable the implementation of appropriate interventions aimed towards the minimisation of the adverse consequences of TRA (Sylaska and Edwards 2014), but also to prevent the occurrence of TRA among young people (Ashley and Foshee 2005).

The context in which violence takes place can pose challenges to the disclosure of abuse and also to the effective prevention of TRA. Hence, by utilising an intersectional approach, this chapter seeks to explore some of the contextual challenges that LGBT young people in Northern Ireland face in relation to seeking and receiving help when in abusive relationships. While the movement to address gender-based violence as well as teenage relationship abuse highlights that violence cuts across all social settings and spaces as a strategic political objective (Nixon and Humphreys 2010), there is a more nuanced approach needed, an intersectional approach, through which to address the different ways that violence is experienced and shapes the realities of various groups in various spaces, such as LGBT youth in Northern Ireland, in order to be able to better respond to their needs. This research is informed by an understanding that one's experiences are related to the spatial and social context one lives in (Hulko 2009). As Valentine (2007, p.19) argues, 'within particular spaces there are dominant spatial orderings that produce moments of exclusion for particular groups'. Researching the intersections of space with LGBT identities in Northern Ireland can offer a more nuanced understanding of the barriers to help seeking that teenagers experiencing teenage relationship abuse face in certain contexts infused with religious beliefs, such as in the case of Northern Ireland.

The concept of intersectionality was first developed and used by black feminist scholars (Collins 1998; Crenshaw 1991) to address the unequal access to education, work and health services that minority women faced. The same approach can be used to further understand and respond to LGBT youth who face TRA. This is a very important approach to apply as it facilitates analysis of the overlap of macro and micro systems, and provides a context for the reality that relationship abuse cuts across social categories including sexual orientation. It also indicates the need to contextualise this abuse and highlight the intersections as these need to become points of intervention. However, this analytical framework is very rarely applied (Bowleg 2012), as both scholarly work and service provision primarily centres on the experiences of the white heterosexual adult middle-class population and ignores or silences the experiences of teenage LGBT youth. So this study is informed by an intersectional approach as it provides 'the best chance for an effective diagnosis and ultimately an effective prescription' (Hancock 2007, p.73).

This chapter reports the preliminary findings from an exploratory pilot study undertaken in 2016, funded by the Improving Children's Lives initiative at Queen's University Belfast.

DESCRIPTION OF THE STUDY

This study utilised a combination of focus groups and interviews with a small community sample of 12 LGBT white teenagers aged between 16 and 22 participating in community youth services. The interviews were conducted with participants who had experienced TRA before they were 18. It is part of a larger pilot study addressing issues surrounding TRA that also includes interviews and focus groups with relevant professionals in order to explore issues surrounding teenage relationship abuse. This chapter reports only on the voices of LGBT young people and on the key barriers, identified by a small group of participants, as undermining their help-seeking behaviour within the context of a city and its surrounding area in Northern Ireland. Northern Ireland presents a unique context, characterised by a history of civil conflict and high levels of religious endorsement and participation. It also has a higher level of homophobic attitudes compared to other Western European countries (Duggan 2012; Hayes and Dowds 2015; Kitchin and Lysaght 2003).

During February and August 2016, six one-to-one interviews were conducted. The average time of the interviews was 52.5 minutes. Furthermore, a two-part focus group comprising ten LGBT young people with their age ranging from 16 to 22 was conducted in August 2016. During the first part that lasted an hour, ten young people participated, while during the second part that lasted two hours, five young people participated. Four of the young people who participated in the focus group were also interviewed. This chapter presents one overlapping theme from the interviews and the focus group, namely barriers to help seeking that LGBT young people survivors of TRA may face.

Relevant ethics procedures were followed as approved by the appropriate research ethics committee at Queen's University Belfast. In order to ensure that the young people could give informed consent, emphasis was placed on the development of age-appropriate information sheets and posters. These were initially emailed to community and youth groups, informing young people about the research. Visits, follow-up emails and phone calls were also made to the agencies asking them for their help to recruit young participants. Despite repeated attempts to recruit, it was in the end just a very small number of young people who participated. The reasons for this may include the sensitive nature of TRA and the high rate of homophobia that exists in Northern Ireland. This may have prevented the LGBT youth population from disclosing their experiences of TRA and from participating in the research, notwithstanding assurances of confidentiality. Furthermore, as Donovan and Hester (2008) have suggested, the excitement of being in their first same-sex relationship might hinder LGBT people from acknowledging an abusive relationship. Last, some key community agency workers who had agreed initially to assist with recruitment were unable to do so, because of the impact of funding cut-backs.

Before the beginning of each interview and focus group, each participant was informed about the nature of the research, their consent was sought and they were reminded that they could withdraw their participation at any time of the research process. Furthermore, the young people were informed that the small financial incentive (£5 and £10 for their participation in the focus group and interview respectively) was theirs to keep even if they decided to withdraw their participation at any time during the research. Each participant reviewed and signed a consent form.

The interviews and focus groups with the young people were conducted at a youth agency and were facilitated by the author who introduced herself as having a minority sexual identity and as having extensive research and professional experience in the area of domestic violence and TRA.

The main youth worker/gate-keeper of the agency that the participants were recruited from was in the building during the time of the interviews/focus group, and remained there after the end in case any of the participants wanted to discuss any issue that arose from the interviews/focus group. A referral list of appropriate specialist agencies along with the email and the phone number of the author/researcher was also prepared and given to the young people and explained to them in case they wanted to address further any TRA-related issue, clarify what they had said or even withdraw their participation at a later date.

The focus group discussions and interviews were transcribed and analysed by two social science researchers (one of which is the author and the other who signed a confidentiality clause) using a thematic analysis (Braun and Clarke 2006) in order to, first, identify the main themes related to help-seeking barriers that emerged and, second, to discuss these key themes.

FINDINGS

This section presents the teenage participants' own narrations based on some of the main themes that were identified. In addition to the themes covered in this chapter, some others were identified, such as lack of knowledge about what constitutes abuse and the rural context. These are discussed elsewhere. To ensure anonymity, the young people's names have been changed.

Barriers to help seeking

The following results are organised in a way that highlights how the young people often felt that they could not ask for help because they did not want to come out to doctors and other health professionals, as they were afraid that their parents would be told; they did not want to be outed to their parents since they were not yet adults. Some said that they had been uncomfortable approaching their school to get help because of previous bad experiences, or because their experiences were silenced and ignored. Other themes that emerged from their narrations were the religious-infused context and the difficulties it poses, as well as the underfunding of support services, which undermines this provision. These factors, along with many others, may contribute to the further marginalisation of LGBT young people in Northern Ireland with experience of TRA.

Fear of double disclosure/being scared to be outed to parents at a young age

The majority of the participants discussed how they were not out to their parents at the time of the abuse. One of the themes that emerged is how the fear of double disclosure about both one's sexuality and being in an abusive relationship can undermine wellbeing and lead to an inability to seek help. Research with older LGBT adults (D'Augelli and Grossman 2001) has highlighted that the anticipation of victimisation once their sexuality becomes known to others is a factor that can lead to hiding one's sexuality in order to avoid harm (D'Augelli and Grossman 2001). Similarly, this fear of anticipated harm can lead to young survivors of abuse from not seeking or receiving effective and appropriate help (Gillum and DiFulvio 2012). This is suggested in Sean's account. Sean (21, gay man) reflected on an abusive relationship he was in when he was 17, which had resulted in injuries that necessitated medical care. He stated that the main challenge he faced in seeking help from the medical services was not being out to his parents:

> '…no one apart from my close friends knew that I was gay, so I didn't want to tell anybody that it had happened because I didn't want to out myself… I dismissed the doctor when, or the nurse, asked me what the bruises were and I just lied and said they were something else and she was like, "Okay", it was in A&E [hospital accident and emergency unit] on, like, a Saturday night which is hectic enough, that nurses head has probably been…it's just a whole mess and like, they and then the Sister didn't know anything about it, I just told her I had fallen… I was just so afraid of being outed…because I was like 17 I thought they would contact my parents and then I would have to explain to my parents what had happened…that was my main worry so I think if there was like guarantee that my parents would never find out… so you could be honest with your doctor so you could get treated… because I never told my doctor that I was sexually assaulted…so they

> never...checked for any like [refers to sexually transmitted diseases]... I didn't realise that until much later – that I had gotten HPV from him...'

Sean's account highlights a fear of double disclosure about sexuality and an abusive relationship, which can lead to healthcare disparity and inequity, undermining and an inability to seek help, not only from the NHS, but also from other institutions and formal sources of support (Gillum and DiFulvio 2012). Sean seems to have decided against self-disclosure through a process of calculating the risks of coming out: 'Concealing is a strategy that individuals often use to avoid stigmatization or negative regard, yet concealment may relate to higher stress over time' (Legate, Ryan and Weinstein 2012, p.146). His sexual orientation intersecting with his age raised questions of confidentiality. Sean continually stressed the importance of confidentiality (Zeitler *et al.* 2006) between the medical professionals and their young patients in order to avoid ineffective treatment/intervention from the healthcare system. The fear of double disclosure, as in Sean's case, may not only lead to survivors being left untreated and their wellbeing undermined, but it may also lead to the perpetrators being left unpunished.

Barriers within the education system

The participants identified barriers within the education sector to include the inability of some teachers to address possible signs of relationship abuse, the abusive experiences of the students, as well as the heteronormative nature of sex education. These themes are acknowledged in other research documenting that same sex attracted young people report poorer experiences in the education sector (Schubotz and O'Hara 2011), and are less likely to say that their school provided them with help when they were bullied (McNamee, Lloyd and Schubotz 2008; Meyer 2015).

Teachers don't address the issues

Teenagers spend much time at school, and the education system has the potential to be a place where the consequences of abuse could be highlighted. However, participants reported on their experiences that some teachers are ill equipped to address issues, either due to a lack of knowledge or due to the religious ethos of the school that they attended.

Anna (a 17-year-old bisexual young woman) discussed how even though she gave some signs to her teachers, the issue of abuse was not addressed:

> 'I was affected by the relationship because I remember at one point, near the end of the relationship, I kinda cracked in class but I'd cracked before and I'd kinda be sitting in the corner of the room just crying and no one would notice and I was ignored a lot, so on top of the bullying I had the relationship thing and it was bothering me but no one noticed even then… So they [the teachers] need to learn how to pay attention, because they pay attention to the people…interrupting the class with all their annoying yelling or just trouble making…'

Anna continued discussing the importance of the teachers in recognising signs of abuse (Pentaraki 2002).

Previous bad experience

Mary (a young trans woman aged 20), reflecting on why she did not seek help, mentioned as a possibility her previously bad experience of bullying in school. So, in response to the direct question of whether she had sought help at a school level, she reported:

> 'I never looked at it, I never put the energy into looking to school for help…possibly, because, like, I was bullied in secondary school which is why I never went on to do A-levels, I preferred to go to Tech [Technical College] which is I felt a lot safer there.'

Furthermore, another participant reported a bad experience relating to the non-confidential nature of help seeking in school. She reported that in the process of seeking help in the relevant school office, she was visible to many people, and felt that she became an object of discussion. This stopped her from seeking help again.

The issue raised by the young participants could be taken into account by schools in order to ensure that students in need of counselling feel that they can go to the relevant professional without so many people knowing. Among other ways forward, Mary above highlights the need for safe spaces in which issues can be discussed confidentially (among others; see Pentaraki 2002 about the role of education).

Heteronormative sex education

Another theme that emerged as a barrier to help-seeking behaviour was the heteronormativity of sex education in faith schools. Help-seeking behaviour is mediated by the heteronormativity of sex education that ignores and marginalises the experiences of LGBT teenagers, and might lead to their alienation and potential secondary victimisation. The participants who had lessons in school about relationships reported that these were heteronormative. The theme of ineffective sex education that is irrelevant to LGBT experiences has been acknowledged in other research (Donovan and Hester 2008; Robinson *et al.* 2013). This theme supports the need for the development of inclusive curricula about which there is growing research evidence (Snapp *et al.* 2015), suggesting that LGBT-inclusive curricula are associated with higher feelings of safety, both at the individual and the school level. The following is an excerpt from the focus group discussion:

> Liam: 'My talk wasn't on domestic violence; it was on heterosexual relationships...'

> Sean: 'I got a talk about the traditional roles in a house... Like, mammy stays home and cooks and looks after the wee [the little] ones and daddy goes out and works and then there was one talk about rape and it was only [about heterosexual] girls...'

To the question of what was excluded from these talks, Liam replied:

> 'Everything, the only thing that they educated us...was how happy straight relationships are.'

Liam's remark raises issues of potential secondary victimisation. When teachers claim that heterosexual relationships are happy and ignore the extent of violence, it may be that young people who are in either same-sex or opposite-sex abusive relationships might assume that the violence they experience is their own fault, which can, in turn, lead to self-blaming. Thus, it is important to discuss the extent of the abuse in all relationships (Donovan and Hester 2008). Schools should be one of the institutions aiming to raise the awareness of the complexities of TRA in order to be able to fulfil their duty to care and protect the students from TRA (Jackson, Bouffard and Fox 2014; Ramos 2010). Otherwise they could potentially be held accountable for not fulfilling their duty of care.

The participants pondered if the heterosexism they experienced was because of a lack of teachers' knowledge of LGBT experiences or because of institutional/cultural constraints. As Sean stated:

> '...like in a Catholic school with a Catholic ethos the board of governors can fire you [the teacher] if you go against their word.'

All of the above, as well as a previous bad experience within the education sector, can lead to devastating effects that undermine LGBT young people's education experience (Meyer 2015). It also raises the need for schools to be inclusive spaces for LGBT youth (for recommendations, see Donovan and Hester 2008 and Meyer 2015, among others) that account for the diversity of the student experience and uphold every young person's rights to equal educational opportunities.

Faith-based contexts

The focus group participants acknowledged the religious nature of a city in Northern Ireland and the surrounding area they were coming from, and then discussed their perceptions about how faith might influence the perpetuation of violence. According to Sean:

> '[The town] is a very religious place but the intensity of the devoutness varies...religion has an impact on all things in society, it's all intertwined in the culture and politics, it's hard to escape from... it's very omnipresent in a lot of society.'

Furthermore, it was suggested that one of the difficulties in addressing violence might be a prevailing 'hush-hush' culture. This closed culture may be associated with the legacy of 'The Troubles' in Northern Ireland. It might also be related to the need to protect the status of the more fundamentalist religious beliefs characterising some families and institutions. As Sean stated:

> 'The religious community infiltrates through the whole relationship so you don't really discuss anything about the relationship, and so if there are issues about abuse or anything like that, then people are less likely to open up about it if they feel they need to be quiet about the relationship in the first place.'

Rylee (a 20-year-old who asked to be identified as 'they') also mentioned that a strong faith can mitigate against the disclosure of abuse, especially when abuse is 'not treated outright as being an awful thing that shouldn't be accepted... And like they down play it and almost accept it...'

Anna elaborated on these points by commenting that people who are abused and approach their priest receive the typical response of 'pray on it, hopefully it gets better'. Anna then mentioned that some of her friends had had these experiences. To this Rylee added that this is more evident in smaller communities where the knowledge of an abusive relationship would be projected by some as a disgrace to the extended family. This can be another reason why help is not sought. One of the difficulties, as Rylee observed, might be that '...it feeds into the helplessness as well because if you're told, like, God does something for a reason, like, and all you can do is pray and hope for the best, like'.

The religious context of Northern Ireland is a factor that needs to be explored further, as its particular specificities may be a potential barrier to help-seeking and help-receiving behaviour.

Austerity

All of the participants recognised how important the community agency with which they engaged was for their wellbeing, but raised concerns about the underfunding of services targeted to LGBT youth, as well as other underfunded and austerity-stricken mainstream services (Bassel and Emejulu 2014) that resulted in long waiting lists.

One participant, Rylee, discussed in detail the austerity conditions and how they affect both the mainstream and specifically LGBT services. 'They' reported among other things:

> '...that [the community agency they attend] itself is, like, so under, like, staffed and the budget is tight and it's just like providing a service for so many people, it's, like, they do an amazing job but at the same time it's, like, one service isn't enough, like, you need so many organisations and charities...'

Austerity is one of the structural conditions that can intensify existing inequalities. It needs to be further explored and be the focus of intervention as there might be further intersections, such as with rural areas. As a couple of the participants mentioned, less urban areas have fewer services appropriate for the needs of young people.

DISCUSSION AND CONCLUSION

Northern Ireland, along with England, Wales and Scotland, has a legal framework that recognises that forms of domestic violence (intimate partner violence) can take place in teenage relationships as well as same-sex relationships. In this framework, it is recognised that 16- and 17-year-olds can experience violent abuse in their interpersonal or sexual relationships (Alldred and Biglia 2015). However, in Northern Ireland, as elsewhere, the legal recognition that this abuse takes place does not necessarily lead to protection, as the disclosure of this abuse may be difficult due to a variety of factors. The findings of this small explorative pilot study suggest that disclosure of teenage relationship abuse/dating violence in Northern Ireland may be mediated by a host of contextual factors including the fear of homophobic reactions, and the institutional silencing of LGBT lives through heteronormative school practises, which can undermine the disclosure of TRA as well as discourage help seeking. The existence of homophobia (Gillum and DiFulvio 2012) may lead to the fear of coming out, which might, in turn, lead to a fear that the abuse will be disclosed. This fear of double disclosure could lead to LGBT young people not seeking support when they need it, such as in the case of Sean in the hospital's A&E unit. This can lead to healthcare disparity and inequity, whereas the institutional expression of heterosexism, as exemplified in the case of heteronormative sex education, might lead to the silencing of LGBT life experiences and lead to young people feeling alienated. More importantly, this could lead to reluctance to seek help due to the TRA they suffer. The preliminary findings of this small pilot research suggest that a heterosexist and religious spatial context, such as that of Northern Ireland, can shape lived experiences and may in turn undermine help-seeking behaviour in general. Therefore, it is vital to recognise the importance of space and time (Monro 2010) and to account for people's experiences that are shaped by heterosexist and faith spaces, etc. The themes that have emerged from this preliminary analysis need now to be analysed in more detail and be explored further in larger studies.

Of course there might be some overlap of the issues that LGBT and heterosexual youth experience, but underlining homophobia can differentiate the experiences of young people. This chapter maintains that an intersectional approach is needed to inform prevention efforts and service provision in order to respond adequately to the needs of

LGBT young people living in a heterosexist and religious context. An intersectional analytical framework can highlight the need to transcend a one-size-fits-all approach by recognising the diversity/heterogeneity of needs (Cho, Crenshaw and McCall 2013). More importantly, however, it enables the identification of the complex and interconnected risks and vulnerabilities LGBT teenagers encounter in settings such as the one in Northern Ireland, where there are increased levels of homophobia as well as more ingrained faith beliefs. One of the issues that this pilot study raises is the importance of addressing the role of religion. However, the adoption of an intersectional approach that recognises patterns of discrimination linked to religion is not only pertinent to Northern Ireland, but also in other European contexts (Lépinard 2014) and elsewhere.

The results of the pilot study suggest the intersections of geography/space (infused with religious beliefs), age and sexual orientation pose help-seeking barriers to young people in such a way that might undermine their wellbeing and reinforce their state and sense of social vulnerability. The barriers to help seeking faced by LGBT young people involve multiple intersecting forms of oppression/marginality/discrimination. LGBT youth are less likely to get the help needed in a Northern Ireland context, not only because of their sexual orientation, but also because of how it intersects with their age, their geographical setting and their religion, among other factors.

These intersections are all areas that need to be explored further in future research. In addition, other intersections that should be studied in more detail include the intersections of rural spaces, and ethnic and racial identities. As this was a small pilot study, the sample tended to be homogeneous. Future research should draw from a more inclusive and diverse sample in order to be able to document the complexity of all intersections (Fish 2008). This is important as each intersection can lead to a form of oppression and a specific need that has to be addressed. These intersections can then inform effective prevention campaigns with multiple levels of interventions in order to address inclusively the diverse needs, concerns and challenges that all young people face. The ultimate goal is intersectionality-informed research that leads to intersectionality-informed practise and policy (Hankivsky 2014).

However, the capacity to do this might be further undermined by the austerity cuts that lead to under-funded prevention projects

(Bassel and Emejulu 2014). Thus, any effective campaigning for inclusive prevention programmes needs to be tied to effective campaigning against austerity cuts (Pentaraki 2013). Current socioeconomic conditions of austerity highlight that an intersectional approach needs to account not only for identities (Carastathis 2008; Donovan and Hester 2015), but also for space, context and, especially, structural conditions. If this does not happen, we will see an increase in the barriers to help seeking and receiving by LGBT youth experiencing relationship abuse in Northern Ireland as well as elsewhere.

Acknowledgements: The author thanks the young participants and the youth workers for their participation in this project. She also thanks the research assistant Arlene Robertson for her help and Janet Speake for suggestions.

REFERENCES

Alldred, P. and Biglia, B. (2015) 'Gender-related violence and young people: An overview of Italian, Irish, Spanish, UK and EU legislation.' *Children and Society 29*, 6, 662–675.

Ashley, O.S. and Foshee, V.A. (2005) 'Adolescent help-seeking for dating violence: Prevalence, sociodemographic correlates, and sources of help.' *Journal of Adolescent Health 36*, 1, 25–31.

Banyard, V.L. and Cross, C. (2008) 'Consequences of teen dating violence: Understanding intervening variables in ecological context.' *Violence Against Women 14*, 998–1013.

Barter, C. (2009) 'In the name of love: Partner abuse and violence in teenage relationships.' *British Journal of Social Work 39*, 2, 211–233.

Barter, C., Stanley, N., Wood, M., Lanau, A.*et al.* (2017) 'Young people's online and face-to-face experiences of interpersonal violence and abuse and their subjective impact across five European countries.' *Psychology of Violence 7*, 3, 375–384.

Bassel, L. and Emejulu, A. (2014) 'Solidarity under austerity: Intersectionality in France and the United Kingdom.' *Politics and Gender 10*, 1, 130–136.

Black, B. and Weisz, A. (2003) 'Dating violence: Help-seeking behaviours of African American middle schoolers.' *Violence Against Women 9*, 187–206.

Bowleg, L. (2012) 'The problem with the phrase women and minorities: Intersectionality – An important theoretical framework for public health.' *American Journal of Public Health 102*, 7, 1267–1273.

Braun, V. and Clarke, V. (2006) 'Using thematic analysis in psychology.' *Qualitative Research in Psychology 3*, 2, 77–101.

Burman, M. and Cartmel, F. (2005) *Young People's Attitudes towards Gendered Violence.* Edinburgh: NHS Health Scotland.

Calton, J.M., Cattaneo, L.B. and Gebhard, K.T. (2016) 'Barriers to help seeking for lesbian, gay, bisexual, transgender, and queer survivors of intimate partner violence.' *Trauma, Violence and Abuse, 17*, 5, 585–600.

Campbell, R. (2008) 'The psychological impact of rape victims' experiences with the legal, medical, and mental health systems.' *American Psychologist 63*, 702–717.

Carastathis, A. (2008) *Feminism and the political economy of representation: intersectionality, invisibility and embodiment.* Ph.D. Thesis, McGill University.

Cho, S., Crenshaw, K.W. and McCall, L. (2013) 'Toward a field of intersectionality studies: Theory, applications and praxis.' *Signs 38*, 4, 785–810.

Collins, P.H. (1998) 'It's all in the family: Intersections of gender, race, and nation.' *Hypatia 13*, 3, 62–82.

Crenshaw, K. (1991) 'Mapping the margins: Intersectionality, identity politics, and violence against women of color.' *Stanford Law Review 43*, 6, 1241–1299.

D'Augelli, A.R. and Grossman, A.H. (2001) 'Disclosure of sexual orientation, victimization, and mental health among lesbian, gay, and bisexual older adults.' *Journal of Interpersonal Violence 16*, 10, 1008–1027.

Donovan, C. and Hester, M. (2008) '"Because she was my first girlfriend, I didn't know any different." Making the case for mainstreaming same-sex sex/relationship education.' *Sex Education 8*, 3, 277–287.

Donovan, C. and Hester, M. (2015) *Domestic Violence and Sexuality: What's Love Got to Do with It?* Bristol: Policy Press.

Donovan, C., Barnes, R. and Nixon, C. (2014) *The Coral Project: Exploring Abusive Behaviours in Lesbian, Gay, Bisexual and/or Transgender Relationships: Interim Report.* Sunderland and Leicester: University of Sunderland and University of Leicester.

Duggan, M. (2012) *Queering Conflict: Examining Lesbian and Gay Experiences of Homophobia in Northern Ireland.* Aldershot: Ashgate.

Elias-Lambert, N., Black, B.M. and Chigbu, K.U. (2014) 'Controlling behaviours in middle school youth's dating relationships: Reactions and help-seeking behaviours.' *Journal of Early Adolescence 34*, 7, 841–865.

Fish, J. (2008) 'Navigating queer street: Researching the intersections of lesbian, gay, bisexual and trans (LGBT) identities in health research.' *Sociological Research Online 13*, 1, 12. Accessed on 3/8/2017 at www.socresonline.org.uk/13/1/12.html

Fortin, I., Guay, S., Lavoie, V., Boisvert, J.-M. and Beaudry, M. (2012) 'Intimate partner violence and psychological distress among young couples: Analysis of the moderating effect of social support.' *Journal of Family Violence 27*, 63–73.

Fox, C.L., Corr, M., Gadd, D. and Butler, I. (2014) 'Young teenagers' experiences of domestic abuse.' *Journal of Youth Studies 17*, 4, 510–526.

Gehring, K.S. and Vaske, J.C. (2015) 'Out in the open: The consequences of intimate partner violence for victims in same-sex and opposite-sex relationships.' *Journal of Interpersonal Violence*, 1–24.

Gillum, T. and DiFulvio, G. (2012) 'There's so much at stake: Sexual minority youth discussing dating violence.' *Violence Against Women 18*, 7, 725–745.

Hancock, A.M. (2007) 'When multiplication doesn't equal quick addition: Examining intersectionality as a research paradigm.' *Perspectives on Politics 5*, 1, 63–78.

Hankivsky, O. (2014) *Intersectionality 101.* Burnaby, BC: Institute for Intersectionality Research and Policy, Simon Fraser University.

Hayes, B.C. and Dowds, L. (2015) 'Religion and Attitudes towards Gay Rights in Northern Ireland: The God Gap Revisited.' In S. Brunn (ed.) *The Changing World Religion Map*, pp.3321–3340. Netherlands: Springer.

Hellevik, P. and Øverlien, C. (2016) 'Teenage intimate partner violence: Factors associated with victimization among Norwegian youths.' *Scandinavian Journal of Public Health.* Accessed on 3/8/2017 at http://journals.sagepub.com/doi/abs/10.1177/1403494816657264

Hulko, W. (2009) 'The time-and context-contingent nature of intersectionality and interlocking oppressions.' *Affilia 24*, 1, 44–55.

Jackson, R.D., Bouffard, L.A. and Fox, K.A. (2014) 'Putting policy into practise: Examining school districts' implementation of teen dating violence legislation.' *Criminal Justice Policy Review 25*, 4, 503–524.

Kitchin, R. and Lysaght, K. (2003) 'Heterosexism and the geographies of everyday life in Belfast, Northern Ireland.' *Environment and Planning A 35*, 3, 489–510.

Legate, N., Ryan, R.M. and Weinstein, N. (2012) 'Is coming out always a good thing? Exploring the relations of autonomy support, outness, and wellness for lesbian, gay, and bisexual individuals.' *Social Psychological and Personality Science 3*, 2,145–152.

Lépinard, E. (2014) 'Impossible intersectionality? French feminists and the struggle for inclusion.' *Politics and Gender 10*, 1, 124–130.

McNamee, H., Lloyd, K. and Schubotz, D. (2008) 'Same sex attraction, homophobic bullying and mental health of young people in Northern Ireland.' *Journal of Youth Studies 11*, 33–46.

Meyer, E.J. (2015) *Gender, Bullying, and Harassment: Strategies to End Sexism and Homophobia in Schools.* New York: Teachers College Press.

Monro, S. (2010) 'Sexuality, space and intersectionality: The case of lesbian, gay and bisexual equalities initiatives in UK local government.' *Sociology 44*, 5, 996–1010.

Nixon, J. and Humphreys, C. (2010) 'Marshalling the evidence: Using intersectionality in the domestic violence frame.' *Social Politics: International Studies in Gender, State and Society 17*, 2, 137–158.
Pentaraki, M. (2002) 'Teenage Relationship Abuse/Dating Violence and Prevention Policies.' In Athens, Gova E. (ed.) *The Undermining of Gender Issues: Proposals Against Sexism and Violence Against Women* (pp.107–122).
Pentaraki, M. (2003) 'The Forms, the Extent and the Consequences of Dating Violence that Greek High School Female Students Face.' Unpublished PhD thesis. Athens, Greece: Panteion University of Social and Political Sciences.
Pentaraki, M. (2004a) 'Physical consequences of violence against [young] women and the necessity of community response of the medical system.' *Greek Journal of Social Work 74*, 101–114.
Pentaraki, M. (2004b) 'Women's unemployment and partner violence against them: Examining the case of lone unemployed mothers.' *Greek Journal of Social Work 76*, 223–244.
Pentaraki, M. (2013) 'Measures to Fight Violence Against Women.' European Commission's Exchange of Good Practises Programme, Spain, 16–17 April. (With contributions by A. Kontothanasi.)
Ramos, J. (2010) 'Defining violence on the blackboard: An overview of the Texas Education Code's approach to teen dating violence.' *Scholar 13*, 105–148.
Robinson, K.H., Bansel, P., Denson, N., Ovenden, G. and Davies, C. (2013) *Growing Up Queer: Issues Facing Young Australians Who Are Gender Variant and Sexuality Diverse.* Melbourne, VIC: Young and Well Cooperative Research Centre.
Schubotz, D. and O'Hara, M. (2011) 'A shared future? Exclusion, stigmatization, and mental health of same-sex-attracted young people in Northern Ireland.' *Youth and Society 43*, 2, 488–508.
Schütt, N.M. (2006) *Domestic Violence in Adolescent Relationships: Young People in Southwark and Their Experiences with Unhealthy Relationships.* Beacon Council and Safer Southwark Partnership.
Silverman, J.G., Raj, A., Mucci, L.A. and Hathaway, J.E. (2001). 'Dating violence against adolescent girls and associated substance use, unhealthy weight control, sexual risk behavior, pregnancy, and suicidality.' *Jama, 286*, 5, 572–579.
Snapp, S.D., McGuire, J.K., Sinclair, K.O., Gabrion, K. and Russell, S.T. (2015) 'LGBTQ-inclusive curricula: Why supportive curricula matter.' *Sex Education 15*, 6, 580–596.
Stonard, K.E., Bowen, E., Walker, K. and Price, S.A. (2015) 'They'll always find a way to get to you: Technology use in adolescent romantic relationships and its role in dating violence and abuse.' *Journal of Interpersonal Violence*, 1–35.
Sylaska, K.M. and Edwards, K.M. (2014) 'Disclosure of intimate partner violence to informal social support network members: A review of the literature.' *Trauma, Violence and Abuse 15*, 1, 3–21.
Valentine, G. (2007) 'Theorizing and researching intersectionality: A challenge for feminist geography.' *The Professional Geographer 59*, 1, 10–21.
Viejo, C., Monks, C.P., Sanchez, V. and Ortega-Ruiz, R. (2015) 'Physical dating violence in Spain and the United Kingdom and the importance of relationship quality.' *Journal of Interpersonal Violence*, 1–23.
Voth Schrag, R.J. and Edmond, T. (2017) 'School sabotage as a form of intimate partner violence: Provider perspectives.' *Affilia 32*, 2, 171–187.
Weisz, A.N., Tolman, R.M., Callahan, M.R., Saunders, D.G. and Black, B.M. (2007) 'Informal helpers' responses when adolescents tell them about dating violence or romantic relationship problems.' *Journal of Adolescence 30*, 5, 853–868.
WHO (World Health Organization) (2013) *Global and Regional Estimates of Violence Against Women: Prevalence and Health Effects of Intimate Partner Violence and Non-partner Sexual Violence.* Geneva: WHO.
Zeitler, M.S., Paine, A.D., Breitbart, V., Rickert, V.I. *et al.* (2006) 'Attitudes about intimate partner violence screening among an ethnically diverse sample of young women.' *Journal of Adolescent Health 39*, 1, 119-e1.

Chapter 8

CARING DADS: SAFER CHILDREN

USING A FOCUS ON FATHERING TO RESPOND TO DOMESTIC VIOLENCE

Nicola McConnell, *Senior Evaluation Officer, NSPCC, UK*

Julie Taylor, *Professor of Child Protection, University of Birmingham/ Birmingham Women's and Children's NHS Foundation Trust, UK*

Matt Barnard, *Head of Crime, Justice and Communities, NatCen, UK*

THE CARING DADS PROGRAMME AND ITS IMPLEMENTATION WITHIN EUROPE

Recent research suggests that using the concept of fatherhood can be a productive and pragmatic way to encourage male perpetrators of domestic abuse to examine their behaviour and to stop further violence (Stanley, Graham Kevan and Borthwick 2012; Stover 2013). However, it is an approach to working with perpetrators that has been contentious within the UK, with some domestic abuse organisations expressing concern that a focus on fathering might be at the expense of addressing men's violence against women (Featherstone and Fraser 2012). Added to this, a recent review found that few fathering interventions for violent fathers have been evaluated, and where they have been evaluated, the evaluations are limited, as was the evidence of their effectiveness (Labarre *et al.* 2016). Given the prevalence of domestic abuse in children's lives (Radford *et al.* 2011), and also the multiple risks of immediate and long-term psychological, physiological and developmental harm caused by children's exposure to domestic abuse (Kimball 2016), approaches to preventing domestic abuse that focus on fathering and co-parenting merit further exploration. One well-known fathering programme is Caring Dads, a programme originating from Canada, which has been implemented within the UK, Ireland, Sweden, Germany and the Netherlands. In this chapter we describe the Caring Dads programme, present our evaluation of Caring Dads: Safer Children and, in keeping with the themes of this book, discuss emerging challenges for policy, practice and research.

The Caring Dads programme

The Caring Dads programme (Scott 2010) uses men's role as a father to motivate them to examine and change their behaviour in seven treatment target areas: anger/hostility/over-reactivity; family cohesion/co-parenting/domestic violence; perceptions of the child as a problem; use of corporal punishment and other aversive behaviours; positive and involved parent–child relationship; self-centredness; and misuse of substances (Scott 2010). The programme has four major goals:

1. To develop sufficient trust and motivation to engage men in the process of examining their fathering
2. To increase men's awareness of child-centred fathering
3. To increase men's awareness of, and responsibility for, abusive and neglectful fathering
4. To consolidate learning, rebuild trust and plan for the future. (Scott 2010)

Fathers attend a two-hour weekly closed group session, usually facilitated by a male and a female practitioner, for 17 weeks. In the latest edition of the programme, two group sessions have been replaced with individual meetings between programme facilitators and fathers to solidify individualised goals for change. Eligible fathers must have abused or neglected their children, exposed them to domestic abuse, or be deemed to be at high risk of these behaviours. However, the programme is not suitable for all: only fathers who provide care or who have regular contact with their children are eligible. In addition, it must also be believed that the father's attendance is in their child's best interests. To ensure that children and partner safety and wellbeing remain paramount, programme delivery is aligned with local child protection and domestic abuse services, family courts and criminal justice systems. Goals identified for each father during the programme must be consistent with those of other professionals working with his family (Scott 2010). When fathers start Caring Dads, other practitioners contact his partner (current or previous) and children to provide information about the programme, make referrals for further support or provide immediate safety planning if required. When partners are willing, practitioners keep regular contact to monitor risk from the father while he attends the programme.

While there is evidence that Caring Dads has the potential to promote positive change in fathers' parenting and co-parenting (Scott and Lishak 2012) and decrease aspects of fathers' parenting stress (a risk factor for child abuse; see Lindsay, Atkins and Matczak 2010), there are mixed findings about whether the programme can affect fathers' aggressive responses (McCracken and Deave 2012; Scott and Lishak 2012), acceptance of responsibility for their actions, or aggression towards women (McCracken and Deave 2012). Most studies outside Canada have been small, with high attrition prior to and during the programme inhibiting achievement of sample sizes sufficient for parametric tests and analysis of subgroups.

Implementation within the UK and Europe

The Caring Dads programme is delivered by approximately 30 different organisations worldwide, including several in north-western Europe. Recognised providers of the programme received training from the programme originators or trainers/practitioners authorised by them to train others.

A recent pilot evaluation by the National Centre on Early Prevention in Germany of the first three programmes delivered in Dusseldorf, Hanover and Groß-Gerau (near Frankfurt) suggests that the programme can work outside of Canada and the UK (Koch, Liel and Eickhorst 2017). Analysis of approximately 40 fathers' and 22 mothers' reports, using the same measures as Scott and Lishak, produced very similar pre- and post-programme results for anger, aggression and problematic parenting. Scores for verbal aggression reduced, but were higher than the Canadian scores at both time points: the authors thought this might be explained by cultural differences, for example direct communication being more usual and not perceived as aggressive in Germany. Results from a postal follow-up survey (50% response) show that most fathers felt that the programme was helpful for them and improved their family relationships.

A diverse range of provider organisations deliver the programme within Europe, including government-led family support and children's services, non-statutory charitable and welfare organisations typically working with families with multiple disadvantages, child protection organisations and organisations involved in the resettlement and rehabilitation of offenders. This variety of providers suggests that the challenge of finding a constructive and engaging way to work with abusive fathers is common to many different sectors and agencies. While this demonstrates that organisations within different settings can run the programme, the originators stress the importance of consistency in the way it is implemented. To be considered a Caring Dads programme, provider organisations must comply with the expectations of running the programme set out on the Caring Dads website.[1] Meeting these standards will ensure that the safeguards and partnership working that were in place within the Canadian programme are translated into the practice and systems elsewhere. For example, process evaluations within the UK have emphasised the importance of retaining social services involvement to manage risk and seeking regular feedback from family members while fathers attend the programme (Hood, Lindsay and Muleya 2014; Kaur and Frost 2014).

CARING DADS: SAFER CHILDREN EVALUATION

A distinctive feature of the evaluation of Caring Dads delivered by the NSPCC (called Caring Dads: Safer Children – or CDSC within the organisation) was the focus on the impact the programme had on partners and children. No previous study of Caring Dads obtained measure data from partners or indeed any data from children, so the fact that the evaluation was successful in recruiting a sample of partners and children sufficient to enable quantitative analysis of their data provided a unique opportunity to explore this aspect of the programme. Surveys, case note analysis and qualitative interviews were

1 See http://caringdads.org/running-the-program.htm

also included in the evaluation design to provide families' perspectives on the programme and greater understanding of how CDSC can influence systems to protect children in addition to the collection of outcomes data from fathers who attended the programme.

Hypothesis

It was anticipated that fathers successfully completing CDSC would be more child-centred in their fathering and willing to take responsibility for previous abusive behaviour. It was therefore hypothesised that after the programme evaluation participants (fathers, partners and children) would report: fathers' attitudes and parenting behaviour being more child-centred; less controlling behaviour by fathers towards their current or former partner; and improvement in children and partners' wellbeing (see Figure 8.1).

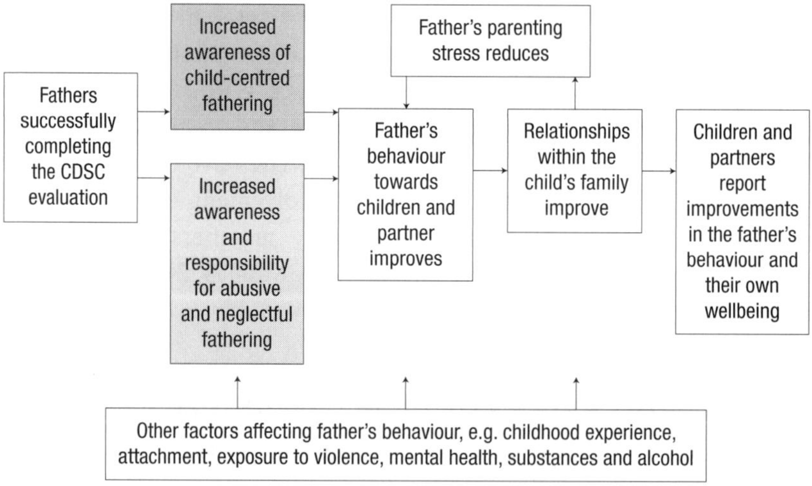

Source: Adapted from Abidin (1995)

Figure 8.1: Theory of change for the Caring Dads: Safer Children evaluation

Participants

CDSC was delivered from five sites located across England, Northern Ireland and Wales between 2010 and 2014. Over two-thirds of fathers were referred by social services; other referrals came via child and family courts and probation and health services. Of fathers referred, 43 per cent went on to attend the first session and over half (53%)

of these fathers completed the programme, attending every group session, or catch-up sessions with facilitators if they missed a week.[2] Nearly 350 fathers were invited to participate in the evaluation. Only nine fathers refused to participate, all of whom eventually dropped out; and only one father who completed the programme refused to provide data post-programme. Table 8.1 presents the number of evaluation participants at each time point. Fathers referred to CDSC ranged in age from between 18 and 66 (M=31.43, SD=8.24); their ethnicity was similar to that of the UK population (ONS 2013), but less diverse than the relevant populations for children in need or on a child protection plan or register (DfE 2014; DHSSPS 2014; Welsh Government 2015). Children's ages ranged from newborn to adult, but most were younger children, with a median age of 4. For nearly half of participating children (47%), contact with their father was unrestricted and unsupervised. Thirty-nine per cent lived with the father, and for nearly three-quarters of the children (74%), the man on the programme was their birth father. Just over two-thirds of partners (69%) were currently in a relationship with the father; the remaining were ex-partners.

Table 8.1: Number of evaluation participants at each time point

Evaluation participant	T1: Pre-programme	T2: Post-programme	T3: Follow-up
Fathers attending community groups completing standardised measures	334	185	49
Case note analysis of fathers' records	Not applicable	178	Not applicable
Partners completing standardised measures	132	71	21
Partners participating in face-to-face survey	109	55	19
Children completing standardised measures	38	22	9
Children participating in face-to-face survey	22	19	6

Note: Figures for partners and children include those who participated at T1 only, at T2 only and also those who participated at each time point.

2 Detailed reasons for attrition prior to and during the programme are described in McConnell *et al.* (2016b).

Procedure

Fathers, their children and partners participated at three time points: at the start of the programme (T1 baseline); at the end of the programme to observe any changes that had occurred (T2); and six months after the programme to observe whether these were maintained (T3). Group facilitators administered measures to fathers, while practitioners working with the families were responsible for the recruitment and involvement of partners and children within the evaluation. Both sets of workers were knowledgeable and experienced in working with child protection and domestic abuse, and thus able to recognise and address issues arising from the completed measures where necessary (McConnell and Taylor 2016). Organisational policy at the time prohibited waiting lists; however, staff shortages at one site led to the postponement of groups, which provided the opportunity to gather and compare data from fathers assessed as suitable but waiting to start the programme with data from other fathers who had completed at the same site. Data were collated and analysed using Microsoft Word, NVivo, Microsoft Excel and SPSS.

Measures

Survey of family members: Partners and children were surveyed at the beginning of the programme about their hopes and expectations of CDSC. After the programme they were asked what changes in the father's behaviour, if any, they had observed or experienced. All surveys with partners and children were administered face-to-face and took place during their meetings with practitioners.

Standardised measures: Participants completed questionnaires that assessed the father's relationship and behaviour towards his children and partner, and any changes in their wellbeing. Where possible family members completed equivalent versions of the questionnaires about the father's behaviour so that the evaluation was not reliant on the father's self-reports. Table 8.2 presents the measures used with each group of respondents.

Table 8.2: Outcomes and measures used in the evaluation of CDSC

Outcomes	Respondents	Measure
Less controlling behaviour by fathers towards their current or former partner	Partners and fathers	Controlling Behaviour Inventory measures emotional abuse, intimidation, economic abuse, isolation, threat/coercion, violence, sexual abuse, injury, using children, denial/minimisation and negotiation
	Children and partners	Survey and qualitative interviews
Fathers' attitudes and parenting behaviour being more child-centred	Fathers	Parenting Stress Index 3rd Edition Short Form measures parental distress, parental–child dysfunctional interaction and perception of the child being difficult (Abidin 1995)
	Children and fathers	Parental Acceptance-Rejection Questionnaire (PARQ) measures warmth and affection, hostility and aggression, indifference, and neglect and rejection (Rohner and Khaleque 2005)
	Children and partners	Survey and qualitative interviews
Improvement in children and partners' wellbeing	Partners	Adult Wellbeing Scale measures depression, anxiety, inwardly directed irritability and outwardly directed irritability (DH 2000)
	Children	Adolescent Wellbeing Scale (DH 2000)
	Child's main carer	Strengths and Difficulties Questionnaire (SDQ) measures a child's pro-social behaviour and emotional and behavioural problems (Goodman 1997)

Qualitative interviews with family members: Qualitative interviews with family members explored partners and children's observations and experiences of CDSC and the effect, if any, they perceived it had had on their lives and their relationship with the father. The qualitative sample was made up of three children aged between 10 and 15, four current partners and four ex-partners.

Analysis of case records: Closing summary statements from the case record system provided information, from the group facilitators' perspective, on each father's progress during the programme or reasons why he may have dropped out of the programme. The case record was checked where the closing summary provided insufficient information.

Ethics

The evaluation was approved by the NSPCC research ethics committee, which is chaired by a researcher independent of the organisation, and which follows the requirements of the UK Economic and Social Research Council (ESRC) and the UK Government Social Research Unit.

FINDINGS

Improvements in fathers' controlling behaviour towards partners

Partners reported statistically significant reductions in the average number of incidents of controlling behaviour (see Figure 8.2). The proportion of partners reporting one or more incidents of controlling behaviour also reduced. Some types of behaviour reduced more than others: partners reporting denials of abuse reduced by a third; abuse using children reduced by more than two-thirds. Four subscales reported by partners had statistically significant reduction over the three time points: violence, injury, denial/minimisation and emotional abuse.

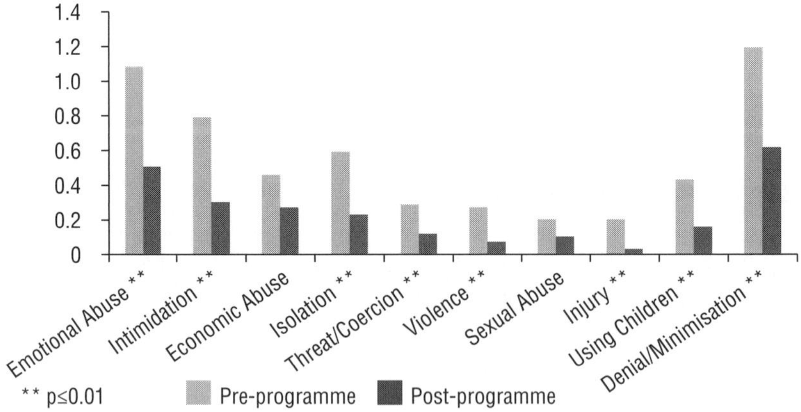

Figure 8.2: Average number of incidents reported by partners via the Controlling Behaviour Inventory, comparing pre- and post-programme scores
Source: CDSC teams October 2010–October 2014

Parenting attitudes and behaviour

Paired sample t-tests indicated significant improvements in fathers' reported parental distress, parent–child dysfunctional interaction, perceptions of their child being difficult and their overall Parenting Stress Index (PSI) score (see Figure 8.3). Moreover, the percentage of fathers whose total scores were within the clinical range, an indicator for higher risk of child abuse, significantly reduced (McConnell *et al.* 2016a), and data from the small group of fathers completing follow-up measures approximately six months after the programme indicated that they had managed to maintain a reduction in stress (see Figure 8.4). A comparison of fathers waiting to start the programme and fathers who had completed the programme at the same service centre indicated that while parenting stress reduced for both groups, there was a larger reduction within the intervention group than in the waiting group (see Figure 8.5).

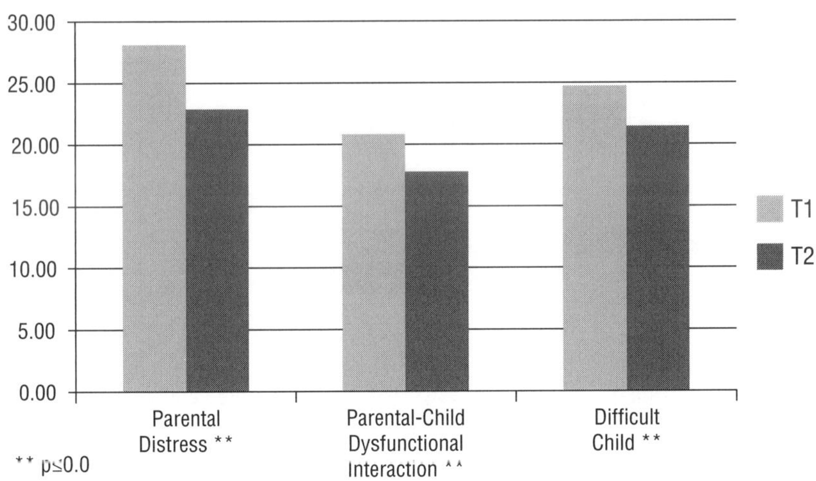

Figure 8.3: Average pre- and post-programme scores for fathers completing the PSI
Source: CDSC teams October 2010–October 2014

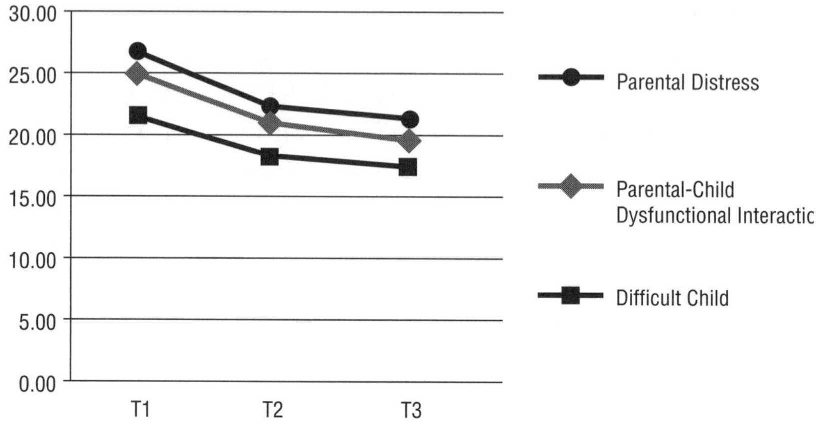

Figure 8.4: Fathers' PSI subscale scores at each time point, *N*=52
Source: CDSC teams October 2010–October 2014

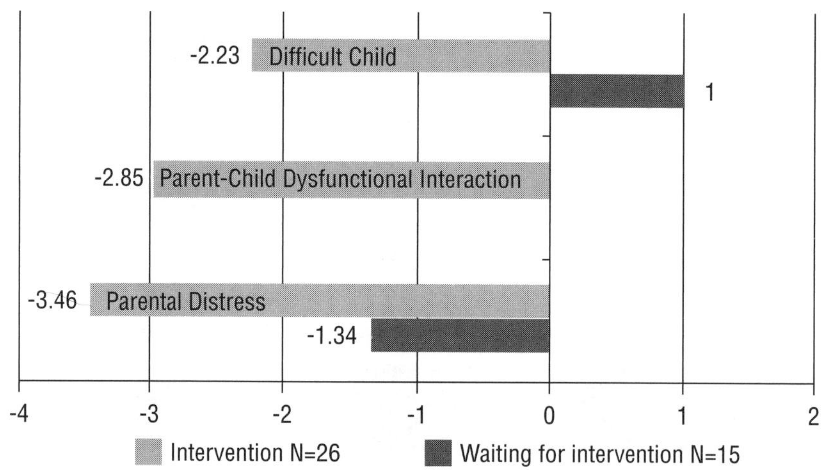

Figure 8.5: Change in mean scores for PSI, comparing fathers who completed programme with fathers who were waiting to start
Source: CDSC teams October 2010–October 2014

Although the fathers' average total and subscale scores for the PARQ reduced post-programme, the only statistically significant reduction found was for hostility and aggression. Peculiarly, fathers' average scores at T1 reported warmer and more accepting parenting behaviour than would be found in the general population, suggesting some response bias, and leaving little room for improvement at T2. Children's reports using the PARQ appeared to be more reliable; being within the normal range and demonstrating bigger decreases in rejecting behaviour, but with a much smaller sample their reported change was not statistically significant.

Children and partners' observations on the father's behaviour

The majority of children surveyed or interviewed (*N*=26) said they had seen an improvement in their father's behaviour after the programme. They talked about seeing him more often and feeling happier and more comfortable around him. Children described fathers demonstrating more child-centred behaviour, for example listening more, taking an interest in their school work, playing with them, praising them and treating them appropriately for their age. Partners similarly commented on the improvement in the father's behaviour in the presence of children, his co-parenting, and his recognition of the impact of his abuse on the children. When asked about the father's behaviour towards themselves, partners talked about him being calmer, more thoughtful and willing to talk through problems. Partners also believed that the father was less likely to escalate disagreements into an argument or become annoyed by the behaviour of others. Nevertheless, it must be noted that some children and partners gave comments that suggested that the father had not changed or that the change was only partial or temporary, describing fathers whose behaviour was still threatening, unreliable or undermining (McConnell *et al.* 2016). These families' experiences underline the importance of providing support to families during the programme and ensuring safety by making sure other agencies working with the family are kept fully informed.

Improvements in partners' wellbeing but findings for children's wellbeing inconclusive

Partners completing the Adult Wellbeing Scale reported statistically significant reductions in depression, anxiety and inward directed irritability (see Figure 8.6), although only the anxiety subscale remained statistically significant over the three time points. For children, comparison of pre- and post-programme scores revealed that although the average scores for behavioural and wellbeing difficulties reduced, none of the differences observed were large or statistically significant. When children's SDQ scores were analysed over the three time points, significant differences were identified for the total difficulties scores and the peer problems scores. However, as the sample over the three time points consisted of only seven children, this finding clearly has limitations (McConnell *et al.* 2016a).

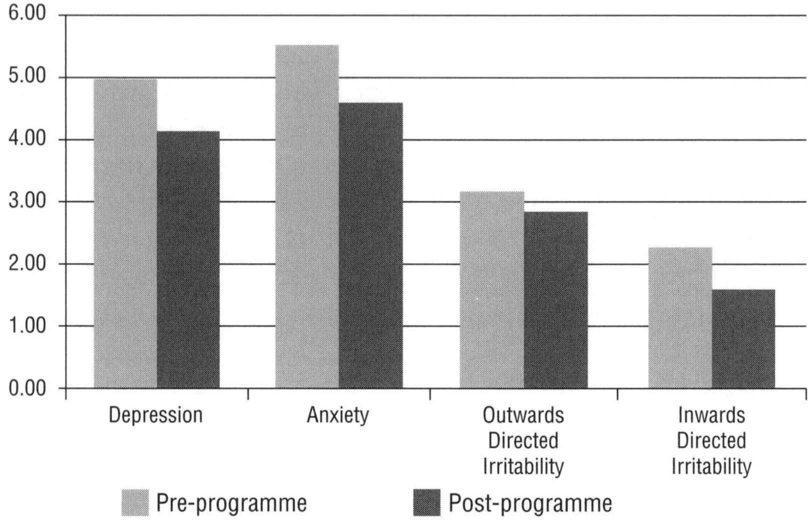

Figure 8.6: Average scores for responses to the Adult Wellbeing Questionnaire, comparing pre- and post-programme scores
Source: CDSC teams October 2010–October 2014

EMERGING CHALLENGES FOR POLICY PRACTICE AND RESEARCH

The findings of the evaluation of CDSC provide promising evidence that the programme can bring about positive changes in the attitudes and behaviour of abusive fathers that can contribute to increased safety and wellbeing within their families. If fathers successfully complete the programme, potential outcomes include a more knowledgeable and child-centred parent; better communication between the father and child; more supportive co-parenting; safer separation or reunification of families; more cooperation with social services or the court process; and greater confidence, freedom and safety for other family members. Even when fathers drop out of the programme or are unable to change, their referral and assessment should make them more visible within the child protection system. Nevertheless, it is important to consider challenges posed by the programme.

Policy challenges

Deciding the appropriate intervention for abusive fathers is a challenge for both referrers and commissioners. One question they need to ask is whether a referral to a programme focused on parenting behaviour could inadvertently support the continuation of perhaps unwanted contact with an abusive parent (Holt 2015). Certainly, any fathering intervention failing to emphasise respectful and non-abusive co-parenting as integral to being a good father, or that does not address ongoing domestic abuse, would be unhelpful and could expose children to further conflict. Some writers emphasise that before attempting to improve fathering, referrers need to ensure children and partners are safe from abuse and are free to make decisions about the extent of their involvement with him (Labarre *et al.* 2016). However, others maintain that achieving this requires intervention *with him*, his role as a co-parent can motivate him to change, and if we do not try to stop abusive and neglectful fathering when we have an opportunity, we merely postpone risk or pass it on to other children in the father's life.

Abusive fathers frequently present a range of different issues that cannot be easily separated and do not necessarily fit existing models of service. As is the case in Canada, where the Caring Dads programmes were set up to work in partnership alongside domestic violence perpetrator programmes (DVPPs), an assessment of a father for Caring Dads can result in a referral for a DVPP or a substance misuse service, if that is judged to be the most appropriate intervention needed at that time. Risks and circumstances differ, and so therefore should interventions. Anecdotally, though, it seems that costs and availability of services determine referral and commissioning decisions as much as considered assessment of evidence and need. There has been much debate within the UK about the extent to which Caring Dads can address partner abuse (Featherstone and Fraser 2012), and what circumstances should determine whether an abusive father is referred to a Caring Dads programme or a DVPP. A joint statement released by Caring Dads and Respect, the organisation that accredits DVPPs within the UK, has tried to address this by stating:

> DVPPs are designed primarily to address violence and abuse in intimate relationships, whereas Caring Dads is designed to focus on the fathering and co-parenting relationships of men who have exposed their children to domestic violence and/or abused or neglected

> their children. (Joint statement between Caring Dads and Respect, November 2016)

This joint statement makes explicit that, while the two programmes have shared goals, they are 'complementary but different interventions. They are not interchangeable and one should not be used as a substitute for the other.' In many locations within the UK, the problem is less that the appropriate intervention for the typology of perpetrators is unavailable, but more likely that no interventions for perpetrators are available. Even if longer programmes like Caring Dads and DVPPs (minimum six months) can demonstrate efficacy, at a time of reduced public spending, commissioners with limited budgets may be inclined to overlook work with perpetrators or consider shorter, cheaper alternatives (HACRO 2016), particularly when funding for refuge and recovery services is also reduced (Women's Aid 2014).

Practice challenges

The two practice challenges identified during the CDSC evaluation were, first, the ability of group facilitators to engage fathers and second, the complex and sensitive work with the fathers' families. It was very important to have a common understanding and a close working relationship between the group facilitators and the partner/family engagement workers within the CDSC team. Together both sides can provide a fuller picture of what is happening within the family, which can inform the group work and also other agencies supporting the family. However, this was difficult to achieve as the two groups of workers were sometimes presented with very different stories that would need to be explored safely and sensitively. CDSC practitioners needed to have a particular set of skills: confident when working with men, a comprehensive understanding of domestic abuse, group work skills and an ability to gain the trust of resistant group participants. Other factors considered useful to practice were: having a non-judgemental attitude; using motivational interviewing techniques to encourage fathers to identify their own positive reasons for changing; retaining a focus on the child's needs to motivate both themselves and the father to persevere; and being able to recognise whether the father is ready to change at the time he is referred. Another challenge to practice identified by UK programmes since is the difficulty in recruiting and retaining suitable male workers.

Research challenges

Providing evidence of effectiveness is problematic for fathering programmes like Caring Dads. As with perpetrator programmes, the evaluation is hampered by high levels of attrition, difficulties in engaging very resistant perpetrators (NICE 2014), and maintaining contact with participants for follow-up measures. Attrition with CDSC, while not atypical for programmes of this type (Donovan and Griffiths 2015), meant that large numbers of men are assessed before sufficient numbers completing the programme are available to be evaluated quantitatively. Problems with sample size are magnified when the evaluation attempts to measure outcomes for the father's children. Not all partners will consent to their participation, and if they do, there are very few measurement tools available to measure outcomes for infants and very young children exposed to domestic abuse, who represented a large proportion of the fathers' children. It is also difficult to compare the effectiveness of different programmes, as there is currently little consensus on outcome measurement for children exposed to abuse (Howarth *et al.* 2016).

Some practitioners felt that the evaluation process inhibited their practise. For example, they felt that the time required explaining the process, informed consent, plus the number and length of the standardised measures, created an unsatisfactory beginning to a programme for a group of fathers who were often already wary and resistant to engage. Similarly for the workers meeting families, the requirement to collect baseline data sometimes meant that practitioners felt they had to introduce questionnaires before they had a chance to build a relationship with the families, with some questions in particular feeling overly intrusive (McConnell and Taylor 2016).

Programme evaluation is often reliant on group participants' self-reports or official data, both of which may underestimate the extent of abuse. Therefore, involving families within the evaluation of CDSC is invaluable, providing it is done in circumstances where they are able to talk freely, and does not increase risks to their wellbeing or compromise their right to privacy and ability to 'get on with their lives' (Gondolf 2000). Involving families enabled the evaluation of the programme from the perspective of its intended beneficiaries. As demonstrated by the differences in scores obtained from fathers and those reported by partners and children using the same measure, father's self-reports on the extent of their abuse alone are unsatisfactory because they frequently minimise the extent of the abuse (Gondolf 2002). Although the sample of children old enough to participate was relatively small, CDSC is unusual because it included the perspectives of children living in a household where the perpetrator of domestic abuse is also still living in the family home. Most studies exclude the broader experience of children living with domestic abuse and its varying severity and forms: either because the study uses adult reports of children's behaviour or because the sample of children recruited are those receiving crisis or post-abuse services, and are therefore more likely to have been exposed to serious physical violence (Kimball 2016).

CONCLUSION

Although not without limitations (McConnell, Barnard and Taylor 2017), the evaluation of CDSC provides a further step towards establishing an evidence base for the Caring Dads programme outside of Canada. Using fatherhood as a way to motivate perpetrators of domestic abuse to reflect on the impact of their behaviour appears to change the behaviour of some fathers who complete the programme, but undoubtedly should be part of a range of approaches needed to prevent and protect against further domestic abuse. Future studies could involve more comprehensive follow-up and stronger research designs, building on what has been learned about outcome measures, likely attrition and participation in the evaluation by fathers' families.

REFERENCES

Abidin, R.R. (1995) *Manual for the Parenting Stress Index*. 3rd Edition. Lutz, FL: Psychological Assessment Resources.

DfE (Department for Education) (2014) *Characteristics of Children in Need: 2013–2014*. SFR 43/2014. London: DfE.

DH (Department of Health) (2000) *Framework for the Assessment of Children in Need and Their Families*. London: The Stationery Office.

DHSSPS (Department of Health, Social Services and Public Safety) (2014) *Children's Social Care Statistics for Northern Ireland 2013/14*. Belfast: DHSSPS.

Donovan, C. and Griffiths, S. (2015) 'Domestic violence and voluntary perpetrator programmes: Engaging men in the pre-commencement phase.' *British Journal of Social Work 45*, 4, 1155–1171.

Featherstone, B. and Fraser C. (2012) 'Working with fathers around domestic violence: Contemporary debates.' *Child Abuse Review 21*, 255–263.

Gondolf, E. (2000) 'Human subject issues in batterer program evaluation.' *Journal of Aggression, Maltreatment and Trauma 4*, 1, 273–297. doi: 10.1300/J146v04n01_12

Gondolf, E. (2002) *Batterer Intervention Systems: Issues, Outcomes, and Recommendations*. Thousand Oaks, CA: Sage Publications.

Goodman, R. (1997) 'The Strengths and Difficulties Questionnaire: A research note.' *Journal of Child Psychology and Psychiatry 38*, 5, 581–586.

HACRO (2016) *Annual Report 2015–16*. Hertford: HACRO.

Holt, S. (2015) 'Focusing on Fathering in the Context of Domestic Abuse: Children's and Fathers' Perspectives.' In N. Stanley and C. Humphreys (eds) *Domestic Violence and Protecting Children: New Thinking and Approaches* (pp.166–181). London: Jessica Kingsley Publishers.

Hood, R., Lindsay, J. and Muleya, W. (2014) *Evaluation of Caring Dads: A Single Site Evaluation in an Urban Local Authority. Interim Report.* London: Faculty of Health, Social Care and Education, Kingston University, and St George's, University of London. Unpublished.

Howarth, E., Moore, T.H.M., Welton, N.J., Lewis, N. *et al.* (2016) 'IMPRoving Outcomes for children exposed to domestic ViolencE (IMPROVE): An evidence synthesis.' *Public Health Research 4*, 10.

Kaur, R. and Frost, N. (2014) *Caring Dads: Helping Fathers Value Their Children. Evaluation of a Pilot Study in Leeds.* Unpublished.

Kimball, E. (2016) 'Edleson revisited: Reviewing children's witnessing of domestic violence 15 years later.' *Journal of Family Violence 31*, 5, 625–637.

Koch, M., Liel, C. and Eickhorst, A. (2017) *Arbeit mit Vätern zur Prävention von Kindesmisshandlung. Eine Pilotevaluation des Caring Dads Programms in Deutschland* [*Working with Fathers to Prevent Child Maltreatment. A Pilot Evaluation of the Caring Dads Programme in Germany*]. Munich: National Centre on Early Prevention.

Labarre, M., Bourassa, C., Holden, G.W., Turcotte, P. and Letourneau, N. (2016) 'Intervening with fathers in the context of intimate partner violence: An analysis of ten programs and suggestions for a research agenda.' *Journal of Child Custody 13*, 1, 1–29.

Lindsay, J., Atkins, C. and Matczak, A. (2010) *Evaluation of the Piloting of the Caring Dads Programme in London, England (2006–2010).* London Probation. Unpublished.

McCracken, K. and Deave, T. (2012) *Evaluation of the Caring Dads Cymru Programme.* Merthyr Tydfil: Welsh Government Social Research.

McConnell, N. and Taylor, J. (2016) 'Evaluating programmes for violent fathers: Challenges and ethical review.' *Child Abuse Review 25*, 183–191. doi: http://dx.doi.org/10.1002/car.2342"10.1002/car.2342

McConnell, N., Barnard, M. and Taylor, J. (2017) 'Caring Dads Safer Children: Families' perspectives on an intervention for maltreating fathers.' *Psychology of Violence*, 23 March. doi:#http://dx.doi.org/10.1037/vio0000105

McConnell, N., Barnard, M., Holdsworth, T. and Taylor, J. (2016a) *Caring Dads: Safer Children. Evaluation Report.* London: NSPCC.

McConnell, N., Cotmore, R., Hunter, D. and Taylor, J. (2016b) *Caring Dads: Safer Children. Learning from Delivering the Programme.* London: NSPCC.

NICE (National Institute for Care and Health Excellence) (2014) *Domestic Violence and Abuse: How Health Services, Social Care and the Organisations They Work with Can Respond Effectively. Gaps-in-the-evidence. I. Guidance and Guidelines.* London: NICE.

ONS (Office for National Statistics) (2013) *Release Edition Reference Tables: 2011 Census, Key Statistics and Quick Statistics for Local Authorities in the United Kingdom – Part 1.* London: ONS.

Radford, L., Corral, S., Bradley, C., Fisher, H.*et al.* (2011) *Child Abuse and Neglect in the UK Today.* London: NSPCC.

Rohner, R.P. and Khaleque, A. (2005) *Handbook for the Study of Parental Acceptance and Rejection.* Storrs, CT: Rohner Research.

Scott, K.L. (2010) *Caring Dad Theory Manual.* Accessed on 3/8/2017 at www.caringdads.org/images/stories/caring-dads-theory-manual.pdf

Scott, K.L. and Lishak, V. (2012) 'Intervention for maltreating fathers: Statistically and clinically significant change.' *Child Abuse and Neglect 36*, 9, 680–684.

Stanley, N., Graham Kevan, N. and Borthwick, R. (2012) 'Fathers and domestic violence: Building motivation for change through perpetrator programmes.' *Child Abuse Review 21*, 4, 264–274.

Stover, C.S. (2013) 'Fathers for change: A new approach to working with fathers who perpetrate intimate partner violence.' *The Journal of the American Academy of Psychiatry and the Law 41*, 1, 65.

Welsh Government (2015) *Children in Need Census.* Cardiff: StatsWales.

Women's Aid (2014) *Why We Need to Save Our Services: Women's Aid Data Report on Specialist Domestic Violence Services in England.* Bristol: Women's Aid.

Part Three

NEW UNDERSTANDINGS ON DOMESTIC ABUSE AND VIOLENCE

Chapter 9

STRENGTH THROUGH SOLIDARITY

PRACTITIONERS AND PARENTS RESISTING CHILD TO PARENT VIOLENCE AND ABUSE IN IRELAND

Declan Coogan, *Lecturer in Social Work, NUI Galway, Ireland*

INTRODUCTION

Child to parent violence and abuse (CPVA) is a pattern of behaviour and an abuse of power through which a son or daughter under the age of 18 coerces, controls or dominates parents or carers. Initially identified as 'battered parent syndrome' (Harbin and Madden 1979), the recent emergence of a growing body of literature research from Ireland, Europe and further afield has enabled us to glance behind the 'veil of silence' surrounding CPVA (e.g. Coogan and Holt 2015; Holt 2016; Ibabe, Jaureguizar and Bentler 2013). Yet there is still a lot to do – the focus of policy, research and intervention development into abuse within familial and intimate relationships has been almost exclusively on child abuse/neglect or domestic violence committed by adults rather than on abusive and violent behaviour within families carried out by children and adolescents (Lyons *et al.* 2015).

In response, this chapter offers practitioners, researchers and those involved with policy development a clear definition of CPVA and focuses on Non Violent Resistance as a model of intervention. This chapter also highlights key messages from European and international literature on CPVA. In particular, this chapter draws on research recently completed by myself, the 'Child to Parent Violence – An Exploration of Non Violent Resistance' (Coogan 2016a) study, hereafter referred to as *Exploring NVR*. This study explored the experiences and perceptions of child and family practitioners in Ireland as they integrate the Non Violent Resistance model into their work with families living with CPVA.

CONTESTED DEFINITIONS OF CPVA

The abusive and/or violent behaviours used by some children towards their parents are part of a continuum of indirect and direct attacks on parents. Indirect attacks can include damage to property and/or threats of self-harm. At their most extreme, direct attacks involve physical assault and/or the use of weapons such as knives that can require medical attention. But there is no single definition of what constitutes CPVA.[1] Difficulties in defining CPVA reflect challenges in the broader field of violence within family relationships; people living with domestic violence may be reluctant to identify their experiences as abusive, while practitioners and researchers frequently highlight the importance of awareness-raising and of identifying as abusive the experiences of those who are targets of abusive and/or violent behaviour. Parents experiencing CPVA tend to speak about fear, shame and being unable to control their child (Coogan 2014; Selwyn and Meakings 2015).[2]

Many definitions of CPVA are based on the work of Cottrell (2001), who described it as a harmful act carried out by a child with the intention to cause physical, psychological or financial pain or to exert power and control over a parent (e.g. Calvete, Orue and Gamez-Guadix 2013; Ibabe *et al.* 2013). This draws attention to the dynamics of power and control and the different types of harm involved in CPVA.

The alternative definition advocated in the introduction to this chapter seems to fit with the complex characteristics of the problem as reflected in accounts emerging from more recent literature derived from research and practise. There are a number of reasons supporting the use of this definition in policy, practise and research.

First, this definition encompasses a wide range of abusive behaviours, including acts of physical violence and controlling tactics. Second, it

---

1 For an overview of the literature on CPVA, see Cottrell and Monk (2004), Coogan (2011, 2016a) and Holt (2013, 2016).

2 For the sake of clarity and to avoid repetition, for the remainder of this chapter, 'parent' or 'child' is used to refer to anyone with parental responsibility for a legal minor or to an individual under the age of 18, respectively.

includes anyone acting in the role of a parent/guardian, such as a step-parent or foster-parent. Third, it underscores the fact that it is the parent who feels disempowered and is the target of the abusive and/or violent behaviour by the child/adolescent under the age of 18. Conceptualising CPVA as an abuse of power also facilitates a self-defining approach to a definition of experiences of violence within the family – that is, a child or adolescent's behaviour should be considered as CPVA if family members feel controlled, intimidated or threatened by it, and if they feel they must adapt their own behaviour because of threats or use of abuse or violence (Paterson *et al.* 2002; Wilcox 2012).

Adolescence can be regarded as a time of tensions between parental authority and an adolescent's increasing need for autonomy and independence when conflict patterns between parents and children become established (Edenborough *et al.* 2008). Pagani *et al.* (2009) draw attention to the heightened tensions between parents and their adolescent children revolving around conflict about responsibilities, money and privileges that can lead to violence and abuse. Pagani *et al.* (2009) and Omer (2004, 2011) suggest that a cycle of escalation and coercion between parent and child may develop, in which higher levels of aggression become part of what had been familiar conflict patterns between the child and the parent within the family. This can lead to the emergence of adolescent violence towards parents and the disempowerment of parents. The definition proposed in this chapter clarifies a distinguishing line between CPVA and troublesome behaviours that could be seen as falling within 'normative' childhood or adolescent behaviour where parental authority is challenged. Parents do not usually feel disempowered by and fearful of their children, as occurs with CPVA.

Finally, this definition removes the concept of 'intention', marking a clear distinction between CPVA and domestic violence while also recognising that CPVA may be used for complicated and for instrumental and/or expressive/reactive reasons. This is consistent with authors such as Gallagher (2008) and Ibabe and Jaureguizar (2010), who suggest that the use of CPVA by a son/daughter may be associated with experiences of trauma or reactive to experiences and/or threats of physical abuse or acts of domestic violence towards mothers.

The following section identifies some key messages from European Union (EU) and international research relating to CPVA.

THE NATURE AND EXTENT OF CPVA

CPVA emerges in a wide range of cultural contexts, family compositions and socioeconomic backgrounds, as reflected, for example, in literature from Canada (Lyons *et al.* 2015), Ireland (Lauster *et al.* 2014), Israel (Weinblatt and Omer 2008), Spain (Calvete *et al.* 2013; Ibabe *et al.* 2013), the UK (Condry and Miles 2014) and the US (Cottrell and Monk 2004; Walsh and Krienert 2009).

Research and interventions relating to CPVA are at the early stages of development (Holt 2016; Wilcox *et al.* 2015). With the exceptions of studies referred to below, there is a lack of contemporary empirical research, a reliance on small sample clinical and case study papers and contradictory and inconclusive findings relating to variables such as gender, race, age, relationship and substance use (Edenborough *et al.* 2008; Walsh and Krienert 2009).

Pagani *et al.* (2009) studied adolescent verbal and physical aggression towards fathers in a randomised sample of 2908 children selected for follow-up annually from kindergarten to mid-adolescence as part of a large longitudinal child development study in Québec. They found that among the male and female 15/16-year-old participants in the study, 12.3 per cent of males and 9.5 per cent of females had been physically aggressive towards their father in the previous six months.

In the first empirical study of CPVA in the UK, Condry and Miles (2014) found that, between April 2009 and March 2010, the London Metropolitan Police recorded 1892 cases of violence from adolescents (aged between 13 and 19) towards their parents. Most incidents involved assaults against the person or criminal damage in the home. The vast majority of adolescents reported to the police for violent offences against parents were male (87.3%), and more than three-quarters of the parents reporting to the police were females/mothers (77.5%).

There have been increasing concerns relating to CPVA in Spain. Calvete *et al.* (2013) report that the number of complaints recorded by the State Public Prosecutor's Office by parents against their children increased from 1627 in 2006 to 5377 only five years later in 2011. There is now legislation in Spain that provides for an order restraining an adolescent, similar to measures applied in cases of domestic violence (Calvete *et al.* 2013).

Between 2013 and 2015, a team of researchers and practitioners from Bulgaria, England, Ireland, Spain and Sweden implemented the EU co-funded action research study, the Responding to Child to

Parent Violence (RCPV) project.[3] It investigated CPVA and responses to it in these five EU nations, reporting that CPVA is increasingly coming to the attention of practitioners in a range of services in those nations, many of whom feel inadequately equipped and resourced to respond effectively to the problems associated with CPVA (Wilcox *et al.* 2015). Practitioners and academics in the study called for the urgent development of policies and practise at EU and national levels to address this problem. Wilcox *et al.* (2015) also reported that some practitioners who spoke to researchers found it difficult to accept that parents could be victimised by their own children, and that many practitioners were not asking about experiences of CPVA, contributing to the hidden nature of the problem.[4]

Although our understanding of gender and CPVA is still evolving, gendered patterns are usually identified in CPVA (Gallagher 2008; Wilcox *et al.* 2015). Mothers seem to be targeted more often than fathers for abusive and violent behaviour from their children. For example, in studies in the US (Boxer, Gullan and Mahoney 2009; Walsh and Krienert 2009) and in the UK (Condry and Miles 2014), mothers report to authorities such as the police and to researchers that they have been targets for CPVA more often than fathers. Cultural norms and values relating to gender and masculinity may affect reports of CPVA where fathers may be more reluctant to report experiences of CPVA (Condry and Miles 2014). Reflecting on the experiences of mothers who were targets of CPVA in Melbourne, Australia, Edenborough *et al.* (2008, 2011) observe that mothers mostly struggled in silence with this problem, and that their experiences were often minimised by their family and community, leaving mothers without support.

A review of relevant literature could lead to the impression that CPVA is primarily a problem for Western cultures and societies. But, as Holt (2016) points out, we cannot view CPVA in this way – it has also been recorded in Colombia, Egypt, South Korea, Sri Lanka and Taiwan.

In the next section of this chapter, practitioners' understanding of the problem in earlier studies in Ireland and the UK are explored, and a description of the Non Violent Resistance intervention model

3 See www.rcpv.eu

4 In the interests of clarity, I draw the attention of the reader to the fact that I was one of the partners involved in the RCPV project.

(hereafter NVR) is provided before our attention turns to the *Exploring NVR* study.

PRACTITIONERS' PERCEPTIONS OF CPVA IN AN EARLIER STUDY IN IRELAND

Although there are no empirical studies relating to the prevalence of CPVA in Ireland, the problem has been explored to some extent in the work of McMahon (2013), O'Rourke (2013), Lauster *et al.* (2014) and by Lauster and myself (Coogan 2014, 2016b; Coogan and Lauster 2015). In the absence of any prevalence data, Parentline, a national telephone support service for parents/carers in Ireland, reports a significant increase in recent years in the number of telephone calls relating to CPVA, with these calls mostly being made by mothers (O'Reilly 2014).

The O'Rourke (2013) study was based on interviews with seven child protection social workers in the North West region of Ireland, all of whom had encountered CPVA in their practise. Participants regarded the child using CPVA as a 'victim', and attributed the use of violence by the child to a variety of factors such as poor parental capacity, the child's earlier experience of violence at home, parental alcohol misuse and attachment and/or learning/mental health difficulties in the child. O'Rourke emphasises the need for specific training for practitioners concerning CPVA. She also argues that the problem would be easier to recognise and constructive responses would be more likely if incidents of CPVA were identified as such in the records of statutory child protection and welfare services.

There are interesting parallels between the observations of participants in the O'Rourke (2013) study in Ireland and the findings of two studies exploring CPVA in the UK. Social work participants in the study by Nixon (2012) and some of the participants in the Holt and Retford (2012) study did not regard children using abusive/violent behaviour towards parents as abusive. Instead, they preferred to use terms such as 'challenging behaviour' and related the problem to 'poor parenting'. The participants in both of these UK studies identified CPVA as a significant practise issue, with a lack of training or interventions specifically designed to address CPVA and the need for a multi-agency response to it.

As in the two UK-based studies described above, increasing referrals relating to CPVA and the absence of training or structured interventions in response to CPVA were identified as concerns by participants in the O'Rourke (2013) study. The *Exploring NVR* study (Coogan 2016a) responds to these concerns by developing training and by exploring in depth the ways in which child and family health and social care practitioners in three geographical areas in Ireland understand and respond to CPVA and to the NVR intervention model.

The section that follows provides an overview of NVR as adapted in Ireland and developed as an integral part of the *Exploring NVR* study.

AN OUTLINE OF THE NVR MODEL IN IRELAND

Weinblatt and Omer (2008), Omer (2011) and Coogan (2017) provide a more comprehensive description of NVR as a response to the abusive/violent behaviour of children and adolescents. In summary, NVR is an evidence-based, non-blaming, systemic and relatively short-term intervention model that empowers parents and practitioners to take action in response to CPVA while respecting and protecting children and adults (Gieniusz 2014; Lauster *et al.* 2014; Weinblatt and Omer 2008).

Within the NVR model there is a clear distinction between understanding a problem (as related, perhaps, to childhood experiences of abuse or to mental health difficulties, for example) and (not) accepting abusive behaviour. The task of the practitioner using NVR in practise is to act as a type of adviser/coach for parents. The practitioner supports parents to develop skills for de-escalation, self-control, resistance and protest, and assists them in recruiting and coordinating the Support Network, empowering parents to take their place as a parent in the family. Parents commit to avoiding all forms of abuse and violence (including humiliation), and make a clear announcement to the family that specific types of behaviour are no longer acceptable. A clear distinction is also made between abusive and violent behaviour (which is rejected and resisted) and the child who is treated with respect and love as a member of the family. Parents increase their positive presence in their child's life and make acts of reconciliation, regardless of the response of a son or daughter.

'New authority' and the Support Network

Implementing NVR is challenging for parents and for practitioners. But the NVR model is underpinned by a robust rationale – the concept of 'new authority'. Reflecting contemporary ideals in Western societies of responsive and sensitive parenting, 'new authority' is based on the authorisation of the parent's role that comes from members of the Support Network – a group of supportive adults chosen by parents (Omer *et al.* 2013). This Support Network encourages the parent to increase their parental presence by resuming emotional closeness and presence in the child's life while taking a determined and persistent stance against any aggressive or violent behaviour. Supporters also provide a forum of accountability, as the parent commits to them to respond in a fair and non-violent way to the child's behaviour. Omer *et al.* (2013) describe this as a process of re-authorisation through which parents' authority is reaffirmed by a support system that also ensures transparency and limits the arbitrary exercise of authority.

After a family announcement by parents about the unacceptability of the use of violence and abuse by anyone in the family, supporters contact or meet the child to let him/her know that they are aware of the impact of violence/abuse in the family and that they support the parent(s') commitment to resist violence and abuse.

Having summarised the NVR model as a response to CPVA, we now focus on the ways in which practitioners who took part in the *Exploring NVR* study conceptualise CPVA and their perceptions of NVR as a response to CPVA.

The Exploring Non Violent Resistance (NVR) study: an action research project

As an intervention model for CPVA, I piloted NVR in Ireland while working with colleagues and families as a social worker and family therapist in a child and adolescent mental health service in Dublin, Ireland. The *Exploring NVR* study was initiated as a response to requests from practitioners for training so that they could adopt the NVR model in their work with families who were also living with CPVA.[5] Building on the work of Omer in Israel (Omer 2004, 2011), I developed a two-day practitioner training programme in NVR for intervention with CPVA.

The *Exploring NVR* study was developed as a constructivist grounded theory action research project. Herr and Anderson (2015) describe action research as research carried out by or in collaboration with practitioners or community members who have a stake or an interest in the problem that is the focus of the research. The research problem (CPVA) was a priority issue for the practitioners who took part in the *Exploring NVR* study. Reflecting the principles of action research, the study design and intervention (the two-day training programme) was developed as a response to the needs of and in collaboration with managers and senior practitioners in the agencies, who asked me to develop and deliver training in NVR for practitioners encountering CPVA in their practise with families.

The study was approved by the Research Ethics Committee at the National University of Ireland (NUI), Galway. The research design incorporated a mixed-methods model; data was gathered through quantitative questionnaires that investigated components of practitioners' perceived self-efficacy. These questionnaires were developed as part of the *Exploring NVR* study and were distributed to all practitioners who attended NVR training at the beginning (Time 1), end (Time 2) and follow-up periods of 3–4 months (Time 3) after the training. Data was also gathered through qualitative interviews that explored practitioners' perceptions and experiences of CPVA and NVR. The issues explored throughout the study were derived from the three central research questions:

1. How do child and family practitioners engage with, assess and intervene with child to parent violence?
2. What is the response of child and family practitioners to the adapted Non Violent Resistance programme?
3. What, if any, is the effect of the two-day training programme on Non Violent Resistance on practitioner self-efficacy in relation to child to parent violence?

---

5 The study and the training programme are described in more detail in Coogan (2016a, b, 2017).

THE RESEARCH POPULATION AND RESEARCH QUESTIONS FOR THE *EXPLORING NVR* STUDY

Recruited from statutory and voluntary services, the research participants were qualified practitioners in social work, psychology, family support or social care with varying levels of experience who had requested training in NVR. In total, 75 practitioners took part in the two-day training programme. The researcher facilitated the training at one site in Dublin and two sites in the West of Ireland. The Self-Efficacy Questionnaires referred to earlier were completed by 63 of the 75 practitioners at Time 1 and Time 2. Participants were also requested to complete and return questionnaires at Time 3.

Everyone who attended the training was invited to volunteer to take part in research interviews. Interviewees were randomly chosen from a list of those who had volunteered. Nineteen practitioners from three different agency contexts in Ireland were interviewed up to four months after their participation in the training. The typed transcripts of the interviews were analysed according to the principles and practises of grounded theory (Corbin and Strauss 2008).

Thirteen of the 19 practitioners who were interviewed as part of the *Exploring NVR* study were female and six were male. Twelve of the interview participants were employed as family workers on four different teams in a voluntary child and family support agency in Dublin; within this agency a further three individuals in this group were managers on different teams, who also worked with parents and children as part of their duties. A further three of the interviewees worked as social workers with the national statutory child protection and welfare service in Ireland. One of the interviewees was a practitioner with a child and adolescent mental health service in the West of Ireland.

The following section draws on the qualitative interview data in the study. The names used to refer to their comments are pseudonyms. The further information in Table 9.1 has been presented in a manner that protects participant identities.

Table 9.1: Qualitative interview, research participants – demographic information

Role (*n*)	Gender	Agency context	Location
Family worker (11)	9 females 2 males	Voluntary service	Dublin, NVR training site 1
Manager, child and family service (3)	3 males	Voluntary service	Dublin, NVR training site 1
Family support worker (1)	1 female	Voluntary service	West of Ireland, NVR training site 2
Clinical psychology (1)	1 female	Statutory service	West of Ireland, NVR training site 2
Children and families social worker (3)	2 females 1 male	Statutory service	West of Ireland, NVR training site 3

FINDINGS FROM THE *EXPLORING NVR* STUDY

Qualitative and quantitative findings indicated that the NVR training significantly increased practitioner understanding of the problem and perceived self-efficacy in responding to CPVA. Interview participants articulated an understanding of CPVA as a complex problem, related to parent–child conflict and in some cases to parenting difficulties and/or family problems such as domestic violence, school attendance and/or mental health difficulties.

Some understood CPVA as one way that children respond to problems within the family. As Carrie, a practitioner with a voluntary child to family service, remarks:

> 'You can often find that, you know, it's always a family problem, it's not the child's problem. You know the violence might be the manifestation of a bigger issue. There might be drinking in the house or there might be triggers there and that's how the child is reacting.'

Participants usually articulated what could be described as a systemic conceptualisation of the problem of CPVA. For example, some understood CPVA as being related to a child or parent's mental health difficulties, which have an impact throughout the family and especially on the parent–child relationship. Although interview participants in the *Exploring NVR* study often explicitly described CPVA as taking place in the context of a range of interpersonal and/or family difficulties, there was never any suggestion by any of the participants that CPVA is an acceptable or excusable response to individual/family difficulties.

Although there are important differences between domestic violence and CPVA, there are some similarities too. For example, the tactics of abuse/violence are similar, as are the effects on the person targeted for abuse/violence and the sense of self-blame, isolation and shame experienced by those who are targeted (Miles and Condry 2015; Wilcox 2012). But participants in the *Exploring NVR* study avoided the use of terms such as 'crime', 'victims' and 'perpetrators', situating the problem within a parent–child conflict/relationship framework and identifying NVR as a method of intervention that assists parents in changing the ways in which they understand and respond to their abusive and/or violent behaviour.

Several participants referred in passing to previous training in responding to domestic violence, but only one referred to CPVA as a form of domestic violence. In Ireland, parents experiencing CPVA are not the primary concern of any service, and any response that is offered is on a localised and ad hoc basis. In this context, the absence of an understanding of CPVA as a form of domestic violence could reflect the blurring of the boundaries of responsibility and blame in CPVA described by Condry and Miles (2014). In domestic violence, the categories of blame, victim/survivor and perpetrator are easily identifiable, but this is not the case in CPVA where children may also be survivors of child abuse and/or domestic violence. Condry and Miles (2014) advocate further work on the utility of different theoretical frameworks to address the complexities of CPVA. If CPVA is considered as a form of domestic violence, then the question of whether feminist conceptual frameworks for domestic violence are applicable to CPVA needs further discussion. CPVA inverts the power dynamic usually expected in parent–child relationships and, apart from exceptional circumstances, parents usually retain legal responsibility to care for their children and are unlikely to leave the family home.

PRACTITIONERS' PERCEPTIONS OF THE SUPPORT NETWORK

Since the research interviews took place up to four months after participants attended the NVR training, practitioners had the opportunity to integrate NVR into their practise, if they so wished.

Interviewees perceived the involvement of a Support Network by parents as playing an essential role in ending CPVA. Participants also believed that, combined with practitioner support, the Support Network empowered parents to respond differently to their child and to resist abusive/violent behaviour. For example, Ellen, a practitioner in a voluntary child and family support service, describes the positive impact on parents of involving supporters:

> 'She [a mother] said she felt afterwards she just felt like for the first time that she felt so held by her family and by people, you know, that she wasn't on her own...that was huge for her...They [the supporters] would take the lead from her because, you know, parents maybe haven't been able to take their place as a parent in their own family quite often and they are quite empowered as well [through their implementation of the NVR model].'

Perhaps a parent's sense of 'feeling held' by others in the Support Network increases her/his self-confidence and legitimises parental authority in cultures where parents may feel blame, shame and stigma when their son or daughter displays violent behaviour. This sense of 'feeling held' could also be related to the ways in which practitioners, among others, can actively support parents by 'doing hope' and by joining in solidarity with parents and supporters in actively resisting abuse and violence. The idea of 'doing hope' (Fredman 2014) refers to creative and hope-filled interactions between practitioners and clients that can help dissolve the hopelessness and paralysis related to complex problems in families and in relationships.

DOES NVR WORK IN IRELAND?

The findings from the qualitative and quantitative data in the *Exploring NVR* study suggest that practitioners in Ireland who attended the training and implemented it in their practise experienced NVR as an empowering, useful and structured response to CPVA. For example, Samantha, a practitioner with a voluntary child and family service, remarks:

> 'You know, it is solution-focused – and it's kind of looking at the strengths of the family. Trying to help the family identify what's

working or what has worked in the past... I suppose overall I found it's been quite positive.'

This is echoed by Ciara, a child protection practitioner, who reflects on the difference NVR can make in family relationships:

> 'You know, this different approach, this different thinking method, can really change the setting of the home environment, you know, and it can alleviate these mad outbursts that lead to such aggression and family breakdown.'

SUPPORT FROM MANAGERS AND PEERS

Participants described the significance of support from management and peers in responding to CPVA and implementing NVR in practise. Some explicitly identified the need for ongoing training and supervision, interagency awareness of the problem and the positive support of managers for responding to CPVA and using NVR. Kate, a child protection practitioner, describes what she identifies as essential supports for any practitioner working with CPVA:

> '...good supervision, that it's, maybe your supervisor is familiar with the model and is supporting the use of it and is clear on how you are using it and is talking you through it in supervision. That would definitely help alright. And maybe I think the agency as a whole having it [NVR] as one of the things we can use.'

RESEARCH AND INTERVENTION LIMITATIONS

As a piece of research, there are a number of limitations that apply to the *Exploring NVR* study described in this chapter. The research participants were not recruited through a random sampling procedure, and a randomised controlled trial design was not adopted for the study. As a small-scale exploratory study, the findings cannot be generalised to other circumstances where practitioners are working with CPVA.

Yet the study does not claim to speak to the perceptions of child and family practitioners anywhere else. Instead, consistent with the principles of grounded theory and action research methods, the *Exploring NVR* study presents credible and convincing accounts of the ways in which the research participants understand and respond to CPVA as practitioners working in the context of health and social care services in Ireland. Central to the perceptions of the practitioners is the idea of 'support'. From their perspectives, the availability of support determined whether or not the problem of CPVA is resolved. Participants also viewed the NVR model and training as support for their practise, providing them with the means of empowering parents to act to resist and respond to CPVA.

The findings of the *Exploring NVR* study could also be limited by the fact that interview participants were self-selecting volunteers and none rejected the model as a method of intervention, perhaps conscious of the fact that they were speaking with the facilitator of the training. However, the data gathered through the anonymously completed quantitative questionnaires lends further validity to the reported overall positive perceptions of the NVR training.

As a model of intervention, NVR is not specifically designed to address issues such as, for example, alcohol/drug abuse and/or homelessness. It does not replace the expertise that individual practitioners or specific agencies have developed to respond to complex difficulties. But NVR can be offered as a model of intervention to parents in addition to interventions and/or advocacy designed to meet a range of different needs (Coogan 2011; Omer 2004). Omer and Dolberger (2015), for example, describe the use of NVR with parents where a child threatens to commit suicide, referring to research that supports the use of NVR where there are severe forms of psychopathology.

CPVA AND NVR: CHALLENGES FOR RESEARCH, POLICY AND PRACTISE

The emergence of CPVA as an increasingly reported social problem challenges us to think differently about violence within the family. Practitioners and parents report that parents frequently feel isolated and fear that reporting CPVA could make matters much worse (Selwyn and Meakings 2015; Wilcox *et al.* 2015). Additional factors that contribute to the challenges in resolving CPVA include the difficulties some practitioners have in accepting that parents can be victimised by their own child and many not asking about CPVA (Wilcox *et al.* 2015), and the reported tendency of practitioners to blame parents when a child needs to be moved from home due to CPVA (Selwyn and Meakings 2015). Such findings are hardly surprising where there are significant gaps in research and where CPVA tends to be absent in policy and training for practitioners in the EU and internationally.

There is a need for the inclusion of CPVA-specific training for practitioners, researchers and policy-makers so that the problem can be better identified and understood, and so that innovative responses such as NVR can be made more readily available for families living with CPVA. Given the lack of visibility of CPVA in policy and practise development, there is also a need for the development of protocols and policies to routinely record incidences and reports of CPVA as distinct from other types of referral categories to a range of children and family services.

An NVR response to CPVA is not the only model of intervention for this type of violence within the family.[6] As a model of intervention, NVR complements the existing knowledge, skills and values of practitioners working in health and social care settings with children and families. Although further research is required, practitioners in the *Exploring NVR* study suggest that an increase in parental presence, a different understanding of parental authority and the active support of individuals chosen by the parent(s) effectively resolves the problem of CPVA in families. Future research could explore the perceptions of parents and children of the problem of CPVA and their experience of a relatively short-term and solution-focused intervention such as NVR.

Thinking about violence in the family from bio-ecological (Bronfenbrenner and Evans 2000) and intersectional perspectives (Sokoloff 2008), NVR seems to effectively activate different levels of support for resisting CPVA, built on the strength and solidarity of a Support Network. This strength embraces rather than excludes the child who uses abusive/violent behaviour as the parent increases their emotional and physical presence in the child's life and resists invitations to return to patterns or habits of escalation. Findings from the Wilcox *et al.* (2015) and the *Exploring NVR* (Coogan 2016a) studies demonstrate that training in non-blaming and solution-focused models such as NVR can significantly enhance practitioners' awareness of CPVA and further develop practitioner skills in working with parents living with CPVA. The NVR model challenges practitioners,

6 Examples of alternatives include the Break4Change (Wilcox *et al.* 2015) and the Power to Change (Cronin *et al.* 2014) models in England and Ireland respectively. Other types of responses are described in Holt (2016).

researchers and policy-makers to shift their focus from the individual child and his/her behaviour to the responses of parents and an extended network, including practitioners. It is time to make easily available to parents, practitioners and researchers the evidence-supported training programmes and intervention models so that they can more fully explore and resolve the problems of CPVA, particularly for the parents and children living with these harsh realities.

Acknowledgements: The author would like to acknowledge and say thanks to the families and colleagues who supported the development of the NVR model in Ireland, the practitioners who took part in the *Exploring NVR* study described in this chapter, and also the reviewers of this chapter. Thanks also to colleagues at the School of Political Science and Sociology and the Social Science Research Institute at NUI Galway, whose support facilitated this chapter.

REFERENCES

Boxer, P., Gullan, R.L. and Mahoney, A. (2009) 'Adolescents' physical aggression towards their parents in a clinical-referred sample.' *Journal of Clinical Child and Adolescent Psychology 38*, 106–116.

Bronfenbrenner, U. and Evans, G.W. (2000) 'Developmental science in the 21st century: Emerging questions, theoretical models, research designs and empirical findings.' *Social Development 9*, 1, 115–125.

Calvete, E., Orue, I. and Gamez-Guadix, M. (2013) 'Child to parent violence: Emotional and behavioural predictors.' *Journal of Interpersonal Violence 28*, 4, 755–772.

Condry, R. and Miles, C. (2014) 'Adolescent to parent violence: Framing and mapping a hidden problem.' *Criminology and Criminal Justice 14*, 3, 257–275.

Coogan, D. (2011) 'Child to parent violence: Challenging perspectives on family violence.' *Child Care in Practise 17*, 4, 347–358.

Coogan, D. (2014) 'Responding to child to parent violence – Innovative practises in child and adolescent mental health.' *Health and Social Work 39*, 2. doi: 10.1093/hsw/hlu011

Coogan, D. (2016a) 'Child to Parent Violence – An Exploration of Non Violent Resistance.' Unpublished PhD thesis. Galway: School of Political Science and Sociology, National University of Ireland.

Coogan, D. (2016b) 'Listening to the voices of practitioners who encounter child to parent violence and abuse: Some findings from an action research project with practitioners in Ireland.' *Irish Social Worker Journal*, Winter, 41–48.

Coogan, D. (2017) *Child to Parent Violence and Abuse: Family Intervention with Non-Violent Resistance.* London and Philadelphia, PA: Jessica Kingsley Publishers.

Coogan, D. and Holt, S. (2015) 'New Challenges and Perspectives in Family Violence.' In A. Christie *et al.* (eds) *Social Work in Ireland: Changes and Continuities (pp.106–124).* Basingstoke: Palgrave Macmillan.

Coogan, D. and Lauster, E. (2015) *Responding to Child to Parent Violence in Europe – Development of Self-Efficacy Tools (Workstream 3).* Brighton. Responding to Child to Parent Violence Project. Accessed on 3/8/2017 at www.rcpv.eu/69-rcpv-ws3-report-final-1-may-2015-pdf/file

Corbin, J.M. and Strauss, A.L. (2008) *Basics of Qualitative Research – Techniques and Procedures for Developing Grounded Theory.* Los Angeles, CA: Sage.

Cottrell, B. (2001) 'Parent Abuse: The Abuse of Parents by Their Teenage Children.' Accessed on 5/4/2016 at www.canadiancrc.com/parent_abuse.htm

Cottrell, B. and Monk, P. (2004) 'Adolescent to parent abuse: A qualitative overview of common themes.' *Journal of Family Issues 25*, 8, 1072–1095.

Cronin, K., Moran, M., Mullen, E., Dully, C. and Byrne, V. (2014) *The Power2Change Programme – A Collaborative Response to Child to Parent Violence.* Parallel Session Paper presented at the Responding to Child to Parent Violence Project International Conference, NUI Galway, Ireland, 12–13 June 2014.

Edenborough, M., Jackson, D., Mannix, J. and Wilkes, L.M. (2008) 'Living in the red zone – The experience of child to mother violence.' *Child & Family Social Work 13*, 4, 464–473.

Edenborough, M., Wilkes, L.M., Jackson, D. and Mannix, J. (2011) 'Development and validation of the Child-to-Mother Violence Scale.' *Nurse Researcher 18*, 2, 63–76.

Fredman, G. (2014) 'Weaving net-works of hope: Families, practitioners and communities.' *Australia and New Zealand Journal of Family Therapy 34*, 1, 54–71.

Gallagher, E. (2008) 'Children's Violence to Parents: A Critical Literature Review.' Unpublished Master's thesis. Monash University.

Gieniusz, B. (2014) 'Examining the effectiveness of non-violent resistance approach as an effective treatment for parents of adolescents with conduct disorder.' *Context – Magazine for Family Therapy and Systemic Practise 132*, April, 42–44. Available at http://nvrpsy.com

Harbin, H. and Madden, D. (1979) 'Battered parents: A new syndrome.' *American Journal of Psychiatry 36*, 1288–1291.

Herr, K. and Anderson, G.L. (2015) *The Action Research Dissertation – A Guide for Students and Faculty.* Second Edition. Thousand Oaks, CA: Sage.

Holt, A. (2009) 'Parent abuse: Some reflections on the adequacy of a youth justice response.' *Internet Journal of Criminology.* Accessed on 16/10/2017 https://docs.wixstatic.com/ugd/b93dd4_5720f359696f4324bdc27b08f8e38803.pdf

Holt, A. (2013) *Adolescent to Parent Abuse – Current Understandings in Research, Policy and Practise.* Bristol: Policy Press.

Holt, A. (2016) *Working with Adolescent Abuse and Violence towards Parents – Approaches and Contexts for Intervention.* Abingdon: Routledge.

Holt, A. and Retford, S. (2012) 'Practitioner accounts of responding to parent abuse – A case study in ad hoc delivery, perverse outcomes and a policy silence.' *Child & Family Social Work, 18*, 3, 365–374.

Ibabe, I. and Jaureguizar, J. (2010) 'Child to parent violence – Profiles of abusive adolescents and their families.' *Journal of Criminal Justice 38*, 4, 616–624.

Ibabe, I., Jaureguizar, J. and Bentler, P.M. (2013) 'Risk factors for child to parent violence.' *Journal of Family Violence 28*, 523–534.

Lauster, E., Quinn, A., Brosnahan, J. and Coogan, D. (2014) 'Practical strategies for coping with child to parent violence – The Non Violent Resistance programme in practise.' *Irish Probation Journal 11*, October, 208–219.

Lyons, J., Bell, T., Frechette, S. and Romano, E. (2015) 'Child-to-parent violence: Frequency and correlates.' *Journal of Family Violence 30*, 6, 729–742.

McMahon, T. (2013) 'Practitioners' Experiences of the Non Violent Resistance (NVR) Approach to Violent and Self-Destructive Behaviours in Children.' Thesis submitted as part requirement for the PhD in Clinical Psychology Programme at the University of Limerick, Ireland.

Miles, C. and Condry, R. (2015) 'Responding to child to parent violence: Challenges for policy and practise.' *British Journal of Criminology 55*, 6, 1076–1095.

Milner, J. and Singleton, T. (2008) 'Domestic violence: Solution focused practise with men and women who are violent.' *Journal of Family Therapy 30*, 1, 29–53.

Nixon, J. (2012) 'Practitioners' constructions of parent abuse.' *Social Policy and Society 11*, 2, 229–239.

Omer, H. (2004) *Nonviolent Resistance – A New Approach to Violent and Self Destructive Children.* Cambridge: Cambridge University Press.

Omer, H. (2011) *The New Authority – Family, School and Community.* Cambridge and New York: Cambridge University Press.

Omer, H. and Dolberger, D.I. (2015) 'Helping parents cope with suicide threats: An approach based on nonviolent resistance.' *Family Process 54*, 3, 559–575.

Omer, H., Steinmeitz, S.G., Carthy, T. and von Schleippe, A. (2013) 'The anchoring function – Parental authority and the parent–child bond.' *Family Process 52*, 2, 193–206.

O'Reilly, R. (2014) 'From a Parent's Perspective.' Keynote paper delivered on 13 June 2014 at the Child to Parent Violence: Innovations in Practise, Policy and Research RCPV Project International Conference, National University of Ireland, Galway.

O'Rourke, E. (2013) 'Child to Parent Violence: The Experience of Child Protection Social Workers.' Unpublished Master's in Social Work dissertation. School of Political Science and Sociology, National University of Ireland, Galway.

Pagani, L., Tremblay, R.E., Nagin, D., Zoccolillo, V.F. and McDuff, P. (2009) 'Risk factors for adolescent verbal and physical aggression toward fathers.' *Journal of Family Violence 24*, 3, 173–182.

Paterson, R., Luntz, H., Perlesz, A. and Cotton, S. (2002) 'Adolescent violence towards parents: Maintaining family connections when the going gets tough.' *Australia and New Zealand Journal of Family Therapy 23*, 2, 90–100.

Selwyn, J. and Meakings, S. (2015) 'Adolescent to parent violence in adoptive families.' *British Journal of Social Work 46*, 5, 1224–1240.

Sokoloff, N. (2008) 'The intersectional paradigm and alternative visions for stopping domestic violence: What poor women, women of colour and immigrant women are teaching us about violence in the family.' *International Journal of Sociology of the Family 34*, 2, 153–185.

Walsh, J.A. and Krienert, J.L. (2009) 'A decade of child-initiated family violence: Comparative analysis of child–parent violence and parricide examining offender, victim and event characteristics in a national sample of reported incidents 1995–2005.' *Journal of Interpersonal Violence 24*, 9, 1450–1477.

Weinblatt, U. and Omer, H. (2008) 'Non-violent resistance: A treatment for parents of children with acute behaviour problems.' *Journal of Marital and Family Therapy 34*, 1, 75–92.

Wilcox, P. (2012) 'Is parent abuse a form of domestic violence?' *Social Policy and Society 11*, 2, 277–288.

Wilcox, P., Pooley, M., Ferrando, M., Coogan, D. *et al.* (2015) *Responding to Child to Parent Violence – Executive Summary of the Responding to Child to Parent Violence Project.* Brighton: Responding to Child to Parent Violence Project. Accessed on 3/8/2017 at www.rcpv.eu/78-rcpv-executive-summary-may-2015-english [In Irish at www.rcpv.eu/60-rcpv-executive-summary-ga/file]

Chapter 10

DIGITAL INTIMATE PARTNER VIOLENCE AND ABUSE AMONG YOUTH

A SYSTEMATIC REVIEW OF ASSOCIATED FACTORS

Per Moum Hellevik, *PhD Candidate, Norwegian Centre for Violence and Traumatic Stress Studies, Oslo, Norway*

INTRODUCTION

New digital technologies, such as smartphones, tablets, laptops and home computers, have become a central part of people's daily lives, with youths[1] among the most avid users of these technologies. In the European Union (EU), 90 per cent of people between the ages of 16 and 29 use the internet daily; 75 per cent of these use a mobile phone to connect to the internet when away from home, a figure that rises to 90 per cent in the eight countries with the highest mobile phone use. Participation on social networking sites is the most common online activity for this age group (Eurostat 2015). Digital media has become part of youths' daily social interactions, and while it provides many opportunities, it also poses certain risks (boyd 2014). One such risk is that digital media might be used in connection with violence and abuse in intimate romantic relationships (Stonard *et al.* 2014), henceforth referred to as 'digital intimate partner violence and abuse' (DIPVA). Although DIPVA is prevalent among European youth (see Chapter 6), relatively little research on factors associated with perpetration or victimisation has been undertaken in Europe. This chapter therefore includes findings from US as well as European research.

1 The UN defines a 'youth' as a person between the ages of 15 and 24 (UN DESA 2013).

Intimate relationships are central aspects of young people's development of identity and social and affective competence (Bouchey and Furman 2008; Collins, Welsh and Furman 2009; Furman 2002; Furman and Shaffer 2003). With much of the social interaction among youth now taking place online, the establishment, maintenance and/or termination phases of their intimate relationships also play out in the digital arena (Lenhart, Smith and Anderson 2015). Intimate relationships are often sources of conflict (Ha *et al.* 2013), and for some, such conflict escalates into violence and abuse (Foshee and Reyes 2011). Perpetration of 'intimate partner violence and abuse' (IPVA) has historically been performed face-to-face, as well as via landline phones and written correspondence (Walker and Meloy 1998). With the digitalisation of intimate relationships, however, IPVA is now thoroughly embedded in the online arena, independent of spatial and time constraints (Stonard *et al.* 2014). At the same time, it is debated whether online and offline forms of violence and abuse belong to separate constructs or are part of the same phenomenon (Marganski and Melander 2015; Schoffstall and Cohen 2011). As will be argued in this chapter, there are clear similarities between the two, strongly indicating that they are, indeed, part of the same phenomenon. However, there are also certain aspects of the digital arena – such as permanence, scope of audience and speed of sharing (Kowalski *et al.* 2014) – that do not exist in 'traditional' forms of IPVA. This can affect the impact of victimisation, with research finding that using digital media in the perpetration of violence and abuse can increase the negative impact on the victim (Brighi *et al.* 2012; Schneider *et al.* 2011).

This chapter is a systematic review of research on factors associated with DIPVA, factors that increase or decrease the likelihood of a person being exposed to such violence and abuse. First, these factors are presented and summarised in Table 10.1. Second, the factors are categorised based on their similarities in order to identify the contexts within which they most commonly appear. And third, the findings are discussed in relation to knowledge about factors associated with offline IPVA. Identifying associated factors can facilitate prevention and intervention work by making it easier to recognise where and how initiatives can be implemented most efficiently. Furthermore, by building on the extensive existing knowledge about traditional forms of IPVA, a deeper insight into their online counterparts can be achieved.

METHODS

This systematic review follows the guidelines of the Preferred Reporting Items for Systematic Reviews and Meta-Analyses (PRISMA) (Moher *et al.* 2009). PRISMA is primarily used in healthcare research, but its clear and concise procedures are applicable to reviews in any research field. To better clarify the review process, the PRISMA flow diagram (Moran *et al.* 2014) has also been included (see Figure 10.1). All peer-reviewed articles written in English that empirically addressed factors associated with DIPVA victimisation and/or perpetration were included. Review papers were excluded. As research on DIPVA is still in its infancy, no publication date limitations were set.

I performed searches using Oria, the University of Oslo's search engine for scientific papers, journals and databases.[2] Additionally, a certified librarian performed searches in the following databases: SveMed+, ProQuest Research, PsycINFO, Medline, Sociological Abstracts, Science Direct and Sage Journals. This ensured that the initial search results were adequate and included all relevant papers. All searches were performed between 9 and 30 January 2017. As there are no commonly agreed-on concepts or definitions to describe DIPVA, a multitude of search terms were used: 'cyber dating[3] abuse',[4] 'cyber dating violence', 'digital dating abuse', 'digital dating violence', 'electronic dating abuse', 'electronic dating violence', 'technology dating abuse', 'technology dating violence', 'online dating abuse', 'online dating violence', tech*[5] 'dating abuse', tech* 'dating violence', sexting AND[6] abuse, sexting AND violence, 'revenge porn', cyber AND dating AND abuse, digital AND dating AND abuse, cyber 'adolescent intimate partner violence', digital 'adolescent intimate partner violence', cyber 'teenage intimate partner violence' and digital 'teenage intimate partner violence'.

---

2 For a list of included search locations, see www.ub.uio.no/bruk/sok-i-hele-biblioteket/pdf/active_pci_resources.pdf.

3 While 'dating' does not accurately describe all types of intimate romantic relationships that adolescents engage in (Furman and Hand 2006), this term is commonly used within this field of research, especially in the US.

4 Quotation marks limit the search to only those results that include the exact words within the quotes.

5 * is a wildcard character, enabling the search to include any word that starts with 'tech'.

6 'AND' shows results that includes both/all three/all four/etc. of the given search words.

After the removal of non-peer-reviewed papers, the initial searches produced 5194 results (see Figure 10.1). An evaluation of all results based on title, scientific journal and topic tags – and abstracts, when needed – reduced the number of included papers to 103. In the next step of the review process, these remaining papers were accessed in their entirety, and evaluated based on their full text versions. This resulted in the exclusion of 73 more papers, leaving a total of 30 papers to be included in the analysis (see Table 10.1). Because the included studies used different definitions, operationalisations and methods of statistical analysis, a quantitative synthesis of the results was deemed inappropriate. Instead, all factors found to be associated with DIPVA were summarised and categorised according to type and their associations with victimisation and/or perpetration (see Table 10.2).

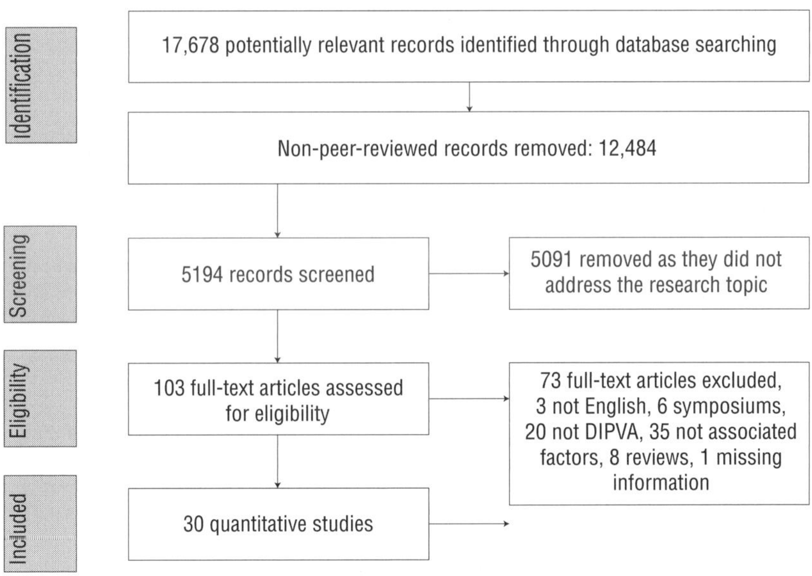

Figure 10.1: PRISMA flow diagram

FINDINGS

Of the 30 included papers, nine (30%) are based on European studies, while the remaining 21 (70%) are based on studies undertaken in the US. The oldest paper was published in 2011 and the rest of the papers were published in 2013 or later, with 12 (40%) having been published within the year prior to the literature search.

Table 10.1: Factors associated with DIPVA

Title	Year	Location	Author(s)	Factors associated with digital dating violence		*N*	Age
				Victimisation	Perpetration		
Cyber-dating abuse among teens using school-based health centres	2014	US	Dick *et al.* (2014)	Being female, sexual CDA <–> non-sexual CDA, physical ARA, psychological ARA, sexual violence by non-partner, contraception non-use, reproductive coercion		1008	14–19
Correlates of cyber-dating abuse among teens	2014	US	Zweig *et al.* (2014)	Being female, delinquent behaviours, having had sex, depressive symptoms, anger/hostility		3745	12–19
The development and validation of the cyber-dating abuse questionnaire among young couples	2015	EU	Borrajo *et al.* (2015)	Physical dating abuse victimisation, cyberbullying victimisation, psychological cyber-dating abuse perpetration, physical dating abuse perpetration, cyberbullying perpetration	Psychological cyber-dating abuse victimisation, physical dating abuse victimisation, cyberbullying victimisation, physical dating abuse perpetration, cyberbullying perpetration	788	18–30
Cyber-dating abuse: prevalence, context and relationship with offline dating aggression	2015	EU	Borrajo, Gámez-Guadix and Calvete (2015a)	Psychological dating aggression victimisation, younger age, same-sex relationship(s), being in a relationship		433	18–30
The rate of cyber-dating abuse among teens and how it relates to other forms of teen dating violence	2013	US	Zweig *et al.* (2013)	Being female, physical dating violence victimisation, psychological dating abuse victimisation, sexual coercion	Being female, physical dating violence perpetration, psychological dating abuse perpetration, sexual coercion	3745	12–19

The temporal association between traditional and cyber-dating abuse among adolescents	2016	US	Temple *et al.* (2016a)	Cyber-dating abuse perpetration, physical dating abuse victimisation	Cyber-dating abuse victimisation	780	18.09 (SD=0.79)
Prevalence and correlates of the perpetration of cyber-dating abuse among early adolescents	2017	US	Peskin *et al.* (2017)		Norms for violence for boys against girls, having a current boyfriend/girlfriend, bullying perpetration	424	12–13
Cyber-dating abuse victimisation among secondary school students from a lifestyle-routine activities theory perspective	2016	EU	van Ouytsel, Ponnet and Walrave (2016)	Engagement in online risk behaviour (e.g. sending personal information to someone that they had never met face-to-face), length of relationship, sexting, amount of social networking site use		466	16–22
Adolescent cyber-dating abuse victimisation and its associations with substance use, and sexual behaviours	2016	EU	van Ouytsel *et al.* (2016)	Males: more frequent alcohol consumption, started drinking at an older age Females: sexual debut at younger age, more sexual partners, unsafe sex Both: episodic drinking		466	16–22
Justification beliefs of violence, myths about love and cyber-dating abuse	2015	EU	Borrajo, Gamez-Guadix and Calvete (2015b)		Offline psychological dating violence perpetration, justification of cyber-dating abuse, myths about love (e.g. jealousy is proof of love)	656	18–30
Snooping and sexting	2016	US	Reed, Tolman and Ward (2016)	Physical abuse, psychological abuse, sexual abuse	Physical violence perpetration	307	17–22

Title	Year	Location	Author(s)	Factors associated with digital dating violence		*N*	Age
				Victimisation	Perpetration		
The co-occurrence of physical and cyber-dating violence and bullying among teens	2015	US	Yahner *et al.* (2015)	Cyberbullying victimisation	Cyberbullying perpetration	5647	12–19
Sticks and stones may break my bones, but abusive text messages also hurt: Development and validation of the Cyber Psychological Abuse Scale	2014	US	Leisring and Giumetti (2014)	Cyber abuse perpetration, being male, psychological abuse victimisation/ perpetration	Cyber abuse victimisation, being male, psychological abuse victimisation/ perpetration	271	19.03 (SD=1.16)
Exploratory investigation on theoretical predictors of the electronic leash	2016	US	Marcum, Higgins and Poff (2016)		Low self-control, race	611	18–26
Dating violence experiences of lesbian, gay, bisexual, and transgender youth	2014	US	Dank *et al.* (2014)	Being lesbian, gay or bi-sexual, identifying as transgender	Being lesbian, gay or bi-sexual, identifying as transgender	3745	12–19
The associations between substance use, sexual behaviours, bullying, deviant behaviours, health, and cyber-dating abuse perpetration	2015	US	van Ouytsel *et al.* (2015)		Had sex, taking alcohol or drugs before sex, alcohol, cigarettes, taking medicine to get high, prescription medicine not from health professional, bad self-reported health, bully victim/ perpetrator, self-reported use of social networking sites, not living with two parents	705	17.96 (SD=0.74)

Keeping tabs: Attachment anxiety and electronic intrusion in high school dating relationships	2016	US	Reed *et al.* (2016)		Being female Girls: length of relationship, current relationship, anxiety Boys: relative age of partner, electronic intrusion victimisation, anxiety	703	13–19
Too close for comfort: Attachment insecurity and electronic intrusion in college students' dating relationships	2015	US	Reed, Tolman and Safyer (2015)		Girls: electronic intrusion victimisation, anxiety, avoidance Boys: electronic intrusion victimisation, anxiety	230	17–22
Cyber aggression within adolescents' romantic relationships: Linkages to parental and partner attachment	2015	US	Wright (2015)		Alienation from mother, anxious partner attachment	326	17.53 (SD=0.51)
Images across Europe: The sending and receiving of sexual images and associations with interpersonal violence in young people's relationships	2015	EU	Wood *et al.* (2015)	Sexting		3299	14–17
Electronic displays of aggression in teen dating relationships: Does the social ecology matter?	2017	US	Smith-Darden *et al.* (2017)		Older age, being black, adverse childhood experiences, parental involvement	727	11–12 and 14–15

Title	Year	Location	Author(s)	Factors associated with digital dating violence		*N*	Age
				Victimisation	Perpetration		
Teenage intimate partner violence: Factors associated with victimisation among Norwegian youths	2016	EU	Hellevik and Øverlien (2016)	Being female, experiencing violence at home, sending sexual messages, generally having older partners		549	14–17
An examination of the Partner Cyber Abuse Questionnaire in a college student sample	2016	US	Wolford-Clevenger *et al.* (2016)	Physical victimisation, psychological victimisation, sexual coercion, injury victimisation, depression		502	18.80 (SD=1.93)
The role of dominance, cyber aggression perpetration, and gender on emerging adults' perpetration of intimate partner violence	2013	US	Schnurr, Mahatmya and Basche III (2013)		Female: physical intimate partner violence, partner's psychological intimate partner violence Male: partner's physical and psychological intimate partner violence	148	17–20
Electronic aggression among emerging adults	2013	US	Kellerman *et al.* (2013)	Family risk (e.g. chaos in the household), support from friends, emotion regulation	Family risk, support from friends, emotion regulation	226	18–23
Sexting, psychological distress and dating violence among adolescents and young adults	2016	EU	Morelli *et al.* (2016)	Sexting	Sexting	1334	13–30
Socially interactive technology and contemporary dating	2013	EU	Marganski and Fauth (2013)	Younger age, country of origin, hooking up (e.g. promiscuous sexual behaviour), sexting	Hooking up, sexting	508	18–30

College students' electronic victimisation in friendships and dating relationships: Anticipated distress and associations with risky behaviours	2011	US	Bennett *et al.* (2011)	Psychological victimisation, physical victimisation, coerced intimacy, being male, female alcohol use		437	18–22
Perpetration of teen dating violence in a networked society	2013	US	Korchmaros *et al.* (2013)		Had sex	615	14–19
Intimate partner violence victimisation in the cyber and real world: Examining the extent of cyber aggression experiences and its association with in-person dating violence	2015	US	Marganski and Melander (2015)	Psychological victimisation, physical victimisation, sexual victimisation		540	18–25

A total of 34 factors were associated with DIPVA victimisation, while 36 factors were associated with DIPVA perpetration. The factors were grouped into seven overall categories based on context (see Table 10.2): prior exposure to violence (online and offline), sexual behaviour, demographic factors, lifestyle choices, relationship factors, psychological factors and social context factors. The number of studies that found a given factor to be associated with DIPVA is indicated by the number within the parentheses in Table 10.2. It is important to note that the studies included in this review did not examine identical factors, but rather investigated factors that each specific study deemed interesting. Therefore, the number of studies that determined the importance of a given factor must not be interpreted as an indication of the strength of the association between the factor and DIPVA. For example, while some studies investigated alcohol consumption or sexting as potentially associated factors, others did not. The frequency of the factors cannot, therefore, be compared directly. Additionally, as all included studies are quantitative and used pre-determined measures, the list of identified factors should not be considered exhaustive. Table 10.2 gives a summarised overview of how the factors were distributed between the categories.

Table 10.2: Categorisation of associated factors

Category	Victimisation (*n*)	Perpetration (*n*)
Prior exposure to violence:		
Offline	Physical IPVA victimisation (9) Psychological IPVA victimisation (8) Sexual violence victimisation (7) Physical IPVA perpetration Psychological IPVA perpetration	Physical IPVA perpetration (4) Psychological IPVA perpetration (3) Psychological IPVA victimisation (2) Physical IPVA victimisation (2) Bullying perpetration (2) Sexual violence victimisation Bully victimisation
Online	Psychological DIPVA perpetration (3) Cyberbullying victimisation (2) Sexual DIPVA victimisation <–> non-sexual DIPVA victimisation Cyberbullying perpetration	Psychological DIPVA victimisation (5) Cyberbullying perpetration (2) Cyberbullying victimisation

Sexual behaviour	Sexting (5) Contraception non-use (2) Same-sex relationship Having had sex Hooking up Sexual debut at younger age More sexual partners	Sexting (2) Having had sex (2) Same-sex relationship Hooking up
Demographic factors	Female gender (4) Younger age (2) Male gender Older age Identifying as transgender Country of origin	Female gender (2) Race (2) Male gender Older age Identifying as transgender
Lifestyle choices	Frequent/high alcohol consumption (2) Delinquent behaviour Online risk behaviour High amount of social networking site use	Alcohol/drug use Bad self-reported health High amount of social networking site use
Psychological factors	Depressive symptoms (2) Anger/hostility Emotion regulation	Anxiety (2) Low self-control Emotion regulation Avoidance
Relationship factors	Being in a relationship Length of relationship	Being in a relationship (2) Age of partner (2) Length of relationship Norms for violence and relationships Anxious partner attachment
Social context factors	Family risk Social support Violence at home	Family risk Social support Not living with two parents Alienation from mother Adverse childhood experiences

Prior exposure to violence

Previous exposure to interpersonal violence – including intimate partner violence, either online or offline – was the factor that appeared most frequently in the reviewed studies. Physical and psychological IPVA victimisation, sexual violence victimisation, physical and psychological IPVA perpetration, psychological DIPVA perpetration and cyberbullying victimisation were factors associated with DIPVA victimisation. Additionally, sexual DIPVA victimisation was associated with non-sexual DIPVA victimisation. Furthermore, physical and psychological IPVA perpetration, physical and psychological IPVA victimisation, (cyber)bullying victimisation and perpetration, sexual violence victimisation and psychological DIPVA victimisation were all associated with DIPVA perpetration.

Comparable results, regarding intricate associations between previous and later violence and abuse exposure in intimate relationships, are found in research on traditional forms of IPVA. In a review of 20 studies that looked at risk and protective factors for adolescent dating violence perpetration, Vagi *et al.* (2013) found that prior IPVA exposure was associated with later IPVA exposure, and that IPVA perpetration was associated with having a history of verbal, sexual and physical aggression perpetration in intimate relationships. Additionally, Dardis *et al.* (2015), in a review of studies researching factors associated with IPVA perpetration, found that IPVA victimisation was associated with IPVA perpetration. Finally, in a review of 61 studies researching risk factors for IPVA victimisation among young women aged 12–24, Vézina and Hébert (2007) found that previous victimisation was associated with later victimisation.

Sexual behaviour

Several of the reviewed studies also found factors related to young people's sexual behaviours to be associated with DIPVA. Sexting,[7] contraception non-use, being in a same-sex relationship, having had sex, hooking up,[8] sexual debut at a younger age and having more sexual partners were factors associated with DIPVA victimisation. Furthermore, sexting, having had sex, being in a same-sex relationship and hooking up were factors associated with DIPVA perpetration. Of these factors – for both victimisation and perpetration – sexting appeared most frequently. As sexting is becoming increasingly common among youth, its association with DIPVA is noteworthy (Wood *et al.* 2015). Also, sexting seems to be related to risky sexual behaviour (Temple *et al.* 2012; Ybarra and Mitchell 2014), and might therefore be part of a pattern of sexual behaviours that entails an increased possibility of adverse outcomes. Interestingly, of the five studies that included sexting as a potential associated factor, four were conducted in Europe. This might

7 Sexting can be defined as 'sexually explicit content communicated via text messages, smartphones, or visual and web 2.0 activities such as social networking sites' (Ringrose *et al.* 2012, p.9).

8 More casual sexual encounters, compared to more serious romantic relationships, such as dating or boyfriend/girlfriend (Marganski and Fauth 2013).

indicate a focus in European research on the interplay between intimacy practises through the use of digital media, and its potential for harmful effects when combined with violent and abusive relationships.

An association between risky sexual behaviour and violence and abuse in intimate relationships is also found in IPVA research. Eaton *et al.* (2007) found, in a study of IPVA and risk behaviours among 15,214 students in the US aged 15–18, that higher levels of risky sexual behaviours were correlated with higher risk of IPVA victimisation. Additionally, in a more recent US study, with a national sample of 879 girls aged 13–21, Alleyne-Green *et al.* (2016) found that more IPVA experience was associated with being less likely to engage in healthy sexual behaviour.

Demographic factors

Gender, being non-white, higher age and identifying as transgender were all categories found to be associated with DIPVA victimisation. These same factors were also associated with DIPVA perpetration. Race, age and transgender identity have similarly been found to be associated with IPVA (Dank *et al.* 2014; Foshee, McNaughton Reyes and Ennett 2010; Wolitzky-Taylor *et al.* 2008). A majority of the studies in this review found that women were more likely to be victims of DIPVA. Two studies found that women were more often perpetrators (Reed *et al.* 2016; Zweig *et al.* 2013), while one study found that perpetrators were more likely to be men (Leisring and Giumetti 2014).

Regarding DIPVA victimisation, research indicates that women are more likely to be victims of such violence. This is found in studies utilising representative samples and studies utilising convenience samples. However, there might be some variation depending on the form of violence and abuse experienced. In a Spanish survey study based on a convenience sample of 656 students between the ages of 18 and 30, Borrajo, Gámez-Guadix and Calvete (2015b) found no gender differences in DIPVA victimisation, overall. However, in another study, they found that men more often than women were victims of DIPVA in the form of relational aggression: a form of aggression directed at the victim's social relations (e.g. spreading rumours) (Borrajo, Gámez-Guadix and Calvete 2015a; Card *et al.* 2008). They argue that this could be because women are more likely to perpetrate relational aggression while men tend to be more inclined to engage in direct aggression.

With regards to DIPVA perpetration, conclusions are difficult to draw, as only three of the studies included in this review found any gender differences. Additionally, as all of these studies were based on convenience samples, the generalisability of their findings is unclear. However, these gender differences should not be completely overlooked. Leisring and Giumetti (2014), in a non-probability online survey of 271 undergraduate students, found that more men than women tended to perpetrate severe DIPVA (which includes behaviour such as threats and public humiliation) rather than minor DIPVA (which includes behaviour such as swearing and insulting). Furthermore, Zweig *et al.* (2013) found more girls than boys to be perpetrators of non-sexual DIPVA, and far more boys than girls to be perpetrators of sexual DIPVA.

Similar gender differences are also found in IPVA research. In a review of 15 empirical studies of gender and IPVA prevalence, Chan (2011) found gender symmetry in studies where context, motives and severity were disregarded, and gender asymmetry where these aspects were included. He argues that, overall, the results indicate that men tend to perpetrate more severe forms of violence when compared to women. For both DIPVA and IPVA, research indicates that the association to gender is present, but might also be dependent on the form of violence experienced. More severe forms of violence are mainly perpetrated by men, while less severe violence is more equally distributed (with some forms being perpetrated more by women than men). The possibility of gendered differences based on the forms and severity of violence perpetrated therefore needs to be further investigated.

Lifestyle choices

High alcohol consumption, delinquent behaviour, online risk behaviour (looking for new friends on the internet, or sending personal information to people/adding people to their online friends lists and address books that they have not yet met in person) and heavy use of social networking sites were associated with DIPVA victimisation. Alcohol and/or drug use, bad self-reported health and heavy use of social networking sites were associated with DIPVA perpetration. Van Ouytsel, Ponnet and Walrave (2016) argue that the high frequency of social network site use increases victims' risk of being contacted by perpetrators. Furthermore, they argue that online risk behaviours might lead to victims neglecting to protect online personal information, which increases the risk of perpetrators accessing this information. Alcohol and drug use was the most frequent factor in this category, with two studies finding an association between high alcohol consumption and DIPVA victimisation (Bennett *et al.* 2011; van Ouytsel *et al.* 2016), and one study finding an association between alcohol/drug use and DIPVA perpetration (van Ouytsel *et al.* 2015). In research on violence and abuse, alcohol and substance abuse is often included in a category of behaviours referred to as 'risky' (van Ouytsel *et al.* 2016). Risky behaviour can be defined as 'any behaviour than can compromise the adolescent's physical and psychosocial health and development...' (Vézina *et al.* 2011, p.815; see also Jessor 1991), and such behaviours have been found to be associated with IPVA victimisation and perpetration (Gover 2004). Risky behaviour, both online and offline, thereby seems to entail an increased risk of exposure to violence and abuse in intimate relationships.

Psychological factors

Factors related to an individual's psychological state were also found to be associated with DIPVA; depressive symptoms, anger/hostility and a lack of emotion regulation were associated with DIPVA victimisation, while anxiety, low self-control, avoidance and a lack of emotion regulation were associated with DIPVA perpetration. Emotion regulation might be a key factor in avoiding escalating negative interactions in the rapid communication characterised by digital media (Kellerman *et al.* 2013). Depression and anxiety were the factors cited most often. However, the studies were unable to make any claims about the direction of the association thus it is unclear whether DIPVA is a cause or an effect of depression and anxiety.

Comparably, in IPVA research, depression and anxiety is found to be associated with both perpetration and victimisation (Cascardi 2016; Vagi *et al.* 2013). Studies on IPVA have been able to look more closely at the directional relationship between experiences of IPVA and depression. In a review of 16 studies on IPVA's correlation with depressive symptoms and suicide attempts, Devries *et al.* (2013) found a bidirectional relationship, wherein experiences of IPVA can result in depression but existing depression can increase the risk of exposure to IPVA. In a longitudinal study of physical IPVA among 2566 students from the US, aged 13–17, Brooks-Russell, Foshee and Ennett (2013) argued that depression can cause feelings of helplessness, increasing the risk of victimisation. Additionally, depression might lead to difficulty identifying cues of threat and danger, which also increases the risk of victimisation (Krause *et al.* 2006). Furthermore, it has been hypothesised that IPVA perpetration can, in itself, lead to internalised issues like anxiety and depression (Temple *et al.* 2016b).

Relationship factors

Specific aspects of the relationship were also found to be associated with DIPVA. Being in a relationship, age of partner and the length of relationship were associated with victimisation, while being in a relationship, age of partner, length of relationship, norms for violence and relationships and anxious partner attachment were all associated with perpetration. Currently being in an intimate relationship, as opposed to having been in an intimate relationship, entails a higher risk of experiencing DIPVA (Borrajo, Gámez-Guadix and Calvete 2015a). In a survey study of 466 Flemish students aged 16–22, van Ouytsel, Ponnet and Walrave (2016) found that the length of the relationship was positively associated with the risk of DIPVA, both for victimisation and perpetration. Additionally, the relative age of the partner also affects the risk of both victimisation and perpetration, with the victims often being much younger than their perpetrators (Hellevik and Øverlien 2016). Peskin *et al.* (2017) looked at norms for violence and relationships by asking whether the respondents agreed to statements such as 'It is okay for a boy/girl to hit his/her girlfriend/boyfriend if she/he did something to make him/her mad' and 'Sometimes boys/girls have to hit their girlfriends/boyfriends to get them back under control'. They found a positive association between agreement with such statements and risk of DIPVA perpetration. Finally, anxious partner attachment – understood as uncertainty about attachment to a partner – was positively associated with DIPVA perpetration (Wright 2015).

Research on IPVA shows similar findings. The length of the relationship has been found to be positively associated with IPVA perpetration (Dardis *et al.* 2015). There is also an increased risk of

IPVA in relationships where one partner is much older than the other (Vézina and Hébert 2007). The degree of trust and agreement between partners is an additional factor associated with IPVA (Rodriguez *et al.* 2015), as are norms of violence in relationships, where youth showing attitudes supporting IPVA is associated with perpetration (Taylor, Sullivan and Farrell 2015).

Social context factors

The final category consists of factors that are linked to social context. Family risks (e.g. chaos in the household or having a substance-abusing family member), lack of social support from friends and violence at home were associated with DIPVA victimisation. Not living with two parents, alienation from their mother and adverse childhood experiences were associated with DIPVA perpetration. Growing up in a hostile and unsupportive home environment might increase the risk of using aggression in situations of conflict, while support from friends seems to moderate those negative effects (Kellerman *et al.* 2013).

In some IPVA research, the association between previous exposure to violence – commonly during childhood – and later victimisation/perpetration is explained by referring to social learning theory (Ali and Naylor 2013). According to Bandura (1977), behaviour is learned through observation and direct instruction from others, and important figures in a person's life often serve as central role models. When a young person is exposed to violence from someone close to him or her (such as a parent), the young person learns that this kind of behaviour is an effective way of managing an unwanted situation. This might result in such behaviour being replicated later in life, thereby continuing the pattern of abuse. While theories focusing on social learning processes are popular in IPVA research, the perspective has faced criticisms, such as a varying use of definitions, lack of theoretical adherence and inconsistency in findings (Ali and Naylor 2013). IPVA research has also found that not living with two parents increases the risk of being exposed to IPVA (Paat and Markham 2016), as does adverse childhood experiences (Miller *et al.* 2011), while social support seems to have a buffering effect (although there might be gender differences) (Richards, Branch and Ray 2014).

CONCLUSION

Digital media has become a central part of young people's interactions within intimate relationships. The possibilities offered by digital media present today's youth with a range of communicative choices that earlier generations have not had. However, this is not without risk. For some young people, intimate relationships become sources of violence and abuse, and the use of digital media is unfortunately not excluded from this. Knowledge about the factors associated with DIPVA provides important insight into who might be vulnerable, and contributes to a better understanding of violence and abuse in general. The ability to more accurately identify the processes underlying victimisation and perpetration will facilitate work to eliminate violence and abuse. Addressing this issue among young people will also decrease the likelihood of violence and abuse continuing at a later stage.

As this review has found, many aspects of online and offline IPVA are similar. While additional research on the specifics of DIPVA is critical, existing knowledge about IPVA can provide important insights into how DIPVA can be better understood and prevented. For policy-makers, a key component in the implementation of prevention and intervention strategies should be a holistic perspective on young people's intimate relationships, sexuality and online proficiency, as these factors are interrelated. Furthermore, as violence and abuse is more than just specific acts and behaviours, a broader understanding of young people's intimacy and sexuality – beyond the mere mechanical aspects of sexual intercourse – should form the basis for sexual education in schools and elsewhere. Thus, a broad approach to DIPVA (with regards to both research and prevention) targeting young people's gender attitudes, use of digital media and understanding of sexuality, boundaries and what it means to be in a healthy intimate relationship is essential.

At the same time, research on DIPVA is in its infancy. This is especially true for European research on DIPVA, with eight of the nine European studies included in this study having been published in 2015 or later. Furthermore, as this book shows, European research on intimate partner violence covers a wide range of topics. Europe is a diverse continent with many nationalities and cultures, and the validity of generalising findings from research performed in the US to European contexts is therefore questionable. For example, while digital media use is quite similar among European and American youth, there are some dissimilarities, such as greater variation within Europe with regards to smartphone ownership (Poushter 2016). Thus, as the majority of research on DIPVA is carried out in the US, an increased focus on this issue in European research is critical for the accurate identification of potential aspects unique to the European context.

REFERENCES

Ali, P.A. and Naylor, P.B. (2013) 'Intimate partner violence: A narrative review of the feminist, social and ecological explanations for its causation.' *Aggression and Violent Behavior 18*, 6, 611–619. doi: http://dx.doi.org/10.1016/j.avb.2013.07.009

Alleyne-Green, B., Grinnell-Davis, C., Clark, T.T., Quinn, C.R. and Cryer-Coupet, Q.R. (2016) 'Father involvement, dating violence, and sexual risk behaviors among a national sample of adolescent females.' *Journal of Interpersonal Violence 31*, 5, 810–830. doi: 10.1177/0886260514556762

Bandura, A. (1977) *Social Learning Theory*. Upper Saddle River, NJ: Prentice Hall.

Bennett, D.C., Guran, E.L., Ramos, M.C. and Margolin, G. (2011) 'College students' electronic victimization in friendships and dating relationships: Anticipated distress and associations with risky behaviors.' *Violence and Victims 26*, 4, 410–429.

Borrajo, E., Gámez-Guadix, M. and Calvete, E. (2015a) 'Cyber dating abuse: Prevalence, context, and relationship with offline dating aggression.' *Psychological Reports 116*, 2, 565–585. doi: 10.2466/21.16.PR0.116k22w4

Borrajo, E., Gámez-Guadix, M. and Calvete, E. (2015b) 'Justification beliefs of violence, myths about love and cyber dating abuse.' *Psicothema 27*, 4, 327–333. doi: 10.7334/psicothema2015.59

Borrajo, E., Gámez-Guadix, M., Pereda, N. and Calvete, E. (2015) 'The development and validation of the cyber dating abuse questionnaire among young couples.' *Computers in Human Behavior 48*, 358–365. doi: http://dx.doi.org/10.1016/j.chb.2015.01.063

Bouchey, H.A. and Furman, W. (2008) 'Dating and Romantic Experiences.' In G.R. Adams and m. Berzonsky (eds.) *Blackwell Handbook of Adolescence* (pp.312–329). Oxford: Blackwell Publishing Ltd.

boyd, d. (2014) *It's Complicated: The Social Lives of Networked Teens*. New Haven, CT: Yale University Press.

Brighi, A., Guarini, A., Melotti, G., Galli, S. and Genta, M.L. (2012) 'Predictors of victimisation across direct bullying, indirect bullying and cyberbullying.' *Emotional and Behavioural Difficulties 17*, 3–4, 375–388. doi: 10.1080/13632752.2012.704684

Brooks-Russell, A., Foshee, V.A. and Ennett, S.T. (2013) 'Predictors of latent trajectory classes of physical dating violence victimization.' *Journal of Youth and Adolescence 42*, 4, 566–580. doi: 10.1007/s10964-012-9876-2

Card, N.A., Stucky, B.D., Sawalani, G.M. and Little, T.D. (2008) 'Direct and indirect aggression during childhood and adolescence: A meta-analytic review of gender differences, intercorrelations, and relations to maladjustment.' *Child Development 79*, 5, 1185–1229. doi: 10.1111/j.1467-8624.2008.01184.x

Cascardi, M. (2016) 'From violence in the home to physical dating violence victimization: The mediating role of psychological distress in a prospective study of female adolescents.' *Journal of Youth and Adolescence 45*, 4, 777–792. doi: 10.1007/s10964-016-0434-1

Chan, K.L. (2011) 'Gender differences in self-reports of intimate partner violence: A review.' *Aggression and Violent Behavior 16*, 2, 167–175.

Collins, W.A., Welsh, D.P. and Furman, W. (2009) 'Adolescent romantic relationships.' *Annual Review of Psychology 60*, 1, 631–652.

Dank, M., Lachman, P., Zweig, J.M. and Yahner, J. (2014) 'Dating violence experiences of lesbian, gay, bisexual, and transgender youth.' *Journal of Youth and Adolescence 43*, 5, 846–857.

Dardis, C.M., Dixon, K.J., Edwards, K.M. and Turchik, J.A. (2015) 'An examination of the factors related to dating violence perpetration among young men and women and associated theoretical explanations.' *Trauma, Violence, and Abuse 16*, 2, 136–152.

Devries, K.M., Mak, J.Y., Bacchus, L.J., Child, J.C., *et al.* (2013) 'Intimate partner violence and incident depressive symptoms and suicide attempts: A systematic review of longitudinal studies.' *PLOS Medicine 10*, 5, e1001439. doi: 10.1371/journal.pmed.1001439
Dick, R.N., McCauley, H.L., Jones, K.A., Tancredi, D.J., *et al.* (2014) 'Cyber dating abuse among teens using school-based health centers.' *Pediatrics 134*, 6, e1560–e1567.
Eaton, D.K., Davis, K.S., Barrios, L., Brener, N.D. and Noonan, R.K. (2007) 'Associations of dating violence victimization with lifetime participation, co-occurrence, and early initiation of risk behaviors among US high school students.' *Journal of Interpersonal Violence 22*, 5, 585–602.
Eurostat (2015) *Being Young in Europe Today – 2015 Edition.* Accessed on 3/8/2017 at http://ec.europa.eu/eurostat/documents/3217494/6776245/KS-05-14-031-EN-N.pdf/18bee6f0-c181-457d-ba82-d77b314456b9
Foshee, V.A. and Reyes, H.L.M. (2011) 'Dating Abuse: Prevalence, Consequences, and Predictors.' In R.J.R. Levesque (ed.) *Encyclopedia of Adolescence* (pp.602–615). New York: Springer.
Foshee, V.A., McNaughton Reyes, H.L. and Ennett, S.T. (2010) 'Examination of sex and race differences in longitudinal predictors of the initiation of adolescent dating violence perpetration.' *Journal of Aggression, Maltreatment and Trauma 19*, 5, 492–516.
Furman, W. (2002) 'The emerging field of adolescent romantic relationships.' *Current Directions in Psychological Science 11*, 5, 177–180. doi: 10.1111/1467-8721.00195
Furman, W. and Hand, L.S. (2006) 'The Slippery Nature of Romantic Relationships: Issues in Definition and Differentiation.' In A.C. Crouter (ed.) *Romance and Sex in Adolescence and Emerging Adulthood: Risks and Opportunities* (pp.171–178). Mahwah, NJ: Lawrence Erlbaum Associates Publishers.
Furman, W. and Shaffer, L. (2003) 'The role of romantic relationships in adolescent development.' *Adolescent Romantic Relations and Sexual Behavior: Theory, Research, and Practical Implications*, 3–22.
Gover, A.R. (2004) 'Risky lifestyles and dating violence: A theoretical test of violent victimization.' *Journal of Criminal Justice 32*, 2, 171–180.
Ha, T., Overbeek, G., Lichtwarck-Aschoff, A. and Engels, R.C.M.E. (2013) 'Do conflict resolution and recovery predict the survival of adolescents' romantic relationships?' *PLOS ONE 8*, 4, e61871.
Hellevik, P. and Øverlien, C. (2016) 'Teenage intimate partner violence: Factors associated with victimization among Norwegian youths.' *Scandinavian Journal of Public Health, 44*, 7, 702–708.
Jessor, R. (1991) 'Risk behavior in adolescence: A psychosocial framework for understanding and action.' *Journal of Adolescent Health 12*, 8, 597–605.
Kellerman, I., Margolin, G., Borofsky, L.A., Baucom, B.R. and Iturralde, E. (2013) 'Electronic aggression among emerging adults.' *Emerging Adulthood 1*, 4, 293–304.
Korchmaros, J.D., Ybarra, M.L., Langhinrichsen-Rohling, J., boyd, d. and Lenhart, A. (2013) 'Perpetration of teen dating violence in a networked society.' *Cyberpsychology, Behavior, and Social Networking 16*, 8, 561–567. doi: 10.1089/cyber.2012.0627
Kowalski, R.M., Giumetti, G.W., Schroeder, A.N. and Lattanner, M.R. (2014) 'Bullying in the digital age: A critical review and meta-analysis of cyberbullying research among youth.' *Psychological Bulletin 140*, 4, 1073–1137.
Krause, E.D., Kaltman, S., Goodman, L. and Dutton, M.A. (2006) 'Role of distinct PTSD symptoms in intimate partner reabuse: A prospective study.' *Journal of Traumatic Stress 19*, 4, 507–516.
Leisring, P.A. and Giumetti, G.W. (2014) 'Sticks and stones may break my bones, but abusive text messages also hurt: Development and validation of the Cyber Psychological Abuse Scale.' *Partner Abuse 5*, 3, 323–341.
Lenhart, A., Smith, A. and Anderson, M. (2015) *Teens, Technology and Romantic Relationships.* Washington, DC: Pew Research Center. Accessed on 3/8/2017 at www.pewinternet.org/files/2015/10/PI_2015-10-01_teens-technology-romance_FINAL.pdf
Marcum, C.D., Higgins, G.E. and Poff, B. (2016) 'Exploratory investigation on theoretical predictors of the electronic leash.' *Computers in Human Behavior 61*, 213–218.
Marganski, A. and Fauth, K. (2013) 'Socially interactive technology and contemporary dating.' *International Criminal Justice Review 23*, 4, 357–377.
Marganski, A. and Melander, L. (2015) 'Intimate partner violence victimization in the cyber and real world.' *Journal of Interpersonal Violence.* doi: 10.1177/0886260515614283
Miller, E., Breslau, J., Chung, W.-J.J., Green, J.G., McLaughlin, K.A. and Kessler, R.C. (2011) 'Adverse childhood experiences and risk of physical violence in adolescent dating relationships.' *Journal of Epidemiology and Community Health 65*, 11, 1006–1013.

Moher, D., Liberati, A., Tetzlaff, J. and Altman, D.G. (2009) 'Preferred reporting items for systematic reviews and meta-analyses: The PRISMA statement.' *BMJ 339*. doi: 10.1136/bmj.b2535

Moran, A.M., Coyle, J., Pope, R., Boxall, D., Nancarrow, S.A. and Young, J. (2014) 'Supervision, support and mentoring interventions for health practitioners in rural and remote contexts: An integrative review and thematic synthesis of the literature to identify mechanisms for successful outcomes.' *Human Resources for Health 12*, 1, 10. doi: 10.1186/1478-4491-12-10

Morelli, M., Bianchi, D., Baiocco, R., Pezzuti, L. and Chirumbolo, A. (2016) 'Sexting, psychological distress and dating violence among adolescents and young adults.' *Psicothema 28*, 2, 137–142.

Paat, Y.-F. and Markham, C. (2016) 'The roles of family factors and relationship dynamics on dating violence victimization and perpetration among college men and women in emerging adulthood.' *Journal of Interpersonal Violence*, 0886260516640544. doi: 10.1177/0886260516640544

Peskin, M.F., Markham, C.M., Shegog, R., Temple, J.R., *et al.* (2017) 'Prevalence and correlates of the perpetration of cyber dating abuse among early adolescents.' *Journal of Youth and Adolescence 46*, 2, 358–375.

Poushter, J. (2016) 'Smartphone ownership and internet usage continues to climb in emerging economies.' Pew Research Center, Global Attitudes & Trends. Accessed on 3/8/2017 at www.pewglobal.org/2016/02/22/smartphone-ownership-and-internet-usage-continues-to-climb-in-emerging-economies/

Reed, L.A., Tolman, R.M. and Safyer, P. (2015) 'Too close for comfort: Attachment insecurity and electronic intrusion in college students' dating relationships.' *Computers in Human Behavior 50*, 431–438.

Reed, L.A., Tolman, R.M. and Ward, L.M. (2016) 'Snooping and sexting.' *Violence Against Women 22*, 13, 1556–1576.

Reed, L.A., Tolman, R.M., Ward, L.M. and Safyer, P. (2016) 'Keeping tabs: Attachment anxiety and electronic intrusion in high school dating relationships.' *Computers in Human Behavior 58*, 259–268.

Richards, T.N., Branch, K.A. and Ray, K. (2014) 'The impact of parental and peer social support on dating violence perpetration and victimization among female adolescents: A longitudinal study.' *Violence and Victims 29*, 2, 317–331.

Ringrose, J., Gill, R., Livingstone, S. and Harvey, L. (2012) *A Qualitative Study of Children, Young People and 'Sexting': A Report Prepared for the NSPCC*. London: NSPCC.

Rodriguez, L.M., DiBello, A.M., Øverup, C.S. and Neighbors, C. (2015) 'The price of distrust: Trust, anxious attachment, jealousy, and partner abuse.' *Partner Abuse 6*, 3.

Schneider, S.K., O'Donnell, L., Stueve, A. and Coulter, R.W.S. (2011) 'Cyberbullying, school bullying, and psychological distress: A regional census of high school students.' *American Journal of Public Health 102*, 1, 171–177.

Schnurr, M.P., Mahatmya, D. and Basche III, R.A. (2013) 'The role of dominance, cyber aggression perpetration, and gender on emerging adults' perpetration of intimate partner violence.' *Psychology of Violence 3*, 1, 70–83.

Schoffstall, C.L. and Cohen, R. (2011) 'Cyber aggression: The relation between online offenders and offline social competence.' *Social Development 20*, 3, 587–604.

Smith-Darden, J.P., Kernsmith, P.D., Victor, B.G. and Lathrop, R.A. (2017) 'Electronic displays of aggression in teen dating relationships: Does the social ecology matter?' *Computers in Human Behavior 67*, 33–40. doi: http://dx.doi.org/10.1016/j.chb.2016.10.015

Stonard, K.E., Bowen, E., Lawrence, T.R. and Price, S.A. (2014) 'The relevance of technology to the nature, prevalence and impact of adolescent dating violence and abuse: A research synthesis.' *Aggression and Violent Behavior 19*, 4, 390–417.

Taylor, K.A., Sullivan, T.N. and Farrell, A.D. (2015) 'Longitudinal relationships between individual and class norms supporting dating violence and perpetration of dating violence.' *Journal of Youth and Adolescence 44*, 3, 745–760.

Temple, J.R., Choi, H.J., Brem, M., Wolford-Clevenger, C. *et al.* (2016a) 'The temporal association between traditional and cyber dating abuse among adolescents.' *Journal of Youth and Adolescence 45*, 2, 340–349.

Temple, J.R., Choi, H.J., Elmquist, J., Hecht, M. *et al.* (2016b) 'Psychological abuse, mental health, and acceptance of dating violence among adolescents.' *Journal of Adolescent Health 59*, 2, 197–202.

Temple, J.R., Paul, J.A., van den Berg, P., Le, V., McElhany, A. and Temple, B.W. (2012) 'Teen sexting and its association with sexual behaviors.' *Archives of Pediatrics and Adolescent Medicine 166*, 9, 828–833.

UN DESA (United Nations Department of Economic and Social Affairs) (2013) *Definitions of Youth.* Accessed on 3/8/2017 at www.un.org/esa/socdev/documents/youth/fact-sheets/youth-definition.pdf

Vagi, K.J., Rothman, E.F., Latzman, N.E., Tharp, A.T., Hall, D.M. and Breiding, M.J. (2013) 'Beyond correlates: A review of risk and protective factors for adolescent dating violence perpetration.' *Journal of Youth and Adolescence 42*, 4, 633–649.

van Ouytsel, J., Ponnet, K. and Walrave, M. (2016) 'Cyber dating abuse victimization among secondary school students from a lifestyle-routine activities theory perspective.' *Journal of Interpersonal Violence.* doi: 10.1177/0886260516629390

van Ouytsel, J., Ponnet, K., Walrave, M. and Temple, J.R. (2016) 'Adolescent cyber dating abuse victimization and its associations with substance use, and sexual behaviors.' *Public Health 135*, 147–151.

van Ouytsel, J., Walrave, M., Ponnet, K. and Heirman, W. (2015) 'The association between adolescent sexting, psychosocial difficulties, and risk behavior: Integrative review.' *The Journal of School Nursing 31*, 1, 54–69.

Vézina, J. and Hébert, M. (2007) 'Risk factors for victimization in romantic relationships of young women: A review of empirical studies and implications for prevention.' *Trauma Violence Abuse 8*, 1, 33–66.

Vézina, J., Hébert, M., Poulin, F., Lavoie, F., Vitaro, F. and Tremblay, R.E. (2011) 'Risky lifestyle as a mediator of the relationship between deviant peer affiliation and dating violence victimization among adolescent girls.' *Journal of Youth and Adolescence 40*, 7, 814–824.

Walker, L.E. and Meloy, J.R. (1998) 'Stalking and Domestic Violence.' In J.R. Meloy (ed.) *The Psychology of Stalking: Clinical and Forensic Perspectives* (pp.140–161). San Diego, CA: Academic Press.

Wolford-Clevenger, C., Zapor, H., Brasfield, H., Febres, J. *et al.* (2016) 'An examination of the Partner Cyber Abuse Questionnaire in a college student sample.' *Psychology of Violence 6*, 1, 156–162.

Wolitzky-Taylor, K.B., Ruggiero, K.J., Danielson, C.K., Resnick, H.S. *et al.* (2008) 'Prevalence and correlates of dating violence in a national sample of adolescents.' *Journal of the American Academy of Child and Adolescent Psychiatry 47*, 7, 755–762.

Wood, M., Barter, C., Stanley, N., Aghtaie, N. and Larkins, C. (2015) 'Images across Europe: The sending and receiving of sexual images and associations with interpersonal violence in young people's relationships.' *Children and Youth Services Review 59*, 149–160.

Wright, M.F. (2015) 'Cyber aggression within adolescents' romantic relationships: Linkages to parental and partner attachment.' *Journal of Youth and Adolescence 44*, 1, 37–47.

Yahner, J., Dank, M., Zweig, J.M. and Lachman, P. (2015) 'The co-occurrence of physical and cyber dating violence and bullying among teens.' *Journal of Interpersonal Violence 30*, 7, 1079–1089.

Ybarra, M.L. and Mitchell, K.J. (2014) '"Sexting" and its relation to sexual activity and sexual risk behavior in a national survey of adolescents.' *Journal of Adolescent Health 55*, 6, 757–764.

Zweig, J., Dank, M., Yahner, J. and Lachman, P. (2013) 'The rate of cyber dating abuse among teens and how it relates to other forms of teen dating violence.' *Journal of Youth and Adolescence 42*, 7, 1063–1077.

Zweig, J., Lachman, P., Yahner, J. and Dank, M. (2014) 'Correlates of cyber dating abuse among teens.' *Journal of Youth and Adolescence 43*, 8, 1306–1321.

Chapter 11

HUMAN TRAFFICKING AND GENDER-BASED VIOLENCE

FROM LIFE AND LIMB TO HEARTS AND MINDS

Nusha Yonkova, *Anti-Trafficking Manager, Immigrant Council of Ireland*

Gloria Kirwan, *Assistant Professor of Social Work, Trinity College Dublin, Ireland*

INTRODUCTION

Despite a range of legal and policy initiatives at national and international levels designed to prevent and combat trafficking in human beings, each year thousands of people are traded as commodities globally, including within and across European borders. The purposes for which human beings are trafficked worldwide include forced labour, prostitution and other forms of adult sexual exploitation, sham or forced marriages, domestic servitude, child soldiers or forced adult recruits, forced begging, benefit fraud, trafficking for organ retrieval and child sexual exploitation (UNODC 2016). Despite increased reporting of other forms of trafficking, such as forced labour (UNODC 2016), trafficking for the purposes of sexual exploitation, which involves mainly female victims, remains the most widely detected form of human trafficking both in Europe and worldwide, according to recent reports (Eurostat 2013; UNODC 2012, p.12, 2014, pp.33–34).

Regardless of the variations that exist, human trafficking involves a chain of actions from recruitment of victims through to the point of exploitation. The strategies employed by traffickers are almost always coercive in nature, often involving threats or the use of violence. Gallagher (2006) also alerts us to the subtler forms of entrapment used by traffickers, including manipulation, coercion, deceit, blackmail or debt agreements that are designed to be impossible to escape from. Whichever form it takes, the entrapment of victims by human traffickers is a form of bondage or modern slavery. Thus, the use of fear combined with physical or psychological control in one form or another is a key component of all human trafficking activity. The motivations that prompt human traffickers to entrap and exploit fellow human beings are diverse, but economic factors underpin much of this activity worldwide; the financial gains associated with human trafficking are generally sufficient motivation for the individuals and the organised gangs that perpetrate this activity.

There is an ever-increasing quantity of data available related to different forms of human trafficking, and this chapter attempts to present an overview of key issues related to human trafficking activity in Europe at the present time, with particular reference to the trafficking of women and its link with gender-based violence. This chapter also highlights the major initiatives in Europe that aim to tackle this growing phenomenon. As will be outlined, much of the policy thrust in Europe is focused on bolstering the detection and legal mechanisms that can be used to root out human trafficking activities, to identify the perpetrators and to bring them to account before the criminal justice system. While considerable effort has been devoted in recent years to coordinating security and legal strategies across Europe, there is still a long way to go before national and European systems are adequately equipped, resourced and harmonised in their laws and implementation to effectively deal with this problem. Therefore, much emphasis continues to be placed on resourcing police and security systems and updating the relevant legislation.

However, there are gaps in the strategies targeting human trafficking, with much of the effort to date concentrated on what we refer to in this chapter as the 'life and limb' dimensions of anti-human trafficking strategies, such as victim rescue, prosecuting traffickers and interrupting the highly organised criminal networks that control different forms of trafficking. In this chapter we argue for more emphasis on awareness-raising initiatives among the wider population that aim to highlight the different forms of human trafficking and its association with gender-based violence. This we refer to as the 'hearts and minds' dimension of human trafficking prevention and intervention because it targets public attitudes and public knowledge. This wider focus is required, it is suggested, because there is a need to address not only the supply end of the trafficking chain, but also to tackle the factors that stimulate the demand for the services provided by trafficking victims. Purchasers of services provided by victims of trafficking are a diverse population, including individuals who may or may not understand that they are involved in trafficking transactions. This chapter argues for more emphasis on awareness-raising strategies that target public awareness and attitudes as a means to shrink the 'marketplace' that traffickers depend on for their cash rewards and that fuels the coercive entrapment of victims by traffickers who stand to benefit financially from the proceeds of trafficking. The chapter concludes with observations on possible future directions in the anti-human trafficking agenda.

DEFINITIONS OF HUMAN TRAFFICKING AND INTERNATIONAL TREATIES

In its *Protocol to Prevent, Suppress and Punish Trafficking in Persons, Especially Women and Children* (UN 2000b), the United Nations General Assembly adopted the following definition of human trafficking that attempts to define the activity in all its different forms:

> 'Trafficking in persons' shall mean the recruitment, transportation, transfer, harbouring or receipt of persons, by means of the threat or use of force or other forms of coercion, of abduction, of fraud, of deception, of the abuse of power or of a position of vulnerability or of the giving or receiving of payments or benefits to achieve the consent of a person having control over another person, for the purpose of exploitation.

Exploitation is a key component of human trafficking, and it is often accompanied by coercion in one form or another. Essentially, it is through an act of exploitation that one person becomes another person's commodity. The link with exploitation and coercion reveals human trafficking as a human rights issue as well as a criminal activity. The United Nation's Protocol (often referred to as the 'Trafficking Protocol') goes on to explain the different dimensions of the term 'exploitation' in the context of human trafficking as follows:

> Exploitation shall include, at a minimum, the exploitation of the prostitution of others or other forms of sexual exploitation, forced

labour or services, slavery or practises similar to slavery, servitude or the removal of organs.

This Protocol, along with the *Protocol against Smuggling of Migrants by Land, Sea and Air* (UN 2000a) and the *Protocol against the Illicit Manufacturing and Trafficking in Firearms, Their Parts and Components and Ammunition* (UN 2001), was adopted as an optional part of the UN *Convention against Transnational Organised Crime* (UN 2004). The Trafficking Protocol, also referred to as the Palermo Protocol after the Italian city where it was opened for signatures, has been useful in bringing a common focus within the international community to the issue of human trafficking and a shared vision of strategies that can be used to combat the long-arm reach of trafficking activity. Achieving agreement on a shared definition at national and international levels is essential for the coordination of anti-human trafficking strategies at all levels including the production of reliable and comparable statistics within and across legal jurisdictions. A lack of agreed definitions at the international level gives rise to differences in the approach to data collection, and this, in turn, leads to an incomplete or inaccurate picture within the international context of the extent and nature of human trafficking activities and the success of anti-trafficking measures.

As indicated in its title, the UN Trafficking Protocol mandates a specific focus on women and children, due to their enhanced vulnerability to abuse and exploitation. Similarly, the UN's (1979) *Convention on the Elimination of All Forms of Discrimination against Women* (CEDAW) is of special significance to trafficking in women because it establishes obligations with regards to legislative, judicial, administrative and other measures to prohibit discrimination and promote equality between women and men. Article 6 of CEDAW explicitly mandates that signatories have to 'take all appropriate measures, including legislation, to suppress all forms of traffic in women and exploitation of prostitution of women'.

THE SPECTRUM OF HUMAN TRAFFICKING

Gallagher (2006, p.163) suggests that human trafficking has moved centre stage, 'from the margins to the mainstream', in the international political landscape. The increased political attention to trafficking is due in part to its scale in terms of the numbers of victims and also its scale in terms of the revenues (mainly undeclared) that it is generating for profiteers and international crime syndicates. For example, UNODC (2010) statistics on trafficking in Europe indicate that approximately 140,000 victims of sex trafficking alone (and not including the many other forms of trafficking already highlighted) are located each year in the European region, among the estimated one million women engaged in transactional sex. The same source suggests that trafficking for sexual exploitation generates income in the region of €2.5 billion each year. Across all different forms of human trafficking, 80 per cent of the detected victims are women or girls (Eurostat 2014). In Europe, trafficking victims constitute a difficult-to-identify population, which is dispersed across urban and rural localities, with victims typically residing in the same home or premises as their trafficker or purchaser (who may or may not be the same person). Because of the complexities involved in identifying victims of trafficking, it is likely that the figures available are an under-estimation of the overall population of trafficked people living within European borders.

FACTORS ASSOCIATED WITH VULNERABILITY TO HUMAN TRAFFICKING

The causes of human trafficking are multiple and complex, but certain factors are associated within the literature with an increased vulnerability to becoming a victim of trafficking. The opportunities for traffickers to locate, identify and entrap potential victims are manifold. It has been found that before they become the victim of trafficking, victims are often already experiencing life contexts that render them particularly susceptible to manipulation, exploitation or abusive coercion. Factors in the countries of origin of trafficking victims may constitute 'push factors', while factors associated with the country of destination are 'pull factors'. Europol (2016, p.10) concludes that push factors not only 'influence victims and exploiters' but also facilitate trafficking. The report goes on to identify these factors to include lack of education, adverse personal circumstances, unemployment, inequalities in the labour market and gender discrimination. Sometimes fleeing abusive family situations and escaping conflict zones also operate as push factors in origin countries.

In a briefing document to the European Parliament, Voronova and Radjenovic (2016) also highlighted the gendered nature of human trafficking and how women and men are trafficked differently and often for different end purposes. They highlighted vulnerability factors associated with female (and children) victims of trafficking, such as a pre-trafficking history of exposure to domestic violence, and highlighted how such histories of violence may affect a woman's confidence and self-esteem, thus depleting her ability to seek help from relevant authorities. They also exposed the commercial nature of prostitution as a form of big business, and as a trade that mainly positions women as the victims. This report also highlighted the relationship between displaced populations and trafficking. Migrant populations, driven from their homelands because of war, poverty and/or famine, are highly vulnerable to traffickers who exploit the experience of displacement that crisis migration will create. Exploitation in this context is likely to include the use of violence, but may also be more nuanced as the victims will be highly dependent on their traffickers for survival.

While the above-mentioned push factors contribute to human trafficking, there are also certain 'pull factors' in the destination countries that similarly fuel human trafficking, such as demand for sexual services and the wider sex industry, the demand for cheap labour, and the globalised movement of migrant populations towards Europe, some of whom are highly vulnerable to exploitation and entrapment by traffickers. Europol (2016) has highlighted subtle factors underpinning the proliferation of trafficking crimes in Europe. These include the lack of public awareness of trafficking, alongside the wider public acceptance of substandard and exploitative conditions in relation to foreign workers. Also, traffickers are adept at utilising new means and methods of avoiding detection. New technologies, in particular, offer traffickers many advantages in terms of identifying potential victims and connecting with potential buyers through advertising and selling (Hughes 2014). Voronova and Radjenovic (2016) report the rise of 'cyber slavery' and the growth in the use of the internet to market sexual services and to sell humans (usually women and children) as sexual commodities. Furthermore, the differences between the EU member states in terms of anti-trafficking policies and legislation enhance opportunities for traffickers to avoid detection and slip through loopholes if apprehended (Europol 2016). Traffickers can be quick to take advantage of legislative gaps, and will relocate their operations to jurisdictions where legislation or security practises are less likely to hold them to account. Europol (2016, p.12) highlights how such legislative gaps operate as pull factors because they facilitate, rather than obstruct or disrupt, the flows of human trafficking.

With reference to the data coming from agencies such as the UN Office on Drugs and Crime (UNODC), it is increasingly clear that gender is a relevant factor in many forms of trafficking, whether it is females into prostitution or males into forced labour (UNODC 2012, 2014, 2016). Common to all trafficking victim groups is the use of coercion, force and violence (or the threat of violence) to bind the victim to the trafficker or to the purchaser(s) to whom the trafficked victim is sold. The UNODC (2012) reported that, in contrast to the global average, Europe, as a world region, has a higher proportion of trafficking for sexual exploitation (an estimated 62%, whereas the global average is 51%) and the lowest proportion of forced labour (an estimated 31%). Hughes (2014, p.2) concludes that the available statistical data and estimations indicate 'the percentage of victims trafficked for sexual exploitation appears to be higher in Europe than in other regions of the world'.

The Eurostat reports corroborate the UNODC findings, exposing Europe as a world region where the sexual exploitation of women is the most prevalent type of trafficking crime. In statistical terms, the Eurostat reports (2013, 2014, 2015) on trafficking in human beings have exposed the high proportion of women and girls among the victims of this crime. According to Eurostat (2015), women are in the majority among those trafficked for sexual exploitation (95%). With the exception of forced labour, women are a combined majority (52%) in all other forms of trafficking. There is also a trend discernible within emerging data to suggest that the percentage of victims of trafficking for sexual exploitation is steadily increasing (Hughes 2014).

The European Commission's *Study on the Gender Dimension of Trafficking in Human Beings* (Walby *et al.* 2016) exposes not only the highly gendered nature of human trafficking in terms of the number of women who are victims, but also in terms of the harms associated with sex trafficking. Walby *et al.* (2016, p.8) point out that the serious nature of harms associated with sexual exploitation is related to the specific ways that the bodies of trafficked women are abused: 'They are severe, brutal and long-term, gender-specific physical, gynaecological and mental health harms, risks to life and traumas from trafficking for purposes of sexual exploitation.'

Europol (2016, p.3) also confirms that the most reported form of human trafficking in the EU is human trafficking for the purpose of sexual exploitation. It records that, in the period 2013–14, 90 per cent of the contributions regarding human trafficking received by Europol concerned organised crime gang activity related to sexual exploitation. In agreement with the reports cited earlier, the gender breakdown of the victims in this category is recorded by Europol (2016) as predominantly female, including a small percentage of female minors. Indeed, of the total cohort of trafficked minors identified by Europol in that two-year period, the report states that many in this group were young girls coerced against their will into prostitution (2016, p.19). In general, victims subjected to trafficking for the purpose of sexual exploitation are identified in Europol's report as coming from many global regions including Asia, Africa and South America. However, the report finds that, in the European context, most victims of trafficking for the purpose of sexual exploitation are female EU nationals from Central and Eastern Europe, a fact which underscores the diverse flows of trafficked victims around the globe and the capacity of traffickers to identify victims across many different geographical contexts.

The findings emerging across all of the reports cited in this chapter agree on the use of violence and coercion as a prevalent means of holding victims in bondage to the traffickers. All the reports highlight the heightened vulnerability of women as victims of trafficking in the context of certain factors. However, the research to date has concentrated, in the main, on the supply end of the trafficking chain and has focused less on the motivations of people who buy services provided by victims of trafficking. A study by Yonkova and Keegan (2014) succeeded in researching the views and attitudes of a sample of people who had bought sex. This transnational study found that attitudes among male purchasers of sex lacked insight into the potential plight of the women they were purchasing sex from, and they were also found to lack awareness concerning their potential role in the human trafficking processes of supply and demand that regularly intersect with the sex industry (Yonkova and Keegan 2014). The study was carried out across five EU member states – Bulgaria, Cyprus, Finland, Ireland and Lithuania – and the data collected included interviews or completed surveys with 763 purchasers of sex (71 face-to-face interviews and 692 online survey responses). The results reveal that the average buyer of sex is male, well educated, with middle to high income, and in a relationship with another adult at the point in time when they engage in the purchase of sex. The data also revealed that the first-time purchase of sex was recalled by the research participants as spontaneous or unplanned, often occurring in conjunction with alcohol or drug consumption and/or in the company of friends who were also purchasing sex. However, the analysis of the face-to-face interviews provided additional information related to the context of subsequent sex purchases that often changed in nature from the unplanned and spontaneous nature of the first sex purchase into a more planned activity. The use of the internet as a medium for locating sex workers and purchasing sex featured strongly in the responses from Finnish and Irish participants. This study also illuminated that first-time experiences of purchasing sex often take place at a relatively young stage of adulthood.

The study canvassed participants on their attitudes towards the women who were involved in these transactions. In the main, the male buyers viewed the females involved in the transactions as consenting adults and were unlikely to conceptualise the women from whom they purchased sex as potential victims of human trafficking, even though almost one-third of male respondents who reported purchasing sex also reported being cognisant of some form of exploitation related to the context of the transaction such as female sellers who were legally under the age of consensual intercourse. These findings suggest a fault line in awareness among the population of purchasers of sex regarding the different routes into prostitution of the women from whom they buy sex and the likelihood that over a number of transactions they are likely to encounter women who are victims of human trafficking. Furthermore, the study found that the purchasers were not deterred by the legislation outlawing the purchase of sex from victims of trafficking (in countries where that exists) because, in general, they did not associate such laws with the activities in which they were engaged.

This reported study provides new knowledge on the attitudes and levels of awareness of trafficking among the potential purchaser population, but clearly more research is needed to better understand the influences on attitudes, motivations and awareness levels among purchasers of services likely to be provided by victims of trafficking, whether it is within the sex industry or other service industries with which human trafficking has come to be associated.

EUROPEAN RESPONSES TO HUMAN TRAFFICKING

In May 2016, in response to the mounting evidence of the extent of trafficking into the European region and the associated high levels of gender-related exploitation of women trafficked for the purposes of sexual exploitation, the European Parliament of the European Union (EU), meeting in plenary session, issued a statement calling for more gender-specific prevention strategies and gender-specific victim support (European Parliament 2016). The statement stands as a recent example of the many initiatives, conventions, agreements and strategies at local, national and regional levels, all of which aim to counteract the trade in human beings. Some years earlier, the Council of Europe (2005) had produced a policy position in the form of the *Convention on Action against Trafficking in Human Beings* (Trafficking Convention), which strongly emphasised the human rights of trafficking victims. It further promoted the issue of gender equality in the context of human trafficking by stipulating in Article 17: 'Each Party shall, in applying measures referred to in this chapter, aim to promote gender equality and use gender mainstreaming in the development, implementation and assessment of the measures.'

The Council of Europe also established the increasingly influential Group of Experts on Action against Trafficking in Human Beings (GRETA) that operates as a monitoring mechanism regarding the implementation of the Trafficking Convention, and is also involved in data gathering and capacity building at national and international levels. GRETA has published six reports of its work since its establishment in 2008 (GRETA 2011, 2012, 2013, 2015, 2016, 2017). In its second report, GRETA (2012, p.11) highlighted the connections between certain forms of human trafficking and gender-based violence, emphasising the need for non-discriminatory strategies to assist all victims of human trafficking in terms of 'protection, assistance and redress'.

The European *Convention for the Protection of Human Rights and Fundamental Freedoms and Protocols* (Council of Europe 1950), generally referred to as the European Convention on Human Rights (ECHR), does not refer explicitly to trafficking in people. However, in 2010, the European Court of Human Rights ruled that trafficking in human beings falls within the scope of Article 4 of the ECHR, making this Convention an essential legal tool in the efforts to stem the spread of trafficking activity in the European context.

The EU has also engaged strategies aimed at the eradication of human trafficking and encouraging increased protection of victims. In 2011, the EU adopted *Directive 2011/36/EU on Preventing and Combating Trafficking in Human Beings and Protecting its Victims* (Trafficking Directive) (EU 2011a). The Trafficking Directive supports anti-trafficking responses across the different EU member states by recognising the rights of victims of crime in general trafficking victims in particular. 'Council Directive 2011/92/EU on combating the sexual abuse and sexual exploitation of children and child pornography' (EU 2011b) is fully synchronised with the Trafficking Directive through its focus on the rights of children exploited through trafficking crimes. This was followed by Council Directive 2012/29/EU that addresses the provision of support and protection to victims of crime (EU 2012). It refers specifically to gender-based violence and violence against women in contemporary societies that it defines in Recital 17 as:

> ...discrimination and a violation of fundamental freedoms, including violence in close relationships, sexual violence (including rape, sexual assault and harassment), trafficking in human beings, slavery and different forms of harmful practises, such as forced marriages, female genital mutilation and so-called 'honour crimes'.

These recent EU Directives develop further the strategies adopted in Directive 2004/81/EC (EU 2004) regarding residency permits for third country national victims of trafficking in human beings, and which provide for periods of recovery and reflection as well as encouraging victim cooperation with the investigation of the trafficking crime(s) committed against them.

In parallel to the various legislative measures, the EU adopted and implemented an ambitious strategy for the period 2012–16, which included priorities such as the identification and assistance of victims, increased prevention and prosecution efforts, and a focus on the generation of new knowledge on the emerging trends and forms of human trafficking. Such efforts at EU level advance the fight against trafficking, particularly on the supply side of the trafficking equation, attempting as they do to interrupt and eliminate trafficking. However, it is argued here that supply follows demand, and that there is a need to match the focus on the supply activities with a focus on the demand side of the trafficking equation. This point is discussed in the next section.

FUTURE DIRECTIONS

Strategic responses to combat human trafficking are best conceptualised as multi-dimensional, involving actions in the areas of prevention, identification of human trafficking crimes, protection, rescue and rehabilitation of victims (and potential victims), prosecution of traffickers and increased research to enable the political systems to stay informed on the constantly changing methods and approaches adopted by traffickers in their efforts to avoid detection.

Law enforcement and prosecution services can do a lot to interrupt the activities of human traffickers. However, based on the estimates of income generation that traffickers gain from this crime, it is clear that many people are paying for services in which people are traded or exploited as commodities. This point applies to many forms of human trafficking, but it is particularly relevant in the context of trafficking for sexual exploitation. It is argued here that directing the bulk of anti-trafficking resources into law enforcement or victim rescue and protection concentrates efforts on the supply side of the trafficking equation but leaves the demand side with a disproportionately small input.

As pointed out earlier, the most widespread form of human trafficking is for the purposes of sexual exploitation of women and girls, a fact that suggests that human trafficking could be dramatically decreased if strategies were successful in preventing the trafficking of women and children for this purpose. It has been internationally agreed that prevention should be based on reduction of the demand that fosters human trafficking, especially of women and children (UN 2000b, Article 9 (5)), which, translated into the particular area of sex trafficking, means the reduction of demand for paid sexual services:

> States Parties shall adopt or strengthen legislative or other measures, such as educational, social or cultural measures, including through bilateral and multilateral cooperation, to discourage the demand that fosters all forms of exploitation of persons, especially women and children, that leads to trafficking.

However, policy aspirations are not enough. There is an urgent need for practical policies informed by reliable research. The transnational research initiative referred to earlier (Yonkova and Keegan 2014) provides an example of the insights that can be gained by conducting targeted research studies in this area. The data that was collected in that study from purchasers of sex offers useful and practical messages regarding buyer attitudes and behaviour. In particular, it highlighted the chilling effect on sex buyers' behaviour when there was any danger to their personal safety, or any likelihood of public identification that they were buying sex, or the possibility of disclosure to their family/partner, or any threat of criminal sanctions such as imprisonment. However, the study authors noted that the laws currently in place that criminalise the purchase of sex from victims of trafficking offer little by way of deterrence, according to the study participants. Therefore, helping potential purchasers to make a link between their purchasing behaviour and the creation of demand for trafficking victims is clearly challenging and difficult to achieve. It is clear, therefore, that devising strategies that educate and raise awareness among the many purchasers of trafficking victims – be it for sex, forced labour, sham marriages, etc. – will require innovation and new ways of connecting with present and potential future purchasers. Such strategies will also need to be informed by a wider research and evidence base that looks beyond trends in trafficking flows and activities and that aims to build knowledge on purchaser motivations and awareness.

CONCLUSIONS

This chapter provides an overview of the global trade in human beings, referred to in the literature as human trafficking and modern slavery. The chapter has also illustrated the scale of the problem with particular reference to the information currently available on human trafficking in the European continent, and it has highlighted the abusive and coercive nature of trafficking activities, particularly with reference to the experience of female and child victims. An elaborate matrix of international agreements, covenants and protocols is now in place to tackle the problem of human trafficking, fuelled by the levels of human suffering it can involve, the exploitative nature of this crime and the detrimental impact on national and international economies that the existence of a black market in human commodities can cause.

The specific nature of human trafficking and the gender-based violence and coercion associated with it are important referents for future strategies on combatting human trafficking. In this context, the chapter has drawn attention to an emerging dimension to preventing trafficking, highlighted by recent results from a study of men who have engaged in the purchase of sex for money in countries of the EU. This research has revealed the importance of raising public awareness about trafficking and exploitation in the minds of individual members of the public, particularly among those members of the public who are likely to become frequent, occasional or potential buyers of services from trafficking victims. It is suggested here that increased attention is urgently needed to inform and educate the general public who may be wittingly or unwittingly the buyers on which the whole market of human trafficking depends. In particular, there is a *need for demand reduction strategies* to target buyers of sex and to heighten their awareness of human trafficking and the gender-based violence that can go hand in hand with it.

Specifically, there is evidence that human trafficking, mediated through the use of violence, exists within the sex industry, and the perception that all women are consenting sellers of sex, and by implication not exploited, needs to be challenged.

Reduction in demand for the services of trafficked humans has to be recognised as a transnational issue, which requires local, national and cross-border responses at European and global levels. National strategies should be informed by the culturally specific context within which individuals become active purchasers of trafficked victims. Targeting purchasers in the trafficking marketplace presents inherent challenges related to the difficulty in identifying who these individuals might be, and the lack of data that persists regarding the profile of purchaser populations. In the meantime, innovation is essential in strategising initiatives that will influence the hearts and minds of those who, wittingly or unwittingly, keep the trafficking industry in business.

REFERENCES

Council of Europe (1950) *European Convention for the Protection of Human Rights and Fundamental Freedoms and Protocols.* Accessed on 3/8/2017 at www.echr.coe.int/Documents/Convention_ENG.pdf

Council of Europe (2005) *Convention on Action against Trafficking in Human Beings.* Strasbourg: Council of Europe. Accessed on 3/8/2017 at www.refworld.org/docid/43fded544.html

EU (European Union) (2004) 'Council Directive 2004/81/EC on residence permit issued to third-country nationals who are victims of trafficking in human beings or who have been the subject of an action to facilitate illegal immigration, who cooperate with the competent authorities.' *Official Journal of the European Union* L 261/19. Accessed on 3/8/2017 at http://ec.europa.eu/anti-trafficking/sites/antitrafficking/files/directive_2004_81_on_residence_permit_en_1.pdf

EU (2011a) 'Council Directive 2011/36/EU on preventing and combating trafficking in human beings and protecting its victims.' *Official Journal of the European Union* L 101/1. Accessed on 3/8/2017 at http://eur-lex.europa.eu/LexUriServ/LexUriServ.do?uri=OJ:L:2011:101:0001:0011:EN:PDF

EU (2011b) 'Council Directive 2011/92/EU on combating the sexual abuse and sexual exploitation of children and child pornography.' *Official Journal of the European Union* L 335/1. Accessed on 3/8/2017 at https://ec.europa.eu/anti-trafficking/sites/antitrafficking/files/directive_2011_92_1.pdf

EU (2012) 'Council Directive 2012/29/EU on minimum standards on the rights, support and protection of victims of crime.' *Official Journal of the European Union* L 315/57. Accessed on 3/8/2017 at http://ec.europa.eu/anti-trafficking/sites/antitrafficking/files/directive_2012_29_eu_1.pdf

European Parliament (2016) *European Parliament of 12 May 2016 on Implementation of the Directive 2011/36/EU of 5 April 2011 on Preventing and Combating Trafficking in Human Beings and Protecting its Victims from a Gender Perspective* (2015/2118(INI)).

Europol (2016) *Situation Report: Trafficking in Human Beings in the EU.* No. 765175. The Hague: Europol Public Information. Accessed on 3/8/2017 at http://ec.europa.eu/anti-trafficking/sites/antitrafficking/files/situational_report_trafficking_in_human_beings-_europol.pdf

Eurostat (2013) *Trafficking in Human Beings 2013.* Luxembourg: Publications Office of the European Union. Accessed on 3/8/2017 at http://ec.europa.eu/anti-trafficking/sites/antitrafficking/files/trafficking_in_human_beings_-_dghome-eurostat_en_1.pdf

Eurostat (2014) *Trafficking in Human Beings 2014.* Luxembourg: Publications Office of the European Union. Accessed on 3/8/2017 at http://ec.europa.eu/anti-trafficking/sites/antitrafficking/files/thb_wp2013-2014_final_161014.pdf

Eurostat (2015) *Trafficking in Human Beings 2015.* Luxembourg: Publications Office of the European Union. Accessed on 3/8/2017 at https://ec.europa.eu/anti-trafficking/sites/antitrafficking/files/eurostat_report_on_trafficking_in_human_beings_-_2015_edition.pdf

Gallagher, A. (2006) 'Recent legal developments in the field of human trafficking: A critical review of the 2005 European Convention and related instruments.' *European Journal of Migration and Law 8*, 163–189.

GRETA (Group of Experts on Action against Trafficking in Human Beings) (2011) *First General Report on GRETA's Activities: Covering the Period from February 2009 to July 2011.* Strasbourg: Council of Europe. Accessed on 3/8/2017 at https://rm.coe.int/16805aa459

GRETA (2012) *Second General Report on GRETA's Activities: Covering the Period from 1 August 2011 to 31 July 2012.* Strasbourg: Council of Europe. Accessed on 3/8/2017 at https://rm.coe.int/16805aa45b

GRETA (2013) *3rd General Report on GRETA's Activities: Covering the Period from 1 August 2012 to 31 July 2013.* Strasbourg: Council of Europe. Accessed on 3/8/2017 at https://rm.coe.int/16805aa45d

GRETA (2015) *4th General Report on GRETA's Activities: Covering the Period from 1 August 2013 to 30 September 2014.* Strasbourg: Council of Europe. Accessed on 3/8/2017 at https://rm.coe.int/16805aa45f

GRETA (2016) *5th General Report on GRETA's Activities: Covering the Period from 1 October 2014 to 31 December 2015.* Strasbourg: Council of Europe. Accessed on 3/8/2017 at https://rm.coe.int/168063093c

GRETA (2017) *6th General Report on GRETA's Activities: Covering the Period from 1 January to 31 December 2016.* Strasbourg: Council of Europe. Accessed on 3/8/2017 at https://rm.coe.int/1680706a42

Hughes, D.M. (2014) 'Trafficking in human beings in the European Union: Gender, sexual exploitation, and digital communication technologies.' *Sage Open 4*, 4, 2158244014553585. Accessed on 28/8/2017 at http://journals.sagepub.com/doi/pdf/10.1177/2158244014553585

UN (United Nations) (1979) *Convention on the Elimination of All Forms of Discrimination against Women.* New York: UN. Accessed on 3/8/2017 at www.unodc.org/pdf/criminal_justice/Convention_on_the_Elimination_of_all_forms_of_Discrimination_against_Women.pdf

UN (United Nations) (2000a) *Protocol against Smuggling of Migrants by Land, Sea and Air, Supplementing the United Nations Convention against Transnational Organized Crime.* New York: UN. Accessed on 3/8/2017 at www.unodc.org/documents/southeastasiaandpacific/2011/04/som-indonesia/convention_smug_eng.pdf

UN (2000b) *Protocol to Prevent, Suppress and Punish Trafficking in Persons, Especially Women and Children, Supplementing the United Nations Convention against Transnational Organized Crime.* 15 November. 2237 UNTS 319 (Palermo Protocol). New York: UN. Accessed on 3/8/2017 at www.osce.org/odihr/19223?download=true

UN (2001) *Protocol against the Illicit Manufacturing of and Trafficking in Firearms, Their Parts and Components and Ammunition, Supplementing the United Nations Convention against Transnational Organized Crime.* New York: UN. Accessed on 3/8/2017 at www.unodc.org/documents/treaties/UNTOC/Publications/A-RES%2055-255/55r255e.pdf

UN (2004) *United Nations Convention against Transnational Organized Crime and the Protocols Thereto.* New York: UN. Accessed on 3/8/2017 at www.unodc.org/documents/treaties/UNTOC/Publications/TOC%20Convention/TOCebook-e.pdf

UNODC (United Nations Office on Drugs and Crime) (2010) *Globalization of Crime: A Transnational Organized Crime Threat Assessment.* Vienna, Austria: UNODC. Accessed on 3/8/2017 at www.unodc.org/documents/data-and-analysis/tocta/TOCTA_Report_2010_low_res.pdf

UNODC (2012) *Global Report on Trafficking in Persons 2012.* No. E.13.IV.1. New York: United Nations. Accessed on 3/8/2017 at www.unodc.org/documents/data-and-analysis/glotip/Trafficking_in_Persons_2012_web.pdf

UNODC (2014) *Global Report on Trafficking in Persons 2014.* No. E.14.V.10. New York: United Nations. Accessed on 3/8/2017 at www.unodc.org/documents/human-trafficking/2014/GLOTIP_2014_full_report.pdf

UNODC (2016) *Global Report on Trafficking in Persons 2016.* No. E.16.IV.6. New York: United Nations. Accessed on 3/8/2017 at www.unodc.org/documents/data-and-analysis/glotip/2016_Global_Report_on_Trafficking_in_Persons.pdf

Voronova, S. and Radjenovic, A. (2016) *The Gender Dimension of Human Trafficking. Briefing, February 2016.* European Parliamentary Research Service, PE 577.950.

Walby, S., Apitzsch, B., Armstrong, J., Balderston, S. et al. (2016) *Study on the Gender Dimension of Trafficking in Human Beings: Final Report.* Luxembourg: Publications Office of the European Union.

Yonkova, N. and Keegan, E. (2014) *Tackling Demand for Sexual Services of Trafficked Women and Girls.* Immigrant Council of Ireland. Accessed on 3/8/2017 at http://ec.europa.eu/anti-trafficking/sites/antitrafficking/files/stoptraffick_full_report_1.pdf

Chapter 12

FEMALE GENITAL MUTILATION

FINDINGS FROM A PORTUGUESE PREVALENCE STUDY

Dalila Cerejo, *Interdisciplinary Centre of Social Sciences (CICS. NOVA-FCSH/NOVA), New University of Lisbon, Portugal*

INTRODUCTION

Female genital mutilation or genital cutting (FGM/C) is a form of gender-based violence and an attack on the rights and freedom of girls and women in many countries. Because of the serious consequences for the physical and psychological health of women and girls who have been subjected to it, FGM/C is considered a human rights and public health issue, unavoidable in most European countries that host migrant populations from countries where FGM/C is practised. In this chapter I define FGM/C, give an overview of the phenomenon's extent throughout the globe, and articulate the subject within the European context, particularly by addressing the creation of legally binding instruments, such as the Istanbul Convention, that urge member states to take measures to prevent and combat all forms of violence against women and gender-based violence, including FGM/C.

Using Portugal as a case study, data from the estimated prevalence of FGM/C and the methods used to estimate that prevalence are also presented. In addition, I discuss the estimated results for women living in Portugal who have undergone FGM/C, as well as prevalence estimations for girls who have undergone or are still at risk of undergoing FGM/C.

FGM/C AS A GLOBAL PROBLEM

FGM/C is acknowledged as a harmful practise and a serious violation of the human rights of women of all ages. It is a worldwide social problem based on gender discrimination and stigmatisation, rooted in power asymmetries that produce and reproduce many forms of gender-based violence, of which FGM/C is one of many. This practise is recognised as having harmful and direct consequences on girls and women's physical, psychological and sexual health (Bansal *et al.* 2013; Campos 2010; DGS 2012; EIGE 2013b, 2015; Frade 2007; Vicente 2007). It is a perennial practise carried out in several countries around the world, and is recognised as a violation of women's human rights and citizenship, and needs to be viewed as both a rights and a public health issue (Council of Europe 2009; European Parliament 2001; UNGA 1948, 1979). FGM/C violates a set of fundamental human rights, gender equality and non-discrimination principles, as well as the inalienable right to life and the right to be free from torture and cruel, inhuman or degrading treatment.

FGM/C is defined as 'all procedures involving the partial or total removal of external female genitalia or any damage to female genitalia for non-medical reasons' (APF 2009, p1). FGM/C is commonly practised on girls aged between 0 and 15, but also on adult women. Depending on the practising community and the sociocultural context, it can occur from the moment a child is born until marriage or after childbirth (APF 2009; Brown, Beecham and Barrett 2013; Mackie 2000; Martingo 2009; WHO 2008, 2009).

According to the World Health Organization (WHO) classification, endorsed by ten United Nations (UN) bodies (WHO 2008), the phenomenon can be divided into four major types of intervention: type I, clitoridectomy: partial or total removal of the clitoris and/or the foreskin of the clitoris; type II, excision: partial or total removal of the clitoris and small labia, as well as a cut to the labia majora; type III, infibulation: narrowing of the vaginal orifice through the creation of a sealant membrane, by the cutting and apposition of the small and/or large lips, with or without excision of the clitoris; and type IV,[1] covering other interventions on the female genitalia for

1 According to WHO, type IV also includes practises such as stretching and the introduction of harmful substances into the vagina.

non-medical reasons, such as puncturing, incisions, cutting, scarring and cauterisation (burns).

WHO estimations indicate that, overall, 90 per cent of FGM/C performed worldwide is of types I, II and IV, with type III representing just 10 per cent. Moreover, WHO reveals that around 130 million girls have been subjected to FGM/C types I, II or IV, and 3 million per year are at risk of undergoing the procedure in the African continent alone (WHO 2000). The practise of types I, II and III is documented in 28 African countries, as well as some Asian and Middle Eastern countries (Equality Now 2012), reminding us that to reduce FGM/C to African countries can be misleading. The II Portuguese Action Programme for the Elimination of Female Genital Mutilation (Grupo de Trabalho Inter-sectorial sobre a Mutilação Genital Feminina 2011–2013) states that FGM/C is also performed in some countries of the Arabic Peninsula (Oman, Yemen, Bahrain and the United Arab Emirates) and in some regions of Indonesia, Malaysia and India (in the Dawoodi Bohra, a small Indian Muslim community). Other variations can be found in Egypt, where FGM/C is often performed in hospitals, despite its ban by the International Federation of Gynaecology and Obstetrics and by WHO. Table 12.1 lists the 37 countries where FGM/C has been documented.[2]

Table 12.1: List of countries where FGM/C is documented

Africa			Asia	Middle East
Benin	Ghana	Central African Republic	India	Oman
Burkina Faso	Guinea-Conakry	Democratic Republic of Congo	Indonesia	Yemen
Cameroon	Guinea Bissau	Senegal	Sri Lanka	United Arab Emirates
Chad	Kenya	Sierra Leone	Malaysia	Iraq
Ivory Coast	Liberia	Somalia		
Djibouti	Mali	Sudan		

2 Not included in this table are other references to indigenous groups in Central and South America, for example in Peru and Colombia. In fact, as of 2007, there was evidence of cases of FGM (type I, clitoridectomy) among the Embera people (Colombia), where, although information is still scarce, it is believed that FGM/C is performed on newborns (UNFPA 2011).

Africa			Asia	Middle East
Egypt	Mauritania	Tanzania		
Eritrea	Mozambique	Togo		
Ethiopia	Niger	Uganda		
Gambia	Nigeria			

Source: Lisboa *et al.* (2015)

Regarding prevalence within these countries, the comparisons of estimations present some variations. According to a UNICEF report on the estimation of FGM/C prevalence, the African countries with the highest prevalence of FGM/C are Somalia (98%), Djibouti (93%), Egypt (91%), Eritrea (89%), Mali (89%) and Sudan (88%) (UNICEF 2013). In these countries, particularly those from the Horn of Africa, FGM/C practise is globally practised, and infibulation its most common type (Macfarlane and Dorkenoo 2014).

However, due to migration flows, FGM/C is not confined to the countries identified above, since cultural frameworks also travel with migrant populations (Martingo 2009; Oberreiter 2008; Otoo-Oyortey 2007). Very often, some of their cultural values, norms and social models clash with the host countries' own cultural and social ideals. Consequently, harmful practises such as FGM/C also become a concern in the various European countries that receive these populations, for whom FGM/C is one of many cultural traditions. Concurrently, new population dynamics have spread the practise of FGM/C to regions and countries with no historic precedents in Europe, North America, Australia and New Zealand (Andro 2016). In countries like England and Wales, FGM/C has become a pressing concern due to the number of girls and women affected by it. The England and Wales FGM/C estimation of the prevalence study for 2011 concludes that 127,000 women were already subjected and 10,000 girls were subjected or at risk of being subjected to FGM/C, the majority of whom were subjected to the practise in the countries of origin (Macfarlane and Dorkenoo 2014). Some European countries have, for many years, hosted migrant communities where FGM/C is practised, while others only now have been confronted with a social problem that needs to be addressed by organisations, authorities and policy-makers, due to recent migratory flows and an unprecedented increase in refugees and asylum-seekers. According to the European Commission, 'the largest groups of women and girls originating from countries in which the practise of FGM is widespread live in the following EU countries: Austria, Belgium, Denmark, Germany, Spain, Finland, France, Ireland, Italy, the Netherlands, Portugal, Sweden, and the United Kingdom'.[3] Due to the phenomenon's global spread and the recognition that the fight to end FGM/C can only be carried out through integrated European policies, several international and European organisations have been developing recommendations and documents encouraging countries to implement strong actions and measures against FGM/C. The work done by these international organisations will be discussed next.

THE EUROPEAN LEGAL FRAMEWORK AND THE ISTANBUL CONVENTION

Several international organisations have been working to combat FGM/C through the implementation of public policies, the sensitisation of practising communities and the prevention and criminalisation of the practise. In 1992, the UN Committee on the Elimination of Discrimination against Women (CEDAW) adopted Recommendation 19, where the word 'mutilation' appeared for the first time. However, the continuation of the harmful practise led to a UN resolution (UN 2013) urging all countries to take any necessary measures to condemn and eradicate FGM/C from their territories. In 2008, an interagency declaration from the UN, alongside WHO, highlighted the need for all countries to develop concerted actions involving different sectors such as education, finance, justice, women's affairs, health, non-governmental organisations (NGOs), advocacy groups and community-based working groups (UN and WHO 2008).

The European Parliament has also been very active in producing resolutions aimed at eliminating the phenomenon. In 2001, it adopted the first resolution on FGM/C (European Parliament 2001), considering the practise to be a serious human rights violation. In 2007, a number of resolutions were issued, focusing on reproductive health consequences resulting from FGM/C as well as the drastic exposure of women from minority groups to all forms of violence (including

3 See http://ec.europa.eu/justice/gender-equality/gender-violence/eliminating-female-genital-mutilation/index_en.htm

FGM/C), making these women, and their offspring, vulnerable, and denying them their full civil and human rights.

In 2011, the creation, by the Council of Europe, of the *Convention on Preventing and Combating Violence against Women and Domestic Violence* (also known as the Istanbul Convention (2011)) represented a historical landmark for the European fight against FGM/C. This was the 'first legally binding instrument in Europe to prevent and combat violence against women as well as the most far-reaching international treaty to tackle serious violations of women rights' (EIGE 2013a, p.35). Member states that signed this Convention (Portugal was one of the first to do so) accepted as their duty to undertake all possible measures to combat and prevent FGM/C, namely through the production of legislative and legal frameworks. In Article 38, the Convention specifically mentions FGM/C, stating that 'parties shall take the necessary legislative or other measures to ensure that the following intentional conducts are criminalized: a) excising, infibulating or performing any other mutilation to the whole or any part of a woman's labia majora, labia minora or clitoris; b) coercing or procuring a woman to undergo any of the acts listed in point a; c) inciting, coercing or procuring a girl to undergo any of the acts listed in point a' (2011, Article 38). To date, 22 Council of Europe member states have signed and ratified the Convention.

In compliance with the Istanbul Convention recommendations, Portugal has adopted measures for the protection of victims, the prevention of the practise and its legal prosecution.[4] Until 2015, FGM was treated as a serious offence against physical integrity (alongside other physical offences) under Article 144 of the Penal Code. However, law 83/2015, Article 144 A, made FGM/C an autonomous crime, stating that 'whoever mutilates part or whole of a female person's genitals through clitoridectomy, infibulation, excision, or any other harmful practise to the female genital organs for non-medical reasons, is punished with imprisonment from 2 to 10 years'.

This new law adds two major improvements. First, preparatory acts (such as organising a trip abroad or hiring someone to come to

4 This new national criminal framework is aligned with the Istanbul Convention, which forces countries to ensure that the practise is criminalised. Currently, less than half of all EU member states (22 out of 47) have ratified the Istanbul Convention. This shows the lack of a transnational criminal and legislative framework that punishes the practise of FGM/C.

Portugal to perform FGM/C) are now punishable, with up to three years of imprisonment. The second major improvement is related to the victim's age. If the victim is a minor, the case only prescribes when she turns 23. Similar to the current laws in the UK and Italy, for example, the Portuguese law also includes acts performed outside the national territory. Until now, no convictions related to FGM/C cases, either practised in Portugal or abroad, have occurred. Only three cases arrived at the Public Prosecution Service of Portugal, all related to girls under 18, and all were closed due to lack of evidence and of witnesses willing to testify (Cerejo 2016).

In order to combat FGM/C from inside the cultural framework of practising communities, given its roots in deep traditional values and models of behaviour, the implementation of legal and criminal measures is not enough, seeing as they do not prevent but rather react to harm already caused through penalising and convicting those who perpetrate these acts. It is necessary to seek a change of behaviour and attitudes towards harmful practises such as FGM/C. In this regard, the Istanbul Convention also states that steps should be taken toward a change in mentality and attitudes (Article 12, paragraph 1), specifically through the deconstruction of gender stereotypes, 'because existing patterns of behavior are often influenced by prejudices, gender stereotypes and gender-biased customs and traditions' (Council of Europe 2014, p.12).

In this matter, this is perhaps the biggest challenge Europe and the various FGM/C-practising communities face today. As discussed next, FGM/C is crystallised in the normative gender roles and models of its practising communities, particularly with regards to women and girls.

FGM/C AS A CULTURAL PRACTISE OF GENDER DISCRIMINATION

It is difficult to pinpoint the historical and geographical origins of the phenomenon. There is some evidence of its early existence in Egypt, revealed by forensic analysis of mummies (Branco 2006). Ancient Egyptians believed that:

> ...the clitoris represented the masculine part of the woman, just as the foreskin represented the feminine part of the man. The removal of one or the other will then be necessary for the establishment of

> gender-defined social roles, allowing individuals to be 'true' men and 'true' women and able to take on the responsibilities and the inherent roles that derive from their biological condition. (Martingo 2009, p.47; author's translation)

This illustrates the beginning of the social organisation of gender roles and gender differentiation in practising communities.

These markedly patriarchal communities are mostly founded on the importance of marriage and the constitution of family; in this sense, 'FGM/C emerges as a way of perpetuating male and familial control and power over women and girls' sexuality' (Lisboa *et al.* 2015, p.27). Rooted in shared social beliefs and myths, such as the promotion of women's purity and fidelity to their husbands, the preservation of virginity, an increase in fertility and the decline of sexual desire, FGM/C is very often considered a prerequisite for marriage. These myths are often regarded as the bases for a 'good marriage' (Lisboa *et al.* 2015, p.26). It is the families', particularly the women's (mothers, grandmothers, aunts[5]), responsibility to ensure their daughters are 'acceptable' for a future husband, making FGM/C a *sine qua non* condition for marriage. Although the decision to subject girls and women to this practise falls on the older women in the family, it is 'a ritual perpetrated by women...by the whim of men' (Branco 2006, p.51; author's translation). Although men from practising communities dislike talking about what is considered a 'women's issue' (Lisboa *et al.* 2015), they play a crucial part in the perpetuation of FGM/C, as many of its cultural foundations uphold male honour values, sexual pleasure and dominance.

In addition to these cultural dimensions, the common, but erroneous, belief that FGM/C is mentioned in the Quran, and thus part of the Muslim cultural tradition, still constitutes an important justification for the practise. Although there is no reference to FGM/C in any of the three Abrahamic religions' holy books (Branco 2006), this practise is commonly associated with Islam. Some authors argue (Branco 2006; Martingo 2009) that it is necessary that Islamic religious leaders speak out and clearly state that FGM/C is not part of Islamic customs or traditions, and that it is not mentioned anywhere in the Quran.

5 Women in the family who exert pressure and submit girls to FGM/C regard the practise as an inevitable ritual to avoid future community stigmatisation processes and social discrimination of the girls and women in their families.

An unambiguous statement such as this from highly esteemed religious leaders within these communities would prevent the use of religion as another tool for facilitating, promoting or potentiating its perpetuation (Johansen *et al.* 2013; Lisboa *et al.* 2015; Martingo 2009). As the European Institute for Gender Equality states, 'any form of female genital mutilation is a harmful tradition practise that cannot be considered part of religion, but an act of violence against women and girls which constitutes a violation of their fundamental rights' (EIGE 2013a, p.38).

FGM/C AS A PUBLIC HEALTH ISSUE

FGM/C is a serious offence against the rights and health of women and girls, not only from a physical and psychological perspective, but also with regard to sexual and reproductive rights and wellbeing (Campos 2010; Frade 2007; Gonçalves 2005; Vicente 2007; WHO 2008, 2009). Its consequences for physical health are very serious and can even endanger the lives of women and girls. Some of the most noteworthy effects on physical, reproductive and sexual health include 'localized infections and septicemia, and other potentially lifelong health issues such as genital and urinary infections, pains and lacerations during sexual intercourse, hemorrhages and obstetric fistulas causing pain, incapacity, infertility' (Gonçalves 2005, p.3); 'sebaceous or inclusion cysts (dermoid cysts), keloid, ulcer, neurinoma and dysmenorrhea' (Vicente 2007, p.91; author's translation); and obstruction of labour, rupture of tissues, prolongation of the expulsive period, increase in the number of caesarean sections, foetal distress or prolonged and painful labour (Campos 2010). In addition, the risk of contracting HIV and other sexually transmitted infections increases significantly (EIGE 2013b), and the possibility of leading a healthy sex life is highly reduced, since FGM/C can cause severe and extensive lesions in vaginal tissue: 'vaginal penetration through injured and scarred genital tissue may be difficult or impossible, with tissue rupture causing new hemorrhages and severe pain' (Gonçalves 2005, p.21; author's translation).

In addition, the use of unsterilised knives, blades and pieces of glass to perform the cut and the absence of anaesthesia and/or antiseptic care in a procedure that can take up to 20 minutes (Frade and Gonçalves no date) greatly increase the aforementioned health risks. A study on the impacts of FGM has revealed that it can lead to obstetric complications and infant death. The study also found that 'children of mothers who underwent more extensive and [invasive] forms of FGM/C were at greater risk of dying during childbirth compared to children of mothers not subject to FGM/C' (Otoo-Oyortey 2007, p.13; author's translation).

The Council of Europe states that the practise, due to its health consequences, 'denies women and girls their right to: physical and mental integrity; freedom from violence; the highest attainable standard of health; freedom from discrimination on the basis of sex; freedom from torture, cruel, inhuman and degrading treatment; and the right to life when the procedure results in death' (2014, p.7).

THE PORTUGUESE PREVALENCE STUDY

In accordance with the recommendations of the Istanbul Convention (Council of Europe 2011), Portugal has adopted measures to understand the phenomenon, in particular by promoting scientific studies for estimating its extent, as evidenced by Programmes of Action for the Elimination of Female Genital Mutilation I, II and III (CIG 2014). In 2015, the first national study on the estimation of the prevalence of FGM/C in Portugal (Lisboa *et al.* 2015) was conducted by an interdisciplinary research team (Interdisciplinary Centre for Social Sciences, Faculdade de Ciências Sociais e Humanas da Universidade Nova de Lisboa (CICS.NOVA-FCSH/NOVA), the Instituto de Higiene e Medicina Tropical (IHMT) and the Faculdade de Ciências e Tecnologia (FCT-UNL)). The data presented next is the result of this research project.

Methodology

The main methodological instrument used for the estimation of FGM/C prevalence in Portugal was the extrapolation method, also used in several other European prevalence studies such as the ones developed in England and Wales (Macfarlane and Dorkenoo 2014), Belgium (Dubourg 2014), Holland (Exterkate 2013), Germany (Bansal *et al.* 2013), Hungary (Kőszeghy 2012) and Italy (Istituto Piepoli 2009). It multiplies the prevalence of FGM/C in the country of origin by the number of women between the ages of 15 and 49[6] born[7] in countries where FGM/C is documented and who are now living in Portugal (Lisboa *et al.* 2015; Teixeira and Lisboa 2016). As such, the prevalence in the countries of origin is applied to the number of women residing in Portugal but who were born in practising countries.

There were many challenges to the estimation of the prevalence of FGM/C in Portugal. The researchers considered many different data sources, foremost of which was the immigration office. However, two major problems arose: on the one hand, it was impossible to access the disaggregated information by age; on the other hand, and most importantly, this dataset only included the foreign population, excluding anyone who already had Portuguese citizenship but was born abroad, as well as daughters from mothers born in the practising countries.

An attempt was also made to consider data on asylum-seekers and refugees from the immigration office and the foreign affairs ministry, but the numbers reported by the UN's Refugee Agency do not regard Portugal as one of the major host countries for these populations. The national employment survey that is conducted by Statistics Portugal every trimester was also not viable for use due to sampling errors regarding these populations.

Given these obstacles, and also because we needed age, sex and country of birth disaggregation, data sources were limited. As such, the last European census (2011) was the main data source for this study. Census data has actually been used for most studies of this kind in Europe, but is not without its flaws: (1) it does not consider the possible impact of migration on cultural processes, namely on the decrease of FGM/C perpetuation in host countries (EIGE 2013b; Lisboa *et al.* 2015); (2) it does not include refugees or asylum-seekers (EIGE 2013b; Lisboa *et al.* 2015); (3) 'ethnicity is not routinely included in census data figures, although it is often a more useful indicator of FGM than nationality' (EIGE 2013b, p.29); (4) it lacks

6 This age group is most commonly used in FGM/C prevalence studies because it refers to women's reproductive age.

7 We have chosen to use the country of birth instead of citizenship in order not to exclude migrants who are already Portuguese citizens, which represent a considerable proportion of those born in Guinea-Bissau, the largest migrant population from a FGM/C-practising country living in Portugal.

'disaggregation by country of origin, by country of birth and by length of stay in a country' (EIGE 2013b, p.29); and (5) it does not allow data comparison between European countries, because censuses (as well as other administrative data) from different countries are not conducted in the same time periods, nor are they carried out using the same methods or information (Cerejo 2016; Teixeira and Lisboa 2016).

Despite these challenges, the chosen extrapolation method enabled us to systematically shed some light on the extension of the phenomenon in Portugal, as presented next.

FGM/C prevalence estimation in Portugal

Among the 28 countries where FGM/C is documented, Guinea-Bissau has the largest population living in Portugal, which represents about 89 per cent of all women originating from practising countries. Next, 3.7 per cent Senegalese live in Portugal followed by Guinean and Nigerian women, representing 1.5 and 1.3 per cent, respectively (see Table 12.2).

Table 12.2: Distribution of women born in practising countries living in Portugal and prevalence of FGM/C in Portugal (women aged 15–49)

Country of origin	Number of women in Portugal	Percentage of women in Portugal	Estimated number of women in Portugal with FGM/C
Benin	2	0.0	0
Burkina Faso	7	0.1	6
Cameroon	36	0.3	1
Central African Republic	42	0.4	12
Chad	5	0.0	2
Côte d'Ivoire	33	0.3	13
Egypt	37	0.3	34
Eritrea	1	0.0	1
Ethiopia	18	0.2	14
Gambia	36	0.3	27
Ghana	57	0.5	3
Guinea	161	1.5	156
Guinea-Bissau	9452	89.0	4747

Yemen	2	0.0	1
Iraq	19	0.2	2
Kenya	28	0.3	10
Liberia	7	0.1	5
Mali	14	0.1	12
Mauritania	5	0.0	3
Niger	1	0.0	0
Nigeria	136	1.3	40
Senegal	395	3.7	104
Sierra Leone	11	0.1	10
Somalia	7	0.1	7
Sudan	34	0.3	29
Togo	19	0.2	1
Uganda	14	0.1	0
United Republic of Tanzania	38	0.4	8
Total	10,617	100	5246

Source: Lisboa *et al.* (2015)

Regarding the estimation of prevalence, the number of women at a reproductive age (15–49) who may have undergone FGM/C is 5246.[8]

The country that most contributes for the FGM/C prevalence estimation in Portugal is Guinea-Bissau. For ages 15–49, this country represents 90 per cent of all women estimated to have been subjected to FGM/C, followed by Guinea (3%) and Senegal (2%). The remaining countries have lower values.

As noted before (see Table 12.2), the prevalence of FGM/C is uneven in the different practising countries. According to the typology used by

8 In addition, some calculations were made for the female population over 49 (representing 2718 women living in Portugal originating from FGM/C-practising countries). Although the definition of prevalence data only includes women of reproductive age, we have extended the analysis to women aged 50 or over in order to achieve a more complete outlook. Using the same extrapolation method, and the 45–49 age-specific prevalence, we estimate that 1330 of these were subjected to FGM. Thus, we have estimated a total of 6576 women living in Portugal. Next, if we take into account all women over 15 years of age, this figure corresponds to 49 per cent of the number of women living in Portuguese territory born in practising countries (for more information, see Lisboa *et al.* 2015).

UNICEF (2013),[9] practising countries are grouped into five different levels of FGM/C prevalence: countries with very high prevalence (FGM/C estimations are ≥80%); countries with high prevalence (51–80%); countries with moderately low prevalence estimations (26–50%); countries with low prevalence (10–25%); and countries with very low prevalence (<10%). As Table 12.3 illustrates, the vast majority of women living in Portugal and who are estimated to have been subjected to the practise (94%) are originally from moderately low prevalence countries, namely Chad, Côte d'Ivoire, Guinea-Bissau, Kenya, Nigeria and Senegal. Only 4 per cent of the prevalence of FGM/C in Portugal refers to very high prevalence countries.

Table 12.3: Prevalence of FGM/C in Portugal (women ≥ 15 years old) by country of origin (*n and %*)

		Estimated number of women in Portugal with FGM/C	Estimated number of women in Portugal with FGM/C per groups of countries	Estimated % of women in Portugal with FGM/C per groups of countries
Very high prevalence countries >80%	Egypt	55	283	4
	Eritrea	2		
	Guinea	163		
	Mali	12		
	Sierra Leone	10		
	Somalia	7		
	Sudan	35		
Moderately high prevalence countries 51–80%	Burkina Faso	7	59	1
	Ethiopia	15		
	Gambia	29		
	Liberia	5		
	Mauritania	3		

9 The UNICEF document (2013) is commonly used as a reference for prevalence studies in Europe that use the extrapolation method. It features the prevalence data for countries that practise FGM/C. This report, which produced an extensive assessment of FGM/C in those countries, drew on several health surveys: DHS (Demographic and Health Surveys), MICS (Multiple Indicator Cluster Surveys), RHS (Reproductive Health Surveys) and SHHS (Sudan Household Health Survey).

Moderately low prevalence countries 26–50%	Chad	5	6185	94
	Côte d'Ivoire	15		
	Guinea-Bissau	5974		
	Kenya	39		
	Nigeria	42		
	Senegal	111		
Low prevalence countries 10–25%	Benin	0	41	1
	Central African Republic	20		
	United Republic of Tanzania	20		
	Yemen	1		
Very low prevalence countries <10%	Cameroon	1	8	0
	Ghana	3		
	Iraq	3		
	Niger	0		
	Togo	1		
	Uganda	1		
Total		6576	6576	100

Source: Lisboa *et al.* (2015)

These results point out an important aspect for the implementation of prevention and protection measures of FGM/C – since 94 per cent of the FGM/C prevalence in Portugal represents only six countries of the 28 where the practise is documented (although most of the Portuguese prevalence data is concentrated in Guinea-Bissau), the focus of public policies towards the elimination of FGM/C should primarily target these six countries' migrant communities.

Girls who have undergone or are likely to undergo FGM/C

Regarding the estimation of FGM/C prevalence for younger women (less than 15 years of age), there is no generally accepted standard methodology. One of the methods is to extrapolate the 15–19 FGM/C prevalence from the country of origin to the number of girls aged 0–14;[10] however, extrapolation using the 15–19 age group prevalence (estimates of the prevalence for the 0–14 age group are neither accurate nor available for every country) was considered to be the most accurate age group for the estimations regarding girls under 15.

10 It is in this age interval (0–14) that girls are most likely to undergo FGM/C (Martingo 2009; UNICEF 2013).

In addition, we also considered the use of the common expression 'girls at risk of FGM' to be a conceptual error. An EIGE report (2013b) uses the 'girls at risk' definition as applicable to (a) girls aged 0–14 born in countries where FGM/C is documented or (b) girls born to a father and/or a mother born in those countries. However, this definition has inherent problems since it includes both girls who have already been cut and girls who may still be at risk of undergoing FGM/C. To overcome this conceptual issue, we used the term 'girls who have undergone or are likely to undergo FGM/C' (Lisboa *et al.* 2015).

Using census data once again, we isolated the girls born in FGM/C-practising countries and the girls born in Portugal to mothers from those countries. Using the same extrapolation method, we considered girls aged 0–14 living in Portugal and who (a) were born in one of the 28 practising countries or, (b) having been born in Portugal, are daughters of mothers born in practising countries.

Table 12.4 presents the prevalence in the country of origin (related to the 15–19 specific prevalence age group), the number of girls living in Portugal and the number of girls who have undergone or are likely to undergo FGM/C. From a total of 3830 girls, 1830 are estimated to have undergone or are likely to undergo the harmful practise. As in the case of the estimation of prevalence for women in the 15–49 age group, the migrant community from Guinea-Bissau again contributes the most for this estimation. Thus, 1628 of the 1830 girls residing in Portugal who were or will be submitted to the practise were born in Guinea-Bissau or are daughters of mothers from that country, which corresponds to 89 per cent of the total estimated prevalence for these girls.

Table 12.4: Girls who have undergone or are likely to undergo FGM/C

Country of origin	Previous country of origin (%)	Girls in Portugal (*n*)	Girls in Portugal with FGM/C or likely to undergo FGM/C (*n*)
Benin	8	4	0
Burkina Faso	58	3	2
Cameroon	0.4	12	0
Central African Republic	18	15	3
Chad	41	2	1

Côte d'Ivoire	28	17	5
Egypt	81	25	20
Eritrea	78	0	0
Ethiopia	62	3	2
Gambia	77	14	11
Ghana	2	13	0
Guinea	89	101	90
Guinea-Bissau	48	3392	1628
Kenya	15	11	2
Iraq	5	8	0
Liberia	44	4	2
Mali	88	12	11
Mauritania	66	0	0
Niger	2	1	0
Nigeria	19	38	7
Senegal	24	111	27
Sierra Leone	80	5	4
Somalia	97	3	3
Sudan	84	14	12
Togo	1	7	0
Uganda	1	0	0
United Republic of Tanzania	7	14	1
Yemen	19	1	0
Total		3830	1830

CONCLUSION

Prevalence studies are fundamental to assess and comprehend the phenomenon of FGM/C, in order to continue to design and implement effective national and international integrated public policies. Until 2016, only 9 of the 28 EU member states had conducted FGM/C prevalence studies: Portugal (2015), Sweden (2015), England and Wales (2014), Belgium (2014), the Netherlands (2013), Germany (2013), Ireland (2013), Hungary (2012) and Italy (2009). Alongside the importance of these studies, it is fundamental to develop common methodologies that allow data comparison between European countries. Because most of the above-mentioned studies used different methodologies, this greatly needed comparison is not possible. Therefore, it is paramount to develop a common transnational methodology for the estimation of the prevalence of FGM/C that can be adopted by all member states (according to EIGE, Council of Europe and EU guidelines) with the aim of producing comparable statistics. This goal is not possible by simply reeling in administrative data that is neither systematically collected nor centrally stored (EIGE 2013b).

Furthermore, prevalence studies and other academic and scientific research are paramount to the design of effective public policies. Drawing from the Portuguese Prevalence Study that also developed several recommendations for the eradication of the phenomenon, Portuguese decision-makers, advocacy groups, NGOs and other organisations are working together in order to implement specific measures to combat FGM/C. In particular, the Commission for Citizenship and Gender Equality (CIG) has developed National Programmes of Action for the Prevention and Elimination of Female Genital Mutilation (PAPEMGF). In its third version (2014–2017) the PAPEMGF foresees the adoption of 42 structured measures around five strategic areas: prevention, integration, training, acknowledgement and cooperation. But the success of these measures depends on three major aspects: (1) the involvement of local communities in the planning of initiatives and in the participation in activities to raise awareness to FGM/C as a harmful practise; (2) 'the strengthening of the intervention of public services in the fields of health, education, social intervention, gender equality, immigration and development cooperation, in order to improve their roles in the referral, prevention and intervention on the occurrences' (PAPEMGF 2014–2017, p.14); and (3) the development of studies and research that continue to shed light on FGM/C idiosyncrasies as well as its multiple sociocultural dimensions since 'Knowledge and research become indispensable instruments in the development of policies for intervention' (PAPEMGF 2014–2017, p.22).

REFERENCES

Andro, A. (2016) 'Methodological Challenges in Estimating FGM Prevalence and Pros and Cons of Some Methods. FGM-Prevalence Study.' Final Seminar. Brussels: University of Ghent.

APF (Associação para o Planeamento da Família) (2009) *Eliminação da Mutilação Genital Feminina – Declaração conjunta OHCHR, ONUSIDA, PNUD, UNECA, UNESCO, UNFPA, ACNUR, UNICEF, UNIFEM, OMS.* Lisboa: APF.

Bansal, S., Breckwoldt, M., Green, S. and Mbugua, S. (2013) *Female Genital Mutilation: Information for Health-Care Professionals Working in Ireland.* 2nd Edition. RCSI, HSE and AkiDwA.

Branco, S. (2006) *Cicatrizes de Mulher.* Lisboa: Público.

Brown, K., Beecham, D. and Barrett, H. (2013) 'The applicability of behaviour change in intervention programmes targeted at ending female genital mutilation in the EU: Integrating social cognitive and community level approaches.' *Obstetrics and Gynaecology International.*

Campos, A. (2010) 'Mutilação genital feminina – A importância de reconhecer e de saber como agir.' *Acta Obstetrica e Ginecologica Portuguesa 4,* 3, 152–156.

Cerejo, D. (2016) *Combating Female Genital Mutilation and Other Harmful Practises: Comment Paper on Portugal and its Situation.* European Union Rights, Equality and Citizenship, European Commission. Brussels: European Union.

CIG (Comissão para a Cidadania e Igualdade de Género) [Commission for Citizenship and Gender Equality] (2014) *III Programme of Action for the Prevention and Elimination of Female Genital Mutilation (2014–2017).* Lisboa: Presidência do Conselho de Ministros.

Council of Europe (2009) *Action to Combat Gender-based Human Rights Violations, Including the Abduction of Women and Girls.* Resolution 1662 (2009). Available at http://assembly.coe.int/nw/xml/XRef/Xref-XML2HTML-en.asp?fileid=17732&lang=en

Council of Europe (2011) *Convention on Preventing and Combating Violence against Women and Domestic Violence.* Available at www.coe.int/en/web/istanbul-convention/home, www.coe.int/en/web/conventions/full-list/-/conventions/treaty/210?

Council of Europe (2014) *Convention on Preventing and Combating Violence against Women and Domestic Violence: A Tool to End Female Genital Mutilation.* Available at www.strategiesconcertees-mgf.be

DGS (Direcção-Geral da Saúde) (2012) *Orientação 005/2012 de 6/02/2012 sobre Mutilação Genital Feminina.*

Dubourg, D.R.F. (2014) *Etude de Prévalence des Femmes Excisées et des Filles à Risque d'Excision en Belgique.*

EIGE (European Institute for Gender Equality) (2013a) *Current Situation of Female Genital Mutilation.* Country Fact Sheets.

EIGE (2013b) *Female Genital Mutilation in the European Union and Croatia.* European Union.

EIGE (2015) *Estimation of Girls at Risk of Female Genital Mutilation in Europe.* European Union.

Equality Now (2012) *Report of a Research Methodological Workshop on Estimating the Prevalence of FGM in England and Wales.* London: City University London, UCL Elizabeth Garrett Anderson Institute for Women's Health, FORWARD (2012).

European Parliament (2001) *Resolution on Female Genital Mutilation (2001/2035(INI)).* 20 September. Available at http://publications.europa.eu/en/publication-detail/-/publication/5dd0b2f0-1a46-421c-8fc8-4c2e5040beb2/language-en

Exterkate, M. (2013) *Female Genital Mutilation in the Netherlands – Prevalence, Incidence and Determinants.* Pharos Centre of Expertise on Health for Migrants and Refugees.

Frade, A. (ed.) Por Nascer Mulher... Um Outro Lado Dos Direitos Humanos. Lisboa: Associação para o Planeamento da Família.

Frade, A. and Gonçalves, Y. (no date) *Mutilação Genital Feminina: Direitos Humanos de Mulheres e Crianças.*

Gonçalves, Y. (2005) *Mutilação Genital Feminina.* Lisboa: Associação para o Planeamento da Família.

Grupo de Trabalho Inter-sectorial sobre a Mutilação Genital Feminina (2011–2013) *II Programa de Acção para a Eliminação da Mutilação Genital Feminina no âmbito do IV Plano Nacional para a Igualdade – Género, Cidadania e Não Discriminação.* Lisboa: CIG.

Istituto Piepoli (2009) *Valutazione Quantitativa e Qualitativa del Fenomeno delle Mutilazioni Genitali in Italia.*

Johansen, R.E.B., Diop, N.J., Laverack, G. and Leye, E. (2013) 'What works and what does not: A discussion of popular approaches for the abandonment of female genital mutilation.' *Obstetrics and Gynecology International* 2013. doi: 10.1155/2013/348248

Kőszeghy, L. (2012) *FGM Prevalence in Hungary – Estimation.*

Lisboa, M., Cerejo, D., Teixeira, A.L., Santana, R. *et al.* (2015) *Mutilação Genital Feminina em Portugal: Prevalências, Dinâmicas Socioculturais e Recomendações para a sua Eliminação.* Vila Nova de Famalicão: Húmus.

Macfarlane, A. and Dorkenoo, E. (2014) *Female Genital Mutilation in England and Wales: Updated Statistical Estimates of the Numbers of Affected Women Living in England and Wales and Girls at Risk. Interim Report on Provisional Estimates.* London: City University London and Equality Now.

Mackie, G. (2000) 'Female Genital Cutting: The Beginning of the End.' In B. Shell-Duncan and Y. Hernlund (eds) *Female 'Circumcision' in Africa* (pp.253–282). Boulder, CO: Lynne Rienner.

Martingo, C. (2009) *O Corte dos Genitais Femininos em Portugal: O Caso das Guineenses.* Lisboa: ACIDI.

Oberreiter, J.A. (2008) 'A Cut for Lifetime: The Case of Female Genital Mutilation among the Community of Guinea Bissau in Lisbon.' Master's thesis in Human Rights and Democratization (Direitos Humanos e Democratização). Faculdade de Direito da Universidade Nova Lisboa.

Otoo-Oyortey, N. (2007) 'Mutilação Genital Feminina. Uma Preocupação da Saúde e Direitos Sexuais e Reprodutivos.' In A. Frade (ed.) *Por Nascer Mulher… Um Outro Lado Dos Direitos Humanos* (pp.10–15). Lisboa: Associação para o Planeamento da Família.

Teixeira, A.L. and Lisboa, M. (2016) 'Estimating the prevalence of female genital mutilation in Portugal.' *Public Health 139*, 53–60. doi: 10.1016/j.puhe.2016.05.002

UN (United Nations) (2013) UN General Assembly Resolution adopted by the General Assembly on 20 December 2012.

UN and WHO (World Health Organization) (2008) *Eliminating Female Genital Mutilation: An Interagency Statement.* Geneva: OHCHR, UNAIDS, UNDP, UNECA, UNESCO, UNFPA, UNHCR, UNICEF, UNIFEM, WHO.

UNFPA (United Nations Population Fund) (2011) *Proyecto Embera-wera – Una Experiencia de Câmbio Cultural para la Eliminación de la Ablación Femenina en Colombia – America Latina.*

UNGA (United Nations General Assembly) (1948) *Universal Declaration of Human Rights.*

UNGA (1979) *Convention on the Elimination of all Forms of Discrimination Against Women.*

UNICEF (United Nations Children's Fund) (2013) *Female Genital Mutilation/Cutting: A Statistical Overview and Exploration of the Dynamics of Change.* New York: UNICEF.

Vicente, L. (2007) 'Intervenção de Profissionais de Saúde em Mulheres Sujeitas a Mutilação Genital Feminina (MGF)/Corte dos Genitais Femininos (CGF).' In A. Frade (ed.) *Por Nascer Mulher… Um Outro Lado Dos Direitos Humanos* (pp.81–92). Lisboa: Associação para o Planeamento da Família.

WHO (World Health Organization) (2000) *Female Genital Mutilation: A Handbook for Frontline Workers.* Geneva: WHO.

WHO (2008) *Eliminating Female Genital Mutilation: An Interagency Statement.* Geneva: OHCHR, UNAIDS, UNDP, UNECA, UNESCO, UNFPA, UNHCR, UNICEF, UNIFEM, WHO.

WHO (2009) *Mutilação Genital Feminina. Integração da Prevenção e do Tratamento nos Curricula de Profissionais de Saúde – Manual de Formação.* Lisboa: Associação para o Planeamento da Família.

Chapter 13

FORCED MARRIAGE IN EUROPE

THE CASE OF BELGIUM

Els Leye, *International Centre for Reproductive Health, Ghent University, Belgium*

INTRODUCTION

This chapter focuses on the issue of forced marriage in Europe, taking the Istanbul Convention and a qualitative study in Belgium as a framework to analyse some of the issues related to this phenomenon.

Forced marriage is widely recognised as a violation of human rights and, because disproportionately more women than men are affected by it, it is seen as a form of violence against women. Forced marriage is a union where one or both spouses have been forced to enter the union against their free will. This also applies for other unions, such as forced legal cohabitation, or unions contracted under customary or religious law.

Defining forced marriage has proven to be problematic, as distinguishing between arranged marriages, marriages of convenience and child marriages is not always straightforward. Crucial elements that can assist in defining whether or not a marriage can be qualified as a child, forced or arranged marriage are the legal age of marriage in a country, the issue of consent, the negotiation space an individual has to refuse proposed marriage partners, and the amount and nature of pressure (or coercion) that is put on that individual to accept the marriage candidate.

Arranged marriages can be described as marriages whereby suitable partners are identified and proposed by others (mostly family members), and whereby there is room for negotiating the proposed marriage candidate. If the options to refuse the proposed marriage candidate are limited, this may result in a forced marriage. Marriages of convenience, on the other hand, are marriages contracted for the sole purpose of enabling the person concerned to enter or reside in a member state (FRA 2014). When women are trafficked for the purpose of being forced into a marriage of convenience, distinguishing between forced marriage and a marriage of convenience is problematic.[1] And finally, child marriages are marriages concluded with persons below the legal age of marriage, which for both boys and girls is 18,[2] although exceptions apply in some countries of the European Union (FRA 2014; Psaila *et al.* 2016). As minors are lacking the legal capacity to consent to marriage, child marriages are, by definition, 'forced'. Figure 13.1 provides an overview of relevant articles of the Istanbul Convention regarding forced marriage.

Providing an overall estimate of the prevalence of forced marriages in Europe is not possible. Some estimations are available, for example in the UK and Germany (FRA 2014), but they are not representative or reliable enough, and cannot be used to provide an overall figure for the EU. The lack of quality data is due to an underreporting of the practise and limitations of the available data (FRA 2014; Psaila *et al.* 2016), difficulties with defining forced marriages that limit systematic and reliable registrations, the taboo, secrecy and loyalty issues that hinder reporting by (potential) victims, and the lack of criminal laws in a number of countries.

This hiatus is problematic given that the systematic collection of reliable data on forced marriage in Europe is an important element of the measurement of all forms of violence against women, as required in Article 11 of the Council of Europe's *Convention on the Elimination of all Forms of Violence against Women*, the so-called Istanbul Convention (Council of Europe Treaty Series, No. 210), that will empower policy-makers and both governmental and non-governmental organisations (NGOs) to address forced marriage more effectively.

---

1 According to the European Agency for Fundamental Rights (FRA), Europol noted an emerging trend of trafficking women to force them into a marriage of convenience (Europol Early Warning Notification 2014).

2 Recommended by the UN Committee on the Rights of the Child, General Comment No. 4, 2003, CRC/GC/2003/4, para. 20, and UN Committee on Elimination of Discrimination against Women General Recommendation 21 (13th session, 1994).

The Istanbul Convention is a landmark policy document that (will) guide(s) national policy-making on violence against women, including forced marriage. The Convention recognised forced marriage as a serious form of violence against women, and all measures proposed in the Convention also apply to forced marriage. It entered into force on 1 August 2014, and as of May 2017, 23 States have ratified it (Council of Europe 2017), including the EU. The Convention legally obliges States to prevent forced marriage, protect victims of this form of violence and prosecute perpetrators as a part of integrated policies (the so-called '4 Ps' approach), which are completed with two other 'Ps': working in partnership between professionals and communities, and prevalence estimations to guide and evaluate policies and other measures (Council of Europe and Amnesty International 2014). Figure 13.1 provides an overview of relevant articles regarding forced marriage.

RELEVANT ARTICLES OF THE ISTANBUL CONVENTION

Article 11 of the Istanbul Convention stresses the need to collect reliable data on a regular basis to measure the prevalence of all forms of violence, including forced marriages.

Article 32 on civil consequences of forced marriages states that 'Parties shall take the necessary legislative or other measures to ensure that marriages concluded under force may be voidable, annulled or dissolved without undue financial or administrative burden placed on the victim'.

Article 37 states that Parties have a duty to criminalise 'the intentional conduct of forcing an adult or a child to enter into a marriage', the 'intentional conduct of luring an adult or child into the territory' with the purpose of forcing the person to enter into a marriage.

Article 59 on residence status demands that Parties ensure victims of forced marriage who are brought into another country for the purpose of the marriage, and who, as a result, have lost their residence status in the country where they habitually reside, may regain their status.

Article 12 states that State Parties must take the necessary measures to encourage all members of society, especially men and boys, to contribute actively to preventing all forms of violence, and that 'culture, custom, religion, tradition or so-called honour shall not be considered as justification for any acts of violence covered by the Convention (including forced marriage)'.

Other relevant articles:

- Article 13: awareness raising at all levels, including with the public at large
- Article 14: the inclusion of teaching materials to prevent violence (and forced marriage) in education curricula
- Article 15: training of relevant professionals
- Article 16: preventive intervention and treatment programmes
- Article 17: participation of the private sector and the media.

Figure 13.1: Relevant articles of the Istanbul Convention

FORCED MARRIAGE IN EUROPE: THE CASE OF BELGIUM

This section highlights some of the findings of a qualitative study on forced marriage in Belgium. The study, entitled 'MATRIFOR', was financed by the European Commission's DG Home Affairs Programme for the Prevention of and Fight against Crime, and was a multi-country study, implemented from 2012 to 2015 in Belgium (Ghent University, International Centre for Reproductive Health), Spain (Universidad Autonoma Barcelona, Antigona Group) and Italy (Le Onde Onlus, Palermo). The main aim was to analyse how EU Directive 2011/36/EU on Trafficking was transposed to national legislation, thereby focusing on forced marriages as a form of human trafficking. The study consisted of qualitative research and combined in-depth interviews (fieldwork) with a legal analysis (desk study). The legal analysis assessed the current legal framework regarding forced marriages and trafficking in human beings (criminal, civil and migration law), while the fieldwork studied the characteristics of forced marriage in Belgium as well as the main obstacles and difficulties in dealing with forced marriage and seeking legal redress. To this end, 25 in-depth interviews were conducted with professionals from various sectors (social, education, judicial and health sectors, non-governmental organisations (NGOs) and policy-makers).

In Belgium, reliable prevalence rates on forced marriage are available for specific geographic areas and a number of specific ethnic communities (Bensaid and Réa 2012; Leye and Sabbe 2015), but national prevalence rates are, as in many European countries, lacking. Databases within the police and prosecutors have not registered many cases of forced marriage since the specific criminal law on forced marriage was adopted in 2007 (see below). The reasons for this are unknown. However, NGOs and other service providers that do keep records have indicated that forced marriages are (highly) present in their areas of work. They also indicate that the blurred line between an arranged and a forced marriage makes it difficult to register a case as a forced marriage. Forced marriages are often registered as 'intrafamilial violence' rather than forced marriage, even though the forced marriage might be the cause of this violence. The under-reporting of the phenomenon was clearly mentioned by the respondents in this Belgian study, and many expressed their concern that the known cases of forced marriage are only the tip of the iceberg. (Potential) victims are very reluctant to report threats of forced marriages, due to loyalty issues and fear of repercussions, and professionals who come across these cases sometimes lack the required knowledge to detect such cases or the capacities and supporting instruments to adequately refer cases.

Belgian legal and policy framework on forced marriages

The Belgian Civil Code (Article 146ter) states: 'There is no marriage when it is entered into without the free consent of both spouses or the consent of at least one of the spouses was given under violence or threat.'[3] Hence, a forced marriage can never be established in a valid manner (de Brabander 2012). Furthermore, to marry in Belgium, a person must have reached the age of 18,[4] although exemptions are possible (Rude-Antoine 2005). The legal framework in Belgium also contains a number of measures to address marriages of convenience, forced legal cohabitation and cohabitation of convenience (Leye and Sabbe 2015).

The Criminal Code of Belgium has criminalised forced marriage since 25 April 2007 in Article 391sexies. The Belgian specific criminal law on forced marriages that entered into force in May of that year states:

> He who forces someone by violence or threats to enter into a marriage, shall be punished with imprisonment from one month to two years or with a fine of one hundred to five hundred euro. The attempt is punished with imprisonment from fifteen days to one year or a fine of fifty to two hundred fifty euro.

Until the end of 2016, Belgium had only one court case related to forced marriage, in 2014.[5] This case involved the forced marriage of two minors (aged 13), with the court convicting the parents of the minors for human trafficking with the aim of sexual exploitation, rape and violation of integrity by means of threats and violence. The mothers were sentenced to 30 months' effective imprisonment, their husbands to 40 months (*De Standaard* 2014).

3 Law of 2 June 2013, Article 146ter, Civil Code. See www.ejustice.just.fgov.be/cgi_loi/change_lg.pl?language=nl&la=N&table_name=wet&cn=2013060208.

4 Article 144 of the Belgian Civil Code.

5 Corr. Verviers, 30 January 2014, 11de Kamer (definitief) (Federal Migration Centre 2014).

Besides these legal provisions, Belgium has also developed a national policy, applicable to forced marriage, that is, the National Action Plan to fight all forms of Gender-related Violence 2015–2019 (Geweld). This 5th national action plan (NAP) on gender-related violence, was launched in November 2015 and is in line with the Istanbul Convention, which was ratified by Belgium. The Federal Agency for Equal Opportunities between Women and Men is responsible for the coordination of the NAP. Forced marriage is one of the specific foci of the NAP, and proposes a number of objectives and activities that follow the '4 Ps' approach of the Istanbul Convention.

In conclusion, Belgium has put in place legal provisions, both in civil and criminal law, and pays particular attention to forced marriage in its NAP. By doing so, the policy framework provides the necessary enabling environment for actions, in line with the Istanbul Convention, that can guide and support prevention and protection activities regarding the abandonment of forced marriages. However, despite a favourable policy framework to tackle forced marriages in Belgium, a number of issues remain, including with the implementation of this policy framework, as highlighted below by the respondents of the study.

Views from professionals on forced marriages in Belgium

Defining forced marriages

As already indicated in the introduction, and confirmed by the respondents, defining forced marriage is problematic. Respondents claimed that making a clear distinction between arranged marriages (not illegal) and forced marriages (illegal) is not always easy and is more complex than that which is defined by the law. Those working with people affected by forced marriage stipulate that it is the victim who defines if it is a problematic situation, and this is taken as a point of departure for action. An important element that was mentioned by many respondents was that arranged and forced marriages are situated in a spectrum of differing levels of consent, pressure and negotiation space. This continuum can range from absolutely no freedom or choice whatsoever to refuse the proposed marriage partner (forced), to different possibilities to negotiate regarding suggested partners or marriage prospects ((strongly) arranged), or to a marriage where both partners consent with the partner who is proposed to them (fully consented arranged marriage).

However, such arranged marriages are not necessarily perceived as problematic, as respondents mentioned that often youngsters agree with the choice made by parents (or others), as they trust their parents' judgement. On the other hand, the perception of marriage can change over time. It might be that an individual has agreed to a marriage in order to be able to migrate, but once in Belgium, the marriage is not what they expected or does not turn out to be good (e.g. due to violence or the threat of violence in that marriage).

Although forced marriage has not been the focus of a specific study by the European Institute for Gender Equality (EIGE), its ongoing work tries to address gaps in data collection on violence against women in the EU (see EIGE 2014, 2016), from which lessons can be learned regarding the collection of data on forced marriage. Furthermore, the importance of defining forced marriage from a gender perspective, whereby it is understood as a form of gender-based violence and a violation of human rights, and that acknowledges the 'specific vulnerability of women and girls', has been underlined by the European Parliament's Committee on Women's Rights and Gender Equality (FEMM) (Psaila *et al.* 2016). When defining forced marriage, the perspectives of the (potential) victims on their definition of their union or marriage should always be the primary concern.

Characteristics of forced marriage

The respondents further indicated a wide range of ethnicities that are confronted with forced marriages, including people coming from Afghanistan, Albania, Algeria, Armenia, Bangladesh, Belgium, Bulgaria (the Turkish community), Chechnya, China, India, Italy, Kosovo (the Roma community), the Kurdish community, Lebanon, Morocco, Pakistan, Russia, Serbia, Thailand, Tunisia and Turkey.

They underlined the role of the family as decision-makers, and in particular, parents. However, pressure can come from the whole community, not only from the family, including family in the country of origin. Pressure can be targeted towards individuals, but equally towards a family. The pressure experienced is mostly psychological, and might be expressed by means of controlling a girl, or for example, by the community punishing a family (e.g. half of the community not showing up at a wedding of one of the children of a particular family of which the daughter married someone not accepted by the community). One of the reasons for keeping up with/accepting this pressure is the fear of being expelled from the community and family, and the fact that it is very hard to break with the safe environment of the family. People also do not want to disappoint parents and scandalise the family's name, so the aspect of loyalty is a vital element here.

When it comes to gender, professionals mentioned that both males and females could be confronted with forced and arranged marriage. It was, however, mentioned several times that males have more opportunities to resist the pressure to accept a marriage candidate, and that other rules apply for men compared to women.

With regard to age, one respondent mentioned that sometimes females are married at age 16 or 17 in countries of origin, and are brought to Belgium once they are 18 in the framework of family reunification, or when certificates are falsified. Child marriages were also noticed in Belgium, in certain communities (Roma and Afghan).

Respondents mentioned a number of reasons for forced or arranged marriages. At the onset of puberty of a girl and when the first signs of femininity appear, having a girl married preserves the honour of the girl and family. Dishonouring the family can also be caused by having an inter-ethnic relation that is not accepted by the parents, by having a too Western attitude, when young people go against family rules, in the case of homosexuality or in the case of 'problematic' young people (drug using, problems at school, criminal history, or having had (multiple) relations prior to marriage). In such cases, a 'therapeutic' marriage is proposed or imposed to 'cure' the person and to put him or her on the right track again. Marriages are equally concluded for financial and/or material reasons or for residence papers. This refers mainly to a marriage that is seen as a financial transaction, whereby parents 'sell' young women, as one respondent put it. Marriages are equally concluded to obtain residence permits, and this causes several problems, as the respondents pointed out. As it is increasingly difficult to enter Belgium, marriages to obtain residence permits are a reality. Marriages are also imposed to protect their own values and against foreign influences. Forced and arranged marriages within same ethnic communities are concluded to protect their own culture and values. Parents might have concerns that their frame of reference, values and language will not be passed on to the next generation. And finally, marriages are imposed to care for the elderly, as senior migrants do not go to residence homes for the elderly, as is common practise in Belgium.

Stakeholders interviewed pointed out a notable change between first and second/third-generation migrants, in terms of more space to negotiate, more freedom to choose the marriage partner and more openness to discuss the issue.

Professionals interviewed brought up numerous consequences of forced marriages. These include psychological problems, early pregnancy, school drop-out for both young men and women, financial repercussions (the bride price as a push factor to accept and/or remain in marriage), problems with integration in the case of a migration marriage (marriage between a partner already living in Belgium and a partner migrating from another country), violence (intimate partner violence, repudiation by the community in case marriage is refused) and extreme isolation.

The ways to cope with forced marriages and its consequences, and/or to escape (a threat of) forced marriage, as indicated by our respondents, included filing a complaint to the police (although rarely done), divorce (although the requirement to remain married for three years for those migrating for marriage purposes is hampering those who want to divorce), refusing to go on holiday to countries of origin in order to avoid pressure to accept marriage candidates, prolonging schooling (e.g. by explicitly failing exams), and psychotherapy. It was again mentioned that mechanisms to escape or to cope with a forced marriage are better for men than for women, as it is accepted for men to have another relationship with a partner of their choice, besides the official marriage.

This summary of the responses from professionals in Belgium with regard to the characteristics of forced marriage indicates that the issue of forced marriage clearly touches a wide range of communities. In order not to stigmatise ethnic communities, the approach towards the issue from a human rights perspective, and acknowledging it as a form of gender-based violence, is advisable, as this will assist in surmounting discussions on the importance of culture, tradition and religion when dealing with forced marriage. The gendered dimension of forced marriage, that is, women and girls are disproportionately affected by it, can also not be ignored, and should be taken into account when developing activities and designing policies and strategies.

Opinions about current provisions of services related to forced marriage

As mentioned by the respondents, *prevention* of forced marriage in Belgium focuses on several aspects: sensitisation, capacity building of professionals, outreach to communities, provision of advice, mediation, counselling and referral, and a telephone helpline, which are further discussed below.

Sensitisation is done through providing information by means of posters, flyers, organisation of colloquia, provision of websites, broadcasting documentaries and movies, theatre plays, educational toolbox, brochures, etc. Sensitisation often focuses on target groups in schools (preferably given before school holidays), newly arrived migrants and the police, according to the respondents.

Capacity building of professionals was mentioned by some respondents as existing, although this seemed to be limited to providing ad hoc training to the police and the development of a training manual. After finishing the study, the Belgian Institute for the Equality of Women and Men developed a manual for service providers on the topic (Institute for the Equality of Women and Men 2015).

Outreach, especially to the Roma communities, was mentioned as a way of building trust with this community, or with a particular family, which is much needed in order to be able to raise issues related to the school attendance of Roma children. It is difficult for young people to attend school once they are married and have children, but outreach workers try to motivate parents to send their children (mainly girls) to school, at least for a couple of weeks or at regular intervals. Another way of dealing with the high school absenteeism of Roma children was the withdrawal of study bursaries or other financial advantages, although this, too, was seen as problematic, as paying back study bursaries was highly problematic for parents.

Mediation is an often-used strategy. It is done, for example, by the police, by teachers (the so-called 'equal opportunity teacher') or by so-called 'cultural' mediators (mediators from the same ethnic community), towards parents, or via the family, the imam or a person trusted by the victim. However, respondents use it with caution, as they consider it complex and problematic. It is often done with the best of intentions by, for example, teachers who discuss a forced marriage with parents, but who are unaware of the serious problems such mediation can cause to the victim (in particular, increasing the risk of violent reactions towards the young person). Moreover, identifying the right person for mediation is equally difficult when considering family members, imams or members from the community, and can work as a deterrent for victims to step forward.

When victims address services, advice, counselling and, if necessary, further referrals are provided. Information is provided on the rights of the victim and the (dis)advantages and risks of each step that could be taken when considering refusing a marriage, and information on referral is equally provided. Shelters are important when it comes to referrals, although the respondents were critical about the insufficient number, the lack of long-term follow-up of those who take the step to break with the family, the lack of specialised care for victims of forced marriage in these shelters and, in particular, the lack of secure shelters for minors.

At the time of the study the Violence and (Child) Abuse Hotline 1712 had just been installed, and it was considered too soon to draw any conclusions.

With regard to the *protection* of victims of forced and arranged marriage, respondents believed that the police, shelters and teachers play a key role here. With regard to the reporting of cases of forced and arranged marriage, such reports come from schools, the police, social workers, teachers, family and friends, welfare departments, centres for pupils' counselling, care providers and health services. Many respondents agreed that victims seldom report cases of forced marriage. It is difficult for victims because, although they do not agree with parents, at the same time they remain loyal to them, and this loyalty conflict makes it very hard for them to denounce and put a complaint in against their parents or family.

Prosecuting forced marriage is equally an option in Belgium. Victims can report to the police, although respondents mentioned that this is not often the case (see above). In the case of reports of a forced marriage, an official report is made and the prosecutor is informed. Court cases might be initiated, and legal actions might include imprisonment or freedom under conditions. As already indicated above, the number of court cases is limited as well as the number of reported cases to the police. Respondents stressed that legal actions should go hand in hand with respectful interventions towards families and communities.

When asked about the services provided, respondents shared insights on their work with victims and on shelters, mediation, referrals, reporting, training and sensitisation. The work with victims ranges from long-term support and follow-up, psychological therapy in their first language, and advice and counselling delivered by peers (women who were former victims, who are now experienced experts, who assist victims in taking a decision). Mediation was also mentioned, although professionals interviewed stressed that their use depends very much on each situation and sometimes it is not recommended at all, as it can put the victim in serious danger. Mediation, as a strategy to work with victims, needs to be tailor-made, not only at crisis moments, but also on a regular basis. Intercultural mediators should be included from the very beginning, when assessing the problem. If these mediators could help service providers in making referrals, respondents thought that help would be much more efficient. Criteria for mediators were equally suggested, and include the following: to have a respectful attitude towards communities, to be respected in the communities, to be known in the communities and to have a wide network in the communities, among other qualities.

Shelters for abused women and their children receive victims of forced or arranged marriages, although the work is the same for all clients, regardless of whether they are victims of forced marriage or not. Shelters provide support for a maximum of three months, and the services provided include mediation, couple counselling, socio-psychological counselling, provision of a security plan for women and children, assisting in reintegration and working with children. Respondents acknowledged that providing adequate support and future perspectives to victims is important. They said that either specialised shelters could be created or that existing structures could be adapted, as long as the victims receive proper accommodation and support.

However, many respondents shared their concerns with regard to the service delivery that is currently available in Belgium. These concerns mainly deal with the attitudes and feelings of professionals and of the communities, or issues related to the activities and strategies of services.

The feelings and attitudes of communities that obstruct adequate service delivery, as expressed by the professionals in the study, refer mainly to fears about shelters and their services, as well as the differences in values and norms concerning issues related to forced and arranged marriages. Respondents stated that the fear of exposing family problems and blaming the family is a barrier to seeking help from services, indicating that they are under-used. It should also not be underestimated that taking the step to seek help in a shelter is extremely difficult for victims, especially minors, who have never lived outside a family setting or community. The threshold to go to services, including the police, was considered high, due to inaccurate knowledge of services or prejudices.

On the other hand, the feelings, attitudes and skills of professionals were equally considered to be an obstacle to adequately tackling forced marriages. Fears of stigmatising communities, stereotypes about ethnic communities, cultural relativism, communication problems due to language barriers and/or differences in value systems were all believed to hinder adequate service delivery. A non-judgemental attitude of professionals and volunteers when dealing with cases of forced marriage was considered paramount, in order not to hinder adequate and early care.

The respondents identified a number of deficiencies in the skills of professionals related to difficulties in assessing the level of danger for a person, diagnosing the situation and taking appropriate action. Moreover, the lack of instructions on how to deal with diversity in our society in the curricula of future professionals (such as teachers or social workers) was also considered problematic, as it results in professionals not being able to act appropriately when confronted with forced marriage cases. In Belgium, the concept of 'diversity' needs to be integrated into services, in the 'heads' of service providers and the public in general, through building competencies to deal with diversity in society. This entails how to deal with diverse values and norms, image building of other cultures, intercultural communication skills, context and background of migration, etc. This should be integrated into every educational curriculum, where diversity should be included as a transversal theme.

With regard to sensitisation, capacity building and training, the need to inform and train prosecutors and magistrates, and other professionals who are likely to interact with forced marriage, was deemed crucial by the respondents. In this respect, it should be noted that, since the study was finished, a number of important initiatives have been taken in Belgium, including a manual for professionals (see above), the risk taxation instrument for so-called honour-related violence (that can be used for forced marriage) that can assist professionals in scoring a situation of honour-related violence and in taking appropriate action (van Vossole 2016), as well as the new circular letter from the Minister of Justice and College of Prosecutors regarding the investigation and prosecution policy of honour violence, female genital mutilation and forced marriages and cohabitations (Openbaar Ministerie 2017).

CONCLUSION

This chapter has provided some insights into how Belgium is dealing with forced marriage cases. The study showed that, in order to comply with the Istanbul Convention, much more needs to be done in order to prevent, protect and support those affected by forced marriages, and to investigate and prosecute it. Measures regarding the prevention, protection and prosecution of forced marriages need to be integrated into a policy that receives sufficient resources to implement them. As other countries have equally developed a number of initiatives to deal with forced marriages, this is why sharing knowledge and expertise across Europe might be very useful. The Istanbul Convention provides useful guidance to develop such a comprehensive policy and subsequent measures to tackle the issue of forced marriage in Europe.

REFERENCES

Bensaid, N. and Réa, A. (2012) *Etude Relative aux Mariages Forcés en Région de Bruxelles-Capitale* [*Study Regarding Forced Marriages in Brussels Capital Region*]. Brussels: Université Libre de Bruxelles – Group for Research on Ethnic Relations, Migrations and Equality.

Council of Europe (2017) 'Georgia ratifies the Istanbul Convention.' Newsroom, 19 May. Strasbourg: Council of Europe. Accessed on 24/5/2017 at www.coe.int/en/web/istanbul-convention/-/georgia-ratifies-the-istanbul-convention

Council of Europe and Amnesty International (2014) *Convention on Preventing and Combating Violence against Women and Domestic Violence. A Tool to End Female Genital Mutilation.* Strasbourg: Council of Europe.

de Brabander, A. (2012) 'De Strafrechtelijke en Criminologische Dimensie van het Gedwongen Huwelijk' ['The Criminal and Criminological Dimension of Forced Marriage']. Master's thesis. Ghent: Ghent University, p.59.

De Standaard (2014) 'Twee Roma-koppels krijgen vijf jaar cel voor gedwongen huwelijk van hun kinderen' ['Two Roma-couples get 5 years of imprisonment for forced marriage of their children']. Accessed on 16/7/2014 at www.standaard.be/cnt/dmf20140130_00954930

EIGE (European Institute for Gender Equality) (2014) *Mapping the Current Status and Potential of Administrative Data Sources on Gender-based Violence in the EU.* Vilnius: EIGE. Accessed on 24/5/2017 at www.eige.europa.eu/gender-based-violence/data-collection#2016

EIGE (2016) *Developing EU-wide Terminology and Indicators for Data Collection on Violence Against Women.* Vilnius: EIGE. Accessed on 24/5/2017 at www.eige.europa.eu/gender-based-violence/data-collection#2016

Europol Early Warning Notification (2014) 'Marriages of Convenience: A Link between Facilitation of Illegal Immigration and THB.' In FRA (European Agency for Fundamental Rights) *Addressing Forced Marriage in the EU: Legal Provision and Promising Practises.* Luxembourg: Publications Office of the European Union, p.9.

Federal Migration Centre (2014) *Traite des Etres Humains. Construire des Ponts. Rapport Annuel 2013 du Rapporteur indépendant Traite des Etres Humains Belgique* [*Human Trafficking. Building Bridges. Annual Report 2013 of the Independent Rapporteur Human Trafficking Belgium*]. Brussels: Federal Migration Centre.

FRA (European Agency for Fundamental Rights) (2014) *Addressing Forced Marriage in the EU: Legal Provision and Promising Practises.* Luxembourg: Publications Office of the European Union.

Institute for the Equality of Women and Men (2015) *Gedwongen Huwelijk? Handleiding voor Dienstverleners* [*Forced Marriage? Manual for Service Providers*]. Brussels: Institute for the Equality of Women and Men.

Leye, E. and Sabbe, A. (2015) *Forced Marriage in Belgium: An Analysis of the Current Situation.* Ghent: ICRH Global vzw.

Openbaar Ministerie (2017) Omzendbrief COL XX/2017 – Gemeenschappelijke Omzendbrief van de Minister van Justitie en het College van Procureurs-Generaal betreffende het opsporings- en vervolgingsbeleid inzake eergerelateerd geweld, vrouwelijke genitale verminkingen, gedwongen huwelijken en wettelijke samenwoningen [Public Prosecutor (2017) Circular letter COL XX/2017 – Joint Circular of the Minister of Justice and the College of Prosecutors concerning investigation and prosecution policy concerning honour-related violence, female genital mutilations, forced marriages and legal cohabitations]. Brussels: Openbaar Ministerie.

Psaila, E., Leigh, V., Verbari, M., Fiorentini, S., Dalla Pozza, V. and Gomez, A. (2016) *Forced Marriage from a Gender Perspective.* Study for the FEMM Committee, EP. PE 556.926. Brussels: European Parliament, Directorate General for Internal Policies, Policy Department C: Citizens' Rights and Constitutional Affairs, Women's Rights and Equalities, pp.17–19.

Rude-Antoine, E. (2005) *Forced Marriages in Council of Europe Member States: A Comparative Study of Legislation and Political Initiatives, Comparison of Law and Political Actions.* Strasbourg: Council of Europe, Directorate General of Human Rights, p.68.

Stop Geweld [Stop Violence] (2015–2019) *Nationaal Actieplan ter Bestrijding van alle Vormen van Gendergerelateerd Geweld* [*National Action Plan to Fight all Forms of Gender-related Violence*]. Accessed on 4/8/2017 at http://www.partnergeweld.be/sites/default/files/content/download/files/uitgebreid_persdossier.pdf

van Vossole, A. (2016) *Risicotaxatie-instrument Eergerelateerd Geweld* [*Risk Taxation Instrument Honour-related Violence*]. Geel: Thomas More, APART.

Part Four

RESPONDING TO DOMESTIC VIOLENCE AND ABUSE

Chapter 14

MODELS ON TREATMENT OF INTIMATE PARTNER VIOLENCE

GENDER-BASED AND TRAUMA-INFORMED WORK AT ALTERNATIVE TO VIOLENCE IN NORWAY

Ingunn Rangul Askeland, *Senior Research Fellow, Norwegian Centre for Violence and Traumatic Stress Studies, and Clinical Psychologist, Alternative to Violence, Oslo, Norway*

Marius Råkil, *Director, Alternative to Violence, Oslo, Norway*

INTRODUCTION

The aim of this chapter is to offer a short description of some of the main theoretical models that have been used to describe the aetiology of violent behaviour towards intimate partners and hence informed the treatment of intimate partner violence (IPV). The idea of offering treatment to people who have committed criminal acts is not novel. This view is explicitly found in philosopher Bertrand Russell's argument for treating the sick and the criminal in similar ways: 'The man who commits a crime from an impulse to violence ought to be subjected to a scientific psychological treatment, designed to elicit more beneficial impulses' (Russell 1919, p.134).

The theoretical paradigms used to explain IPV can broadly be divided into three main fields: *sociocultural models, systemic models* and *individual-focused models.* These models present competing understandings of why IPV occurs and what sustains it. Most of the IPV programmes have been developed in the US within a sociocultrual framework, based on pro-feminist, cognitive-behavioural or psychodynamic approaches (Gondolf 2002). However, many seem to integrate elements from all of these treatment modalities (Dalton 2007). Furthermore, there is substantive support in the literature that a fruitful way forward might be that treatment approaches should correspond more closely to different types of violence and the individual's varying treatment needs (e.g. Gilchrist and Kebbell 2010; Taft, Murphy and Creech 2016). In a study of IPV treatment in European Union (EU) countries, it was found that over-half (54%), in fact, adopted a combination of cognitive-behavioural, pro-feminist and psychodynamic approaches, with the most common form comprising cognitive-behavioural and pro-feminist techniques (41%) (Hamilton, Koehler and Lösel 2012). More specifically, it appeared that cognitive-behavioural approaches more often were implemented as a component, rather than an alternative, to a pro-feministic approach (Hamilton *et al.* 2012).

We discuss some aspects of the above-mentioned models and how these have been integrated in the treatment of IPV within the specific context of the work of Alternative to Violence (ATV), a large non-profit non-governmental organisation (NGO) that provides treatment and professional expertise on violence with a particular focus on IPV in Norway. Although several parts of this chapter are relevant to both men and women, the chapter is written with a particular focus on men in treatment for IPV against a female partner.

SOCIOCULTURAL MODELS

While there are several types of sociocultural models, they concur in their focus on how shared cultural beliefs, socialisation factors and common norms contribute to and encourage violent behaviour. In the 1970s several countries experienced pressure from the women's movement that focused on systematic gender inequalities in society. In the US, women's advocates noted the lack of reactions and sanctions against men who used violence against their partners as being symptomatic of this gender inequality (Schecter 1982). Interventions for male batterers in the US developed as part of a larger movement addressing the rights and needs of battered women, and evolved as a component of a coordinated community response to men's IPV.

The Domestic Abuse Intervention Project, commonly referred to as the Duluth Model, was the first multi-disciplinary programme to coordinate agencies addressing domestic violence (Pence and Paymar 1993). According to this model, the primary cause of violent behaviour is patriarchal ideology, and the model states that 'battering is a pattern of actions used to intentionally control or dominate an intimate partner'.[1] Violent behaviour is perceived as originating in the societal norms that support men's power over women and enable them to establish superiority over their partners (DeKeseredy 2016; Pence 2002). Interventions within this approach aim to change the societal conditions that support men's use of power and control, and to offer opportunities to change through court-ordered educational group interventions (Gondolf 2012). Duluth-type models have developed since its initiation, and are often now described as 'a gender-based cognitive-behavioural approach to counselling and/or educating men arrested for domestic violence and mandated by the courts to domestic violence programs' (Gondolf 2007, p.645). The Duluth approach still occupies a strong position within the field, and the majority of men in treatment for IPV in the US and Europe are mandated by the legal system to undergo treatment within this tradition. Thus most intervention programmes in both Europe and the US are based on group treatment, with a substantial focus on psychoeducation regarding power and control (Hamilton *et al.* 2012; Maiuro and Eberle 2008; Stover, Meadows and Kaufman 2009).

Such programmes, particularly the most gendered and feminist versions such as the Duluth Model, have been broadly criticised (Dutton and Corvo 2006). Some authors would claim that the sociocultural models are merely ideological and dogmatic, overlooking research that women tend to perpetrate IPV at nearly the same rate as men (Dutton and Nicholls 2005; Stets and Straus 1992; Straus and Gelles 1992). Large national surveys have found approximately equal levels of victimisation rate for men and women, at least on 'mild' IPV (Straus 1979, 1990; Thoresen and Myhre 2014). However, 'severe' male-perpetrated physical violence is consistently reported at much higher rates, and male-perpetrated sexual violence is reported up to six to nine times as often (Haaland, Clausen and Schei 2005; Pape and Stefansen 2004; Thoresen and Myhre 2014). In a meta-analytic review, Archer (2000) concluded that women were slightly more likely than men to report physical violence toward their partners, whereas in agency samples, men were more likely than women to perpetrate violence. The overall tendency to find that women are victimised at higher rates than men in relationships has been found in

1 See www.theduluthmodel.org/about/index.html

other national studies in the US, such as the National Violence Against Women Survey (NVAWS) and the National Crime Victimization Survey (NCVS) (Catalano 2012; Tjaden and Thoennes 2000).

Although prevalence rates may provide important information regarding IPV, there are several problems with such data and how they are interpreted. Given that prevalence rates for men and women are the same, it does not mean that the actual acts are equivalent. For instance, a slap might be rather 'mild' or it might be delivered with substantial force and cause severe damage. Additionally, merely counting what tend to be equal acts of violence fails to ignore important features such as the nature, context and consequences of the violence (Mahoney, Williams and West 2001). Several studies have found that more women than men are injured by their partner, and that women are more severely injured than men (Archer 2000; Caldwell, Swan and Woodbrown 2012). Men more often start the violence, and report more frequently laughing and feeling amused at their partner's initiated assaults (Hamberger and Guse 2002). Research undertaken in both clinical and laboratory settings has found women reporting more fear than men (Hamberger and Guse 2002; Phelan *et al.* 2005), and that men are more likely than women to report frightening their partners with their violent behaviour (Ansara and Hindin 2011). Further, more men tend to use violence to control or dominate their partner; women, on the other hand, tend to assault their partners to protect themselves or to escape (Bair-Merritt *et al.* 2010). Among bi-directionally violent couples, women express higher levels of PTSD (post-traumatic stress disorder) and depression compared to the men (Cascardi, O'Leary and Schlee 1999; Vivian and Langhinrichsen-Rohling 1994). Across studies and nations women are far more often injured and killed by their partners than men (Cooper and Smith 2011). In line with these findings, a recent literature review of clinical samples found that women are more victimised, frightened and injured by their partner compared to men, that women are more likely to use violence in response to IPV, and that sexual violence is perpetrated predominantly by men (Larsen and Hamberger 2015).

Although men and women report similar rates of using what is referred to as 'mild violence', at least in community samples and if one simply counts acts of violence, there are some crucial differences; overall, compared to women's use of IPV, men's use of IPV is more likely to be severe, have different purposes and have more adverse consequences for their partners.

SYSTEMIC MODELS

A significant controversy in the field has been about whether it is appropriate to use systemic approaches and practise couples therapy in cases of IPV. Systemic models explaining IPV share a common focus on explaining individual behaviours in interpersonal contexts, such as the family system or as a couple dynamic. Relationship conflicts are perceived as stemming from the reciprocal exchange of behaviours and negative emotional expressions between the partners (Gurman and Jacobson 2002; Spencer, Mendez and Stith 2016). When one member of a family uses violence, it is understood as behaviour derived from problems within the family or the couple's system. From a systemic point of view, then, violence typically emerges from a reciprocal exchange of negative behaviours (Gurman and Jacobson 2002). Thus, the solution is to help the members of the system find new constructive ways of relating to each other.

A significant view within the literature on IPV has been that treatment should never be offered in the format of couples treatment. The criticisms of a systemic approach to IPV can be distilled into two points: a pragmatic position focusing on security issues, and a more philosophical objection regarding responsibility (McCollum and Stith 2008). Typically, there are concerns that the female partner's treatment-session revelations about the male partner's violence could trigger violent responses (Stith and McCollum 2011). The more philosophical objection targets the systemic theory, that is, the basis of couples counselling. Analysing violence in an interactional perspective leads to a risk of not holding the violent partner responsible, and ending up blaming the non-violent partner (Gauthier and Levendosky 1996). Moreover, the substantial empirical research as described above has demonstrated that IPV in general is not a 'mutual' phenomenon between two equal partners. Treating both partners when there has been IPV will risk putting the two parts into an equal position when, in fact, they are not.

In spite of such concerns, several variations of couples counselling have been developed for treatment of IPV (La Taillade, Epstein and Werlinich 2006; Stith *et al.* 2012). As mentioned above, a number of studies have found that within some couples both partners engage in physical violence (Archer 2000; Whitaker *et al.* 2007), and nearly 80 per cent of partners in clinical samples report a bi-directional pattern of violence (Cantos, Neidig and O'Leary 1993; Cascardi, Langhinrichsen and Vivian 1992; Langhinrichsen-Rohling, Neidig and Thorn 1995). Additionally, research shows that those who engage in violence are at a higher risk of being subjected to violence (Archer 2000). Bi-directional violence has also been found to be associated more often with injury than one-directional IPV, regardless of the violent partner's gender (Whitaker *et al.* 2007). Exposure to violence has been found to be the strongest predictor of committing violence against a partner (O'Leary and Slep 2012; O'Leary, Slep and O'Leary 2007). Moreover, low levels of marital satisfaction and high levels of conflict have been found as predictors of IPV (Murphy and Eckhardt 2005; Stith *et al.* 2004). Increased levels of problematic communication between partners are highly related to arguments and distress, factors that have been shown to predict IPV (Babcock *et al.* 1993). Another argument for couples treatment comes from research demonstrating high levels of violence among couples seeking regular family treatment (Jose and O'Leary 2009), and that many couples wish to stay together and want help with their relationship (Stith and McCollum 2011).

Taking everything into consideration, there is substantial empirical research demonstrating that IPV is not only a one-dimensional phenomenon (Holtzworth-Munroe and Meehan 2004) and that there may be cases suitable for couples interventions.

INDIVIDUAL AND PSYCHOLOGICALLY BASED MODELS

One of the main objections towards the sociocultural model has been how it has ignored or reduced the role of trauma and its consequences. Living with violence in the family affects children's physical, psychological, cognitive and behavioural development (Graham-Bermann and Edleson 2001; Holden, Geffner and Jouriles 1998; Margolin 2005). Research on adults engaging in IPV has repeatedly shown high levels of exposure to trauma and especially violence within the family (Askeland, Evang and Heir 2011; Delsol and Margolin 2004; Taft *et al.* 2016). Different theoretical models have been used to explain *how* childhood experiences of family violence contribute to adult IPV. One of these models is Bowlby's (1969) attachment theory. Experiences of threats and violence will impact negatively on the child's attachment system. Paradoxically, when a parent is both the source of threat and the source of protection and survival, the child will experience a double negative effect. The normal anger response when attachment needs are not met will turn into aggression and will be triggered so frequently that the response becomes integrated into the child's self-structure (Fonagy 1999; Fong, Hawes and Allen 2017). This view finds support in research on neurobiology and its long-term effects of trauma. Traumatic events, especially those experienced repeatedly and early in life, are connected to difficulties with affect regulation (e.g. Briere and Spinazzola 2009). Put simply, in a threatening environment those parts of the brain called 'the limbic system' or 'the emotional brain' will be highly and easily activated, and the more advanced parts, such as the neocortex, which mainly involves language, logic and consciousness, will be less developed (McCrory, Puetz and Viding 2017). The result may be a low threshold for immense emotional reactions and, at the same time, impaired development in the areas of the brain that help us regulate emotions. Several researchers have specifically described how insecure attachment and trauma generate affect dysregulation (Schore 2001, 2002; Schore and Schore 2008; van der Kolk 1988). Repeated exposure to violence from a parent will produce extreme dysregulation (van der Kolk 2005; van der Kolk, McFarlane and Weisaeth 2012) and might have long-term effects. Furthermore, children's working models are shown to be fairly stable and to predict adult attachment styles (Main, Hesse and Kaplan 2005; Sroufe 2005), and may become the source of the adult male's violent outburst (Dutton *et al.* 1994). Relative to non-violent men, violent men tend to be less likely to be securely attached and have elevated levels of anxious attachment (Dutton 2006; Dutton *et al.* 1994, Holtzworth-Munroe, Stuart and Hutchinson 1997; Lawson 2008). Moreover, several studies have shown how different insecure attachment styles seem to predict violent behaviour and how violence seems to function as a way to increase or decrease proximity to a partner accordingly (Allison *et al.* 2007; Babcock *et al.* 2000; Landolt and Dutton 1997).

Another theory used to explain how childhood trauma increases the risk for using IPV is the *social information-processing (SIP) model* (Crick and Dodge 1994; Lemerise and Arsenio 2000). On a basic level this model concurs with the attachment model. The basic elements of the SIP model are based on the belief that social information is transformed into responses founded in a 'database' of memories constructed on past experiences and transformed into responses through decoding skills, decision skills and enactment skills (Crick and Dodge 1994). Put briefly, studies have found that trauma such as exposure to violence negatively affects how people process social information, enhances the probability of developing biased and dysfunctional patterns, a bias to attribute hostile intentions to others, and a lack of functional behavioural strategies to solve interpersonal problems and a reduced ability to enact social competence (Dodge 1993; Dodge, Bates and Pettit 1990). In sum, over a hundred studies have found measures of the SIP model to be significantly associated with child and adolescent aggressive behaviour (Dodge *et al.* 2003). Research on adults has provided additional support for a social-processing model. Holtzworth-Munroe and colleagues have conducted a series of studies comparing non-violent and violent men on several SIP constructs, finding that violent men attribute more negative intentions to their female partners compared to non-violent men (Holtzworth-Munroe and Hutchinson 1993). They tend to have hostile cognitive biases, and these are most intense among severely violent men (Clements and Holtzworth-Munroe 2008). Problems at the decoding stage have been shown to affect the decision-making stage in such a way that violent men tend to formulate responses that are less socially competent (Holtzworth-Munroe and Anglin 1991), and to express less supportive and more aversive responses to different partner behaviours (Holtzworth-Munroe and Smutzler 1996). Theoretically, emotion processes comprise part of the SIP model, even if the role of emotions is not explicitly described in the model (Crick and Dodge 1994). In line with the above-mentioned research, exposure to violence between parents and direct exposure to violence suggests that these experiences influence one's ability to regulate emotions and the interpretation of interpersonal relationships as an adult (Ehrensaft *et al.* 2003), and that children who experience violence fail to develop an adequate capacity to regulate emotions and form stable and well-functioning relationships over time (Moffitt *et al.* 2001; Taft *et al.* 2008).

There is a growing focus on the association between PTSD and IPV perpetration. Among men in IPV treatment it has been found that those classified with PTSD are more frequently and severely aggressive than men without PTSD (Rosenbaum and Leisring 2003). Further, the effects of exposure to inter-parental violence on the physical and psychological perpetration of IPV have been found to be primarily indirect, and expressed through PTSD symptoms and information-processing deficits (Taft *et al.* 2008), as will be further explained in the following. PTSD symptoms have been linked to dysfunctional information processing, such as a heightened perception of threats and negative interpretations (Constans 2005), and PTSD may lead to a context-inappropriate activation of the cognitive processes related to 'survival mode' (Novaco and Chemtob 1998). Earlier traumatic experiences may prime those with PTSD to be more inclined to perceive negative intentions and threats from others, which results in a higher level of arousal and cognitive bias associated with heightened anger, hostile appraisal, inclination to confirm a threat and sensitivity to threat recognition; ultimately, it also leads to a lowered barrier to respond to a threat. In accordance with this model, one might expect the hyperarousal symptom cluster of PTSD, that is characterised by heightened physiological reactivity, an exaggerated startle response and difficulties with anger, to be specifically related to perpetrating IPV. In line with this, compared with the other two PTSD symptom clusters, hyperarousal symptoms have been shown to have the strongest positive relationship with aggressive behaviour (Taft *et al.* 2007).

Over the years several different *typologies of violent behaviour* have been developed (e.g. Holtzworth-Munroe 2005; Johnson 2006). This work has aimed at explaining the differences in prevalence rates across samples and to offer a framework to differentiate between types of violent relationships. Johnson developed a typology of violent relationships describing couples who experience violence: situational couple violence, intimate terrorism, violent resistance and mutual violent control (Johnson 2006). Typically, intimate terrorism involves physical violence embedded in a general pattern of coercive control, and the violence is primarily unidirectional, whereas situational couple violence is more frequently bi-directional, typically connected to specific issues, and does not include coercion or control. Violent resistance is used in response to an intimate terrorist, often motivated by self-protection, whereas mutual violent control is defined by two partners engaging in intimate terrorism (Johnson 2006, 2011). Most systemic approaches to IPV are designed to stop and prevent low-level violence that would typically be labelled as situational couple violence

(Stith *et al.* 2012), with couples who do not fear each other and where both partners consider the violence to be a problem they want to resolve (La Taillade *et al.* 2006).

An important thing to point out in this context is how typologies, and especially models like Johnson's, can, and have, been misused. The two terms 'episodic partner violence' and 'intimate terrorism' are often used as two extremes on a scale, as if there are only two distinct forms of violence. A direct consequence of this is the risk of ending up perceiving the IPV not labelled as intimate terrorism as 'not dangerous and severe'. As Johnson himself points out, all types of violence can occur rarely and frequently in a relationship, and can range from relatively mild to killing another person. However, intimate terrorism is the type of violence that is more often frequent and brutal (Johnson 2008). By defining something 'not-intimate terrorism', one risks perceiving all other forms of violence as low-frequent and not severe. Johnson's typology does not, in itself, offer a categorical division into 'dangerous' or 'harmless' violence – he emphasises that single acts of violence in episodic partner violence can be severe and harmful (Kelly and Johnson 2008). On the other hand, the physical violence in intimate terrorism can be 'less severe', but still have a strong and pervasive impact on the exposed partner. This may be because the physical violence occurs in combination with control strategies, or because one incident of violence may have created such a strong fear that this in itself makes the victim comply with the violent partner (Johnson and Leone 2005; Meier 2015). The risk of the violence escalating over time is less in cases labelled as episodic partner violence than for intimate terrorism, but violence can still escalate (Kelly and Johnson 2008). Furthermore, there may be questions as to whether the categories can be used as distinct groupings. For instance, surveys of shelter-based women have shown that almost half of them would have been categorised as episodic partner violence following Johnson's criteria (Johnson 2008). Such results indicate that cases which, according to Johnson's criteria, would be classified as episodic partner violence hold, in fact, many of the same characteristics as intimate terrorism.

These objections to Johnson's typology call for caution. Johnson himself never intended that this typology should be used to define how severe the violence in a relationship is, or used to determine the risk situation of the person(s) exposed to the violence. Although the model can be used to differentiate between what is likely to be two extremes of partner violence, it is important to keep in mind that relationships with violence cannot be reduced so they can easily fit into one of these categories. The model is not suitable for assessing risk and dangerousness at the individual level, and is therefore not suitable as a tool when deciding what type of treatment to offer. Such assessments must be based on an extensive evaluation, including a broad assessment of violence, risk assessment, partner information, current life situation and different measures of psychological functioning.

Given that IPV is a heterogeneous phenomenon and varies along dimensions such as type, severity, gender and function, it seems likely that some approaches are better suited to address specific forms of IPV. Thus it seems clear that treatment should be tailored to the individual case. In addition, as for all human behaviour, men's violence against a current or former partner might best be explained by several factors. Consequently, all perspectives may be valuable and integrated in assessing, approaching and working therapeutically with the individual man. This is in line with a more ecological approach as, for example, described by the Violence Prevention Alliance (VPA)[2] and as described in a recent book on evidence-informed responses to domestic violence by Devaney and Lazenbatt (2016). As an example of a treatment approach combining the different models, we will describe some of the central themes in treatment of IPV at Alternative to Violence in Norway.

ALTERNATIVE TO VIOLENCE

Norway was the first European country to offer therapeutic work by professional therapists explicitly for men who engage in IPV when the first Alternative to Violence (ATV) treatment centre opened in 1987. Within the Nordic countries, a fairly strong psychotherapeutic tradition has evolved, emphasising mainly sociocultural and individual psychological perspectives on IPV. Today, ATV has 13 offices in Norway, four in Sweden, one in Denmark, one in Iceland and a group treatment in Åland.

2 See www.who.int/violence_injury_prevention/violence/alliance/en/vpa_tor.pdf?ua=1

Norwegian IPV interventions can broadly be divided into two sectors: programmes for those serving inside prisons, and those available for the general population. Very few men in Norway are court-mandated to attend treatment; thus all IPV treatment is essentially based on voluntary admittance. Prison officers often lead the prison-run programmes, while treatment outside prison, such as ATV, is offered by healthcare providers. ATV is a low-threshold treatment programme intended to reach a variety of men using violence. Treatment targets violent behaviour and is based on general psychological knowledge and operates within the psychotherapeutic tradition. However, the fundamental basis for this treatment is based on an awareness of how gender, power and control issues relates to the violent behaviour. The above models previously discussed and empirical knowledge derived from research on IPV have inspired and formed the fundamental basis for the treatment approach. The treatment can be described as multimodal violence-specific psychotherapy, provided by professional therapists, primarily clinical psychologists, all working with IPV on a full-time basis. ATV works with men, women and adolescents who use violence, adult and adolescent victims of violence, and children living with violence in their families. Most adult clients at ATV using violence are men, accounting for approximately eight out of ten clients.

The previously mentioned individual and psychological perspective plays a central role in the treatment work at ATV. A core question is, *what* is it in the personal history of individuals that contributes to their violent behaviour, and in *what way, through what mechanisms*? About eight out of ten men attending treatment at ATV have a history of growing up in a family with violence or neglect (Askeland *et al.* 2011, 2012), and there is an elevated rate of other trauma exposure among the group as a whole (Askeland *et al.* 2012). Furthermore, about seven out of ten male participants have at least one ongoing psychiatric diagnosis consistent with the long-term effects of trauma, including high levels of PTSD symptoms (Askeland and Heir 2014).

The trauma-informed treatment is embedded in the work on the men's personal explicit and implicit views and feelings on *gender and power*. This includes beliefs and 'schema' of themselves as a man, partner and father, his partner as a woman and mother, and men and masculinity and women and femininity, in general. A focus on the sociocultural aspects of IPV is perceived as essential but not sufficient. To help men change in substantial ways, it is necessary to work therapeutically with the personal psychological history and specifically on how it is connected to their violent behaviour and beliefs of himself and others.

ATV adopts a low threshold, requiring only a phone call to register with the programme. Approximately 50 per cent of the men are self-referred, often after being encouraged by their partner, with the remaining half referred through public services (e.g. child protection services, social workers, family doctors, women's shelters, outpatient psychiatric services, emergency units, the police, prisons, etc.). Treatment at ATV is both individual and group-based. Time in treatment is not time-limited but based on the therapist's evaluation of the therapeutic need of the individual man.

Before entering treatment, all men undertake a systematic *individual assessment* based on a range of different assessment tools. This includes a broad assessment of the nature of the client's violent behaviour and its consequences, alcohol or substance abuse, his current life situation, trauma history and indicators of psychiatric symptomatology. The assessment forms the basis for considering whether treatment at ATV is the right intervention, and whether individual treatment or group treatment should be offered. Exclusion criteria would be the presence of severe mental illness, or alcohol and substance abuse, to the extent that these conditions need to be addressed before work on violence is appropriate. Those with the most significant mental health issues and with extreme levels of violence would most likely profit from individual treatment and will be offered such treatment. The assessment covers known risk factors included in such measures as the Spousal Assault Risk Assessment (SARA) Guide (Kropp and Gibas 2010; Kropp and Hart 2000). The wellbeing and safety of the adult victim and children is a primary ethical concern. Assessment therefore also incorporates a session with the client's partner or former partner, if they have children together. This broad assessment creates a reasonable base for making a risk assessment in each case. Risk assessment, though, is an ongoing process throughout the whole treatment. The partner session also includes partner safety planning, comprising such aspects as her and the children's general wellbeing, dangerousness, if she intends to continue the relationship, resources (such as family, friends), specific escape plans and removal of weapons and such like.

THE ATV THERAPEUTIC TREATMENT MODEL

As discussed previously in this chapter, there is a strong debate as to whether systemic models are useful in the context of IPV. Couples treatment is not the primary form of treatment at ATV. Several of the couples seen at ATV report bi-directional patterns of violence. However, looking closer into these relationships, it becomes obvious that, in the majority of these cases, the relationships are primarily characterised by one aggressor and one victim who is usually both afraid and traumatised by the violence. Thus couples treatment would neither be ethical nor professional. Conjoint treatment is used in ATV when both partners want it, if the therapist finds it useful, if there are no issues concerning safety and the violent partner has been in treatment and both partners consider treatment as successful. These couple sessions are very well prepared and highly structured, and will typically include two therapists.

The ATV treatment model revolves around four essential themes: *violent behaviour*, *responsibility*, *psychological connections* and *consequences* (Råkil 2006). The overall purpose is to help the men cease their violence and to develop a strong sense of responsibility for their violent behaviour. Additionally, a central aim is to assist the men in developing non-violent, healthy and respectful ways of relating to others. The following description does not intend to describe specific therapy techniques, but focuses on the four overarching themes in the treatment of IPV.

The work on the first theme involves a *focus on the violence*. From the first session, throughout the treatment, violent behaviour is explicitly addressed. The main aim of this therapeutic work is helping the man to acknowledge his violence as an unquestionable actual reality. The violence has to be 'reconstructed' in a very detailed way, in terms of what happened, where it happened, how it happened, and to whom. This includes recognising the wide variety of ways in which men commit violent acts, including physical, psychological, sexual, latent and material violence, and more specifically, how he has been violent. In this way the therapist helps the client to see himself as an *active agent* – he is the person who is using violence. The goal of the work is to increase the client's acceptance of his problem and to help him to understand that the solution is for him to change. The work on this theme is also indirectly working on addressing the issues of responsibility. Additionally, it is important to map the overall pattern of his violence, such as frequency and severity, and for how long the violence has been going on over time. Further, such a meticulous focus on violence enables the therapist to work on the issues of risk and safety planning with the male client. This work is done in addition to the work on risk and safety planning with his partner. The work requires an awareness by the therapist regarding language, and it is of vital importance that the violence is talked about specifically and not reformulated into concepts like 'we had a fight or we were quarrelling', which defocuses the power and abusing features of the violence. This process also includes detailed questioning about the children – their presence, if they were not present, where they were, and their reactions to the violence. The work requires a persistent focus on violence. At the same time, it is crucial to develop an alliance, so this work must be done in a respectful and empathic way. Previous research has emphasised that activation of the client's motivational goals fosters a working alliance and thus enhances the possibility of a positive outcome of therapy, while activating the avoidant goals early in treatment can lead to ruptures (Flückiger and Grosse Holtforth 2008; Gassmann and Grawe 2006). A study of men in treatment at ATV has shown a variety of ways in which the clients might present themselves to form a working alliance during the first treatment session (Lømo, Haavind and Tjersland 2016). This study offers a conceptual model of client-offered gateways and invitations to an early alliance. This conceptual model has the potential to increase therapists' awareness on what can be seen as a client's invitation to work on some kind of personal change. The researchers suggest therapists search for and explore the strongest invitations, as these might activate the client's approach to motivational goals (Lømo *et al.* 2016).

The second theme is work on the client's sense of *responsibility*. Through the process of detailed reconstruction of the violent behaviour, it becomes apparent that the violent acts are rational and controllable, indicating that the violence is actually a chosen act among many other alternative actions. This implies that the client has the option of choosing other, non-violent, acts instead. Part of the work on responsibility includes focusing on denial, minimisation, externalising and fragmentation, which are common features of men's talk about their violent behaviour (Adams 1988; Isdal 2000; Isdal and Råkil 2002). This part of the work also includes getting hold of the man's intentions governing his use of violence. These cognitive mechanisms are, together with the focus on responsibility, made central issues throughout the entire treatment process.

The work of the two first themes forms the necessary framework for the work process focusing on the *psychological connections* aimed at connecting his personal history, his present inner working models on interpersonal relationships and his beliefs on gender to his use of violence. Topics such as the man's current life situation, attitudes regarding men and women, his perceptions of gender roles and his life experiences are explored. To what extent the man understands his violence to be something he is entitled to, and to what extent he sees the violence to be a part of his masculine identity, are explored. Equally, his awareness of his relative and physical power position is addressed. As previously mentioned, the majority of clients attending ATV report high scores on trauma exposure (Askeland, Evang and Heir 2011; Askeland *et al.* 2012). The effects of such experiences go far beyond social learning and imitation, and include a broad spectrum of long-term consequences and have a profound effect on the way these men view the world, themselves and others. Typically, the men will express some distorted and incorrect ways of thinking. Further, they will show difficulties with regulating their emotions. Some of the frequent issues revolve around trust, lack of self-esteem and subsequent lack of respect and confidence in others. Additionally, their past has often been full of experiences of feeling inferior, helpless, lack of control and with overwhelming feelings of powerlessness, which are all factors known to be associated with trauma exposure. Therapeutic work connected to their trauma histories, how these affect their thinking and feelings today, is seen as crucial in preventing recidivism in the long term. However, this work should always be related to how the man's experiences affect his feelings and thinking today, and how this is interconnected to his violence. This work also helps the client to actually see how the violence is affecting his children as well as his current or former partner.

The fourth theme entails an increased focus on the harmful *consequences* of violence. Through the processes described above, the client experiences that the violent behaviour is not the result of a loss of control or simply a response to his partner's behaviour. The client becomes enabled to acknowledge that the violence is about him, his attitudes and his own emotional and social self-perceptions and perceptions of others, which, in turn, is often rooted in the lack of recognition of his own feelings of powerlessness, shame and inferiority. The difficulties in recognising the effects of violence and abuse are seen to be linked to both to the client's own personal history and to the cultural context with its imperatives regulating the standards for masculinity and femininity. Taking full responsibility for the violence and all the negative aftermaths it has caused for his partner, children and other people including himself can be emotionally challenging. Thus many men have strong emotional reactions connected to this process, such as guilt, shame and sorrow. Therapists must acknowledge these reactions and offer support while simultaneously avoiding harmful self-pity or anger connected to these strong emotions.

One additional theme is connected to the *men as fathers*. A study measuring mentalisation capacity among a group of men in treatment at ATV found this to be low, and concluded that these factors need to be screened for and addressed in treatment with men using IPV who are fathers (Mohaupt and Duckert 2016). ATV offers specific work for men who are fathers. The intention of this work is to develop the men's understanding of children's perspectives in the work and to focus more on fatherhood as an element of their IPV. Part of this is to eschew their often 'split image' as both being abusive towards their partner and still perceiving themselves as loving fathers. Work on men's violence needs to include the men's perceptions of themselves as fathers, how the violence is affecting the father–child and mother–child relationships, how the child is affected by the violence on both a short and long-term basis, the basic psychological needs of the child in a developmental perspective, and how these needs are violated by the presence of violence (Råkil 2006).

FINAL COMMENTS

Still, there is an intense debate demonstrating rather strong disagreements on both the causes of men's violence towards intimate partners and their children, and so what would be good and effective interventions in order to help men stop using violence. The presented ATV model illustrates that it is possible to make integrated approaches combining a focus on gender and power with a focus on individual psychological factors, all central aspects contributing to why the violent behaviour has developed and how it is maintained. As pointed out in the survey on domestic violence perpetrator programmes in

Europe (Hamilton *et al.* 2012), most programmes combined multiple treatment modalities. However, it was not clear how programmes are tailored to the participants' varying profiles of risk and need, and it seemed that tailoring was rarely based on empirically validated assessment tools (Hamilton *et al.* 2012). To enhance knowledge on important elements in the treatment at ATV, and to gather evidence about who seems to benefit from treatment, there is an ongoing process and outcome study of men in treatment at ATV, carried out by the Norwegian Centre for Violence and Traumatic Stress Studies (NKVTS). Data has been collected from both men and their partners, before treatment, repeatedly during treatment, at the end of treatment and at follow-up 18 months after ending treatment. Data includes auditory records of treatment sessions, measures of mental health (Mini-International Neuropsychiatric Interview (MINI); Sheehan *et al.* 1998), lifetime trauma experiences (Traumatic Experiences Checklist (TEC); Nijenhuis, van der Hart and Kruger 2002), working alliance (Working Alliance Inventory (WAI); Horovath and Symonds 1991) in addition to the outcome measure (Outcome Questionnaire-45 (OQ-45); Lambert *et al.* 1996), and measures of violence, alcohol and substance abuse (Violence, Alcohol, and Substance Abuse Questionnaire (VAS); Askeland and Heir 2014; Askeland *et al.* 2012). Hopefully the results from this study will give more insight to what constitutes effective therapeutic processes, and what seems to work for whom.

REFERENCES

Adams, D. (1988) *Treatment Models of Men Who Batter. A Profeminist Analysis.* Newbury Park, CA: Sage Publications, Inc.

Allison, C.J., Bartholomew, K., Mayseless, O. and Dutton, D.G. (2007) 'Love as a battlefield: Attachment and relationship dynamics in couples identified for male partner violence.' *Journal of Family Issues 29*, 1.

Ansara, D.L. and Hindin, M.J. (2011) 'Psychosocial consequences of intimate partner violence for women and men in Canada.' *Journal of Interpersonal Violence 26*, 8, 1628–1645.

Archer, J. (2000) 'Sex differences in aggression between heterosexual partners: A meta-analytic review.' *Psychological Bulletin 126*, 5, 651–680. doi: 10.1037/0033-2909.126.5.651

Askeland, I.R. and Heir, T. (2014) 'Psychiatric disorders among men voluntarily in treatment for violent behaviour: A cross-sectional study.' *BMJ Open 4*, 4. doi: 10.1136/bmjopen-2013-004485

Askeland, I.R., Evang, A. and Heir, T. (2011) 'Association of violence against partner and former victim experiences: A sample of clients voluntarily attending therapy.' *Journal of Interpersonal Violence 26*, 6, 1095–1110. doi: 10.1177/0886260510368152

Askeland, I.R., Lømo, B., Strandmoen, J.-F., Heir, T. and Tjersland, O.A. (2012) *Kjennetegn hos menn som har oppsøkt Alternativ til Vold (ATV) for vold i nære relasjoner: Alternativ til Vold-terapiprosjektet.* Oslo: Nasjonalt kunnskapssenter om vold og traumatisk stress.

Babcock, J.C., Jacobson, N.S., Gottman, J.M. and Yerington, T.P. (2000) 'Attachment, emotional regulation, and the function of marital violence: Differences between secure, preoccupied, and dismissing violent and nonviolent husbands.' *Journal of Family Violence 15*, 4, 391–409.

Babcock, J.C., Waltz, J., Jacobson, N.S. and Gottman, J.M. (1993) 'Power and violence: The relationship between communication patterns, power discrepancies and domestic violence.' *Journal of Consulting and Clinical Psychology 61*, 6, 40–50.

Bair-Merritt, M.H., Shea Crowne, S., Thompson, D.A., Sibinga, E., Trent, M. and Campbell, J. (2010) 'Why do women use intimate partner violence? A systematic review of women's motivations.' *Trauma, Violence, and Abuse 11*, 4, 178–189.

Bowlby, J. (1969) *Attachment: Attachment and Loss.* New York: Basic Books.

Briere, J. and Spinazzola, J. (2009) 'Assessment of the Sequelae of Complex Trauma.' In C. Courtois and J. Ford (eds) *Treating Complex Traumatic Stress Disorders: An Evidence-Based Guide* (pp.104–123). New York: Guilford Press.

Caldwell, J.E., Swan, S.C. and Woodbrown, V.D. (2012) 'Gender differences in intimate partner violence outcomes.' *Psychology of Violence 2*, 1, 42–57.

Cantos, A.L., Neidig, P.H. and O'Leary, K.D. (1993) 'Men and women's attributions of blame for domestic violence.' *Journal of Family Violence 8*, 4, 289–302. doi: 10.1007/BF00978094

Cascardi, M., Langhinrichsen, J. and Vivian, D. (1992) 'Marital aggression: Impact, injury, and health correlates for husbands and wives.' *Archives of Internal Medicine 152*, 6, 1178–1184.

Cascardi, M., O'Leary, K.D. and Schlee, K.A. (1999) 'Co-occurrence and correlates of posttraumatic stress disorder and major depression in physically abused women.' *Journal of Family Violence 14*, 3, 227–249.

Catalano, S.M. (2012) *Intimate Partner Violence, 1993–2010.* Washington, DC: US Department of Justice, National Crime Victimization Survey (NCVS).

Clements, K. and Holtzworth-Munroe, A. (2008) 'Aggressive cognitions of violent versus nonviolent spouses.' *Cognitive Therapy and Research 32*, 3, 351–369.

Constans, J.L. (2005) 'Information-processing Biases in PTSD.' In J.J. Vasterling and C.R. Brewin (eds) *Neuropsychology of PTSD: Biological, Cognitive, and Clinical Perspectives* (pp.105–130). New York: Guilford Press.

Cooper, A. and Smith, E. (2011) *Homicide Trends in the US, 1980–2008.* Washington, DC. Available at www.bjs.gov/content/pub/pdf/htus8008.pdf

Crick, N.R. and Dodge, K.A. (1994) 'A review and reformulation of social information-processing mechanisms in children's social adjustment.' *Psychological Bulletin 115*, 74–101.

Dalton, B. (2007) 'What's going on out there? A survey of batterer intervention programs.' *Journal of Aggression, Maltreatment and Trauma 15*, 59–74.

DeKeseredy, W.S. (2016) 'Understanding woman abuse in intimate heterosexual relationships: The enduring relevance of feminist ways of knowing.' *Journal of Family Violence 31*, 8, 1043–1046.

Delsol, C. and Margolin, G. (2004) 'The role of family-of-origin violence in men's marital violence perpetration.' *Clinical Psychological Review 24*, 99–122.

Devaney, J. and Lazenbatt, A. (2016) *Domestic Violence Perpetrators – Evidence-informed Responses.* Routledge Advances in Social Work. Abingdon: Routledge.

Dodge, K.A. (1993) 'Social-cognitive mechanisms in the development of conduct disorder and depression.' *Annual Review of Psychology 44*, 1, 559–584.

Dodge, K.A., Bates, J.E. and Pettit, G.S. (1990) 'Mechanisms in the cycle of violence.' *Science, New Series 250*, 1678–1683.

Dodge, K.A., Lansford, J.E., Burks, V.S., Bates, J.E. *et al.* (2003) 'Peer rejection and social information-processing factors in the development of aggressive behavior problems in children.' *Child Development 74*, 2, 374–393.

Dutton, D.G. (2006) *The Abusive Personality: Violence and Control in Intimate Relationships.* New York: Guilford Press.

Dutton, D.G. and Corvo, K. (2006) 'Transforming a flawed policy: A call to revive psychology and science in domestic violence research and practice.' *Aggression and Violent Behavior 11*, 5, 457–483. doi: 10.1016/j.avb.2006.01.007

Dutton, D.G. and Nicholls, T. (2005) 'The gender paradigm in domestic violence research and theory: Part I – The conflict of theory and data.' *Aggression and Violent Behavior 10*, 6, 680–714.

Dutton, D.G., Saunders, K., Starzomski, A. and Bartholomew, K. (1994) 'Intimacy anger and insecure attachment as precursors of abuse in intimate relationships.' *Journal of Applied Social Psychology 24*, 1367–1386.

Ehrensaft, M.K., Cohen, P., Brown, J., Smailes, E., Chen, H. and Johnson, J.G. (2003) 'Intergenerational transmission of partner violence: A 20-year prospective study.' *Journal of Consulting and Clinical Psychology 71*, 4, 741–753.

Flückiger, C. and Grosse Holtforth, M. (2008) 'Focusing the therapist's attention on the patient's strengths: A preliminary study to foster a mechanism of change in outpatient psychotherapy.' *Journal of Clinical Psychology 64*, 7, 876–890. doi: 10.1002/jclp.20493

Fonagy, P. (1999) 'Male perpetrators of violence against women: An attachment theory perspective.' *Journal of Applied Psychoanalytic Studies 1*, 1, 7–27.

Fong, V.C., Hawes, D. and Allen, J.L. (2017) 'A systematic review of risk and protective factors for externalizing problems in children exposed to intimate partner violence.' *Trauma, Violence, and Abuse.* doi: 10.1177/1524838017692383

Gassmann, D. and Grawe, K. (2006) 'General change mechanisms: The relation between problem activation and resource activation in successful and unsuccessful therapeutic interactions.' *Clinical Psychology and Psychotherapy 13*, 1, 1–11.

Gauthier, L.M. and Levendosky, A.A. (1996) 'Assessment and treatment of couples with abusive male partners: Guidelines for therapists.' *Psychotherapy 33*, 3, 403–417. doi: 10.1037/0033-3204.33.3.403

Gilchrist, E. and Kebbell, M.R. (2010) 'Intimate Partner Violence: Current Issues in Definitions.' In J.R. Adler (ed.) *Forensic Psychology: Debates, Concepts, Practice* (pp.351–377). Cullompton: Willan Publishing.

Gondolf, E.W. (2002) *Batterer Intervention Systems: Issues, Outcomes, and Recommendations.* Thousand Oaks, CA: Sage Publications, Inc.

Gondolf, E.W. (2007) 'Culturally-focused batterer counseling for African-American men.' *Criminology and Public Policy 6*, 2, 341–366.

Gondolf, E.W. (2012) *The Future of Batterer Programs: Reassessing Evidence-based Practise.* Lebanon: UPNE.

Graham-Bermann, S.A. and Edleson, J.L. (2001) *Domestic Violence in the Lives of Children: The Future of Research, Intervention, and Social Policy.* Washington, DC: American Psychological Association.

Gurman, A.S. and Jacobson, N.S. (2002) *Clinical Handbook of Couple Therapy.* New York: Guilford Press.

Haaland, T., Clausen, S.E. and Schei, B. (2005) *Vold i parforhold – ulike perspektiver. Resultater fra den første landsdekkende undersøkelsen i Norge.* Oslo: NIBR.

Hamberger, L.K. and Guse, C.E. (2002) 'Men's and women's use of intimate partner violence in clinical samples.' *Violence Against Women 8*, 11, 1301–1331. doi: 10.1177/107780102762478028

Hamilton, L., Koehler, J.A. and Lösel, F.A. (2012) 'Domestic violence perpetrator programs in Europe. Part I: A survey of current practise.' *International Journal of Offender Therapy and Comparative Criminology 57*, 10, 1189–1205.

Holden, G.A., Geffner, R. and Jouriles, E.N. (1998) *Children Exposed to Marital Violence: Theory, Research and Applied Issues.* Washington, DC: American Psychological Association.

Holtzworth-Munroe, A. (2005) 'Male versus female intimate partner violence: Putting controversial findings into context.' *Journal of Marriage and Family 67*, 5, 1120–1125.

Holtzworth-Munroe, A. and Anglin, K. (1991) 'The competency of responses given by maritally violent versus nonviolent men to problematic marital situations.' *Violence and Victims 6*, 257–269.

Holtzworth-Munroe, A. and Hutchinson, G. (1993) 'Attributing negative intent to wife behavior: The attributions of maritally violent versus nonviolent men.' *Journal of Abnormal Psychology 102*, 2, 206–211.

Holtzworth-Munroe, A. and Meehan, J.C. (2004) 'Typologies of men who are maritally violent: Scientific and clinical implications.' *Journal of Interpersonal Violence 19*, 12, 1369–1389. doi: 10.1177/088626050426

Holtzworth-Munroe, A. and Smutzler, N. (1996) 'Comparing the emotional reactions and behavioral intentions of violent and nonviolent husbands to aggressive, distressed, and other wife behaviors.' *Violence and Victims 11*, 4, 319–339.

Holtzworth-Munroe, A., Stuart, G.L. and Hutchinson, G. (1997) 'Violent versus nonviolent husbands: Differences in attachment patterns, dependency, and jealousy.' *Journal of Family Psychology 11*, 3, 314–331.

Horvath, A.O. and Symonds, B.D. (1991) 'Relation between working alliance and outcome in psychotherapy: A meta-analysis.' *Journal of Counseling Psychology 38*, 2, 139.

Isdal, P. (2000) *Meningen med volden.* Oslo: Kommuneforlaget.
Isdal, P. and Råkil, M. (2002) 'Volden er mannens ansvar- behandling av mannlige voldsutøvere som tiltak mot kvinnemishandling.' In M. Råkil (ed.) *Menns vold mot kvinner – behandlingserfaringer og kunnskapsstatus* (pp.100–128). Oslo: Universitetsforlaget.
Johnson, M.P. (2006) 'Conflict and control: Gender symmetry and asymmetry in domestic violence.' *Violence Against Women 12*, 11, 1003–1018.
Johnson, M.P. (2008) *A Typology of Domestic Violence: Intimate Terrorism, Violent Resistance, and Situational Couple Violence.* Boston, MA: Northeastern University Press.
Johnson, M.P. (2011) 'Gender and types of intimate partner violence: A response to an anti-feminist literature review.' *Aggression and Violent Behavior 16*, 4, 289–296.
Johnson, M.P. and Leone, J.M. (2005) 'The differential effects of intimate terrorism and situational couple violence: Findings from the National Violence Against Women Survey.' *Journal of Family Issues 26*, 3, 322–349.
Jose, A. and O'Leary, K.D. (2009) 'Prevalence of Partner Aggression in Representative and Clinic Samples.' In K.D. O'Leary and E.M. Woodin (eds) *Psychological and Physical Aggression in Couples: Causes and Interventions* (pp.15–35). Washington, DC: American Psychological Association.
Kelly, J.B. and Johnson, M.P. (2008) 'Differentiation among types of intimate partner violence: Research update and implications for interventions.' *Family Court Review 46*, 3, 476–499. doi: 10.1111/j.1744-1617.2008.00215.x
Kropp, P.R. and Gibas, A. (2010) 'The Spousal Assault Risk Assessment Guide (SARA).' In R.K. Otto and K.S. Douglas (eds) *Handbook of Violence Risk Assessment* (pp.227–250). New York: Routledge.
Kropp, P.R. and Hart, S.D. (2000) 'The Spousal Assault Risk Assessment (SARA) Guide: Reliability and validity in adult male offenders.' *Law and Human Behavior 24*, 101–118.
Lambert, M.J., Burlingame, G.M., Umphress, V., Hansen, N.B. *et al.* (1996) 'The reliability and validity of the Outcome Questionnaire.' *Clinical Psychology and Psychotherapy 3*, 4, 249–258.
Landolt, M.A. and Dutton, D.G. (1997) 'Power and personality: An analysis of gay male intimate abuse.' *Sex Roles 37*, 5–6, 335–359. doi: 10.1023/A:1025649306193
Langhinrichsen-Rohling, J., Neidig, P. and Thorn, G. (1995) 'Violent marriages: Gender differences in levels of current violence and past abuse.' *Journal of Family Violence 10*, 2, 159–176.
Larsen, S.E. and Hamberger, L.K. (2015) 'Men's and women's experience of IPV part II: A review of new developments in comparative studies in clinical populations.' *Journal of Family Violence 30*, 1007–1030. doi: 10.1007/s10896-015-9730-x
La Taillade, J., Epstein, N.B. and Werlinich, C.A. (2006) 'Conjoint treatment of intimate partner violence: A cognitive behavioral approach.' *Journal of Cognitive Psychotherapy 20*, 4, 393–410.
Lawson, D.M. (2008) 'Attachment, interpersonal problems, and family of origin functioning: Differences between partner violent and nonpartner violent men.' *Psychology of Men and Masculinity 9*, 2, 90.
Lemerise, E.A. and Arsenio, W.F. (2000) 'An integrated model of emotion processes and cognition in social information processing.' *Child Development 71*, 1, 107–118.
Mahoney, P., Williams, L.M. and West, C.M. (2001) 'Violence Against Women by Intimate Relationship Partners.' In C.M. Renzetti, J.L. Edleson and R.K. Bergen (eds) *Sourcebook on Violence Against Women* (pp.143–178). London: Sage Publishers.
Main, M., Hesse, E. and Kaplan, N. (2005) 'Predictability of Attachment Behavior and Representational Processes at 1, 6, and 19 Years of Age.' In K.E. Grossmann, K. Grossmann and E. Waters (eds) *Attachment from Infancy to Adulthood: The Major Longitudinal Studies* (pp.245–304). New York: Guilford Press.
Maiuro, R.D. and Eberle, J.A. (2008) 'State standards for domestic violence perpetrator treatment: Current status, trends, and recommendations.' *Violence and Victims 23*, 2, 133–155.
Margolin, G. (2005) 'Children's exposure to violence: Exploring developmental pathways to diverse outcomes.' *Journal of Interpersonal Violence 20*, 1, 72–81.
McCollum, E.E. and Stith, S.M. (2008) 'Couples treatment for IPV: A review of outcome research literature and current clinical practises.' *Violence and Victims 23*, 2, 187–201.
McCrory, E., Puetz, V.B. and Viding, E. (2017) 'The Neuroscience and Genetics of Childhood Maltreatment.' In D. Skuse, H. Bruce and L. Dowdney (eds) *Child Psychology and Psychiatry: Frameworks for Clinical Training and Practice* (pp.187–194). Chichester: John Wiley & Sons.
Meier, J.S. (2015) 'Johnson's differentiation theory: Is it really empirically supported?' *Journal of Child Custody 12*, 1, 4–24. doi: 10.1080/15379418.2015.1037054

Moffitt, T.E., Caspi, A., Rutter, M. and Silva, P.A. (2001) *Sex Differences in Antisocial Behavior: Conduct Disorder, Delinquency, and Violence in the Dunedin Longitudinal Study.* New York: Cambridge University Press.
Mohaupt, H. and Duckert, F. (2016) 'Parental reflective functioning in fathers who use intimate partner violence: Findings from a Norwegian clinical sample.' *Nordic Psychology.* doi: 10.1080/19012276.2016.1162107
Murphy, C. and Eckhardt, C. (2005) *Treating the Abusive Partner: An Individualized Cognitive-behavioral Approach.* New York: Guilford Press.
Nijenhuis, E.R.S., van der Hart, O. and Kruger, K. (2002) 'The psychometric characteristics of the Traumatic Experiences Questionnaire (TEC): First findings among psychiatric outpatients.' *Clinical Psychology and Psychotherapy 9,* 3, 200–210.
Novaco, R.W. and Chemtob, C.M. (1998) 'Anger and Trauma: Conceptualization, Assessment, and Treatment.' In V.M. Follette, J.I. Ruzek and F.R. Abueg (eds) *Cognitive-behavioral Therapies for Trauma* (pp.162–190). New York: Guilford Press.
O'Leary, K.D. and Slep, A.M.S. (2012) 'Prevention of partner violence by focusing on behaviors of both males and females.' *Prevention Science 13,* 4. doi: 10.100-7/S1121-011-0237-2
O'Leary, K.D., Slep, A.M.S. and O'Leary, S.G. (2007) 'Multivariate models of men's and women's partner aggression.' *Journal of Consulting and Clinical Psychology 75,* 5, 752–764.
Pape, H. and Stefansen, K. (2004) *Den skjulte volden? En undersøkelse av Oslobefolkningens utsatthet for trusler, vold og seksuelle overgrep.* Oslo: Nasjonalt Kunnskapssenter om vold og traumatisk stress.
Pence, E. (2002) 'The Duluth Domestic Abuse Intervention Project.' In F. Mederos and E. Aldarondo (eds) *Programs for Men Who Batter: Intervention and Prevention Strategies in a Diverse Society, 6,* 1–46. Kingston, NJ: Civic Research Institute.
Pence, E. and Paymar, M. (1993) *Education Groups for Men Who Batter: The Duluth Model.* New York: Springer Publishing Company.
Phelan, M.B., Hamberger, L.K., Guse, C.E., Edwards, S., Walczak, S. and Zosel, A. (2005) 'Domestic violence among male and female patients seeking emergency medical services.' *Violence and Victims 20,* 2, 187–206. doi: 10.1891/0886-6708.2005.20.2.187
Råkil, M. (2006) 'Are Men who Use Violence Against Their Partners and Children Good Enough Fathers?' In C. Humphries and N. Stanley (eds) *Domestic Violence and Child Protection: Directions for Good Practise* (pp.190–202). London: Jessica Kingsley Publishers.
Rosenbaum, A. and Leisring, P.A. (2003) 'Beyond power and control: Towards an understanding of partner abusive men.' *Journal of Comparative Family Studies 34,* 7–22.
Russell, B. (1919) *Roads to Freedom: Socialism, Anarchism and Syndicalism.* London: Allen & Unwin Ltd.
Schecter, S. (1982) *Women and Male Violence: The Visions and Struggles of the Battered Women's Movement.* Boston, MA: South End Press.
Schore, A.N. (2001) 'Effects of a secure attachment relationship on right brain development, affect regulation, and infant mental health.' *Infant Mental Health Journal 22,* 1–2, 7–66.
Schore, A.N. (2002) 'Dysregulation of the right brain: A fundamental mechanism of traumatic attachment and the psychopathogenesis of posttraumatic stress disorder.' *Australian and New Zealand Journal of Psychiatry 36,* 1, 9–30.
Schore, J.R. and Schore, A.N. (2008) 'Modern attachment theory: The central role of affect regulation in development and treatment.' *Clinical Social Work Journal 36,* 1, 9–20.
Sheehan, D.V., Lecrubier, Y., Sheehan, K.H., Amorim, P. *et al.* (1998) 'The Mini-International Neuropsychiatric Interview (MINI): The development and validation of structured diagnostic psychiatric interview for DSM-IV and ICD-10.' *Journal of Clinical Psychiatry 59,* 22–33.
Spencer, C., Mendez, M. and Stith, S. (2016) 'Couple Violence in Couple and Family Therapy.' In J. Lebow, A. Chambers and D.C. Breunlin (eds) *Encyclopaedia of Couple and Family Therapy* (pp.1–4). New York: Springer.
Sroufe, L.A. (2005) 'Attachment and development: A prospective, longitudinal study from birth to adulthood.' *Attachment and Human Development 7,* 4, 349–367.
Stets, J. and Straus, M.A. (1992) *Gender Differences in Reporting Marital Violence: Physical Violence in American Families.* New Brunswick, NJ: Transaction Publishers.
Stith, S.M. and McCollum, E.E. (2011) 'Conjoint treatment of couples who have experienced intimate partner violence.' *Aggression and Violent Behaviour 16,* 312–318.
Stith, S.M., McCollum, E.E., Amanor-Boadu, Y. and Smith, D. (2012) 'Systemic perspectives on intimate partner violence treatment.' *Journal of Marital and Family Therapy 38,* 1, 220–240.

Stith, S.M., Rosen, K.H., McCollum, E.E. and Thomsen, C.J. (2004) 'Treating intimate partner violence within intact couple relationships: Outcomes of multi-couple versus individual couple therapy.' *Journal of Marital and Family Therapy 30*, 3, 305–318.

Stover, C.S., Meadows, A.L. and Kaufman, J. (2009) 'Interventions for intimate partner violence: Review and implications for evidence-based practise.' *Professional Psychology: Research and Practise 40*, 3, 223–233.

Straus, M.A. (1979) 'Measuring intrafamily conflict and violence: The conflict tactics (CT) scales.' *Journal of Marriage and the Family 41*, 1, 75–88.

Straus, M.A. (1990) 'Ordinary Violence, Child Abuse, and Wife Beating: What Do They Have in Common?' In M.A. Straus, R.J. Gelles and C. Smith (eds) *Physical Violence in American Families: Risk Factors and Adaptions to Violence in 8,145 Families* (pp.403–424). New Brunswick, NJ: Transaction Publishers.

Straus, M.A. and Gelles, R.J. (1992) 'How Violent Are American Families?' In M.A. Straus and R.J. Gelles (eds) *Physical Violence in American Families* (pp.95–108). New Brunswick, NJ: Transaction Publishers.

Taft, C.T., Kaloupek, D.G., Schumm, J.A., Marshall, A.D. *et al.* (2007) 'Posttraumatic stress disorder symptoms, physiological reactivity, alcohol problems, and aggression among military veterans.' *Journal of Abnormal Psychology 116*, 3, 498–507. doi: 10.1037/0021-843x.116.3.498

Taft, C.T., Murphy, C.M. and Creech, S.K. (2016) *Trauma-informed Treatment and Prevention of Intimate Partner Violence.* Washington, DC: American Psychological Association.

Taft, C.T., Schumm, J.A., Marshall, A.D., Panuzio, J. and Holtzworth-Munroe, A. (2008) 'Family-of-origin maltreatment, posttraumatic stress disorder symptoms, social information processing deficits, and relationship abuse perpetration.' *Journal of Abnormal Psychology 117*, 637–646.

Thoresen, S. and Myhre, M.C. (2014) *Vold og overgrep i barndommen* [*Violence and Abuse in Childhood*]. Oslo: Nasjonalt kunnskapssenter om vold og traumatisk stress.

Tjaden, P. and Thoennes, N. (2000) *Extent, Nature, and Consequences of Intimate Partner Violence: Findings from the National Violence Against Women Survey.* Rockville, MD: National Institute of Justice.

van der Kolk, B.A. (1988) 'The trauma spectrum: The interaction of biological and social events in the genesis of the trauma response.' *Journal of Traumatic Stress 1*, 3, 273–290.

van der Kolk, B.A. (2005) 'Developmental.' *Psychiatric Annals 35*, 5, 401.

van der Kolk, B.A., McFarlane, A.C. and Weisaeth, L. (2012) *Traumatic Stress: The Effects of Overwhelming Experience on Mind, Body, and Society.* New York: Guilford Press.

Vivian, D. and Langhinrichsen-Rohling, J. (1994) 'Are bi-directionally violent couples mutually victimized? A gender-sensitive comparison.' *Violence and Victims 9*, 2, 107–124.

Whitaker, D.J., Haileyesus, T., Swahn, M. and Saltzman, L.S. (2007) 'Differences in frequency of violence and reported injury between relationships with reciprocal and nonreciprocal intimate partner violence.' *American Journal of Public Health 97*, 5, 941–947.

Chapter 15

HEALTHCARE RESPONSES TO DOMESTIC VIOLENCE

WHY AND HOW?

Lucy Potter, *Academic Clinical Fellow, University of Bristol, UK*

Gene Feder, *Professor of Primary Care, University of Bristol, UK*

INTRODUCTION

The Council of Europe definition of domestic violence and abuse encompasses 'all acts of physical, sexual, psychological or economic violence that occur within the family or domestic unit or between former or current spouses or partners, whether or not the perpetrator shares or has shared the same residence with the victim' (Council of Europe 2011). Domestic violence and abuse (DVA) is a violation of human rights and a global public health epidemic. Most of the studies we refer to in this chapter focus on intimate partner violence (IPV), which affects one in three women worldwide (Garcia-Moreno *et al.* 2013) and 25.4 per cent of women in Europe (FRA 2014). The health sector, alongside other sectors and civil society, has a crucial role to play in prevention in response to violence against women and children, but too frequently health systems are failing to recognise or adequately address the problem. This chapter explores why there must be a healthcare response to DVA, and provides evidence-based guidance as to how this can be achieved.

DVA is a gendered issue that disproportionately affects women. Men inflict the majority of the abuse on women, and the majority of serious harm. Compared with male survivors of DVA, female survivors are more likely to suffer more severe forms of DVA, more likely to experience severe injury and three times more likely to fear for their life (AuCoin 2005; Walby, Allen and Simmons 2004). Women are much more likely to be killed by their partner or ex-partner than men (44% of female victims compared with 6% of male victims) (Flatley 2016). Despite the gender difference in prevalence and severity of DVA, men in heterosexual and same-sex relationships also experience abuse from their partners. In a study of 1368 men attending English general practises, 162 reported having experienced DVA, 93 reported having perpetrated DVA and 117 reported having both experienced and perpetrated DVA (Hester *et al.* 2015). The high prevalence of DVA poses a challenge to society as a whole and, given that most abuse is illegal, the criminal justice system. But why do we need a specific health service response? There are three key reasons: the impact of DVA on health and healthcare; the expectations of DVA survivors; and evidence of intervention effectiveness after disclosure to clinicians.

Domestic violence and abuse is bad for health and a challenge to health systems

Experiencing DVA damages health and reduces quality of life in European men and women (Costa *et al.* 2015), as in the global population. Survivors of DVA experience higher rates of chronic physical health problems including chronic pain, infectious illnesses, neurological symptoms, gastrointestinal disorders, higher cardiovascular risk and gynaecological problems. Compared to women who have not experienced physical or sexual violence from an intimate partner, survivors have higher rates of self-reported poor or very poor health, difficulty with daily activities, memory loss, dizziness and vaginal discharge (Ellsberg *et al.* 2008).

The mental health consequences of DVA are substantial. Women exposed to DVA compared to those who are not are 2.8 times more likely to suffer depression, 7.3 times more likely to suffer post-traumatic stress disorder (PTSD) (Trevillion *et al.* 2012) and 5.6 times more likely to abuse alcohol (Golding 1999). Exposure to DVA, both over a woman's lifetime and during pregnancy, is associated with a higher prevalence and increased risk of perinatal mental health disorders (Howard *et al.* 2013). Women who have been exposed to physical or sexual violence from a partner or ex-partner are 2.9 times more likely to have ever had suicidal thoughts and 3.8 times more likely to have attempted suicide (Ellsberg *et al.* 2008).

DVA in the home is damaging to children and young people. There is an increased risk that they will also experience child abuse. A study from the US showed children exposed to DVA were 15 times more likely to experience physical and/or sexual assault compared to the national average (Volpe 1996), which has similarly been found in several other countries (Krug *et al.* 2002). Early exposure to the stress of DVA can impair cognitive and sensory neurodevelopment (Perry 2001). Children exposed to DVA at home compared to children from non-violent homes suffer poorer physical health and development, higher rates of externalising behaviours, such as aggression and conduct problems, and higher rates of internalising behaviours, such as depression, anxiety and low self-esteem, carrying poorer outcomes that can persist through the lifespan (Fantuzzo and Mohr 1999).

In addition to other societal costs, DVA is costly to health systems, costing the UK National Health Service (NHS) £1.2 billion a year for physical injuries and an additional £176 million in mental healthcare (Walby 2004). Women who are or have experienced DVA use considerably more healthcare services (Bonomi *et al.* 2009).

Women experiencing DVA want clinicians to ask about it and respond appropriately

The prevalence of DVA is higher in clinical populations than the wider population (Bonomi *et al.* 2009; Boyle and Todd 2003; Roberts, Hegarty and Feder 2006). Eighty per cent of women in the UK experiencing DVA are in contact with the health service (DH 2000). A study of 2500 women accessing DVA services in the UK showed that, prior to receiving specialist help, just under half had attended primary care an average of 5.3 times, and one in five had attended emergency departments as a result of the abuse (CAADA 2012). People experiencing DVA identified in healthcare settings are more likely to be from vulnerable, hard-to-reach groups (CAADA 2012), presenting an opportunity for clinicians to identify and support those who may not disclose to other professionals, such as social workers.

Women who have been exposed to DVA report that a clinician is one of the few people they can disclose violence to, and want them to respond appropriately (Feder *et al.* 2006). Are clinicians currently equipped for asking about and responding to DVA? A relatively recent cross-sectional study from the UK would suggest not: less than a third of clinicians reported feeling prepared to ask appropriate questions on DVA, and less than a quarter reported feeling able to refer a patient to DVA services. Knowledge gaps were identified, such as heightened risk on leaving an abusive relationship (Ramsay *et al.* 2012).

There are effective interventions after disclosure of DVA to clinicians

A recent Cochrane review on advocacy interventions for DVA showed some benefit, but noted that most studies were under-powered (Rivas *et al.* 2015). The authors concluded that intensive advocacy might improve the short-term quality of life and reduce physical abuse one to two years after intervention; however, this was only studied in women recruited from domestic violence shelters or refuges. They found brief advocacy provided small short-term mental health benefits and could reduce abuse, particularly in pregnant women and for less severe abuse. A systematic review of trauma-focused interventions for DVA survivors concluded that individualised, culturally informed, brief interventions were of benefit to survivors (Warshaw, Sullivan and Rivera 2013). The review highlighted important components to be information on DVA dynamics and safety concerns, cognitive reframing, skill enhancement and social connection.

THE CURRENT HEALTHCARE RESPONSE TO DVA IS INADEQUATE

There are criticisms at a number of levels where healthcare could do better in addressing the problem of DVA. A cross-sectional study of UK primary healthcare clinicians' knowledge and attitudes towards women experiencing domestic violence revealed a positive attitude towards engaging with the issue, but that most felt poorly prepared to ask about it, and 80 per cent felt they did not have adequate knowledge of local DVA resources (Ramsay *et al.* 2012). In the UK, every domestic violence murder results in a domestic homicide review, examining the circumstances in which it occurred – an opportunity to identify and apply lessons to prevent future cases. Health is the most frequently mentioned sector in domestic homicide reviews in which there are missed opportunities for intervention, and successive reviews highlight the need for appropriate healthcare professional training, organisational policies and multi-agency working (Home Office 2016).

Perhaps this is not surprising when DVA has not historically been part of medical curricula or postgraduate training programmes. According to a recent survey of UK medical schools, DVA is starting to become part of medical curricula in the UK, but three-quarters of curriculum representatives who do provide teaching DVA felt it was 'inadequate' or 'not quite enough' to prepare future doctors (Potter and Feder 2017). DVA is damaging to health, survivors would like to be able to disclose to clinicians and there is evidence of effective interventions; there is an imperative to improve the response, both at individual clinician and health system levels. This has been recognised at an international level with the adoption of the 67th World Health Assembly resolution 'Strengthening the role of the health system in addressing violence, in particular against women and girls, and against children' (WHO 2014). What follows is a summary of current available evidence and guidance on how this can be achieved.

WHAT CAN HEALTH SYSTEMS AND CLINICIANS DO?

Evidence-based guidance has been developed by the World Health Organization (WHO 2013), the UK National Institute for Health and Care Excellence (NICE 2014) and a series published in *The Lancet* on violence against women (*The Lancet* 2014), providing a series of recommendations of how clinicians and health systems should respond to DVA and violence against women. Although men also experience DVA, women experience substantially more DVA, and suffer a much greater impact on morbidity and mortality, and so the majority of the research and thus guidance is based on women experiencing DVA. It is these recommendations that we discuss, followed by an example of a healthcare response in UK primary care that implements some of these recommendations.

IDENTIFICATION OF SURVIVORS OF DVA

Clinicians should use selective or clinical enquiry to identify survivors of DVA. A Cochrane review concluded that while screening may improve the identification of women experiencing DVA, it has not been shown to be more effective in identifying survivors than selective enquiry, nor does it reduce further abuse or improve women's health outcomes (O'Doherty *et al.* 2014). Possible harms of screening have not been adequately assessed, and it tends to deter clinicians from engaging with DVA. Thus it has been concluded that there is insufficient evidence for screening in healthcare settings. Instead, clinicians should ask about exposure to DVA selectively, when assessing conditions that may be caused or complicated by it (see below).

EXAMPLES OF CLINICAL CONDITIONS ASSOCIATED WITH INTIMATE PARTNER VIOLENCE

- Symptoms of depression, anxiety, post-traumatic stress disorder (PTSD), sleep disorders
- Suicidality or self-harm
- Alcohol or other substance misuse
- Unexplained chronic pain, gastrointestinal symptoms, neurological or genitourinary symptoms
- Adverse reproductive outcomes, including multiple unintended pregnancies
- Repeated vaginal bleeding and sexually transmitted infections
- Traumatic injury, particularly if repeated
- Repeated health consultations with no clear diagnosis
- Intrusive partner in consultations

Source: WHO (2013)

In order to ensure asking about DVA does not put the survivor at higher risk, clinicians and services must ensure this conversation is in private, confidentiality is ensured, the clinician has had training and there is a system for referral in place. These are stated as minimum requirements in international guidance (WHO 2013). The frontline clinician must also be able to identify children or young people affected by DVA, offer support and, when appropriate, refer to local child protection services.

TAILORED SUPPORT

People experiencing DVA will have different backgrounds, vulnerabilities, strengths and needs. They may be experiencing different forms of abuse, be at different levels of risk and be in different stages of recognition of this abuse. Clinicians need to respond appropriately to that individual's needs at that time. At a minimum, this would be direct support from frontline clinicians to patients disclosing abuse. A meta-analysis of qualitative studies of women survivors of DVA suggests that this support should include non-judgemental, sensitive enquiry about their needs, validation of the disclosure without pressure, assisting the woman in increasing the safety of her and her children, and provision of support to access ongoing care (Feder *et al.* 2006). The meta-analysis also highlights unhelpful responses, including judging, pitying, blaming and trivialising, which must be avoided by the clinician.

Once identified, survivors of DVA may benefit from a range of support, some of which may be from the identifying clinician, and some through referral to other specialists or DVA services. Evidence-based interventions exist for mental health conditions such as depression and PTSD that the patient may be experiencing associated with the abuse. Cognitive behavioural therapy is recommended as an intervention for women who have PTSD and who are no longer experiencing DVA, although the evidence of benefit is insufficient to recommend it if she is still exposed to the abuse (WHO 2013). Advocacy interventions aim to help those who have or are experiencing DVA by connecting them with community resources, such as legal, housing, police or financial services, and many also include psychological support (Garcia-Moreno *et al.* 2014). There is some evidence of the efficacy of these interventions (Rivas *et al.* 2015); recommendations for a structured programme of advocacy, support and/or empowerment are currently limited to women who have spent at least a night in a shelter, or during prenatal care, as the evidence for improved outcomes is uncertain outside of these contexts (Feder, Wathen and MacMillan 2013).

Psychotherapeutic interventions for children exposed to DVA are recommended based on evidence from trials in North America (Cohen, Mannarino and Iyengar 2011). These are likely to be applicable to high-income countries in Europe, but not necessarily to low- and middle-income settings.

Mandatory reporting of DVA to the police from clinicians is not recommended (WHO 2013); clinicians could offer to report to the police or other authority if the victim would like this and they are aware of their rights, but should not do this without the victim's consent as long as they are deemed to have capacity for this decision. Child exposure to DVA is more challenging in terms of mandatory reporting. There is a growing consensus internationally that DVA is a form of child maltreatment. While there is no evidence that reporting all children in that situation to relevant authorities improves outcomes for children, the health sector has an important role in information sharing for children they deem to be at risk. In many European countries and globally, child protection services are patchy and poorly funded (WHO 2013). This must be improved for the protection of children.

CLINICIAN TRAINING, RESOURCES AND CAPACITY

For clinicians to be able to deliver informed frontline support, they must understand the dynamics of DVA, be able to recognise the signs, sensitively ask about it and be able to respond appropriately with knowledge of how to respond and what services are available locally to provide specialist support. It is recommended that this training be included in curricula for clinicians at both undergraduate and postgraduate levels (NICE 2014). Clinicians must have an appropriate environment to enable them to use their training on asking about and supporting those experiencing DVA, with functioning referral pathways. They must have appropriate support and mentoring mechanisms in place and, where feasible, be able to access a lead or specialist in the field (Garcia-Moreno *et al.* 2014). Sustainable change must be part of a comprehensive systems approach, in which the health system supports clinicians in this work, and acts beyond the patient–clinician interaction in its response to DVA. Further exploration of how this can be achieved is explored below.

LEADERSHIP AND GOVERNANCE

Health systems afford a vital opportunity to provide supportive care to those experiencing DVA as well as contributing to prevention efforts and a society-wide message that DVA is unacceptable. Political will is essential to acknowledge the harm and prioritise a healthcare response to DVA in policies, budgets and service commissioning. Health sector organisations are large employers and should promote healthy relationships in their workplace policies and environments (Garcia-Moreno *et al.* 2014). In these ways health systems can contribute to the wider climate shift of improving the response for those experiencing DVA, and preventing it from happening in the first place.

COMPREHENSIVE, COORDINATED, MULTISECTORAL CARE

Care for survivors of DVA must be integrated into existing health services. People who experience DVA have complex needs, including safety, medical, social, economic, housing and legal aspects, so a multisectoral response is necessary (Garcia-Moreno *et al.* 2014). Coordination within and between these systems is essential for the holistic care of survivors of abuse; intervention models where the health system has taken a lead role in the response to DVA in European countries have been reviewed (Bacchus *et al.* 2012). Relationships with community-based organisations (CBOs) or non-governmental organisations (NGOs) is often necessary and advantageous, but should not replace the State's responsibility to ensure provision of services (WHO 2013). There should be clear protocols and methods for referrals and information sharing between providers and sectors, considering data protection, consent, confidentiality and safety (NICE 2014). The WHO has recommended minimum requirements for a health sector response to violence against women (WHO 2013), which could be considered a start-point in developing those for DVA (see Table 15.1).

Table 15.1: Minimum requirements for a health sector response to violence against women

Policies and protocols	Local policies and protocols defining roles, responsibilities and procedures related to identification and management of survivors need to be developed and implemented (with appropriate training and continual support)
Management support	Management backing, often with financial support, is important, especially for the long-term sustainability of the response

Comprehensive care	Ensure the provision of all aspects of medico-legal care either by the provider/linked providers in health services, or through the support of NGOs or CBOs or community efforts, in a way that minimises the number of contacts required
Links with CBOs/NGOs	Build relationships with local NGOs and CBOs
Intersectoral collaboration	Establish clear working protocols, including the referral pathway of survivors, between services offered by the same facility or by different sectors, and establish regular (monthly) meetings to ensure coordination
Resource material	Ensure the availability of some resource material (posters, pocket cards and/or leaflets)
Surveillance and recording	Develop systems for maintaining records and conducting surveillance that are confidential and do not put women at risk
Monitoring and evaluation	Implement a system for monitoring and evaluation, based on local policy and procedures, including considerations related to safety
Support for clinicians/care providers	Provide support to those delivering care

Source: Adapted from WHO (2013)

MONITORING AND EVALUATION

In order to strengthen the healthcare response to DVA, appropriate monitoring and evaluation activities should be embedded in healthcare systems. This can provide training to clinicians, for example feeding back referral data, tracking adherence to evidence-based guidance, contributing to resource allocation decisions, and ultimately monitoring and driving progress. The UK has a set of quality standards that provide an example of how the healthcare response to DVA can be monitored (NICE 2014).

HEALTHCARE RESPONSE IN EUROPE

Variation in the structure of European health services and in the resourcing of domestic violence specialist services means that it is impossible to generalise on the development of the healthcare response across the continent. A scoping study of DVA interventions in primary and maternity healthcare settings shows significant innovation in seven European countries: the UK, Germany, the Netherlands, Spain, Belgium, Finland and Serbia (Bacchus *et al.* 2012). The initial survey identified 81 programmes, of which seven were studied in depth as case studies. These had achieved the engagement of clinicians in identifying women experiencing domestic violence and giving access to specialist domestic violence support, implementing key recommendations of the WHO intimate partner and sexual violence guidelines (WHO 2013).

Conclusions from the survey included the importance of clinical leadership in establishing DVA training and treatment/referral protocols for driving change within healthcare organisations. These clinical leaders or champions sensitised their colleagues to their role in identifying and supporting patients experiencing DVA, in addition to dealing with resistance within the healthcare setting towards implementation of a response to the problem. The case studies also highlighted that implementation also depends on a national framework of legislation, national guidelines and national action plans to support change within healthcare settings. In all seven countries there is acknowledgement of violence against women as a public health and clinical issue, with strategies for addressing it developed by inter-ministerial collaboration. Their national action plans include specific targets for healthcare professionals and for addressing DVA in the health sector. Although the case studies were exemplars of good practise, the absence of secure funding, even before the full impact of austerity that we are currently experiencing across the European public sector, threatens the sustainability of a healthcare response integrated with the domestic violence sector. There is insufficient funding of that sector, often based on NGOs or charities, and healthcare organisations find it easier to disinvest in DVA services than, say, diabetes treatment. Having said that, the survey found striking examples of how DVA programmes in healthcare settings had found innovative ways of sustaining their training and referral pathways.

IDENTIFICATION AND REFERRAL TO IMPROVE SAFETY (IRIS)

In the UK we have developed a national programme of training and support for general practise that has now been implemented in 36 areas of England and Wales and more than 1000 practises. This programme is based on collaboration between primary care and specialist DVA services; a key feature is that the training to doctors and nurses within the practises is delivered by the DVA advocate (together with a local GP), who also receives the referral of the women experiencing abuse. That advocate-educator provides an initial assessment of the needs of the patient referred, safety advice and linkage to further services. This intervention was tested in a randomised controlled trial of 48 practises in East London and Bristol, showing a six-fold increase in referrals to the advocate-educator in intervention practise (Feder *et al.* 2011) and strong approval from clinicians and patients (Malpass *et al.* 2014). Crucially, in terms of securing funding for the programme from health services, we conducted an economic analysis that estimated that the intervention was highly cost-effective and probably cost-saving to the NHS (Norman *et al.* 2010). Other factors that promoted the implementation of IRIS was its naming in national DVA guidelines and Department of Health policy documents, a (small) national coordinating organisation that trained the local advocate-educators, and systematic data collection on the functioning of the programme (IRIS 2012). Although developed for responding to the needs of women experiencing DVA in general practise, further research has adapted the scope of the model to include the needs of men in general practise (Williamson *et al.* 2015), of patients in mental health services (Trevillion *et al.* 2014) and of patients in sexual health services (Sohal *et al.* 2017).

CHALLENGES

This chapter has provided an overview of current evidence-based guidance on the healthcare response to DVA and implementation in European contexts. There is growing evidence of effective health responses to DVA and widespread, but not necessarily systematic and secure, implementation in Europe. We conclude with our views on emerging research questions that need answering and contextual challenges that need considering for a more effective response that improves outcomes for the survivors of DVA and their families.

DVA has historically been hidden, tolerated or ignored at community, national and international levels (Garcia-Moreno *et al.* 2015). This chapter has highlighted the increasing efforts to confront, understand and shine a light on this damaging phenomenon. Yet, progress to shift patriarchal norms has been slow (Carter 2014) and remains a challenge to the implementation of healthcare responses to DVA. There is a need to better understand how healthcare systems can be involved in primary prevention efforts, for example public health campaigns and challenging the societal attitudes of male dominance and normalisation of violence (Carter 2014). The current evidence for those interventions is weak.

Health systems are large, complex and heterogeneous organisations. Currently, to varying extents in different European countries, they are overworked and sometimes overwhelmed. For them to engage with DVA as a health problem, when it has traditionally been seen as lying outside healthcare, requires political will, training, financial support and structural change. As highlighted in this chapter, there are examples where this engagement and change has been achieved, and proven to be valuable. A lot of work is required to make this the norm of health systems, rather than the exception.

The health system needs to have functioning and effective support services, housing and trauma-informed mental health services to refer survivors of DVA to. There is a need for services for perpetrators and children exposed to DVA. Many of these crucial roles are often fulfilled by NGOs. A major provider of these services in the UK, Refuge, has experienced cuts to 80 per cent of its services, with some being cut by up to 50 per cent since 2011 (Refuge 2016). With politically imposed austerity, cuts to these services risk a destructive step backwards, at precisely the point when healthcare systems in Europe are finally waking up to the public health and clinical challenge of DVA. Perhaps also related to austerity, domestic violence is increasing in the UK. Walby's re-analysis of English and Welsh crime survey data has found an increase in violent crime since the economic crisis, reversing the long-run fall (Walby, Towers and Francis 2016). This is driven by violence committed by domestic relations and acquaintances and by violence against women. A multisectoral response to DVA is only as strong as its weakest link; an improvement in the health sector response can only make a difference if it is enabled by the wider political climate.

Most of the research on healthcare interventions for DVA has been conducted in high-income countries, and predominantly for women accessing antenatal care. We cannot assume that these findings are transferable: we need to better understand the feasibility, delivery and efficacy of advocacy or empowerment interventions and shelter provision for survivors of DVA in resource-poor settings, and for people who may not be accessing antenatal services.

The European refugee crisis adds a further appalling challenge to DVA prevention and response efforts. Refugees experiencing unsafe and insecure living conditions are at higher risk of DVA and have poorer access to services, both in transit and resettlement (IRC 2016; McCracken, Cook and Chantler 2013). Many of these women have already experienced gender violence before coming to the UK. In a survey of asylum-seekers detained in Yarl's Wood, three-quarters had been raped (Feder and Hester 2015). Urgent action is called for in all sectors to improve protection for these women and girls. In the English Chief Medical Officer's 2014 report, the Istanbul Convention requires State governments to promote and protect the rights of women to live free from DVA, and to ensure that survivors have access to services facilitating their recovery without discrimination on grounds of migrant or refugee status (Council of Europe 2011).

We need to better understand how to identify and support survivors of DVA who are men or transgender and people in lesbian and gay relationships. DVA is gendered, but that does not mean men do not experience DVA. It does mean that we need to understand those needs that may require a modification of our strategies and services. Marginalised groups, such as migrants, may experience unique challenges in seeking help or accessing services. We need research to articulate evidence-informed identification and intervention strategies among diverse populations. There is very little evidence to inform how health services and clinicians should respond to perpetrators of abuse, and in how to talk to and support children and other members of a household experiencing DVA.

There is scope for further work on developing more specific psychological therapy for survivors of DVA. An example is trial work testing advocacy/empowerment interventions that are enhanced with trauma-informed psychological therapy. This includes integrating brief psychological interventions into advocacy support (Brierley *et al.* 2013).

MOVING FORWARD

Awareness of DVA is increasing in Europe, and there is support for European-level action on this (Eurobarometer 2010). The Istanbul Convention represents an opportunity to improve the legal framework to prevent and address DVA. The health sector, alongside other sectors, can be an effective part of prevention and response to DVA. This requires prioritisation, infrastructure, funding, training and coordination. There are success stories of how this can be achieved, and the benefits to health and society such investment can carry. Health policy-makers, healthcare organisations and individual clinicians need to show leadership and raise awareness of the health burden and cost. We should use evidence to drive policy, and there are still areas where we need to do more research, but the evidence is enough to inform our actions for now.

REFERENCES

AuCoin, K. (2005) *Family Violence in Canada: A Statistical Profile.* Statistics Canada, Canadian Centre for Justice Statistics.

Bacchus, L., Bewley, S., Fernandez, C., Hellbernd, H. *et al.* (2012) *Health Sector Responses to Domestic Violence in Europe: A Comparison of Promising Intervention Models in Maternity and Primary Care Settings.* London: London School of Hygiene and Tropical Medicine.

Bonomi, A.E., Anderson, M.L., Rivara, F.P. and Thompson, R.S. (2009) 'Health care utilization and costs associated with physical and nonphysical-only intimate partner violence.' *Health Services Research 44,* 3, 1052–1067.

Boyle, A. and Todd, C. (2003) 'Incidence and prevalence of domestic violence in a UK emergency department.' *Emergency Medicine Journal 20,* 5, 438–442.

Brierley, G., Agnew-Davies, R., Bailey, J. *et al.* (2013) 'Psychological advocacy toward healing (PATH): Study protocol for a randomized controlled trial.' *Trials 14,* 1, 221.

CAADA (2012) *CAADA Insights 1: A Place of Greater Safety.*

Carter, J. (2014) 'Patriarchy and violence against women and girls.' *The Lancet 385,* 9978, e40–e41.

Cohen, J.A., Mannarino, A.P. and Iyengar, S. (2011) 'Community treatment of posttraumatic stress disorder for children exposed to intimate partner violence: A randomized controlled trial.' *Archives of Pediatrics and Adolescent Medicine 165,* 1, 16–21.

Costa, D., Hatzidimitriadou, E., Ioannidi-Kapolou, E., Lindert, J. *et al.* (2015) 'Intimate partner violence and health-related quality of life in European men and women: Findings from the DOVE study.' *Quality of Life Research 24,* 2, 463–471.

Council of Europe (2011) *Convention on Preventing and Combating Violence Against Women and Domestic Violence (Istanbul Convention), 11. V. 2011.*

DH (Department of Health) (2000) *Domestic Violence. A Health Response: Working in a Wider Partnership.* London: DH.

Ellsberg, M., Jansen, H.A., Heise, L., Watts, C.H. *et al.* (2008) 'Intimate partner violence and women's physical and mental health in the WHO multi-country study on women's health and domestic violence: An observational study.' *The Lancet 371,* 9619, 1165–1172.

Eurobarometer (2010) *Domestic Violence against Women.* Eurobarometer 73.2, European Commission.

Fantuzzo, J.W. and Mohr, W.K. (1999) 'Prevalence and effects of child exposure to domestic violence.' *The Future of Children,* 21–32.

Feder, G.S. and Hester, M. (2015) 'Gender-based Violence Against Women.' In S.C. Davies (ed.) *Annual Report of the Chief Medical Officer, 2014, The Health of the 51%: Women,* 17–29. London: Department of Health.

Feder, G.S., Davies, R.A., Baird, K. *et al.* (2011) 'Identification and Referral to Improve Safety (IRIS) of women experiencing domestic violence with a primary care training and support programme: A cluster randomised controlled trial.' *The Lancet 378,* 9805, 1788–1795.

Feder, G.S., Hutson, M., Ramsay, J. and Taket, A.R. (2006) 'Women exposed to intimate partner violence. Expectations and experiences when they encounter health care professionals: A meta-analysis of qualitative studies.' *Archives of Internal Medicine 166,* 1, 22–37.

Feder, G.S., Wathen, C.N. and MacMillan, H.L. (2013) 'An evidence-based response to intimate partner violence: WHO guidelines.' *JAMA 310,* 5, 479–480.

Flatley, J. (2016) *Homicide: Findings from Analyses Based on the Homicide Index Recorded by the Home Office Covering Different Aspects of Homicide.* London: Home Office.

FRA (European Union Agency for Fundamental Rights) (2014) *Violence Against Women: An EU-wide Survey – Main Results Report.* Luxembourg: Publications Office of the European Union. Available at http://fra.europa.eu/sites/default/files/fra-2014-vaw-survey-main-results-apr14_en.pdf

Garcia-Moreno, C., Hegarty, K., d'Oliveira, A.F.L., Koziol-McLain, J., Colombini, M. and Feder, G. (2014) 'The health-systems response to violence against women.' *The Lancet 385*, 9977, 1567–1579.

Garcia-Moreno, C., Pallitto, C., Devries, K., Stockl, H., Watts, C. and Abrahams, N. (2013) *Global and Regional Estimates of Violence Against Women: Prevalence and Health Effects of Intimate Partner Violence and Non-partner Sexual Violence.* Geneva: World Health Organisation.

Garcia-Moreno, C., Zimmerman, C., Morris-Gehring, A., Heise, L. *et al.* (2015) 'Addressing violence against women: A call to action.' *The Lancet 385*, 9978, 1685–1695.

Golding, J.M. (1999) 'Intimate partner violence as a risk factor for mental disorders: A meta-analysis.' *Journal of Family Violence 14*, 2, 99–132.

Hester, M., Ferrari, G., Jones, S., Williamson, E. *et al.* (2015) 'Occurrence and impact of negative behaviour, including domestic violence and abuse, in men attending UK primary care health clinics: A cross-sectional survey.' *BMJ Open 5*, 5, e007141.

Home Office (2016) *Key Findings from Analysis of Domestic Homicide Reviews.* London: Home Office.

Howard, L.M., Oram, S., Galley, H., Trevillion, K. and Feder, G. (2013) 'Domestic violence and perinatal mental disorders: A systematic review and meta-analysis.' *PLoS Med 10*, 5, e1001452.

IRC (International Rescue Committee) (2016) *Europe Refugee Crisis: Urgent Action Needed for Protection of Women and Girls.* IRC Briefing, August 2016.

IRIS (Identification and Referral to Improve Safety) (2012) 'About IRIS.' Available at www.irisdomesticviolence.org.uk/iris/about-iris/about

Krug, E.G., Mercy, J.A., Dahlberg, L.L. and Zwi, A.B. (2002) 'The world report on violence and health.' *The Lancet 360*, 9339, 1083–1088.

Lancet, The (2014) 'Violence against women and girls' Series.

Malpass, A., Sales, K., Johnson, M., Howell, A., Agnew-Davies, R. and Feder, G. (2014) 'Women's experiences of referral to a domestic violence advocate in UK primary care settings: A service-user collaborative study.' *British Journal of General Practise 64*, 620, e151–e158.

McCracken, K., Cook, K. and Chantler, K. (2013) *Access to Shelters of Undocumented Migrant Women Fleeing Domestic Violence: The Legal and Practical Situation in the Member States.* European Union. Brussels: European Parliament.

NICE (National Institute for Health and Care Excellence) (2014) *Domestic Violence and Abuse: Multi-agency Working.* Public health guideline PH50.

Norman, R., Spencer, A., Eldridge, S. and Feder, G. (2010) 'Cost-effectiveness of a programme to detect and provide better care for female victims of intimate partner violence.' *Journal of Health Services Research and Policy 15*, 3, 143–149.

O'Doherty, L.J., Taft, A., Hegarty, K., Ramsay, J., Davidson, L.L. and Feder, G. (2014) 'Screening women for intimate partner violence in healthcare settings: Abridged Cochrane systematic review and meta-analysis.' *BMJ 348*, g2913.

Perry, B.D. (2001) 'The neurodevelopmental impact of violence in childhood.' In D. Schetky and E.P. Benedek (eds.) *Textbook of Child and Adolescent Forensic Psychiatry* (pp.221–238). Washington, DC: American Psychiatric Press.

Potter, L. and Feder, G. (2017) 'Domestic violence teaching in UK medical schools.' *The Clinical Teacher.* Under review: Manuscript ID TCT-2017-0047.

Ramsay, J., Rutterford, C., Gregory, A., Dunne, D. *et al.* (2012) 'Domestic violence: Knowledge, attitudes, and clinical practise of selected UK primary healthcare clinicians.' *British Journal of General Practise 62*, 602, e647–e655.

Refuge (2016) *Refuge Annual Report 2015–2016.* London: Refuge.

Rivas, C., Ramsay, J., Sadowski, L., Davidson, L.L. *et al.* (2015) 'Advocacy interventions to reduce or eliminate violence and promote the physical and psychosocial well-being of women who experience intimate partner abuse.' *The Cochrane Database of Systematic Reviews 12*, CD005043.

Roberts, G., Hegarty, K. and Feder, G. (2006) *Intimate Partner Abuse and Health Professionals: New Approaches to Domestic Violence.* Amsterdam: Elsevier.

Sohal, A., Pathak, N., Berry, J., Apea, V. *et al.* (2017) 'Improving the healthcare response to domestic violence and abuse in sexual health clinics: Feasibility study of a training, support and referral intervention.' *Sexually Transmitted Infections.*

Trevillion, K., Byford, S., Cary, M., Rose, D. *et al.* (2014) 'Linking abuse and recovery through advocacy: An observational study.' *Epidemiology and Psychiatric Sciences 23,* 1, 99–113.
Trevillion, K., Oram, S., Feder, G. and Howard, L.M. (2012) 'Experiences of domestic violence and mental disorders: A systematic review and meta-analysis.' *PloS ONE 7,* 12, e51740.
Volpe, J. (1996) *Effects of Domestic Violence on Children and Adolescents: An Overview.* The American Academy of Experts in Traumatic Stress.
Walby, S. (2004) *The Cost of Domestic Violence.* London: Department of Trade and Industry.
Walby, S., Allen, J. and Simmons, J. (2004) *Domestic Violence, Sexual Assault and Stalking: Findings from the British Crime Survey.* London: Home Office Research, Development and Statistics Directorate.
Walby, S., Towers, J. and Francis, B. (2016) 'Is violent crime increasing or decreasing? A new methodology to measure repeat attacks making visible the significance of gender and domestic relations.' *British Journal of Criminology 56,* 6, 1203–1234.
Warshaw, C., Sullivan, C.M. and Rivera, E.A. (2013) *A Systematic Review of Trauma-focused Interventions for Domestic Violence Survivors.* National Center on Domestic Violence, Trauma and Mental Health.
WHO (World Health Organization) (2013) *Responding to Intimate Partner Violence and Sexual Violence Against Women: WHO Clinical and Policy Guidelines.* Geneva: WHO.
WHO (2014) *Strengthening the Role of the Health System in Addressing Violence, in particular against Women and Girls, and against Children.* 67th World Health Assembly Resolution. Geneva: WHO.
Williamson, E., Jones, S.K., Ferrari, G., Debbonaire, T., Feder, G. and Hester, M. (2015) 'Health professionals responding to men for safety (HERMES): Feasibility of a general practise training intervention to improve the response to male patients who have experienced or perpetrated domestic violence and abuse.' *Primary Health Care Research and Development 16,* 3, 281–288.

Chapter 16

OLDER WOMEN'S EXPERIENCES OF DOMESTIC VIOLENCE

Elizabeth Martin, *PhD Candidate, Queen's University Belfast, UK*

John Devaney, *Centenary Chair of Social Work, University of Edinburgh, Scotland*

Gemma Carney, *Lecturer in Social Policy, Queen's University Belfast, UK*

INTRODUCTION

While Europe is undergoing significant political change, it is also changing demographically, with a consequent impact on the need for particular services, including support for victims of domestic violence. In this chapter we explore the intersection between ageing and domestic violence, and examine the research evidence on the scale and nature of this issue. In doing so we pose two fundamental questions: How visible are older women who experience domestic violence? And does the impact of domestic violence on older women differ in significant ways from the impact on younger victims?

Over the last 50 years the rise in the size of the European population has occurred on the basis of improvements in infant and child survival, with declining mortality rates in particular for people aged 65 and over being mainly responsible for gains in life expectancy in the last 50 years (Marin 2013). Additionally, the population is ageing, with the median age in the European Union (EU) having increased from 34 in 1985 to 42 in 2014 (Eurostat 2015). As a consequence, there has been an increasing recognition of the need to ensure that aspects of ageing, and in particular ageing well, are a central concern within policy spheres (Foster and Walker 2015; UN 2012). In advanced economies such as the UK, 7 out of every 10 90-year-olds are female (ONS 2015), but government research into population ageing is rarely subjected to analysis for gender impact (Carney 2017). Until recently the voices of older women have been missing from research literature in regards to domestic violence. This is due, in part, to assumptions made by policy-makers and service providers that domestic violence ends at around 50 years (Lazenbatt, Devaney and Gildea 2010). It is our contention that older women are doubly disadvantaged as a consequence of society's antipathy towards both being old and being a victim of domestic violence and abuse.

AGEING

Ageing itself is a biological process, and as such, although factors such as social class, gender and lifestyle can influence it somewhat, as human beings our lifespan is relatively 'fixed'. However, recent medical advances and improvements in social protection have resulted in increases in life expectancy, leading to an extension of this for many (see Harper 2016). However, it needs to be recognised that our older population is not a homogeneous group (Gray and Dowds 2010). Despite the fact that frequency of disability and levels of frailty increase greatly with age, many people over 90 are as 'functionally able' as people of 50 (Bond, Coleman and Peace 2000). Nevertheless, ageing is often seen as a negative, stigmatising process, with such individuals being viewed as 'dependent, sick, frail and incompetent' (Hurd 1999, p.421). Lynott and Lynott discuss how some approaches to researching age can produce an alienating discourse resulting in the issues faced by old people being viewed mainly 'in terms of their private troubles' (Lynott and Lynott 1996, p.775). This means that the focus is placed on immediate concerns, such as social isolation or lack of support, rather than examining the underlying reasons for these. Because of this, they argue, the relationship between what Mills (1959) would describe as 'private troubles and public issues' is not addressed, with the focus being placed on dealing with causal arguments, rather than tackling more complex structural concerns.

The First World Assembly on Ageing was held in Vienna, Austria, in 1982. Called for in response to a rapidly ageing world population, the Assembly introduced the International Plan of Action on Ageing. To mark the 20th anniversary of what became known as the Vienna Plan, the Second World Assembly on Ageing was held in Madrid, Spain, in 2002. The purpose of the second meeting was to review the implementation and progress of the recommendations that had been established by the Vienna Plan. The goal of the groups and the committees involved in the formulation of the Madrid Plan was to create a fresh plan of action that reflected the new social, cultural, political, economic and demographic realities of the 21st century. The Madrid Plan sought to extend and enhance the initiatives of the Vienna Plan, such as significantly mainstreaming ageing issues in all aspects of development, interagency cooperation and interdependence between generations (UN 2002). The Madrid Plan has served as a guide to member states on their roles and responsibilities for upholding and enforcing the rights of older people. Included within the plan are three priority areas for action: (1) older people and development, (2) advancing health and wellbeing into old age and (3) ensuring enabling and supportive environments.

AGEING AND GENDER

The Madrid Plan recognises that the experience of ageing is impacted by a number of factors at both a structural and individual level. Arber and Ginn argue that the degenerative discourse on ageing is especially harmful to women, leading to 'stereotypes of elderly women [which] are particularly negative and demeaning' (Arber and Ginn 1991, p.1). Lips describes a theme that she calls 'cultural preparedness for powerlessness' (Lips 1994, p.90), whereby, from early childhood, socialisation from parents, teachers and peers combine to create gender stereotypes, resulting in girls and women becoming ever more ready to 'learn' powerlessness in new situations they find themselves in.

Throughout their lives, women continue to face numerous social and structural constraints, and although the process of ageing has been socially constructed as a problem for both males and females, it has been argued that becoming old is more problematic for women than it is for men (Cruikshank 2013), with many women rendered 'invisible' as a result (Bell 2012).

Recent work suggests that gender is an important aspect in ageing, with women outnumbering men in older age groups across all EU member states (Eurostat 2014; Harper 2016). Gender is a significant indicator of elder abuse in older age groups, with most research suggesting women are more at risk of being victims of this than men (de Donder *et al.* 2016). Women under 65 describe more recurring and serious abuse (Ansara and Hindin 2010; Jonson and Akerstrom 2004), and women over 65 are at greater risk of being victims of domestic violence than men (Freel and Robinson 2004, 2005; O'Keefe *et al.* 2007). However, as we discuss later in this chapter, there is a need to differentiate between what is defined as elder abuse and domestic violence.

SCALE OF DOMESTIC VIOLENCE AGAINST OLDER WOMEN

The existence and extent of domestic violence has been largely hidden within all societies, compounded by a dearth of systematic and nationally representative information on the prevalence and impact of domestic violence among both women and men (Holt and Devaney 2015). While it is now widely acknowledged that domestic violence is common (FRA 2014) and presents significant social, health and legal issues to society as a whole (WHO 2000, 2013), the policy response has been more fragmented, and in particular to the differential experience and impact of domestic violence on specific sub-groups. At a transnational level, the European Commission and the Council of Europe have devoted considerable effort to discussing the issue of violence and abuse within intimate relationships, and agreeing how these issues should be tackled (Council of Europe 2011). However, an important starting point in developing a policy response is knowing the scale and nature of the issue to be addressed.

A number of studies have specifically looked at older women's experiences of domestic violence. Brandl and Cook-Daniels (2002), in a review of 54 research articles published between 1988 and 2002, examined how the needs of older women who have been victims of domestic violence are often not being met as a result of certain perceptions and expectations of ageing and confusion over classifications of domestic violence and elder abuse. In fact, they go as far as arguing that instead of domestic violence in later life being 'covered' by research into the areas of elder abuse, older victims of domestic violence are often excluded. Many domestic violence studies focus on women aged 18–59, while elder abuse research looks at broader areas such as self-neglect, institutional abuse and financial exploitation, as well as family violence (Brandl and Cook-Daniels 2002). Because of this, underlying concerns of domestic violence, such as male violence and issues of power and control, are often not addressed. As a consequence older women as a group become invisible in our society (Calasanti and Slevin 2006; Gullette 2004; Jonson and Akerstrom 2004).

In North America, Bonomi and colleagues (2007) randomly sampled a total of 370 English-speaking women (aged 65 and older) from a healthcare system to participate in a cross-sectional telephone interview. Many of the abused women reported more than 20 episodes of violence in their lifetime (from 18.1% for physical violence to 61.2% for controlling behaviour). The median duration ranged from three years (forced sexual contact) to ten years (controlling behaviour). The proportion of abused women rating their abuse as severe ranged from 39.1 per cent (forced sex or sexual contact) to 70.7 per cent (threats).

In the prevalence study of Abuse and Violence against Older Women (AVOW), data was collected through surveys and interviews from a random selection of 2880 women aged 60 or older living in private households in Austria, Belgium, Finland, Lithuania and Portugal (Luoma *et al.* 2011). The study found that, across the five participating European countries, the prevalence rate of abuse of these women was 30.1 per cent. Factors such as marital status were significantly associated with those who were married being at greater risk of severe abuse.

De Donder *et al.* (2016) reviewed 19 prevalence studies of elder abuse that had been conducted within Europe, identifying that prevalence rates varied between 0.8 and 29.3 per cent across Europe. This broad range was as a result of the different definitions, study designs and inclusion and exclusion of various types of abuse used in the various studies, demonstrating the difficulties faced by researchers trying to compare such data.

Given the paucity and variable quality of data in Europe on women's experiences of abuse and violence, a survey was undertaken of 42,000 women aged 18 to 74 across the 28 EU member states. Of particular note was the upper age range for inclusion of participants. The data from this survey has highlighted that gender-based violence is highly prevalent and disproportionately affects women (FRA 2014; see also Chapter 1). The survey asked women about their experiences of physical, sexual and psychological violence in both childhood and as adults, including incidents of intimate partner violence ('domestic violence'), and also asked about issues relating to stalking, sexual harassment and the role played by new technologies in women's experiences of abuse. The survey found that 19 per cent of respondents aged 60 and above reported having experienced physical and/or sexual violence since the age of 15 by a partner, with 3 per cent having experienced such abuse within the previous 12 months.

However, while such surveys highlight the significant prevalence of abuse in later life, there is a dearth of research into older women's experiences of domestic violence, and the supports required to offer appropriate and effective protection. It is to this issue we now turn.

OLDER WOMEN'S EXPERIENCES OF DOMESTIC VIOLENCE

Lazenbatt *et al.* (2010) conducted a study in Northern Ireland with 18 participants aged between 53 and 70. All of these women had experienced domestic violence, with 11 reporting an ongoing relationship with the abusive partner. In addition to the qualitative interviews that were conducted with these participants, a focus group was held with professionals and service providers who work to support older women who have experienced domestic abuse.

While some studies that have focused on abuse against older adults have not clearly distinguished abuse perpetrated by intimate partners from abuse perpetrated by significant others (e.g. relatives or other caregivers) (Bonomi *et al.* 2007), Lazenbatt *et al.* (2010) highlight two specific sub-groups of older women with experience of domestic violence by intimate partners. The first, and larger, group are those who have experienced domestic violence earlier in life, and therefore have lived with this issue and the consequences for their health and social wellbeing for a large portion of their life. As one respondent in their qualitative study reported, 'violence in my early years was extremely physical, he battered me emotionally and physically but violence in my latter years has been more psychologically threatening and devastating for my life in general' (quoted in Lazenbatt *et al.* 2010, p.41).

In some instances women have remained living with their abusive partner, while for others this relationship may have finished through separation or death. The second, and smaller, group are women who in later life enter a new relationship that is abusive. These women often feel ill prepared for dealing with this abuse and violence, and may have a more limited network of family and social support on which to draw. Differentiating between these populations becomes important for service providers in seeking to identify those who are being victimised, and in considering how best to respond in both keeping women safe, while also addressing the impact of the abuse (Beaulaurier *et al.* 2007).

Finally, as highlighted by McGarry, Simpson and Hinchliff-Smith (2011), the experiences of women from minority ethnic groups remain to date largely invisible in studies of domestic violence among older women. However, as part of a study exploring the assumptions made by service providers towards women from minority ethnic backgrounds, Burman, Smailes and Chantler (2004) did include the accounts of older women from minority ethnic groups. They undertook an 11-month action research project with 26 services in one part of England that supported victims of domestic violence, as well as interviewing 23 women who self-identified as being from minority ethnic groups. In so doing they highlighted the cultural misconceptions that exist which normalise certain behaviours, and inhibit recognition and access to services and support. Participants spoke about fear of bringing their whole community into disrepute by reporting violence, while others discussed being almost dismissed by authorities due to pre-existing assumptions of violence within their communities.

THE IMPACT OF ABUSE ON OLDER WOMEN

The negative health sequelae of domestic violence have been well documented in younger women, and show that symptoms of post-traumatic stress disorder (PTSD) and other psychological stress reactions are long-term mental health consequences. Women who have been abused by their partners are three times more likely to be diagnosed with mental illness and to report depression (Calvete, Estivez and Corral 2007); five times more likely to attempt suicide (Pico-Alfonso *et al.* 2005); nine times more likely to misuse drugs; and 15 times more likely to experience problematic alcohol use (Dutton, Green and Kaltman 2006). Depression and PTSD, which have substantial co-morbidity, are the most prevalent mental health sequelae of domestic violence (Sormanti and Shibusawa 2008), with low self-esteem and feelings of inferiority heightening the risk of re-victimisation (Simmons and Baxter 2010). Long-term effects for older women who may have experienced trauma over a number of decades include permanent physical damage, disability, self-harm, self-neglect, loss of confidence, mental health problems, reliance on substances and a significant link to suicide risk and risk of homicide (Lazenbatt and Devaney 2014; McGarry *et al.* 2011; Zink *et al.* 2006). As noted by one respondent in the study by McGarry and Simpson (2011, p.296), '"I'm waiting for a hearing aid…I got severely bashed on my ear, and I'm told that I can't hear at all in this ear, and I've been told that it is a perforated eardrum" (Participant 8: 76 years).'

A review of the research on the impact of domestic violence on health concluded that the physical health of older victims might be more severely affected than younger victims. In contrast, there is evidence that older victims may experience less psychological distress in response to domestic violence than younger victims (Knight and Hester 2016).

Evidence suggests that psychological violence is the most common form of abuse for older women (Bows 2015; Sormanti and Shibusawa 2008). In addition to the direct psychological effects, the abuse may also negatively affect the factors that could improve mental health and wellbeing, such as contact with family and friends, and being in a supportive and caring relationship (Calvete *et al.* 2007). In relation to the ageing process, older victims of domestic violence report the increasing isolation over time that they face. This takes a number of forms, including children growing up and moving out of the family home, retirement from work outside the family home, and the decease of close family members and friends who offered emotional and practical support in relation to the abuse and violence experienced.

THE SERVICE RESPONSE

The majority of research into older women's experiences of domestic violence reveals the significant difficulty they experience with coping and seeking help (McGarry and Simpson 2011). Coping is not meant to imply that individuals should 'accept' the difficult situation they are experiencing – rather, it acknowledges that all individuals may, at some point in their lives, need to deal with the psychological and physiological consequences of stressful situations, requiring the need to call on and utilise both external and internal resources.

Economic dependence and family support are regularly cited as the most significant barriers to seeking support, or leaving an abusive relationship (Lazenbatt *et al.* 2010; Straka and Montminy 2006), although traditional attitudes towards marriage and gender roles also appear to be influential factors, particularly for older women (Scott *et al.* 2004). Respondents often cite a significant lack of support from the police and their GP:

> 'My doctor knew that I was living with a violent partner but he never really got involved – he would get all the letters from the hospital with my injuries itemised and prescribed drugs but never provided any help or support. He never took the situation seriously or talked about my safety or my children's safety.' (Quoted in Lazenbatt *et al.* 2010, p.31)

This is compounded by a lack of supportive programmes or settings that would allow older women to 'tell their stories' safely and in private (McGarry and Simpson 2011; Rogers 2016). Complicating service delivery for older women are the artificial boundaries that have been created in the service sector. Protective service systems designed for older people have few methods for dealing with domestic violence among older women, while women report domestic violence refuges as being unfamiliar with ageing issues and the special needs of older women, such as dealing with chronic illness, disabilities or alcohol dependence, and very few have separate programming targeting this group (Lazenbatt *et al.* 2010; Straka and Montminy 2006).

The failure by some professionals to identify the abuse that women are suffering in later life appears to be related to sexist and ageist assumptions that domestic violence does not exist for this age group (McGarry and Simpson 2011). It has been argued that there is a need for greater professional awareness and support services that cater for the additional needs of older women as their physical health deteriorates. Development of services, support groups and community outreach specifically suited to the needs and desires of older women who experience domestic violence have been identified as vital, such as the use of preventive healthcare that would allow GPs the opportunity to screen and make referrals during routine, non-emergency check-ups (Rogers 2016). Professionals in all service sectors must more fully understand the help-seeking barriers that older victims face. To this end, the research community can assist in replacing myths and stereotypes about the nature and prevalence of domestic violence among older people with research-based knowledge. A good place to start would be to acknowledge that age segregation across social policy and service planning (illustrated by the existence of separate children's, women's and ageing strategies and directorates in many agencies and societies) makes it difficult for policy-makers to produce a person-centred approach to issues such as domestic abuse that can affect people across the life course.

CONCEPTUALISATIONS OF THE ISSUE OF OLDER WOMEN'S EXPERIENCE OF DOMESTIC VIOLENCE

As noted by Straka and Montminy (2006), violence against older women has been constructed through one of two paradigms, as either domestic violence or elder abuse. Scott *et al.* refer to the 'ideological gulf' between those working in domestic violence services and those providing aged care. Scott *et al.* suggest that while domestic violence is viewed as a gendered abuse of power, in later life domestic violence is treated as a 'sub-set' of abuse against older people, and therefore the particular experiences of older women and the particular difficulties that they face may often be ignored within the wider consideration of care needs (McGarry *et al.* 2011). Moreover, the presumptions that have pervaded elder abuse, and which further ignore the significance of power and gender, fail to appreciate the significance of the underlying complexities of the nature of power relations within abusive relationships in later life (Penhale 1999). Once institutionalised ageism is taken into account, the powerlessness of older, abused women is all the more apparent (Carney and Gray 2015).

The strengths of the feminist-informed domestic violence paradigm are grounded in its structural analysis of gender–power relations, the specificity of its focus and an empowerment approach to supporting women to make informed choices on their own terms about what help should look like. Of particular note is supporting women to name and understand the dynamics of power and control that have kept them in situations of violence and abuse. This paradigm has informed the growth of a range of services designed to support female victims of domestic violence such as refuges and outreach services. While this has been extremely helpful in supporting victims of domestic violence, traditional domestic violence services have largely been poorly designed for the specific needs of older service users (Lazenbatt *et al.* 2010; Straka and Montminy 2006).

Conversely, the strengths of the elder abuse paradigm are grounded in its ability to serve the range of needs related to ageing. For example, it is estimated that rates of severe aggression by dementia care recipients against caregivers are estimated at greater than 20 per cent (Wharton and Ford 2014). Practitioners responding to elder abuse are concerned with questions of competency and how cognitive impairments may play a role in abusive situations. In recognising the diminution of family and social networks associated in later life, this approach remains open to attempting to salvage family relationships, if so desired by the abused woman, and if it is possible to create a safe situation for her (Chisnell and Kelly 2016).

Where caregiving stresses and illness play a role in the violence and abuse (Boye and Yan 2016), the elder abuse response does well in putting supports and resources into place. However, it is argued that the problem of domestic violence is rarely identified or understood by such professionals, who often have their primary focus on physical health needs and maintaining family integrity (Salwen, Gray and Mona 2016). For example, there is often an expectation that women will provide care for their elderly partners, even in situations involving domestic violence. Issues relating to gender-based violence are often overlooked, and interventions are informed by the paternalistic principle of intervening to keep victims safe, rather than empowering victims to make decisions that see safety as only one dimension of their needs (SafeLives 2016). This is unsurprising given that many of the policy and practise responses informing the professional response to elder abuse and adult safeguarding have drawn on child protection processes (Montgomery *et al.* 2016).

INTERSECTIONALITY

There is an increasing recognition within the domestic violence literature of the issue of intersectionality. This refers to the idea that individuals are multifaceted, and that the power relations within society are mediated by factors as diverse as age, gender, disability, ethnicity and sexual orientation, to name a few. As such, some individuals may find they are multiply disadvantaged, especially if those who are attempting to provide services are not mindful of the intersection between these issues (Devaney and Lazenbatt 2016). Intersectional theory views the influence of these characteristics as an intersecting process within a structural and historical context (e.g. disability *and* gender; gender *and* ageing), therefore creating 'pillars of privilege and domination' (Parker and Hefner 2015, p.224). As Brownell (2014) notes, the concept of intersectionality draws on a human rights framework. This states that human rights are interdependent and the level of enjoyment of any one right is dependent on the level of realisation of other rights. The *Convention for the Elimination of all Forms of Discrimination Against Women* (CEDAW) and CEDAW General Recommendation 27 (human rights of older women) lay out the rights of older women to live lives of dignity free of any form of discrimination or abuse. As Choi, Brownell and Moldovan (2017) note, the Madrid Plan identified issues of violence towards elders in 'Priority area III, Issue 3: Neglect, abuse and violence'. The abuse of older women was not specifically addressed within the Vienna Plan in 1982, and where it did, it was framed as a social problem that affected the care of the dependent, frail elderly. The abuse of older people was also seen as a problem to be addressed by professionals in the fields of gerontology and geriatrics. However, this perspective has changed significantly between the First and Second World Assemblies on Ageing. By 2002, neglect, abuse and violence against older people were understood to take many forms – physical, psychological, emotional and financial – and occur in every social, economic, ethnic and geographic sphere, and occurring within both caring and intimate relationships (UN 2002). It was also recognised that older women in particular faced a greater risk of physical and psychological abuse, not because of dependency and high care needs, but because of discriminatory social attitudes and the non-realisation of the fundamental human rights of women (UN 2012).

CONCLUSION

One in nine people in the world is aged 60 or over, and this is projected to increase to one in five by 2050, with women forming the majority of older people (UN 2017). We also know that men and women experience old age differently. Gender relations structure the entire life course, influencing access to resources and opportunities, with an impact that is both ongoing and cumulative. It is recognised that in many situations older women are typically more vulnerable to discrimination, including poorer access to healthcare and jobs, subjection to greater levels of abuse, denial of the right to own and inherit property, and lack of a basic minimum income and social security, whereas older men, particularly after retirement, may also become vulnerable due to their weaker social support networks and can also be subject to abuse, particularly financial abuse. These differences have important implications for public policy and programme planning, and the important distinctions that are required linked to different genders and different types of harm likely to be experienced. Older people are not a homogeneous group for which one-size-fits-all policies are sufficient. It is important not to reduce the characteristics and needs of older people to a single category, but to recognise that the older population is just as diverse as any other age group, in terms of, for example, age, sex, ethnicity, education, income and health. The AVOW study (Luoma *et al.* 2011), for instance, suggests that structural inequalities can be a factor that increases the risk that women will be abused. Not only must we start to recognise the abuse of older women, we must also acknowledge society's obligations to both protect and support victims of domestic violence, and the particular needs brought on by being older for both the experience of and response to domestic violence. While we now have good data in Europe to highlight both the lifelong impact of domestic violence across the life course, and the continuing experience of it in later life, professionals working in health, social care and criminal justice as a whole have a central role in both identifying domestic violence, and understanding the particular experiences and needs of older women affected by this issue. A pivotal part of this challenge, therefore, lies first in recognising at an organisational and service level that domestic violence among older women is a substantial issue, and second in developing services and support that are currently largely absent, to meet the particular needs of this group. At present there is a dearth of evidence that highlights what interventions, delivered in which ways, are most likely to keep older victims of domestic violence safe, while also helping them address the impact of the abuse that they have suffered. This is a challenge we should now start to meet.

REFERENCES

Ansara, D.L. and Hindin, M.J. (2010) 'Exploring gender differences in the patterns of intimate partner violence in Canada: A latent class approach.' *Journal of Epidemiology and Community Health 64*, 849–854.

Arber, S. and Ginn, J. (1991) *Gender and Later Life: A Sociological Analysis of Constraints.* London: Sage Publications.

Beaulaurier, R., Seff, L., Newman, F. and Dunlop, B. (2007) 'External barriers to help seeking for older women who experience intimate partner violence.' *Journal of Family Violence 22*, 8, 747–755.

Bell, C. (2012) *Visible Women: Tales of Age, Gender and In/visibility.* Newcastle upon Tyne: Cambridge Scholars Publishing.

Bond, J., Coleman, P. and Peace, S. (2000) *Ageing in Society.* 2nd Edition. London: Sage Publications.

Bonomi, A.E., Anderson, M.L., Reid, R.J., Carrell, D. *et al.* (2007) 'Intimate partner violence in older women.' *The Gerontologist 47*, 1, 34–41.

Bows, H. (2015) 'Domestic violence "grown old": The unseen victims of prolonged abuse.' *The Conversation.* Accessed on 19/5/2017 at https://theconversation.com/domestic-violence-grown-old-the-unseen-victims-of-prolonged-abuse-43014

Boye, F. and Yan, E. (2016) 'Abuse of older persons with dementia: A review of the literature.' *Trauma, Violence, and Abuse.* Online First.

Brandl, B. and Cook-Daniels, L. (2002) *Domestic Abuse in Later Life.* Harrisburg, PA: National Resource Center on Domestic Violence.

Brownell, P. (2014) 'Neglect, abuse and violence against older women: Definitions and research frameworks.' *South Eastern European Journal of Public Health 1*, 1. doi: 10.4119/UNIBI/SEEJPH-2014-28

Burman, E., Smailes, S. and Chantler, K. (2004) 'Culture as a barrier to service provision and delivery: Domestic abuse services for minoritized women.' *Critical Social Policy 24*, 3, 332–357.

Calasanti, T. and Slevin, K. (2006) 'Introduction: Age Matters.' In T.M. Calasanti and K.F. Slevin (eds) *Age Matters: Realigning Feminist Thinking* (pp.1–17). London: Routledge.

Calvete, E., Estivez, A. and Corral, S. (2007) 'Intimate partner violence and depressive symptoms in women: Cognitive schemas as moderators and mediators.' *Behaviour Research and Therapy 45*, 791–804.

Carney, G.M. (2017) 'Towards a gender politics of aging.' *Journal of Women and Aging.* Firstview. Accessed on 19/5/2017 at www.tandfonline.com/doi/pdf/10.1080/08952841.2017.1301163?needAccess=true

Carney, G.M. and Gray, M. (2015) 'Unmasking the "elderly mystique": Why it is time to make the personal political in aging research.' *Journal of Aging Studies 35*, 125–134.

Chisnell, C. and Kelly, C. (2016) *Safeguarding in Social Work Practise: A Lifespan Approach.* Exeter: Learning Matters.

Choi, M., Brownell, P. and Moldovan, S.I. (2017) 'International movement to promote human rights of older women with a focus on violence and abuse against older women.' *International Social Work 60*, 1, 170–181.

Council of Europe (2011) *Convention on Preventing and Combating Violence Against Women and Domestic Violence.* Strasbourg: Council of Europe.

Cruikshank, M. (2013) *Learning to Be Old: Gender, Culture, and Aging.* Lanham, MD: Rowman & Littlefield.

de Donder, L., Lang, G., Ferreira-Alves, J., Penhale, B., Tamutiene, I. and Luoma, M-L. (2016) 'Risk factors of severity of abuse against older women in the home setting: A multinational European study.' *Journal of Women and Ageing 28*, 6, 540–554.

Devaney, J. and Lazenbatt, A. (2016) *Domestic Violence Perpetrators – Evidence-informed Responses.* Abingdon: Routledge.

Dutton, M.A., Green, B.L. and Kaltman, S.I. (2006) 'Intimate partner violence, PTSD, and adverse health outcomes.' *Journal of Interpersonal Violence 21*, 955–968.

Eurostat (2014) *Main Scenario – Population on 1st January by Age and Sex [proj_13npms].* Accessed on 19/5/2017 at https://data.europa.eu/euodp/en/data/dataset/lZgn7QrvVQ23lqxIzMBo9Q

Eurostat (2015) *Population: Structure Indicators.* Accessed on 19/5/2017 at http://ec.europa.eu/eurostat/data/database

Foster, L. and Walker, A. (2015) 'Active and successful ageing: A European policy perspective.' *The Gerontologist 55*, 1, 83–90.

FRA (European Union Agency for Fundamental Rights) (2014) *Violence Against Women: An EU-wide Survey*. Luxembourg: FRA.

Freel, R. and Robinson, E. (2004) *Experience of Domestic Violence in Northern Ireland: Findings from the 2001 Northern Ireland Crime Survey*. Research and Statistical Bulletin 1/2004. Belfast: Northern Ireland Office, Statistics and Research Branch.

Freel, R. and Robinson, E. (2005) *Experience of Domestic Violence in Northern Ireland: Findings from the 2003/2004 Northern Ireland Crime Survey*. Research and Statistical Bulletin 5/2005. Belfast: Northern Ireland Office, Statistics and Research Branch.

Gray, A.M. and Dowds, L. (2010) 'All our futures: Attitudes to age and ageing in Ireland.' Research Update, No. 68. Londonderry, University of Ulster. Accessed on 10/4/2017 at www.ark.ac.uk/publications/updates/update68.pdf

Gullette, M. (2004) *Aged by Culture*. Chicago, IL: University of Chicago Press.

Harper, S. (2016) *How Population Change Will Transform Our World*. Oxford: Oxford University Press.

Holt, S. and Devaney, J. (2015) 'Understanding Domestic Abuse and Sexual Violence: Prevalence, Policy and Practise.' In D. Healy, C. Hamilton, Y. Daly and M. Butler (eds) *The Routledge Handbook of Irish Criminology* (pp.70–88). Oxford: Routledge.

Hurd, L. (1999) 'We're not old! Older women's negotiation of ageing and oldness.' *Journal of Ageing Studies 13*, 4, 419–439.

Jonson, H. and Akerstrom, M. (2004) 'Neglect of elderly women in feminist studies of violence, a case of ageism?' *Journal of Elder Abuse and Neglect 16*, 1, 47–63.

Knight, L. and Hester, M. (2016) 'Domestic violence and mental health in older adults.' *International Review of Psychiatry 28*, 5, 464–474.

Lazenbatt, A. and Devaney, J. (2014) 'Older women living with domestic violence: Coping resources and mental health and wellbeing.' *Current Nursing Journal 1*, 1, 10–22.

Lazenbatt, A., Devaney, J. and Gildea, A. (2010) *Older Women Coping with Lifelong Domestic Violence*. Belfast: Institute Governance, Queen's University Belfast.

Lips, H. (1994) 'Female Powerlessness: A Case of "Cultural Preparedness?"' In H. Radtke and H. Stam (eds) *Power/Gender: Social Relations in Theory and Practise* (pp.89–107). London: Sage Publications.

Luoma, M.-L., Koivusilta, M., Lang, G., Enzenhofer, E. *et al.* (2011) *Prevalence Study of Abuse and Violence against Older Women: Results of a Multi-cultural Survey in Austria, Belgium, Finland, Lithuania, and Portugal (European Report of the AVOW Project)*. Finland: National Institute for Health and Welfare.

Lynott, R. and Lynott, P. (1996) 'Tracing the course of theoretical development in the sociology of aging.' *The Gerontologist 36*, 6, 749–760.

Marin, B. (2013) *Welfare in an Idle Society? Reinventing Retirement, Work, Wealth, Health and Welfare*. Aldershot: Ashgate.

McGarry, J. and Simpson, C. (2011) 'Domestic abuse and older women: Exploring the opportunities for service development and care delivery.' *The Journal of Adult Protection 13*, 6, 294–301.

McGarry, J., Simpson, C. and Hinchliff-Smith, K. (2011) 'The impact of domestic abuse for older women: A review of the literature.' *Health and Social Care in the Community 19*, 1, 3–14.

Mills, C.W. (1959) *The Sociological Imagination*. New York: Oxford University Press.

Montgomery, L., Anand, J., Mackay, K., Taylor, B., Pearson, K.C. and Harper, C.M. (2016) 'Implications of divergences in adult protection legislation.' *The Journal of Adult Protection 18*, 3, 149–160.

O'Keeffe, M., Hills, A., Doyle, M., McCreadie, C. *et al.* (2007) *UK Study of Abuse and Neglect of Older People Prevalence Survey Report*. Accessed on 16/6/2017 at https://www.kcl.ac.uk/sspp/departments/sshm/geront/research/elderlyabusestudy.pdf

ONS (Office for National Statistics) (2015) 'Estimates of the very old (including centenarians), UK: 2002 to 2015.' Statistical Bulletin. Accessed on 19/5/2017 at www.ons.gov.uk/peoplepopulationandcommunity/birthsdeathsandmarriages/ageing/bulletins/estimatesoftheveryoldincludingcentenarians/2002to2015

Parker, K.F. and Hefner, M.K. (2015) 'Intersections of race, gender, disadvantage, and violence: Applying intersectionality to the macro-level study of female homicide.' *Justice Quarterly 32*, 2, 223–254.

Penhale, B. (1999) 'Bruises on the soul: Older women, domestic violence and elder abuse.' *Journal of Elder Abuse and Neglect 11*, 1, 1–22.

Pico-Alfonso, M.A., Garcia-Linares, M.I., Celda-Navarro, N., Blasco-Ros, C., Echeburua, E. and Martinez, M. (2005) 'The impact of physical, psychological, and sexual intimate male partner violence on women's mental health: Depressive symptoms, posttraumatic stress disorder, state anxiety, and suicide.' *Journal of Women's Health 15*, 5, 599–611.
Rogers, M. (2016) 'Older Women's Experiences of Domestic Violence and Abuse.' In A. Ahmed and M. Rogers (eds) *Working with Marginalised Groups: From Policy to Practice* (pp.134–150). London: Palgrave.
SafeLives (2016) *Safe Later Lives: Older People and Domestic Abuse.* Accessed on 19/5/2017 at http://safelives.org.uk/sites/default/files/resources/Safe%20Later%20Lives%20-%20Older%20people%20and%20domestic%20abuse.pdf
Salwen, J.K., Gray, A. and Mona, L.R. (2016) 'Personal assistance, disability, and intimate partner violence: A guide for healthcare providers.' *Rehabilitation Psychology 61*, 4, 417–429.
Scott, M., McKie, L., Morton, S., Seddon, E. and Wosoff, F. (2004) *Older Women and Domestic Violence in Scotland...and for 39 Years I Got on With It.* Edinburgh: Health Scotland.
Simmons, B. and Baxter, J.S. (2010) 'Intimate partner violence in older women: What home healthcare physicians should know.' *Home Healthcare Nurse 28*, 2, 82–89.
Sormanti, M. and Shibusawa, T. (2008) 'Intimate partner violence among midlife and older women: A descriptive analysis of women seeking medical services.' *Health and Social Work 33*, 1, 33–41.
Straka, S.M. and Montminy, L. (2006) 'Responding to the needs of older women experiencing domestic violence.' *Violence Against Women 12*, 3, 251–267.
UN (United Nations) (2002) *Political Declaration and Madrid International Plan of Action on Aging.* Accessed on 11/3/2017 at https://social.un.org/index/Portals/0/ageing/documents/Fulltext-E.pdf
UN (2012) *Aging in the Twenty-First Century: A Celebration and a Challenge.* Accessed on 11/3/2017 at www.unfpa.org/webdav/site/global/shared/documents/publications/2012/Ageing-Report_full.pdf
UN (2017) *Ageing.* Accessed on 19/5/2017 at www.un.org/en/sections/issues-depth/ageing/index.html
Wharton, T.C. and Ford, B.K. (2014) 'What is known about dementia care recipient violence and aggression against caregivers?' *Journal of Gerontological Social Work 57*, 5, 460–477.
WHO (World Health Organization) (2000) *World Report on Violence and Health.* Geneva: WHO.
WHO (2013) *Global and Regional Estimates of Violence Against Women: Prevalence and Health Effects of Intimate Partner Violence and Non-partner Sexual Violence.* Geneva: WHO.
Zink, T., Jacobsen, C.J. Jr., Pabst, S., Regan, S. and Fisher, B.S. (2006) 'A lifetime of intimate partner violence: Coping strategies of older women.' *Journal of Interpersonal Violence 21*, 5, 634–651.

Chapter 17

WHOSE MOVEMENT IS IT ANYWAY? REFLECTIONS FROM THE FIELD

Davina James-Hanman, *Independent Violence Against Women Consultant, Lisbon, Portugal*

INTRODUCTION

In the past 10–15 years in England and Wales, as in many jurisdictions across Europe and elsewhere, the response to domestic violence has changed radically (Stanley and Humphreys 2015), in that more agencies – particularly statutory agencies – are now recognising and responding to domestic violence, new services have been developed and legislation has been passed. However, despite these many changes, the number of victims is still rising (Walby *et al.* 2017), and the overall number of homicides has only slightly decreased (ONS 2016). This chapter charts that journey throughout the UK, including the drive to 'professionalise' the domestic violence sector, and asks whether we are heading in the right direction, or have we simply ended up in a cul-de-sac? To this end the chapter reflects on my three decades of experience of working on domestic violence in the UK in local, regional and national roles. These included in local and national government, as CEO of a national charity, and as an Associate Tutor for the National Police Training College. Utilising my extensive network of contacts, this chapter is presented in a historical narrative format, drawing on empirical evidence where appropriate and available. In the main, however, it reflects on my personal experience over that time period.

PRE-2000

Prior to the new century, the women's movement had worked on domestic violence for several decades, raising awareness and demanding that the State fulfil its responsibility to protect its citizens. From a frontline perspective, there were some successes at a local level, most notably in establishing a nationwide network of refuges – albeit not in every local authority area – and at a national level in campaigning for changes in the law, both civil and criminal. The refuge movement grew out of the consciousness-raising groups of the 1970s, and was founded on recognition that domestic abuse could happen to any woman. Initially run without paid workers, refuges relied heavily on volunteers, often survivors, and were structured as collectives with everyone having an equal say. Campaigning was a critical part of the work and was focused on convincing statutory authorities and wider society that issues such as domestic abuse should be of public concern.

Throughout the 1990s, a multi-agency approach to domestic violence was promoted, but this rarely resulted in any significant commitment beyond around 20 local authorities (there are over 170 in England and Wales). In these exceptions, a Domestic Violence Forum was often established, but my experience was that many of these struggled to attract senior agency representatives or indeed any representative at all from some important quarters such as health or education. Some of the more pioneering local authorities employed Domestic Violence Coordinators who worked across their local areas to implement training of frontline staff, produce good practise manuals and organise awareness-raising events. Allocated budgets were often miniscule, limiting the scope of work that could be undertaken, and at a national level, there was a single civil servant in the Home Office, a post created in the mid-1990s, with responsibility for domestic violence policy across Government. At a national level, domestic violence was frequently described as an issue that was 'everywhere and nowhere'; its impacts were felt in every Government Department, but from my experience, there was little appetite for practising the inter-departmental approach that was preached. Even today, the national strategy is resource-lite when it comes to commitments from other Government Departments.

Following the success of two trial units in the late 1980s (Edwards 1989), the police were encouraged from 1990 onwards to improve their responses to domestic violence (Home Office 1990). With two exceptions, these were usually limited to a small Domestic Violence

Unit with two to three low-ranking staff whose job almost exclusively focused on victim support rather than investigation and prosecution preparation. It was common knowledge across the sector at that time that these tended to be staffed by policewomen who had recently had a baby and who wanted a 9–5, Monday to Friday job, and to work in one was not perceived as a career-enhancing move. Nor were such units universal across all police forces. The two exceptions took place in West Yorkshire Police (Killingbeck division only) (Hanmer, Griffiths and Jerwood 1999) and the Metropolitan Police (Islington division only) (Kelly *et al.* 1999). In West Yorkshire, a system of enhanced responses to reduce repeat victimisation was implemented whereby increasing levels of intervention were made to protect the victim and demotivate the offender based on re-attendance by police officers. In Islington, central government funding was used to create a team of crisis intervention workers based within the local police station. In essence, this was the prototype for what would later become Independent Domestic Violence Advisers/Advocates, although all women who reported domestic violence to the police were offered support rather than only those assessed as 'high risk'.

In 1998, the Crime & Disorder Act was passed. While not about domestic violence at all, its provisions were to have far-reaching impacts for the field. This new law specified that local government and their local police were to produce, in partnership, a three-year crime reduction strategy, and made monies available from central government if certain targets were met. This led to each local area analysing their local crime patterns, and for the first time, it became clear that domestic violence was a significant proportion of reported crime in each area, with many reports being made repeatedly by the same victim against the same perpetrator. The simple act of making the scale of the issue visible was to galvanise local areas into more coordinated and concerted action. Over the next few years, the number of local areas with a specific strategy for domestic violence went from a few dozen to over 140, driven by a central government target known as Best Value Performance Indicator 225 (Home Affairs Select Committee 2008).

Policing of domestic violence began to shift around this time, pioneered by the Metropolitan Police. Former employees of the Metropolitan Police Authority (subsequently replaced with the Mayor's Office for Policing and Crime (MOPAC)) assert that the initial shift was as a consequence of needing to make radical changes towards their policing of racially motivated crime in the wake of the Stephen Lawrence Inquiry. With finite resources to do this, a decision was made instead to expand Domestic Violence Units to include 'hate' crime (racist and homophobic), and detectives were assigned to investigate crimes. As such, the 'tea and sympathy' model described above was largely abandoned; the focus was now on investigations, and victim support was referred out to other agencies. For any career police officer, anecdotal evidence in the field asserted that some time spent working in one of these units was now seen as essential.

THE NEW CENTURY

Changes in the way that refuges were funded in 2003 further expanded the refuge network (although see below for unintended consequences), and three independent reviews of different component parts of the criminal justice system (HM Crown Prosecution Service Inspectorate and HM Inspectorate of Constabulary 2004; HM Inspection of Court Services 2005; HM Inspection of Probation 2004) laid bare the poor level of protection most survivors received, and identified a range of proposed improvements that focused on, among others, improved training, record keeping, evidence gathering and witness care. Together with the publication of a particularly in-depth analysis of the British Crime Survey with respect to domestic violence (Walby and Allen 2004), these led directly to the publication of the first national report and action plan on domestic violence in 2005 (Home Office 2005). This marked a paradigm shift in central government policy that was most clearly set out on page 3 where the Government noted the contribution of statutory and voluntary organisations, and announced that it would now become a full member of that partnership. The national report made 17 commitments to developing the response of public services to domestic violence, and included new measures such as Specialist Domestic Violence Courts and Independent Domestic Violence Advocates/Advisers. The objectives were to reduce the prevalence of domestic violence and domestic violence-related homicides, to increase reporting to the police, to bring more offenders to justice and to provide support and protection to victims. While this commitment was a step in the right direction, it was also criticised, most notably by the Home Affairs Select Committee (2008), that noted that the approach was disproportionately focused on criminal justice responses and that efforts to prevent domestic violence needed more attention. It would take another six years for this critique to have any effect on Government policy.

THE DOMINANCE OF THE CRIMINAL JUSTICE SYSTEM LENS

The emphasis in these years (driven by the aforementioned targets) was to reduce 'repeat victimisation'; in other words, the number of times a victim experienced an 'incident' of domestic violence. From a frontline perspective, this was experienced as a problematic concept that dominated the debates for almost a decade.

This incident-based lens necessarily made physical assaults the principal focus of attention and conversely made less visible acts of control. If one is subjected to constant deprivation of money or freedom of movement, then how can an 'incident' be measured? As such, physical abuse became the focus even as survivors consistently insisted that this was not the worst part of their abuse (WNC 2009). Other forms of abuse were often framed as 'warning signs', thereby creating a hierarchy where only physical abuse was seen as 'real'. The incident-based lens also paved the way for the obsessive focus on risk and risk management that not only starved prevention initiatives of funding for over a decade, but which became so dominant that services for anyone not at risk of death or serious injury all but disappeared across huge swathes of the country (End Violence Against Women Coalition 2007).

Multi-Agency Risk Assessment Conferences (MARACs) and Independent Domestic Violence Adviser (IDVA) services were established across England, while drop-ins, outreach, resettlement and recovery services closed. In 2015, Women's Aid England found that refuges were forced to turn away two-thirds of all women fleeing domestic violence, most often because of a lack of available space. For women of black and minority ethnic (BME) origin, the number of refusals rose to four in five (Women's Aid England Annual Survey 2015). Both MARACs and IDVAs only worked with the 10 per cent of survivors who were assessed as being most at risk of death or serious injury. In many areas, only refuges remained for the 90 per cent of victims who were not deemed to be 'high risk' and, even here, the range of services narrowed as funding disappeared, especially for recovery work. State funding for work with children in refuges was excluded from 'Supporting People' (the funding stream for refuges), and funds to undertake awareness-raising and campaigning work dried up. The focus on risk management led to short-termism, the solidifying of the criminal justice system as being at the centre of the State's response, and survivors feeling (being) blamed. Recovery became secondary, with the purpose of IDVAs and MARACs being only to manage risk. Once this had been achieved, services were withdrawn. If risk couldn't be or wasn't 'managed', anecdotal evidence suggests that survivors often ended up being labelled 'intractable cases'.

The year 2005 also saw the start of the development of Specialist Domestic Violence Courts (SDVCs) across England and Wales. Loosely based on a model from New York State, these involved tracking cases across the criminal justice system, specially trained magistrates and specially trained prosecutors. IDVAs also attended court to support the victim, and where they existed, a representative from the local perpetrator programme. While these did produce much improved conviction rates for women using the criminal justice system (always a minority), the SDVCs in England and Wales were a far cry from the original model that integrated family court systems with criminal cases under the mantra 'One Family: One Judge'. While it was undoubtedly a relief for the victim in SDVCs to have their case heard and dealt with by properly trained professionals, it still failed to address the fundamental problems that victims raised when recounting their experiences of the courts; namely, that the split between civil and criminal law allowed the abuser to gain an advantage in each (Home Affairs Select Committee 2008). In the family court, the victim could be portrayed as vindictive, seeking to criminalise the father of her children; in the criminal courts, her testimony could be muted or even withdrawn by his promises to back down on the family court proceedings. The 'three planets' model described by Marianne Hester (2011) showed clearly how, despite welcome advances in each 'planet', progress was made in silos. The failure to integrate and coordinate systems meant that all progress was limited in its potential, and often made little differences to the lived experience of abused women and children.

EXPANDING SECTOR, CONTRACTING POLITICS

From the start of the new century, I recall that references to the need to 'professionalise' the domestic violence 'sector' began to gather momentum. Definitions were never specifically provided and were certainly not debated in any meaningful way. From the perspective of the specialist women's sector, professionalising turned out to mean depoliticising the women's anti-male violence movement and burying them in paperwork. It meant reshaping services so that they met less of survivors' needs and looked more like those provided by the State. 'Professionalising the sector' was targeted solely at voluntary sector organisations (who were increasingly referred to as the 'third sector' with its unhelpful echoes of 'third world'). It invariably resulted in putting agency objectives – especially those of the criminal justice system – at the centre rather than the needs of survivors. With many parts of the women's movement reacting in equal parts of frustration and outrage, refusing to competitively bid for poorly drawn-up contracts that favoured costs over quality of service, a vacuum was created into which generic service providers eagerly stepped. This is not to say that women's organisations just 'threw in the towel', but with each round of contract letting, services that the State were prepared to fund shrank still further along with the unit costs for the support that was deemed necessary.

MARACs became sacred cows, in part because, in many instances, they were the only experience of multi-agency work that members had. Beloved by statutory agencies as their 'evidence' that they were 'doing something' about domestic violence, to question their cost, their focus on 'high risk' and indeed their effectiveness in meeting their raison d'être of reducing domestic violence homicides has become heresy. The cost of running a MARAC has been estimated as approximately £120,000 per annum, and research found that the sheer number of cases and time pressures have resulted in MARACs becoming 'an increasingly managerialist response to a personal crisis... There was no room for discussion of unintended consequences, or a more holistic assessment of a particular case' (McLaughlin *et al.* 2014, p.4). Survivors whose cases were heard at MARAC reported 'feeling they were done "to" rather than "with"' (p.2). Although not originally intended in this way, risk assessment is increasingly the main gateway to support, and management of risk is the main criterion of success. This does not promote long-term positive outcomes, as risk can be managed without meeting survivors' and their children's needs (Women's Aid 2015).

A study tracking 100 women and their children over three years after they left the refuge found that:

> ...across all agencies, domestic violence was still being reduced to incidents of physical assault, which led not only to an exclusion of some women from services and support when their abuse was more characterised by coercive control, but also a minimising of post-separation abuse. This misunderstanding also meant that many professionals underestimated the toll living with abuse had on women and children, expecting that separation, in and of itself, would not just create safety but also lift all the other burdens. (Kelly, Sharp and Klein 2014, p.7)

Despite official MARAC guidance stating that 'consent should always be sought if possible and it is safe to do so',[1] in practise this frequently does not happen. Research into a select number of MARAC sites reported that while members believed gaining consent was 'good practise', in the majority of the cases referrals were made without the survivor's consent or knowledge (McCoy and Kelly 2011). The drive towards greater information sharing has been a key theme of the past decade. Unfortunately, the narrative has been dominated by legal considerations, with very little thought given to the ethics involved. In my experience of delivering training to hundreds of professionals, asking people to identify ethical considerations involved in sharing information usually results in rows of blank faces and long silences. This has resulted in survivors' worst fears being realised: if they disclose their abuse to a professional, they may well lose control of what happens next, with this being especially true for mothers. The constant emphasis to social workers to 'think child' has often resulted in a myopic focus that holds abused mothers as equally culpable as the abuser (Lapierre 2008). Indeed, the perpetrator is often invisible within child protection with the notable exception of the 'Hackney model' (Phillips 2013), although this has yet to become widespread. This is not to argue that children living with domestic violence do not need protection, but the mantra of the women's sector – 'the best form of child protection is support and empowerment of the non-abusing parent' – has rarely been translated into practise. Instead, women are told they must leave or their children will be removed with little support to do so or apparent recognition that abuse of children, and

1 See www.safelives.org.uk/practise-support/resources-marac-meetings

their mother, often continues long after separation due to the Family Courts routinely granting unsupervised access (Holt 2016).

There are personal, institutional and cultural barriers to leaving. These can and do include a lack of money, a lack of housing, an inability to access legal protection, insecure immigration status, fear of being ostracised by one's community, a fear of further violence and a lack of childcare among others, yet this is still seen as the 'optimum option' by most professionals, even as they also hold a new awareness in their heads as this being the time when the woman is most likely to be killed (Richards 2003). Due to the myopic focus on risk (where risk *only* means risk of death or serious harm), scant attention is paid to enabling women to rebuild their lives and to re-connect with their children. Erin Davis (2015) argues that this is a consequence of a failure of agencies to recognise a feminist understanding of the nature of domestic abuse and its inherent gendered nature. Implicit in this is the importance of recognising the key role of women who are/have experienced abuse in managing their own safety. The failure of this can undermine the attempts at safeguarding put into place.

Many of the interventions now in existence have resulted in survivors following the 'rules' by disclosing their experiences only to have every resulting interaction with statutory agencies focus on the woman's children or to get the perpetrator convicted with little concern or thought for the woman's needs (Women's Aid 2016).

Time and again, consultation with survivors highlights issues and concerns that domestic violence services have simply not addressed (or where it was being addressed in the past, funding has shrunk to leave only skeleton provision or none at all). Survivors frequently identify that their most intractable issues are money (or rather lack of it), Family Court proceedings/contact issues and dealing with isolation. While it is acknowledged that a few partnerships include debt advice agencies, this is not the same as, for example, employment advice. There is not currently a single domestic violence partnership that includes agencies that might enable survivors' financial freedom; while there is some – albeit rapidly disappearing – support and special measures[2] within the criminal justice system, there are no matching

2 Special measures are steps that can be taken to enable vulnerable or intimidated witnesses to give better evidence in the criminal court. This might include a pre-visit to the court, a screen between the witness and defendant, or even giving evidence via video link. They are not automatic for domestic violence victims, and must be applied for from the judge.

services in the Family Courts. Evan Stark (2007) eloquently argues that physical and sexual abuse in intimate relationships is interwoven with three equally important tactics: control, intimidation and isolation. It is their toxic combination that entraps abused women, leading Stark to argue that domestic violence is not a simple crime of assault, but a 'liberty crime' that creates conditions of un-freedom. Recovery, therefore, must create 'space for action' (Kelly *et al.* 2014), that is, to restore personal and financial autonomy as well as social and relational networks. This especially includes (but is not limited to) survivors' relationship with their children. Many women derive a sense of self-worth from their role as mothers and, as such, it commonly becomes a specific target of abusers to undermine the mother–child bond. A recent evaluation of a befriending scheme in South London (Sutton Women's Aid and Jigsaw4U 2017) that provided support with all three of these issues found that survivors deeply appreciated this support that was not forthcoming from anywhere else. This 'recovery work' is now relatively rare in domestic violence service provision, another consequence of the preoccupation with risk.

THE AGE OF AUSTERITY

Since the financial crisis and the 'age of austerity', specialist provision has shrunk still further. The concept of providing gender-specific provision has come under sustained attack with many services forced to also work with male victims or lose their funding. Even before the cuts, the specialist sector was poorly funded. A study in 2008 estimated that the income of the 'richest' 200 specialist Violence Against Women agencies was £87 million per annum, with £17 million of that being shared among just three charities. As a comparison, Barnardo's annual income in the same year was £147 million (Kail, Blaythwayt and Jarvinen 2008). Since then, income – and provision – has shrunk at an alarming rate. Women's Aid England has stated that 17 per cent of women's refuges have closed since 2010, with BME refuges particularly badly affected. Of the original 34 ethnic-specific refuges, only half are still open, and 11 of these face deep uncertainty about their future survival. More than 155 women a day are being turned away from refuges because there are not enough suitable places available (Women's Aid England Annual Survey 2013). Only recently the media reported that victims wait on average two years to receive financial compensation, double the amount of time recommended by the Criminal Injuries Compensation Authority. Only a fifth of women using domestic abuse services see criminal proceedings brought against their perpetrators (ONS 2016), and the health service, a key help-seeking route for survivors, is stretched beyond capacity. In this context, the recent announcement by Prime Minister Theresa May that she will oversee a wide-ranging review and pass yet more laws on domestic abuse rings hollow. She is implying that woeful service responses are due to confusion about the legislation rather than as a consequence of ongoing public sector cuts and stubbornly persistent victim-blaming attitudes.

As IDVAs and MARACs have expanded, a shift has occurred in the dynamics. Domestic violence service providers lost their politics, the issue became de-gendered (Neate 2015) and was de-coupled from other forms of male violence,[3] and started to be referred to as a sector rather than as a movement. In particular, the focus of intervention moved away from empowering survivors – and arguably even listening to them describe their needs and experiences – and became focused on risk, prosecution and information sharing. When the last Labour Government finally capitulated to demands for a national Violence Against Women strategy in 2009, it was notable how much of the content was criminal justice system-focused, even though this was utilised by a minority of survivors (Home Office 2009). Even by 2015, only 21 per cent of survivors contacted the police (WNC 2009).

Although lobbying did result in an extensive survivor consultation taking place to inform the first national Violence Against Women and Girls strategy (WNC 2009), the results were all but ignored. Even taking into account progress made since then, almost a decade later there has only been some limited progress on less than a quarter of their key recommendations. Along the way, 'we' has become 'them and us', and the drive to 'professionalise' the domestic violence 'sector' has resulted in paternalistic attitudes where women are deemed to be 'in denial' if they do not want to take the course of action professionals have decided they should. Conversations with survivors reveal that they are encouraged (and sometimes coerced) by social workers to 'prove'

3 Until 2009, central government strategies addressed each form of male violence separately. Although there is now one overarching strategy, each form is still addressed separately within it, and domestic abuse dominates the actions.

their commitment to protecting their children, to attend groups where they can 'learn about abuse' as if their lived experience wasn't sufficient, and with the victim-blaming implication that if only they 'knew' about abuse, they would be able to select non-abusive relationships in the future (Zannettino and McLaren 2014). This ignores, of course, that the majority of survivors did not experience abuse for at least a year into their relationship; they were not 'attracted to abusers', but to partners who presented themselves as non-abusive. From my perspective, survivor involvement, a strengths-based approach and being needs-led are all now being presented as 'new' ideas, erasing the history of the anti-male violence movement and survivors' role within it. Even the term 'survivor' has been co-opted; originally devised as a way of acknowledging women's strengths and the many and varied ways in which they coped with and managed abuse, it is now more commonly presented as a 'journey' that victims make until, at some undefined stage, they 'become' a survivor, thereby erasing their resistance while being abused. Instead it would seem that survivors are portrayed as cowering in corners with bruises who need knowledgeable professionals to intervene for their own good, even if this means forcing them into actions against their will, such as summonsing them to court to give evidence, sharing information without their consent (McCoy and Kelly 2011) or threatening them with the removal of their children due to their 'failure to protect' (Scourfield and Welsh 2003).

In a recent training session that I gave for frontline professionals, participants struggled to know what to do with a case study about a single woman whose abuse fell below the threshold of being designated 'high risk'. Without a trace of irony, participants mused about how the absence of children hampered their ability to force the victim into taking action. Such attitudes are rife; a paternalistic approach of 'the professionals know best', coercive interventions and victim-blaming when the system doesn't work to protect her or the children has been enhanced and cemented during the 'progress' of the past 15 years.

It is interesting to note that when the role of the IDVA was first created, the 'A' stood for 'Advocate', not 'Adviser'. Mirroring one of the major trends of the past 15 years, this role has shifted from being one that enabled and empowered women to realise their rights to one that gave out information to women on what was available. A subtle, but telling, difference.

Nowhere can the co-option of the movement against men's violence be seen more clearly than in the re-naming of UN International Day of Action against Violence against Women (25 November) as 'White Ribbon Day'. 25 November was chosen to honour three women who were killed for their politics, and signals the start of 16 days of activism, linking violence against women with International Human Rights Day on 10 December. In the UK this has all but been forgotten. Instead, it is widely marked as White Ribbon Day, a Canadian campaign encouraging men to speak out about male violence following the Montreal massacre of 14 women on 6 December 1991. In both instances, the origins are not about domestic abuse, and while not disputing the benefits of men speaking out about male violence, it is interesting to note that a day intended to honour women's political activity has been reframed as all about the men.

There is an intense frustration among specialist domestic violence service providers at the pace of change in the statutory sector; issues on which specialist services campaign take between 10 and 15 years to gain traction and a further period of time to be fully implemented. Meanwhile, women die.

SOME HOPE?

Of course not all of the changes in the past 15 years have been negative. Despite the largely hostile environment, specialist feminist organisations and campaigns continue to exist, albeit many of them hanging on by their fingertips. Strengths-based interventions[4] and 'change that lasts'[5] are gaining traction, and even those who pioneered the risk-based approach are backing away from it and focusing on early intervention. After a lengthy campaign, sex and relationship education is finally to be part of the national curriculum,[6] although, as ever, the more progressive political landscape in Scotland offers a more visionary idea of what prevention work could look like (Scottish Government 2016).

---

4 See www.scie.org.uk/care-act-2014/assessment-and-eligibility/strengths-based-approach

5 See www.womensaid.org.uk/our-approach-change-that-lasts

6 See www.gov.uk/government/news/schools-to-teach-21st-century-relationships-and-sex-education

The concept of coercive control is also starting to be better understood, and the long-term health impacts of domestic abuse are finally galvanising the health service into action (NatCen 2015). Standards have been developed for specialist services, and the Home Office (2016) has issued a national statement of expectations, setting out what local areas are expected to provide across both statutory and voluntary sector services. The expectations include taking a gendered approach and listening to survivors, and as such is a welcome intervention from central government, albeit a document without any 'teeth'. However, the Istanbul Convention inches towards ratification in the UK, which will add some much-needed accountability with regard to the funding of services.

There is a growing understanding that survivors with complex needs are being routinely failed, often perceived as a set of problems that in turn are each addressed individually. There is a nascent recognition that effective outcomes might be more readily achieved if the survivor was treated as a vulnerable person with a range of issues that are connected and interlocked. For example, it is common for refuges to decline access to women with substance use issues. It is equally common for drug and alcohol services to work with women to reduce their substance use without any recognition of the underlying causative factor of domestic abuse (AVA Project 2014). Work by the Stella Project[7] has been challenging this disconnect, and there are a growing number of services equipped to deal with both issues simultaneously. Work within the women's centres for those at risk of offending, and services for women exiting prostitution or street homeless women – all of whom tend to have multiple issues including high rates of domestic violence – are also showing how trauma-informed approaches can produce positive outcomes, even among seemingly 'intractable cases'. If there is one factor that links all of these, it is that each really 'sees' the client, and that the relationship between them and their worker is critical to success.

The key to getting back 'on track' with domestic violence responses is simple, yet deeply challenging. It requires services to relinquish control to survivors, to stop labelling them as 'hard to reach' but

7 The Stella Project was established in 2003 and works to build partnerships between drug and alcohol services and domestic violence services. In more recent years, it has extended to include other forms of violence against women and disadvantage. See https://avaproject.org.uk/ava-services-2/multiple-disadvantage

admitting that they are 'hard to hear'. It means treating survivors as whole people with complex lives, of which domestic violence may only be a part. It means being needs-led rather than risk-focused, and it means addressing all of the abuse a woman experienced and not just the physical assaults. It means sharing power and building relationships based on respect rather than simply giving the survivor another experience of being the voiceless and powerless. As Audre Lorde (1984, pp.110–113) so famously commented, 'the master's tools will never dismantle the master's house'.

REFERENCES

AVA (Against Violence & Abuse) Project (2014) *Case by Case: Refuge Provision in London for Survivors of Domestic Violence Who Use Alcohol and Other Drugs or Have Mental Health Problems.* Available at https://avaproject.org.uk

Davis, E. (2015) 'Survivor-led ethics in multi-agency work.' *DVRCV Advocate 1*, Autumn/Winter, 28–33.

Edwards, S.S. (1989) *Policing 'Domestic' Violence: Women, the Law and the State.* London: Sage Publications, Inc.

End Violence Against Women Coalition (2007) *Map of Gaps – The Postcode Lottery of Violence Against Women Support Services.* London: Equality and Human Rights Commission.

Hanmer, J., Griffiths, S. and Jerwood, D. (1999) *Arresting Evidence: Domestic Violence and Repeat Victimisation.* No. 104. London: Home Office, Policing and Reducing Crime Unit.

Hester, M. (2011) 'The three planet model: Towards an understanding of contradictions in approaches to women and children's safety in contexts of domestic violence.' *British Journal of Social Work 41*, 5, 837–853.

HM Crown Prosecution Service Inspectorate and HM Inspectorate of Constabulary (2004) *Violence at Home: A Joint Thematic Inspection of the Investigation and Prosecution of Cases Involving Domestic Violence.*

HM Inspectorate of Court Services (2005) *Domestic Violence, Safety and Family Proceedings.*

HM Inspectorate of Probation (2004) *An Inspection of National Probation Service Work with Domestic Violence Perpetrators.*

Holt, S. (2016) '"Quality" contact post-separation/divorce: A review of the literature.' *Children and Youth Services Review 68*, 92–99.

Home Affairs Select Committee (2008) *Domestic Violence, Forced Marriage and 'Honour'-Based Violence.* Appendix 60. London: The Stationery Office.

Home Office (1990) *Domestic Violence.* Circular 60/1990. London: Home Office.

Home Office (2005) *Domestic Violence – A National Report.* London. Home Office.

Home Office (2009) *Together We Can End Violence Against Women and Girls Strategy.* London: Home Office.

Home Office (2016) *Violence Against Women and Girls: National Statement of Expectations.* London: Home Office.

Kail, A., Blaythwayt, I. and Jarvinen, J. (2008) *Hard Knock Life.* London: New Philanthropy Capital.

Kelly, L., Bindel, J., Burton, S., Butterworth, D., Cook, K. and Regan, L. (1999) *Domestic Violence Matters: An Evaluation of a Development Project.* Home Office Research Study 193. London: Home Office.

Kelly, L., Sharp, N. and Klein, R. (2014) *Finding the Costs of Freedom: How Women and Children Rebuild Their Lives after Domestic Violence.* London: Solace Women's Aid.

Lapierre, S. (2008) 'Mothering in the context of domestic violence: The pervasiveness of a deficit model of mothering.' *Child & Family Social Work 13*, 4, 454–463.

Lorde, A. (1984) *Sister Outsider: Essays and Speeches.* Trumansburg, NY: Crossing Press.

McCoy, M. and Kelly, L. (2011) *Islands in the Stream: An Evaluation of Four London Independent Domestic Violence Advocacy Schemes.* London: London Metropolitan University.

McLaughlin, H., Banks, C., Bellamy, C., Robbins, R. and Thackray, D. (2014) '*Domestic Violence, Adult Social Care and MARACs: Implications for Practice*.' NIHR School for Social Care Research. Available at www.sscr.nihr.ac.uk/PDF/Findings/RF44.pdf

NatCen (2015) *Responding Effectively to Violence and Abuse (REVA Project)*. Available at http://natcen.ac.uk/our-research/research/responding-effectively-to-long-term-consequences-of-violence-and-abuse-(reva)

Neate, P. (2015) 'Domestic abuse could not be further from gender neutral: Wake up Britain.' *The Telegraph*, 11 June. Available at www.telegraph.co.uk/women/womens-life/11666990/Domestic-abuse-and-violence-is-not-gender-neutral.-Wake-up-Britain.html

ONS (Office for National Statistics) (2016) *Domestic Abuse in England and Wales: Year Ending March 2016*. London: ONS.

Phillips, R. (2013) *DVIP's Co-location in Hackney Children's Services: A Process Evaluation*. London: London Metropolitan University.

Richards, L. (2003) *Findings from the Multi-agency Domestic Violence Murder Reviews in London*. London: Metropolitan Police.

Scottish Government (2016) *Equally Safe: Scotland's Strategy for Preventing and Eradicating Violence Against Women and Girls*. Edinburgh: Scottish Government.

Scourfield, J. and Welsh, I. (2003) 'Risk, reflexivity and social control in child protection: New times or same old story?' *Critical Social Policy 23*, 3, 398–420.

Stanley, N. and Humphreys, C. (eds) (2015) *Domestic Violence and Protecting Children*. London: Jessica Kingsley Publishers.

Stark, E. (2007) *Coercive Control: How Men Entrap Women in Personal Life*. New York: Oxford University Press.

Sutton Women's Aid and Jigsaw4U (2017) *Supporting Families Affected by Domestic Violence*. Available at http://cyp.mertonpartnership.org.uk/januaryfebruary-2017/positive-contribution/supporting-families-affected-by-domestic-violence

Walby, S. and Allen, J. (2004) *Domestic Violence, Sexual Assault and Stalking: Findings from the 2001 British Crime Survey*. Home Office Research Study 276. London: Home Office.

Walby, S., Towers, J., Balderston, S., Corradi, C. *et al.* (2017) *The Concept and Measurement of Violence Against Women and Men*. Bristol: Policy Press.

WNC (Women's National Commission) (2009) *Still We Rise – Report from WNC Focus Groups to Inform the Cross-government Consultation: 'Together We Can End Violence Against Women and Girls'*. London: WNC.

Women's Aid (2015) *Change that Lasts*. Available at www.womensaid.org.uk/our-approach-change-that-lasts

Women's Aid England Annual Surveys (2013, 2015, 2016) Both available at www.womensaid.org.uk/womens-aid-annual-survey-reports

Zannettino, L. and McLaren, H. (2014) 'Domestic violence and child protection: Towards a collaborative approach across the two service sectors.' *Child & Family Social Work 19*, 4, 421–431.

CONCLUDING REMARKS

PROGRESSING THE DEBATE ON DOMESTIC VIOLENCE IN EUROPE

Stephanie Holt, *Associate Professor of Social Work, Trinity College Dublin, Ireland*

John Devaney, *Centenary Chair of Social Work, University of Edinburgh, Scotland*

Carolina Øverlien, *Associate Professor, Stockholm University, Sweden, and Researcher, Norwegian Centre for Violence and Traumatic Stress Studies, Oslo, Norway*

This book is a product of the inaugural European Conference on Domestic Violence held at Queen's University Belfast in September 2015. The conference drew together over 500 delegates from 32 countries involved in research, policy and practice, and this book similarly reflects a sample of those contributions across the three areas of interest, with contributions from across Europe. The conference was arranged in response to a need to gather together European researchers, practitioners and policy-makers in the field of domestic violence, as there are limited platforms and meeting points, on a European level, where these discussions can take place. Although there is plenty to learn from each other's work, prior to 2015 there was no European journal on domestic violence, no standing conference on domestic violence in Europe, and no edited book on European perspectives on domestic violence. The intent with this book was to fill part of that void, and to contribute to a growing and vibrant debate about how to understand and respond to domestic violence in all its myriad forms.

In the two years between that first conference and the second European Conference on Domestic Violence in Porto in September 2017, the political landscape across Europe has changed, some would say critically, and with a concerning degree of instability. Against the backdrop of this uncertainty, this book celebrates achievements and developments in domestic violence research, policy and practice.

In collaboration with our contributors, this book provides a much-needed platform to discuss what we understand to be the key issues, debates and challenges, for researchers, policy-makers and practitioners alike, in domestic violence in a European context. While it is not possible, as we have acknowledged earlier, to include every geographical area, or indeed the many manifestations of domestic violence, what we have sought to achieve in this volume is to provide a collection of significant knowledge across the 17 preceding chapters. Having done so, we begin by briefly reflecting on progress at a European level, before drawing some wider conclusions. We end this chapter signposting some opportunities and challenges for continued developments in the field of domestic violence research, policy and practice.

THE STORY SO FAR...

Until relatively recently across the European Union (EU), domestic violence was viewed as a private matter demanding minimal state intervention (FRA 2014). It is now widely acknowledged, however, that domestic abuse is common (FRA 2014), and that it presents significant social, health and legal issues to society as a whole (WHO 2013). Prior to the publication of the FRA survey (2014), those working to understand and address domestic violence at the EU and member state levels were confronted by an absence of comprehensive, robust and comparable data on its extent and nature. Existing police and criminal justice statistics, or evidence from case law, paint only a partial picture of the 'true' extent and nature of domestic violence. This is partly because victims under-report a broad range of incidents, and also because many criminal justice systems have difficulty in bringing offenders to account and accurately serving the needs and rights of victims. For example, where criminal justice data are available for analysis, they have traditionally shown high 'attrition rates' for domestic violence offences; in other words, conviction of perpetrators of domestic violence is low in comparison with the number of reported incidents of domestic violence (Devaney 2014). In addition, how incidents of domestic violence are counted tends to minimise the real scale of the issue (Walby, Towers and Francis 2016).

While the knowledge base on domestic violence has grown exponentially with policy and practice becoming more sophisticated and grounded empirically, to date there has been a limited focus on domestic abuse through a European lens. There is a need to explore how issues of violence, abuse and gender are understood within the context of Europe, with all of its diversity in terms of culture, ethnicity, prosperity and political orientation. Europe is not a single entity, and even within political institutions such as the EU, there is a wide disparity in terms of how the issue of domestic violence is conceived of and responded to.

Inspired by the breadth and depth of new knowledge captured by the FRA survey, this book, designed around three interconnected strands – policy, research and practice – seeks to promote the evidence base informing policy and practice developments relating to domestic violence in Europe at both the level of individual countries and as a continent.

CONNECTING RESEARCH, POLICY AND PRACTICE

In this final part of the book, we draw attention to the need for stronger linkages and relationships between research, policy and practice, arguing that these are critical, particularly in areas concerned with sensitive and challenging issues such as domestic violence. Awareness of the need to effectively use knowledge to improve policy has grown and evolved in recent years. This increased interest is frequently reflected in legislation, such as the Istanbul Convention, and sometimes supported by governmental funding for relevant research, monitoring and evaluation requirements in order to support policy developments.

Internationally, academic institutions are driven by research agendas, service providers are increasingly required to produce evidence of efficacy in their interventions and policy is questioned about how evidence-informed and transparent it is. To respond to each of these competing demands, the actors in each field – across research, policy and practice – need to collaborate and contribute to each other's efforts. That triangular relationship between research, policy and practice is neither always evident nor is it linear, particularly where each sphere is at a different developmental stage with differential levels of history and sophistication. This is particularly evident in the field of domestic violence; as Stanley and Devaney (2017, p.330) have articulated, 'practice has galloped ahead of the evidence'. With the gap between research and policy slowly closing, the preceding chapters evidence the achievements to date in research, policy and practice on long-standing issues such as violence against women, alongside more emergent issues of concern such as child-to-parent violence. New knowledge has also been garnered on new populations within the broader field of domestic violence, but at opposite ends of the lifespan. In this volume, these include a focus on older women experiencing domestic violence and also violence in teenage relationships.

The rising sophistication of technology brings new challenges for addressing violence in relationships, while fluid borders, movement and migration make women and children particularly vulnerable to violence in the form of, for example, trafficking and sexual exploitation. At the same time, in many European countries, legal statutes and regulatory frameworks that are meant to protect citizens from violence and abuse are in place, but are, for a number of reasons, not properly implemented. An example of this is the UN Convention on the Rights of the Child (UNCRC), ratified by all European countries, and in some countries embedded in legislation. Article 19 states that all children should be protected from violence and abuse, and if maltreatment has occurred, States should provide the necessary support and treatment. Yet many children who seek shelter in refuges for abused women seldom receive any form of support or treatment, although research clearly shows that these children are at risk of developing a broad spectrum of psychological, behavioural and social difficulties (Øverlien 2011). Hence, research and policy can also be understood at times as having developed ahead of practice.

FUTURE DIRECTIONS

The preceding chapters have identified many challenges in addressing the societal problem of domestic violence, challenges that are both long-standing and, as such, familiar, while also charting new and emerging territory. In looking to the future, we have four final points to make before concluding with a focus on the connectivity between research, policy and practice. First, a thread throughout this book and indeed the focus of the first chapter by Goodey is the necessity to continue to frame domestic violence as a human rights issue. In this way, it is understood as a priority for States across Europe, regardless of governmental or political positions at an individual country level. For this to be possible, the level of awareness, not only of domestic violence, but also of women and children's rights, and the State's obligations to prevent and protect its citizens from domestic violence and its consequences, needs to be enhanced. The level of general awareness of domestic violence against women has increased, but this awareness varies significantly from country to country (FRA 2014). Also, there are clear opportunities for new generations of boys and girls to learn, at an early age, that all forms of domestic violence violate human rights and are not acceptable.

Reflective of this rights-based position, our second point responds in part to Houghton's (2006) call for us to 'listen louder' to the views and experiences of children and young people, recognising children as 'experts' in their own lives. This value accorded to their subjective experiences is at the core of the UNCRC and, indeed, has substituted the notion of 'the vulnerable and dependent child' with that of the 'competent child' who is given the right to participate (Kjorholt 2002, p.64). This sensitivity to children's rights includes the right to hold and express an opinion; to have that opinion taken seriously and respected; the right to be consulted in all matters that affect them; and to participate in decisions that impact on their individual lives. Engaging in the practice of 'listening louder' empowers us to focus on those who are or have been excluded, unseen or unheard in the domestic violence debate. Our commitment to this process is reflected in a focus on children and young people (to varying degrees) in seven of the preceding chapters. We argue going forward that this focus needs to be strengthened and embedded firmly in domestic violence research, policy and practice, with particular attention to those groups of children and young people vulnerable to additional adversities.

Related to this is our next point, which encourages those involved in research, policy and practice to incorporate an intersectional analysis to facilitate an understanding of how those who experience domestic violence are also shaped by the interaction of different social positions, for example ethnicity, gender, class, age and sexuality, and, indeed, by the differing social and political contexts within which they live. As James-Hanman argues in the previous chapter, we must see individuals as being multifaceted, and therefore policy and service responses need to be able to deal with this complexity.

Finally, we need to step back from viewing domestic violence as essentially a criminal justice issue. While there is a need to have a well-functioning legal system to both protect victims and hold perpetrators to account, the contributions in this book highlight that all sectors of society must see domestic violence as important and relevant. The criminal justice system cannot, by itself, reduce the prevalence and incidence of domestic violence, and may even make it more complicated to respond in ways that victims find helpful.

We conclude with a final challenge going forward: the need to make research, policy and practice inform each other, intertwine and cooperate in ways that are simultaneously effective and beneficial, both in terms of prevention as well as support and treatment for those in need. In rising to meet this challenge, we reflect on Chris Argyris's assertion (2002, cited in Chaskin and Rosenfeld 2008, p.167) that 'some people want to explain the world, others want to change it'. We contend that the connection between the two is not dichotic and incompatible. Rather, there is real potential for logical synergy, with each informing and being informed by the other. Focusing on that process of informing and being informed, we hope this volume will usefully contribute to inspiring those concerned about and involved in applying knowledge to policy and practice in the field of domestic violence, and play some part in contributing to more effective social change. This process involves the critical task of bridging the utilities of knowledge generation and its application in the domain of social policy and intervention. We recognise that the process of building the connectivity between evidence and action is a complex one. Nonetheless, we conclude this volume with the assertion that this complexity needs to be embraced as an opportunity, and not perceived simply as a problem.

REFERENCES

Chaskin, R.J. and Rosenfeld, J.M. (eds) (2008) *Research for Action: Cross-national Perspectives on Connecting Knowledge, Policy and Practise for Children.* New York: Oxford University Press.

Devaney, J. (2014) 'Male perpetrators of domestic violence: How should we hold them to account?' *The Political Quarterly 85*, 4, 480–486.

FRA (European Agency for Fundamental Rights) (2014) *Violence Against Women: An EU-wide Survey.* Luxembourg: Publications Office of the European Union.

Houghton, C. (2006) 'Listen Louder: Working with Children and Young People.' In C. Humphreys and N. Stanley (eds) *Domestic Violence and Child Protection: Directions for Good Practise* (pp.82–94). London: Jessica Kingsley Publishers.
Kjorholt, A.T. (2002) 'Small is powerful: Discourses on "children and participation" in Norway.' *Childhood 9*, 1, 63–82.
Øverlien, C. (2011) 'Women's refuges as intervention arenas for children who experience domestic violence.' *Child Care in Practise 17*, 4, 375–391.
Stanley, N. and Devaney, J. (2017) 'Gender-based violence: Evidence from Europe.' *Psychology of Violence 7*, 3, 329–332.
Walby, S., Towers, J. and Francis, B. (2016) 'Is violent crime increasing or decreasing? A new methodology to measure repeat attacks making visible the significance of gender and domestic relations.' *British Journal of Criminology 56*, 6, 1203–1234.
WHO (World Health Organization) (2013) *Global and Regional Estimates of Violence Against Women: Prevalence and Health Effects of Intimate Partner Violence and Non-partner Sexual Violence.* Geneva: WHO.

CONTRIBUTOR BIOGRAPHIES

Ingunn Rangul Askeland is educated as a clinical psychologist and holds a PhD in Psychology. She works as a senior researcher at the Norwegian Centre for Violence and Traumatic Stress Studies. Her research focus is mainly on men attending therapy for violent behaviour. She has worked at Alternative to Violence as a therapist for many years, with both men and women who use violence in intimate relationships. Further, she works as a teacher and lecturer, both nationally and internationally.

Matt Barnard is head of the Crime, Justice and Communities teams at NatCen Social Research, the UK's leading independent social research organisation. He is currently leading studies on developing an outcomes framework for children's social care services, evaluating two initiatives as part of the Department for Education's Innovation Programme, and undertaking research into women's asylum appeals. His previous roles include Head of the Child Outcomes Research Consortium, and Head of Evaluation at the NSPCC.

Gemma Carney is a lecturer in Social Policy on the ARK Ageing programme at Queen's University Belfast. Her research career began in gender and politics, and has grown into a focus on ageing and older people, with feminism as a strong philosophical basis. Her work has been published in *Gender & Society*, *Ageing & Society*, the *Journal of Women and Aging* and the *European Journal of Ageing*. She is a member of the editorial board of *Ageing & Society* and a member of the executive committee of the British Society of Gerontology. She is currently principal investigator on The Lively Project, a project that uses art and literature to communicate the value of living a long life.

Dalila Cerejo PhD is an integrated researcher at CICS.NOVA and the National Observatory on Violence and Gender at the Faculty of Social and Human Sciences at the New University of Lisbon. She is an assistant professor and is an invited researcher at the Interdisciplinary Centre of Social Sciences (CICS.NOVA). She is currently developing her postdoctoral research. In the last 13 years, her professional career has been marked by research in the area of gender violence in Portugal, namely domestic violence, intimate partner violence and female genital mutilation. She studies gender-based violence from a sociology of emotions perspective.

Declan Coogan, PhD, is a lecturer in Social Work at the School of Political Science and Sociology at the National University of Ireland (NUI), Galway, and a research fellow with the UNESCO Child and Family Research Centre at NUI Galway, Ireland. He is also a member of the Social Science Research Institute at NUI Galway. He is a registered social worker and psychotherapist with practise experience in community child and adolescent mental health and child protection and welfare services. His research interests include child-to-parent violence and abuse, domestic violence, mental health, action research and grounded theory research methods.

John Devaney, PhD, is the Centenary Chair in Social Work at the University of Edinburgh. He moved into academia in 2006 after a working as a social worker and senior manager in social care in Northern Ireland. He has published widely on issues related to domestic violence and child abuse and neglect. His most recent book Domestic Violence Perpetrators - Evidence informed responses is published by Routledge.

Gene Feder is a GP in Bristol and professor of Primary Care at the University of Bristol. Gene led the first epidemiological study of domestic violence (DV) in primary care in Europe, systematic reviews on DV screening and on survivors' expectations of clinicians, and trials of DV interventions. He has led two DV research programmes: PROVIDE and REPROVIDE. Gene chaired the 2013 World Health Organization intimate partner violence guideline development group and the 2014 NICE (National Institute for Health and Care Excellence) DVA programme development group. From 2011 to 2014 he was the Royal College of General Practitioners DV clinical champion.

Gene currently leads an MRC Global Challenges project on DV in Brazil and Palestine.

Joanna Goodey, PhD, is head of the Freedoms and Justice Department at the European Union Agency for Fundamental Rights, Vienna. Prior to this she was a research fellow at the UN Office on Drugs and Crime. In the 1990s she held lectureships in criminology and criminal justice at British universities, and was also a regular study fellow at the Max Planck Institute for Foreign and International Criminal Law in Freiburg. To date, she has published numerous academic journal articles and book chapters on subjects ranging from masculinities and crime through to racism, and is author of the book *Victims and Victimology: Research, Policy and Practise* (2005).

Per Moum Hellevik is a PhD candidate at the Norwegian Centre for Violence and Traumatic Stress Studies and the Institute for Media and Communication at the University of Oslo. He is a sociologist specialising in internet and social media use among young people in connection with violent and abusive behaviour. This includes topics such as teenage intimate partner violence and abuse, cyberbullying and interpersonal behaviour in online games.

Stephanie Holt is an associate professor in the School of Social Work & Social Policy, Trinity College Dublin. Her academic and research interests include domestic violence, intimate partner homicide and risk assessment, child contact, child care and family support. She has a particular interest in ascertaining and representing the voice of the child in research. She is currently chair of the Irish branch of BASPCAN (British Association for the Study and Prevention of Child Abuse and Neglect).

Claire Houghton is currently Expert Adviser to the Scottish Government on Gender-based Violence and Children's Rights. She has worked in the domestic abuse field for 30 years, as a practitioner and national policy worker with Women's Aid, in Government coordinating domestic abuse policy, and now as a researcher at the University of Edinburgh. Over the past 15 years she has undertaken a series of participatory action research projects with young survivors of domestic abuse that have significantly influenced policy.

Davina James-Hanman has worked on violence against women for over 30 years in various capacities including frontline service delivery, as a campaigner, conference organiser, strategy developer, policy officer, project manager, researcher, trainer and writer. She has worked in both local and national NGOs, in local and national government, and in health and criminal justice settings. Much of her work over this period has been ground-breaking.

Gloria Kirwan is assistant professor of Social Work at Trinity College Dublin. She is also a registered social worker and has worked in mental health and child welfare services in the past. She teaches both undergraduate and postgraduate social work modules, and as part of her teaching portfolio in recent years she has been involved in developing teaching inputs on anti-human trafficking strategies.

Sibel Korkmaz is a PhD candidate at the Department of Social Work at Stockholm University, Sweden. She is part of a mixed-methods research project on teenage intimate partner violence in Sweden, drawing on survey data as well as qualitative interviews in her thesis. Of particular interest is how specific cultural and social conditions of teenage life may play an important factor to consider when discussing intimate partner violence among teenagers, also exploring concepts of resilience and responses.

Els Leye is a postdoctoral fellow attached to the International Centre for Reproductive Health at Ghent University and the Centre for Gender, Diversity and Intersectionality at the Free University in Brussels, and holds a position as professor in Global Health/Gender-related Practises at the Faculty of Medicine at Ghent University. She has senior expertise in research on female genital mutilation, and child and forced marriages, and on gender-based violence in general. She has many publications in her name on the topic of female genital mutilation, forced marriages and violence against women in general.

Nicola McConnell is a senior evaluation officer within the NSPCC, the leading children's charity in the UK specialising in child protection. Nicola has over 20 years of experience of evaluating health and social care services for children and families, as well as training and supporting others to do this work. She has researched and published within the fields of child protection, domestic abuse, interventions to prevent child abuse and working with fathers.

Philip McCormack is a research officer with Cosc – Ireland's National Office for the Prevention of Domestic, Sexual and Gender-based Violence – and is responsible for the overseeing of all work related to the research unit at Cosc. His background is in Anthropology, and his research skills include both qualitative and quantitative research methodologies in applied social sciences. His recent research interests have included domestic and sexual violence service provision in Ireland and domestic violence perpetrator programmes.

Elizabeth Martin, MA, is a PhD candidate within the School of Social Sciences, Education and Social Work at Queen's University Belfast. Elizabeth has a particular interest in researching marginalised populations, and in giving a voice to the more vulnerable members of society. Her doctoral work relates to an exploration of the substance use of older women who have been victims of domestic violence.

Zuzana Ocenasova, PhD, works as a research and monitoring expert at the Coordination and Methodological Centre for Prevention of Violence against Women in Bratislava, Slovakia. Her research interests are intimate partner violence, sexual violence and gender equality policies. She also teaches a graduate course on gender equality policies at the Faculty of Social and Economic Sciences, Comenius University.

Carolina Øverlien is associate professor of Social Work, Stockholm University, Sweden, and researcher at the Norwegian Centre for Violence and Traumatic Stress Studies, Oslo, Norway. Carolina has published extensively in academic journals, published two books and co-edited one book, all in the field of children and adolescents experiencing violence and trauma. She is particularly interested in children and adolescents' own strategies and responses to violence, research ethics and narrative theory and analysis. She is currently involved in two research projects on teenage intimate partner violence.

Maria Pentaraki has, for almost 30 years, been actively involved in the women's movement in different countries, including Canada, the US and Greece, addressing primarily gender-based violence, including the educational sabotage of women survivors of domestic violence, femicides/domicides, sex trafficking, etc. Her PhD research (2003) on dating violence/teenage relationship abuse (TRA) has informed TRA prevention programmes implemented in Greek high schools. Part of her diverse professional experience has been with the world-renowned

Duluth Model of Domestic Abuse Intervention Project in Minnesota, USA. She has held social work academic positions in three countries, and has been appointed by the European Commission as an independent gender violence country expert for Greece.

Lucy Potter is a GP in Bristol, UK, with a specialist interest in domestic violence and abuse. She is clinical lead for IRISi (Identification and Referral to Improve Safety; www.irisdomesticviolence.org.uk/iris) in Bristol, and has conducted research into domestic violence and abuse in medical education and the impact of different types of abuse on health.

Marius Råkil is educated as a specialist in Clinical Psychology and is executive director of Alternative to Violence in Norway. He has 27 years of experience in treating men who use violence in intimate relationships. He works as lecturer and speaker both nationally and internationally. He has published articles or book chapters in Sweden, Italy, England and the US, and edited a Norwegian textbook on men's violence against women. He has been a member of governmental committees on men, equality and violence in Norway.

Hana Smitkova, PhD, is a lecturer in the Department of Psychology, Faculty of Arts, Comenius University, Bratislava, Slovakia with a Counselling Psychology specialisation. Her teaching/research interests include a person-centred approach, ethics in the counselling setting, gender and LGBT issues. She is a psychotherapist, facilitator and supervisor in training programmes for helping professions.

Julie Taylor, PhD is a nurse scientist specialising in child maltreatment. She is professor of Child Protection in the Institute of Clinical Sciences at the University of Birmingham, in partnership with Birmingham Women's and Children's NHS Foundation Trust. She has held previous chairs at the Universities of Edinburgh (NSPCC Child Protection Research Centre) and Dundee (School of Nursing and Midwifery). For three years she was head of Strategy and Development (Abuse in High Risk Families) with the NSPCC.

Nusha Yonkova is the anti-trafficking manager at the Immigrant Council of Ireland. She is conducting employment-based postgraduate research with University College Dublin, sponsored by the Irish Research Council, exploring gender-sensitive approaches to the assistance of trafficked victims. Nusha has been working exclusively in the area of human trafficking for the last nine years, and has authored a range of reports as well as coordinated national and transnational research teams.

SUBJECT INDEX

AUTHOR INDEX